All that is native and fine

The Fred W. Morrison
Series in Southern Studies

David E. Whisnant

ALL THAT IS
NATIVE & FINE

The Politics of Culture in an

American Region

The University of North Carolina Press

Chapel Hill and London

Library of Congress Cataloging in Publication Data

Whisnant, David E., 1938–
All that is native and fine.

(The Fred W. Morrison series in Southern studies)
Bibliography: p.
Includes index.
1. Appalachian Region, Southern—Popular culture.
2. Social classes—Appalachian Region, Southern.
3. Appalachian Region, Southern—Social life and customs.
I. Title. II. Series.
F217.A65W47 1983   306'.0974   82-24851
ISBN 0-8078-1561-6

Both the initial research and the publication of this work
were made possible in part through grants from the
National Endowment for the Humanities,
a federal agency whose mission is
to award grants to support education, scholarship,
media programming, libraries, and museums,
in order to bring the results of
cultural activities to a broad general public.

*For my daughters
Beverly and Rebecca*

Contents

List of Illustrations

Preface

THIS IS A BOOK about cultural "otherness," about how people perceive each other across cultural boundaries—especially those boundaries that correlate with social class. It is also about cultural anxiety, cultural manipulation, cultural change, and cultural survival (and *re*-vival). It is about cultural assumptions and cultural images, about the purposeful translation and willful transformation of culture.

More specifically, it is about how mostly educated, urban, middle- and upper-class, liberal "culture workers" perceived, manipulated (I use the term here in a purely descriptive sense), and projected the culture of mostly rural, lower-class working people in the southern mountains during the half-century after 1890. It is about how those culture workers assessed the "threat" or "danger" to what they understood to be traditional culture in the mountains—dangers they thought emanated from coal mine and cotton mill life; from Tin Pan Alley and the radio and recording industries; from automobiles and face-powder and high heels. It is about what they tried to do to offset those perceived dangers: the schools and festivals, fund-raising tours and newsletters, ballad-singing clubs and dance teams, handicraft workshops and guilds, demonstration herds and cooperative creameries, Maypoles and recorder consorts.

Indeed, if I had to choose two images to suggest what this book is about, one would probably be novelist Lucy Furman's portrait of a hell-raising mountain boy ("Fighting Fult Fallon"), tamed and stuffed into a purple plumed hat and velvet knee-britches, playing the title role in a dramatized version of "Lord Lovel" at a mountain settlement school. The other might be of a talented mountain girl, a reluctant scholarship student at a mission school, hitching a ride across the river on a ferry and striking out back across the mountains on foot—home to her folks.

In a single phrase, this book is about the politics of culture. Not politics at the formal level of legislative act, judicial decision, or policy directive, but at the more basic level of individual values and assumptions, personal style and preference, community mores and local traditions. It is thus about the relatively intimate—but socially and politically significant—differences between the ways people talk and see, think and feel, believe and act, understand and structure their experience. It is those things, after all, upon which formal politics always rest—in the area of culture as in all other areas of human activity.

Writing a scholarly book is probably as good a way as any to grasp the concrete meaning of human interdependence. Novels can be written out of the author's accumulated personal experience; a poem can be composed out of a momentary private vision. But a scholarly book cannot. One knows what one knows, indeed one sees and learns the way one does, partly because of the work of those who have gone before. Thus one daily gives thanks for the marginal but essential efficiencies of so fundamentally messy and unpredictable a process as scholarship.

In the notes to each chapter, I have acknowledged the formal debts I am aware of to specific scholars and scholarly works. But there are so many others which by their nature cannot be acknowledged in detail: scraps of imperfectly remembered conversations, a reader's note in the margin, a chance encounter with a colleague, a nurturing friendship.

This book was more than three years in the making, and during that time I benefited greatly from the goodwill and generous help of many individuals and institutions. Archie Green has been my Mark Hopkins for more than a decade now, as he has been to so many others. Gordon Ebersole remains not only one of my most important sources of encouragement but also a prime model of the committed and humane public servant.

I am also indebted to Roger Abrahams, Francis Atkins, John Blakemore, Beverly Boggs, Mia Boynton, J. Charles Camp, Anne Campbell, Richard Chase, Norman Cohen, Harold Hensley, Mrs. W. M. Hensley, Joseph C. Hickeron, Esther Hyatt, Loyal Jones, James Klotter, Debora Kodish, Helen Lewis, Kip Lornell, J. Roderick Moore, Michael Mullins, Eric Olson, Gerald Parsons, Daniel Patterson, Charles L. Perdue, Jr., Elizabeth C. Powers, Neil Rosenberg, John Stephenson, Fredericka Teute, Elizabeth Watts, Cratis Williams, Jerry Williamson, and Joseph T. Wilson.

Major archival materials were made available to me at the University of North Carolina's Southern Historical Collection, Alderman Library at the University of Virginia, the Library of Congress, Hindman Settlement School, and the John C. Campbell Folk School. Crucial items were also supplied by libraries at Duke University, Berea College, Wellesley College, Vassar College, the Sayre School (Lexington, Kentucky), Utah State University, and the Historical Department of the Church of Jesus Christ of Latter Day Saints. Valuable assistance was also rendered by the Charles A. Cannon Memorial Library at Concord, North Carolina; the Bergen County (New Jersey) Historical Society; and Pack Memorial Public Library in Asheville, North Carolina.

The bulk of my work on this book was generously supported by two grants from the National Endowment for the Humanities (RS-29670-79-273 and RS-20060-80-1667). For the period of the grants, I was a Fellow in Residence in the Folklife Program at the Smithsonian Institution, where I enjoyed the warmly collegial support of the program's director, Ralph Rinzler. My work was concluded at the Woodrow Wilson International Center for Scholars, where I was a Fellow in the American Society and Politics Program, directed by Michael J. Lacey. Both the Smithsonian and the Woodrow Wilson Center made splendid facilities and staff support available to me, and afforded me invaluable intellectual stimulation and guidance. The University of Maryland Baltimore County, and especially its American Studies Department, bent all of its normal rules and regulations to allow me an extended period of uninterrupted leave.

Every author should have the good fortune to work with the splendid staff of the University of North Carolina Press. Their help, cooperation, and understanding have been both remarkable and unfailing.

I am deeply grateful to all of these people and institutions; the views I set forth here are of course entirely my own, and I accept full responsibility for them.

It should be clear from the foregoing that my work on this book was supported largely by public funds. Given the regressive tax policies of which we are perennially so fond, the money I spent came mainly from the pockets of the common working people of the United States. I hope I have been a good steward of those funds, and that the major benefits of the book—if indeed any ensue—will return to those who made my work possible. At the very least, I hope what I have written will lend some point and urgency to the phrase "the politics of culture."

Baltimore, Maryland
March 1982

All that is native and fine

Introduction

Another potent asset, that should appeal to the lover of America and American institutions, is that these southern Appalachian mountains are giving to the nation every year 100,000 new citizens of the purest American type, which is no inconsiderable item when we know that fifty per cent. increase in many of our large cities is made up of a low type of immigrants from the slums of Europe.

The Carolina Churchman, March 1910

IN SARAH S. GIELOW'S brief little novel *Uncle Sam* of 1913, a surveyor named William Vincent stops at a mountain cabin. He tells the mountaineer who lives there that the outside world is coming to the mountains, and will soon destroy the virgin forests that surround his home. If mountain people are to survive, Vincent advises, they will have to plant fruit trees and become orchard keepers. Luckily, he says, they can apply to Uncle Sam (a.k.a. the U.S. Department of Agriculture [USDA]) for fruit tree slips. The mountaineer's lack of immediate enthusiasm leads Vincent to conclude that he has stumbled upon "a shut-in community with a shut-in mentality."[1]

In true liberal fashion, however, Vincent goes ahead and acts unilaterally. Back in Washington, he gets seed corn, tree slips, and flower seeds from the USDA and sends them to the mountaineer, along with small gifts of soap and other items he considers necessities for self-respecting Americans. Unbidden though they were, the slips and seeds are welcomed by the mountaineer's wife, whose mentality is not quite so shut in. "Yo' Uncle Sam," declares Aunt Cindy, "air a plumb sho' giver." Through the surveyor's initiative, "a new era of living by better work" has been inaugurated.

So grateful is the mountaineer that he embarks for Washington—taking "a settin' of aigs" as a gift—to thank his Uncle Sam. Fortunately (in fiction, mountaineers live lives shot through by marvelous coincidence), he meets his surveyor friend on the street, and is taken to the White House. There he meets the president's daughter, who has "read of mountain people, [and] also heard interesting talks by Mountain Mission workers before her church guild." After puzzling over the unaccustomed mysteries of nightgowns and bathtubs, the mountaineer retires to sleep before his breakfast audience with Uncle Sam.

At length the surveyor's sister (it was usually the women who were so moved) goes to the "shut-in community" to open a mission school because, she reasons, "Uncle Sam needs lots of mountain boys to replenish his ranks of workers and soldiers."[2] The mountaineer's twin sons become "a power [*sic*] of strength" in her work, "leading the boy brigade of embryo soldiers preparing to give their services, as their ancestors did, to fight, bleed, and die for Uncle Sam."

Gielow's little novel would be simply ludicrous if it did not reflect so accurately so much that was actually going on in (and beyond) the southern mountains at the time. However crude the plot, thin the characterization, and bald the didacticism, most of the actual historical patterns are there: the arrival of resource-hungry, northeastern-based entrepreneurs and their (always male) agents; the puny liberal nostrums of federal agencies that mapped the resources of the mountains at public expense and then swapped mountaineers USDA apple tree slips for virgin tulip poplars six feet in diameter twenty feet above the ground; the simple-minded cultural dualism that ranged bathtubs and nightgowns against settin's of aigs; the consensus mythology of the mountains purveyed on the missionary guild lecture circuits throughout the liberal and Protestant northeast; the women (almost always it was the women—literal and symbolic sisters of the advance-agent surveyors) who trooped in to found the mission schools, settlement schools, folk schools, and handicraft programs—psychic, educational and cultural aid stations for the bruised and dislocated victims of an advancing industrial capitalism; and always and always the overarching ideological appeal to the value of mythicized old-stock mountaineer Americans who could be diked against the unkempt (and possibly radical) European riffraff flotsaming into the cities. And who could in time of national need be sent into the trenches to "fight, bleed and die for Uncle Sam"— each one another potential Sergeant York from Fentress County, Tennessee, carrying within him the indomitable spirit of King's Mountain and the Battle of New Orleans.

Viewed broadly, there were four profoundly important, interrelated processes going on in the mountains—and in the South generally—at the end of the nineteenth century: economic colonization by northeastern capital; the rise of indigenous resistance among workers and farmers; the discovery of indigenous culture by writers, collectors, popularizers, and elite-art composers and concertizers; and the proliferation of (mostly Protestant) missionary endeavors. Gielow's *Uncle Sam* hints at them all, but all have been—or are presently being—chronicled in more elaborate and convincing detail.[3]

In the dominant northeastern intellectual and cultural centers, a self-congratulatory resistance to the notion of a South or an Appalachia that could (and did) give birth to and nurture progressive and radical social movements and institutions has long been so strong that those aspects of southern and Appalachian history are still generally unknown among all but a few specialists, such as historians of agrarian and labor movements, analysts of educational reform, and the like.[4]

But in those same centers, it has long been accepted as established truth that the mountains and the rest of the South are laden with fascinating cultural traditions. Many are the urban sophisticates who have found their attention unexpectedly riveted by Delta blues, New Orleans jazz, mountain ballads and banjo pickers, coverlet weavers and chair makers, Cajun fiddlers, and Ozark storytellers. Nor did the flood of interest abate as the years passed. The adoption of southern music, musicians, and musical forms by a mainstream starved for rooted cultural energy and authenticity has helped shape much of American musical history since World War II.[5]

What is needed, it seems to me, is a new and more analytically sophisticated understanding of the relationship between the cultural history of the mountains (and of the South generally—though my focus cannot be that broad here), its own economic history, and the essentially political history of its economic and cultural interaction with the rest of the country. In short, I am convinced that to understand culture in the mountains—or indeed in any culturally enclaved area within a larger, formally pluralistic but essentially assimilationist social system—one must inevitably talk about the politics of culture.

Look, for example, at what was happening in the mountains during the two decades on either side of the century marker: Most of the coal and timber land was bought by northeastern-based entrepreneurs and corporations; a few score miles of railroads lengthened to many hundreds, as timber and coal production shot up at a dizzying rate in county after previously isolated county; textile mills moving south in search of nonunion labor congregated in the foothills and the Piedmont and made the pie-in-the-sky promises to mountaineers that were later satirized in Gastonia mill worker Dave McCarn's immortal "Cotton Mill Colic No. 3":

> Lots of people with a good free will
> Sold their homes and moved to the mill.
> We'll have lots of money they said,
> But everyone got hell instead.
> It was fun in the mountains rolling logs,
> But now when the whistle blows we run like dogs.

At the same time that mountaineers were trading virgin poplars for fruit tree slips, rolling logs for mill whistles, and one-horse farms for a miner's dinner pail, the culture industry was also booming in the mountains. Vassar graduate Susan Chester opened her Log Cabin Settlement in Asheville, North Carolina before 1895; at about the same time, Berea College started its "fireside industries" crafts program. Also in the same year, Frances Goodrich (another New England woman) started her Allanstand cottage industries project near Asheville, and Katherine Pettit made the first of her exploratory visits to eastern Kentucky that led to the founding of Hindman Settlement School in 1902 and Pine Mountain Settlement School in 1913. The years immediately after 1900 witnessed the founding of countless schools, academies, and institutes in the mountains, many of which had a pronounced cultural preservation and revival focus: Hazel Green and Oneida in Kentucky, Pleasant Hill in Tennessee, the Berry Schools in Georgia, Dorland-Bell in North Carolina, and many others. In addition, there were many crafts-revival efforts not attached to schools: Mrs. Vanderbilt's Biltmore Industries; numerous small enterprises around the tourist centers of Tryon and Saluda, North Carolina; the later Pi Beta Phi settlement in Gatlinburg, Tennessee; and the Crossnore and Penland programs in North Carolina.[6]

Scores of ballad collectors also roamed the newly opened mountains. Articles on the musical lore of the mountains began to appear in the earliest volumes of the new *Journal of American Folklore* in the early 1890s. By 1908, Massachusetts-born Olive Dame Campbell, accompanying her husband on his Russell Sage Foundation-funded social survey of the mountains, was systematically collecting ballads. She was followed by many another, most notably of course the English collector Cecil Sharp, whom she convinced to come to the mountains in 1916.

As one looks closely at some of these cultural endeavors—especially if one attempts to understand them in the context of the region's economic history—one becomes gradually aware that the manipulation of culture (at least, of culture construed in certain ways) inevitably reflects value and ideological differences as well as the inequalities inhering in class. Thus one must sooner or later consider the *politics* of culture, which show some signs of being reasonably predictable, even in widely separated circumstances.

In the eighteenth century in Scotland, to cite a fairly well-known example, the Highland lairds forcibly cleared the indigenous population from the land in order to introduce large-scale sheep farming and other economic "improvements." To legitimize their actions, they denigrated local people culturally and purged their own lives of any trace of local dialect, dress, or style. Later sensing the loss entailed in having done so, however, they attempted to "revive" the displaced culture, formed the Society of True Highlanders, learned to speak Gaelic again, and staged nostalgic cultural festivals among the few remaining indigenous highlanders.[7]

But there are other examples closer by which are instructive—especially those in which the politics of culture were worked out in the context of some missionary endeavor. At the close of the Civil War, scores of Northerners went south to teach in the freedmen's schools conducted under the aegis of the American Missionary Association (AMA) and the Freedmen's Bureau. Their work was eerily predictive of what was to happen among mountain whites a generation later.[8]

Nearly 80 percent of the teachers who went were women, and more than half of those were in their twenties. Nearly two-thirds were from Massachusetts, Connecticut, and New York, and over 40 percent were the daughters of manufacturers, merchants, or professionals. They thus belonged, concluded scholar Jacqueline Jones, to the "literate (and literary) self-conscious Protestant middle-class," whose world view "provided the philosophical basis for . . . [the] belief that they . . . had both the duty and the ability to rectify certain moral and institutional evils." In general, they subscribed to the ideals of self-sacrifice and "social guardianship" that were widespread among middle-class Victorian women.[9]

These "soldiers of light and love" went south, says Jones, "to save and be saved," and the work they did was "an intricate web spun with the threads of race, class, sex, and culture." The religious programs, educational classes, and self-improvement efforts they inaugurated among Georgia blacks led W. E. B. Dubois, in his *Souls of Black Folk* (1903), to call them "saintly souls." But in *The Mind of the South* (1941), W. J. Cash dismissed what they did as "meddlesome stupidity."

However that polar disagreement is to be resolved, several things are reasonably clear: The work of these particular soldiers of light and love was fraught with cultural conflict; it was linked to a conservative concept of social change; and it projected seriously misleading images of the world of Georgia blacks to the world outside.

The relationship between blacks and the Freedmen's Bureau and its teachers and schools, Jones concluded, was "fraught with tension." Arriving in Georgia, the teachers were shocked when they attended black worship services and encountered passion, intense rhythms, and shouts instead of the cool exegesis they were accustomed to.[10] The schools they established became patently "culture-bound" attempts to "Yankeeize" the freed people.[11] The curriculum was based on "[northern] values that were alien to the former slaves," and reading lessons "consisted of short stories about good children who loved God and obeyed their parents." Geography lessons "contrasted the energetic North with the lazy South." The one text which portrayed blacks positively—Lydia M. Child's *Freedmen's Book*, which contained biographical sketches of the heroes of black liberation—got very limited use. Like the Massachusetts common schools after which they were patterned, the freedmen's schools emphasized an "ethos of efficiency, manipulation, and mastery."[12]

As daughters of the upper middle class, the soldiers of light and love "shared with Republicans the vision of a truly unified American society in which competing interests would be cemented together in a national purpose by the tenets of Protestantism and capitalism." They also shared the general Protestant unease about the "dangerous classes" and about the stresses in the moral fabric of society arising out of rapid social change. A major goal of the schools they ran, then, was "to effect moral character reform and thereby guarantee social stability in the face of increasing fragmentation based on class, political, religious and racial tensions." Not surprisingly, the primary mechanisms of both "personal and group advancement" and broader social change were conceived to be education and moral suasion.[13]

Having built their enterprise partly upon a credulous acceptance of antebellum stereotypes of blacks, the freedmen's schools and their AMA associates continued to promote the stereotype among their potential contributors in order to justify their efforts. In a survey of official AMA correspondence, Jones found that editors of AMA journals sometimes edited and rewrote "letters to the editor" in order to change the image of both blacks and AMA work among them. They "sought to impress upon journal readers," Jones found, "the black man's degraded position in southern society and his total dependence upon northern support." An 1867 AMA circular on the preparation of photographs of freedmen's work for publicity purposes suggested images that would be appropriate for northern audiences: black students gathered around a "neatly, not fancifully dressed" teacher; and a black family respectfully listening to a northern teacher read the Bible in their modest but orderly home.[14]

As the difficulties and intractabilities of remaking southern blacks in the image of the Protestant, Republican northeast became apparent toward the end of the century, home mission boards and philanthropic groups cast about for a more promising field. One of the most attractive (and closest at hand) was the southern mountains. Newly thrust upon the public consciousness by a stream of post–Civil War local-color fiction and the burgeoning coal and timber industries, the mountains began to claim a greater and greater share of missionary attention.[15]

As that shift occurred, many of the working assumptions, operational patterns and methods, and effects of the earlier mission enterprise were manifested in the new one. Historian James Klotter has shown that even the established stereotypic images of southern blacks were carried over and used to characterize mountain whites. Once established in their new context, such patterns proved remarkably durable. As late as 1928 the Russell Sage Foundation's Mary Routzhan was still asking a gathering of mountain mission workers—who had mailed out thousands of photographs of barefooted mountain children to potential donors—whether more honest if less heart-rending images might better be chosen. "Perhaps in real life," she noted, "Lizzie Ann is no longer barefooted."[16]

The pages that follow do not by any means explore the whole of the multifaceted church and secular missionary enterprise in the mountains. That task will eventually require many hands. Rather, they focus on the cultural drama that was central to the entire undertaking. From the scores of episodes afforded by the history of the mountains during the half-century between 1890 and World War II, I have chosen three for intensive analysis: Hindman Settlement School (founded in 1902), the cultural work of Olive Dame Campbell (covering the period from 1908 to the early 1950s), and the White Top (Virginia) Folk Festival (1931–39). Each was important in itself; each highlighted the most important issues with special clarity and force; each was in some ways typical of many other analogous efforts. And by no means least important, each is accessible through existing archival material.

Hindman Settlement School was one of the earliest (not *the* earliest, as often asserted) attempts to create a social and educational settlement institution in the mountains. It was modeled partly upon the urban social settlements of major midwestern and northeastern cities and partly upon the "industrial" schools prominent among southern blacks at the end of the nineteenth century. Guided primarily by upper-middle-class, genteel women from the Kentucky Bluegrass and New England, Hindman Settlement School developed an elaborate array of cultural endeavors as a central feature of its educational program. Those endeavors (as I will show) were based upon a flawed reading of local culture, as well as upon a naive analysis of the relationship between culture, political and economic power, and social change.

Olive Dame Campbell's diverse cultural activities in the mountains spanned more than forty years—from her first trips with her husband, John C. Campbell, to Hindman Settlement School in late 1907, to her subsequent work with English ballad collector Cecil Sharp, her efforts to establish a mountain "folk school" based upon Scandinavian models, and her more than twenty-five years of work with the Southern Highland Handicraft Guild. Mrs. Campbell's cultural work, while more sensitive to political-social-economic context than that of most of her peers and coworkers, nevertheless partook of many of the ironies and confusions that have characterized most organized cultural work in the mountains.

By all odds the most bizarre and confused of the three examples chosen for analysis here is the White Top Folk Festival. On the surface, the festival would appear to have been simply a celebration of local culture in a picturesque area of southwest Virginia in the 1930s. Upon closer inspection, however, the event turns out to have been an extraordinary example of manipulative cultural intervention. It blended the entrepreneurial aspirations of the local lawyer who owned White Top Mountain, the mostly sensitive and generous cultural and social concern of a brilliant and productive but vulnerable woman, and the insane racial-cultural-political agendas of a posturing elitist composer and pianist who tried to use WASP southern mountaineers and their culture in an effort to forestall the national cultural suicide he believed would follow inevitably from any instance of race mixing.

Culture was so central to missionary work in the mountains for two reasons. The first is that, in the interaction of such disparate groups as northeastern missionaries and southern blacks or mountain whites, culture—that is, the entire range of belief, attitude, value, characteristic behavior, posture, and so on, which makes up the individual and collective identity of an ethnic, regional, or socioeconomic group—generally proves to be the most available touchstone, the handiest standard to which everything may be referred, by which everything may be measured. Thus in the management of the missionary enterprise, which is formally oriented toward introducing preselected changes in individual and collective behavior and social organization, judgments about family and community structure, forms of worship, school curricula, entertainment, and a host of other matters are rendered finally in terms of the cultural nuances that inhere in such things as bodily postures and rhythms, vocal cadence, and interactional style. Pedagogical or economic theory, political or hygienic principle, theological or moral dogma may be formally offered as a rationale, but to the careful observer, culture usually proves to be the operative basis for most judgments and agendas. Thus the women that Jacqueline Jones studied were conversant with the educational theories and experiments of Horace Mann, but first, last, and always they were the Protestant, Victorian daughters of conservative New England business and professional men.

The second reason has to do with a fortuitous conjunction between the particular socialization of women in the mid- and late-nineteenth century, and part of the popular image of the southern mountains during the same period. As Ann Douglas has recently argued in *The Feminization of American Culture* (1979), both women and the clergy were systematically disestablished in American life in the early nineteenth century. Nineteenth century clergymen who were excluded from political office were but pale copies of their seventeenth- and eighteenth-century predecessors, who had not only held office and participated in political debates but had supplied much of the language and conceptual apparatus for those debates. But as the years passed, Douglas shows, clergymen were required "to be more agile in an ever shrinking space."

Like ministers, women were also systematically disestablished—losing, for example, the right to vote that many of them had had earlier. The etiquette books of the 1820s and 1830s stressed that "women were to cultivate domestic piety behind closed doors while [males] were to face . . . the competitive world of commerce." So conditioned, Douglas argues, such women "[represent] nothing finally but a state of susceptibility to very imprecisely conceived spiritual values."[17]

In sum then, women and their ministerial counterparts had claimed what was essentially a narrowly conceived *culture* as their special concern only a few decades before the southern mountains became popularly known as a vast unmapped repository of valuable cultural survivals—beliefs, sayings, manual skills, language, values, and such other intangibles as Mrs. Gielow depicted at the sun-drenched, flag-draped end of *Uncle Sam.*

Historically, the fact that so many of the women missionaries to the mountains focused on culture is important for two major reasons. In the first place, their culture-bound cultural goals and programs had a substantial and long-lasting impact upon *indigenous* culture in the mountains (as the following case studies will make clear). But equally important, culture (as the women defined it in limited and romantic terms) became a diversion, a substitute for engaging with the political and economic forces, processes, and institutions that were altering the entire basis of individual identity and social organization in the mountains.

Thus to this day there are a thousand people who "know" that mountaineers weave coverlets and sing ballads for every one who knows that millions of them have been industrial workers for a hundred years, have organized unions and picketed state and national capitols in pursuit of their constitutional rights, and have laid their bodies in front of strip-mine bulldozers and overloaded coal trucks. Or that, today, they shop at the K-Mart and Radio Shack, drive Camaros, and watch as much television as people anywhere.

When I speak of the politics of culture in the following pages, therefore, I mean principally two things: (1) the interaction of disparate cultural systems *as* systems, and (2) the function of a fixation *upon* a romantically conceived "culture" within the broader social, political, and economic history of the mountains.

In order to make the first dimension of the politics of culture somewhat clearer and more precise, I have employed the notion of *systematic cultural intervention.* By that I mean simply that someone (or some institution) consciously and programmatically takes action within a culture with the intent of affecting it in some specific way that the intervenor thinks desirable.

The action taken can range from relatively passive (say, starting an archive or museum) to relatively active (like instituting a cultural revitalization effort). Its intent can be either positive (as in a sensitive revitalization effort) or negative (as in the prohibition of ethnic customs, dress, or language). Moreover, a negative effect may follow from a positive intent, and vice versa.

Since Appalachia is by no means the only place where systematic cultural interventions have occurred, one can look to earlier instances to sharpen one's sense of what intervention is. In *Sinful Tunes and Spirituals: Black Folk Music to the Civil War* (1977), Dena Epstein notes that a French monk sent as a missionary to Martinique in 1694 judged the African dances he found among slaves there to be indecent and lascivious, and suggested that they be replaced by the minuet and the courante, "which would satisfy their love of dancing in an innocent way." [18]

The effects of such high-handed tactics have frequently been judged to be positive. Epstein quotes a remarkably candid letter from a Charleston, South Carolina man in 1851 who compared Cuban Negroes in their "savage, original state" to Christianized black slaves in the United States. There remains, wrote Frederick Bremer,

> no longer a doubt in my mind as to the beneficial influence of Anglo-American culture upon the negro. . . . The sour crab is not more unlike our noble, Astrachan apple, than is the song of the wild African to the song of the Christian negro in the United States. . . . And low and sensual is that lawless life and intoxication of the senses in those wild negro dances, and those noisy festivities to the beat of a drum, compared with that life, and that spiritual intoxication in song and prayer, and religious joy, which is seen and heard at religious festivals of the people here. [19]

Epstein comments at length upon the Port Royal experiment, which of course produced the first great collection of slave songs in this country, but which also as an episode of cultural intervention had some unfortunate results. A southern-born white clergyman from Massachusetts wrote to Port Royal in 1863 that "we have heard these [native songs] long enough, and we hope the good taste of the refined young ladies at Port Royal will substitute others more sensible and elevated in language." A visitor in one of the Sea Islands schools wrote of "these little barbarians . . . circling round in this fetish dance." These people, the visitor told friends back home, "are receiving an education through their songs which is incalculable. Our teachers discourage the use of their old barbaric chants, and besides our beautiful, patriotic and religious hymns teach the virtues of industry, truth, honesty and purity in rhyme and meter."[20]

But the Port Royal teachers themselves were apparently divided concerning the cultural merits of the enterprise. One teacher wrote in 1863, "I wish I could introduce you to this school as it appears in the morning, and let [the students] sing to you one of their own native songs; afterwards one which they have just learned—'Rally round the Flag.' They are delighted with our songs, and catch them readily." But a black teacher from Philadelphia who went to a Negro funeral there in 1863 saw the process differently. "We could see the crowd of people," she said, "and hear them singing hymns;—not their own beautiful hymns, I am sorry to say. I do so fear these will be superseded by ours, which are poor in comparison, and which they do not sing well at all."[21]

Clearly, cultural intervention is a complex process which has taken many forms and whose results are subject to a variety of interpretations. We will begin to understand these episodes and processes in our cultural history only when we look at them in detail *as* intervention, and not as benign incidents which produced a collection of slave songs, or a revival of handweaving, or a colorful festival. In short, we must begin to understand the politics of culture—especially the role of formal institutions and forceful individuals in defining and shaping perspectives, values, tastes, and agendas for cultural change.

The second dimension of the politics of culture as I discuss it also has roots that reach back beyond and outside the period of southern Appalachian history I am specifically concerned with. Ann Douglas has shown that the exclusive focusing of disestablished women and ministers upon culture had its social and political effects, especially insofar as their approach to social change was concerned. Leading clergymen such as Horace Bushnell (1802–76) supported "essentially private and personal causes—missions, prison reform, temperance—whose potential to hurt vested economic interests was real but limited." Thus, Douglas observes, "they depoliticized not just the content but the method of reform."[22]

Like the clergymen, women of the period in general took a very cautious approach to social issues. They were persuaded that the main instrument available to them was a vague "influence" which, from their special sphere, they might exert for good. But as Douglas points out, "Participation in radical causes on the part of the practicioners of 'influence' was strikingly low." Women such as Catherine Beecher and Emma Willard "took neutral or conservative stands on crucial public issues," and Harriet Farley advocated "the politics of politeness." Farley later rebuked Orestes

Brownson for his attack on New England factory conditions and became editor of the *Lowell Offering*, a magazine for Lowell factory girls, in which she opposed strikes and suggested that women "do good by stealth."[23]

For such a conception of social change to be imported to the southern mountains, cloaked in a mantle of romantic cultural revitalization, and legitimized for the general public at the very time when the region was undergoing convulsive social, economic, and political upheaval became an enormously important fact in its history. It is finally the implications of that fact which interest me most in the analysis that follows.

1

'Hit sounds reasonable'

Culture and Social Change at Hindman
Settlement School

"Wimmen, I jist want to know . . . what *is*
you'ns here for anyway?"
"[We are] simply here . . . to learn all we can and
teach all we can."
"Waal, now, hit *sounds* reasonable."

Katherine Pettit's diary account of a visit with Mrs. Green,
George's Branch, Kentucky, 1901

We had heard so many stories of the ignorance of the
mountaineers that we were somewhat disappointed by their
familiarity with a good many things we had expected them not
to know.

George E. Vincent, "A Retarded Frontier," *American Journal of
Sociology* 4 (July 1898): 15

ON AN EVENING in mid-September 1917, the English ballad collector Cecil Sharp sat before a fire in the comfortable library of Hindman Settlement School in remote Knott County, Kentucky, and listened to mountain children sing ballads that, though nearly extinct in England, still thrived in the mountains of eastern Kentucky. Initially doubtful that he would find what he was looking for in a well-established school located in a county seat, Sharp nevertheless collected sixty ballads in five days of roaming the countryside in the daytime and gathering with the settlement school children before the fire at night. "Judging from their faces, voices, and manners," he told their teachers, "these children of yours might belong to the very best of English families. . . . It would be a great mistake ever to try to change the mountain people. They should be developed along the lines of their natural culture."[1]

However desirable Sharp's agenda for developing mountain people in harmony with their "natural culture," it was not to be.[2] For eastern Kentucky in 1917 was a developmental powder keg at the end of a short—and already lighted—fuse. And the norms and values by which development would proceed contrasted dramatically with the people's "natural culture" as Sharp perceived it. The railroad, which when the school opened fifteen years earlier had terminated forty-five miles away in Jackson—a hard two-day trip by horseback—was now only twenty miles away in Hazard and was pushing ever deeper into Knott County. The treasure that Sharp sought was cultural, but the railroads were following the veins of coal that lay under virtually every road, trail, and creek bed he tramped in search of the unexpected vestigial outcroppings of an ancient and now finally imperiled cultural tradition.

And yet the scrubbed and well-mannered children who sang for him each evening were part of an experiment designed to use that very imperiled cultural tradition as part of an educational program to help fit mountain children for life in the emerging new order without destroying the personal and social characteristics that made them at once so attractive and so vulnerable. It was a delicate balance.

Founded in 1902 by Katherine Pettit and May Stone, two well-born women from the Kentucky Bluegrass, Hindman by the time Sharp visited it had survived several major fires and floods and perennially precarious finances to become one of the two or three most substantial of the "church and independent schools" that were springing up throughout the mountains.[3] As an independent "settlement" school, however, its conceptual origins lay not primarily in the evangelicalism of the Protestant church, but in an uneasy amalgam of the progressive social vision embodied in the ur-

ban settlement houses of the closing years of the nineteenth century and
the conservatism of the "industrial schools" that were springing up in various parts of the country, but especially among blacks in the South.[4]

At the simplest level, urban settlement houses were seeking to provide a
basic educational program, but beyond that to conserve—as a resource for
personal identity and growth, family cohesion, and social development—
what was perceived as valuable in the received culture of urban immigrants. The settlement itself was to be both a buffer against social and economic exploitation and a tool for self-directed social betterment.

If it was to take such a model seriously, Hindman Settlement School
would inevitably enmesh itself in the strategic political, social, and value
questions faced by the urban settlement houses: What are the limits of
"education" as an approach to progressive social change in the midst of a
rapidly expanding industrial economic and social order? What ethical warrant has one to decide what is "good" or "bad," progressive or not, "useful" or not, in a culture other than one's own? How may one conserve certain cultural traits, values, and practices (handicraft skills, or religious
observances, or music) while partitioning them off from others (male dom-
inance in the household, or parental authoritarianism) to which they are
intimately tied but which are judged undesirable or nonfunctional? May
cultural traditions that flourished amidst one set of historical circumstances be "preserved" or "reinforced" amidst another set? And if so, with
what costs and benefits? And to whom?

However these political and ethical questions are to be answered, the
historical example of Hindman Settlement School poses some quite specific questions for the historian: What may one learn from Hindman about
the movement of the settlement idea from urban to rural areas early in this
century (and the industrial school idea from deep South to mountain
South), and how was each idea modified by the movement, particularly in
its cultural aspect? More specifically, how did Hindman Settlement School
arise and function in the midst of a resource-rich area long known for its
cultural riches and long since marked out for entrepreneurial exploitation?
And finally, to what extent may the institution and the new mass culture it
helped to bring to the mountains actually have facilitated the exploitation
it sought to forestall?

Urban and Rural Settlements:
The Migration of a Concept

The story of the origins of the social settlement in England in the 1880s, and its movement to the United States a few years later, has been told so often that it need not be repeated here except in barest outline.[5]

The settlement idea arose out of a complex of social reform ideas, experiments, and movements in late nineteenth century England. It spoke to some of the concerns expressed earlier in the Reform Bill of 1832 and the Chartist Demonstration of 1848 and drew ideas from such diverse social theorists and reformers as Robert Owen (1771–1858), Thomas Carlyle (1795–1881), John Stuart Mill (1806–73), Charles Dickens (1812–70), Lord Shaftesbury (1801–85), and others. These concerns included improving the wretched lives of the poor (Dickens), factory reform (Owen and Shaftesbury), society as a moral organism (Carlyle), and more equitable distribution of wealth (Mill). Nor was the social settlement the first institutional form into which some of these ideas were cast; it was preceded by such organizations as the Society for Promoting Workingmen's Associations (1850), Charles Kingsley's Workingmen's Clubs, the London Workingmen's College (1854), and the college missions founded later in London's slums.

The first social settlement in England was founded in 1884 by John R. Green and Canon Samuel Barnett, who brought several Oxford students together to "learn to sup sorrow with the poor" in the industrial quarter of East London. They named it Toynbee Hall, in honor of an influential student leader who had died the year before. The social settlement was, as Allen Davis has characterized it, "the culmination of a diverse reform movement, closely allied with Romanticism, that sought to preserve humanistic and spiritual values in a world dominated by materialism and urban industrialism."[6]

The settlement idea spread to America quickly. In 1886 the American Stanton Coit went to live at Toynbee Hall. Returning to New York in 1887, he established what has usually been called the first American social settlement (Neighborhood Guild) on Forsythe Street in New York's Lower East Side. The guild's purpose was "the cultivation of friendly relations between the educated and the uneducated, and the gradual uplifting of the latter by the better influences thus brought to bear upon them." Guild workers were confident that "educated men and women, living and working among the poor, associating with them as equals, but introducing . . . all that trained intelligence and friendly sympathy have to give, can make themselves a most efficient means of bettering and elevating the mental, moral and physical condition of the people."[7]

By 1891 there were six social settlements in the United States; six years later there were seventy-four. There were more than a hundred by 1900, and the number doubled in each of the next five-year periods, to more than four hundred by 1910.[8]

The prime exemplar of the social settlement in the United States was of course Jane Addams's Hull House, founded in Chicago in 1889.[9] An "ugly, pigeon-toed little girl," Addams described herself, "whose crooked back obliged her to walk with her head held very much upon one side." Born on the eve of the Civil War, she imbibed the "Quaker tendencies" of her father, whom she acknowledged as the dominant influence in her early life, and the humanitarianism of Abraham Lincoln, whom she read and reread as a young woman. Later she read all of Tolstoy's books as they appeared, and was moved by his ability to "lift his life to the level of his conscience." After graduating from Rockford College in 1881, Addams spent a short while at the Woman's Medical College of Philadelphia, but withdrew because of illness. In 1888 she visited Toynbee Hall, and in the fall of the next year established Hull House.

From the beginning, she said, Hull House was "ready to perform the humblest neighborhood services" among Chicago's polyglot immigrant groups. In its early years it carried out studies of diet, organized young people's clubs and a coffeehouse, set up a "co-operative coal association" to provide fuel for the poor, established cooperative apartments for working girls, ran adult education classes and recreation programs, and helped to get streets paved in immigrant neighborhoods. As the years passed, Hull House programs branched out to embrace studies of the link between high mortality rates and poor garbage collection in slums; efforts to improve building codes, housing conditions, and landlord-tenant relations; juvenile court reform; reform of public education; lectures for working people; and classes in language, cooking, gymnastics, and trades.[10]

Despite their proliferation and undeniable success, the urban settlement houses began to experience some retrenchment as early as 1910. In an article in the *Harvard Theological Review* in 1911, Gaylord White noted the closing of a settlement in New York the previous year and said "the relatively permanent value of the social settlement" was open to question.[11] White concluded that the settlements were likely to survive for a long while, but his tone was nevertheless defensive. In fact, the settlements' very success was rendering them obsolete, as many of the reforms they sought were achieved and the services they pioneered in providing were increasingly "municipalized." "Hull House has always held its activities lightly," Jane Addams said, "ready to hand them over to whomever would carry them on properly." [12]

Even as the urban settlements relinquished their functions to public agencies, a move was afoot to transpose the settlement idea from urban to rural areas—as it had earlier moved from England to America. Allen Davis has pointed out that many urban settlement house workers, having been raised in comfortable homes in well-to-do residential neighborhoods, "had an ambivalent attitude toward the city." [13] It was also common at the turn of the century for rural areas to be seen as a possible haven for the lower classes who were being brutalized by life in the city. "Fresh air funds," for example, were common mechanisms for offering urban newsboys a few days of rustic rejuvenation. [14]

As early as 1899, John P. Gavit proposed formally that rural social settlements be established. [15] Noting that few such attempts had been made in the dozen years since Coit's Neighborhood Guild opened, Gavit argued that social settlements would benefit "wilderness bound" families. The "barren life of a rural community would make welcome almost any variety of intelligent provocation to social action," he said. "Imagine," he continued, "a versatile young couple, weary of city streets and dirt and artificiality, determining to transfuse their personal lives and culture and moral purpose into the life of a self-neglectful village and its contributing community." Like its urban predecessor, a rural settlement, Gavit suggested, "would take for granted the goodness, the aspiration, the self-serving power of the community, and would offer for these place and initiative of self-expression."

Gavit envisioned converting a church or schoolhouse to settlement use—the "emancipation of the people's building," he called it—and the organization of recreation, clubs, traveling libraries, "summer excursions," and "co-operative farming or dairying." "Why should not the sleepless conscience of a Rockefeller or a Pearsons," he concluded, "provoke the establishment of a fund to send a brilliant, resourceful group to the inspiration and salvation of some obscure country region, to set the example for the gradual uplift of rural communities throughout the land? . . . There needs to be now an evangelism to the socially and intellectually lost among the hills and valleys and on the prairies of this land." [16]

One of the larger contingents of those popularly considered to be "socially and intellectually lost" were the hill-bound people of southern Appalachia. Beginning with a few fragmentary accounts in the late eighteenth and early nineteenth century, and continuing in the torrent of "travels on horseback" narratives and popular fiction of the post–Civil War era, the region had been brought forcibly to popular awareness.[17] Among the most benighted of the "lost," the public was encouraged to believe, were the mountaineers of Kentucky's easternmost counties—Harlan and Breathitt, Perry and Letcher, Knott, Pike, Floyd, and Leslie—racked for years by feuds between the Frenchs and Eversoles, the Turners and the Sizemores, and many another family.[18] In the popular view Kentucky was, as George Vincent called it in his 1898 *American Journal of Sociology* article, "a retarded frontier." But it was less that than it was a frontier on the verge of convulsive industrial development which would shortly see internecine feuds replaced by bloody industrial warfare.[19]

In the center of eastern Kentucky lay Knott County, and at the center of it the county seat of Hindman. The story of how the first "settlement school" in the southern mountains came to be established there in 1902 reveals much about the accommodation of an urban institution to rural conditions. More significant, however, it is one of the most important chapters in the history of the relationship between indigenous culture and social change in Appalachia.

"To Learn All We Can and Teach All We Can": Founding a Rural Settlement

In the same month that Gavit's call for rural settlements appeared in the *Commons* (May 1899), the Kentucky Federation of Women's Clubs, meeting in Frankfort, heard a report from its Traveling Library Committee, which was sending boxes of books around the state. A questionnaire had been sent out with the books to assess how the program was working, and to it the Reverend J. T. Mitchell from Hazard (in Perry County, adjacent to Knott) replied that books were fine, but what was really needed was some women to teach mountain women cooking, sewing, and similar skills.[20]

As early as 1895, federation member Katherine Pettit had spent a week with six other women at a hotel in Hazard, forming some initial impressions of eastern Kentucky. She returned the next year with the state president of the Women's Christian Temperance Union (WCTU) and reported to the WCTU's annual meeting in the fall that formal work in the mountains should be undertaken. Nothing came of it, however, until the Federation of Women's Clubs meeting three years later.

Shortly after that meeting, four women went to Hazard—more than forty miles beyond where the railroad ended at Jackson—to set up what they called Camp Cedar Grove.[21] They erected borrowed tents, decorated them with pictures cut from magazines, arranged their cots and dining table, and welcomed all who came. "We hear a great deal of the sturdy, strong mountaineers," observed one, "but we saw few of them. Most of the people are tall, thin, sallow, and far from vigorous." For six weeks the women ran a kindergarten for the children, passed out books, magazines, and newspapers, and gave lessons in cooking (especially making beaten biscuits), sewing, and reading. There were also, Madeline McDowell Breckinridge wrote, "classes in many of the intermediate grades of knowledge." Although Breckinridge noted that the effort was derided in some quarters as the "beaten biscuit crusade," to her it seemed that local people valued the experience greatly. "One father came with the request," she wrote, "that the settlementers should take his daughter to the country they came from and bring her up to be such a woman as they were. . . . The settlementers left amid the sorrow of the whole countryside. . . . The women wept and begged them to come back the next summer. . . . The children clung to them and one man said to them, . . . 'You will go away and forget us, but we will never forget you and the good you have done will remain with us.'"[22]

The experiment was repeated the following year (1900), but on a larger scale. Six women—May Stone and Eva Bruner of Louisville; Madeline Breckinridge's sister-in-law Curry, Katherine Pettit, and "Miss Christian" of Lexington; and "Miss Campbell" of Philadelphia—stepped from the train at Jackson on 12 June and loaded their equipment and provisions on five wagons for the forty-five mile trip to Hindman.[23]

Passing out newspapers and magazines along the way, they followed Buckhorn Creek on the final leg of their trip to Hindman. By 15 June they had pitched their three tents on a high bluff above the little town. On a rope stretched between the tents, they hung Japanese lanterns. Bookcases and cupboards for dishes were set up, tent walls were covered with magazine pictures, and wooden tent platforms were spread with red carpets. The women cleared a playground from the underbrush, and every day twenty-five to fifty children arrived for kindergarten classes and recreation. "I wonder and wonder at the bright minds of these children," Pettit wrote in her diary. Using rooms in a local school building, the women offered classes similar to those of the previous year. Sixty-seven people entered the morning cooking classes, and more than a hundred (including about thirty-five boys) came for the two-hour afternoon sewing class. Pettit and Stone conducted Sunday school classes; Curry Breckinridge taught temperance songs; and Philadelphian Laura Campbell held music classes.[24]

FIGURE I-I
Town of Hindman as seen from settlement school grounds, ca. 1900
(Hindman Settlement School Archive).

FIGURE I-2
Summer settlement teachers and students
(Hindman Settlement School Archive).

FIGURE I-3
*Interior of summer settlement teacher's tent, showing magazine pictures used as
model decoration
(Hindman Settlement School Archive).*

Although frequently depicted in the popular press as reticent, suspicious, and hostile to outsiders, local people again, as they had the previous year, proved eager for and open to opportunities for human contact, color, novelty, and the learning of new skills. At a picnic Pettit and her associates gave ten days before they left at the end of August, nearly 350 local people showed up to express their appreciation. In his *Lexington Morning Herald* article at the end of the summer, French Combs called the camp "the mecca of all within reach."

After hearing Katherine Pettit's report on the summer's work, the Kentucky Federation of Women's Clubs decided at its 1901 meeting to conduct a third "social settlement in the mountains."[25] Less than three weeks later, Pettit and Stone and their two co-workers, Rae M. McNab and Mary E. McCartney, were met at the train in Jackson by Uncle Noah Spencer, who took them in wagons to Hindman. Welcomed by children and adults they had taught the summers before, Pettit and Stone climbed to their "Old Camp Ground" to find their favorite view of the valley "changed by the ugly new frame houses that were dotted here and there."

The 1901 summer settlement was actually set up not at Hindman but at Sassafras, in Carr's Fork Valley near the juncture of Letcher, Perry, and Knott counties, sixty miles from the nearest railroad. The *Lexington Morning Herald* asserted that there was "no charity similar in its methods and ends . . . in the United States or indeed in the world."[26] The program was similar to that of the two previous years, except that the women traveled more widely in the area and visited extensively in homes and neighborhoods. Perhaps drawing to some degree upon McCartney's experience as principal of a Presbyterian mission school among Mormons at Richmond, Utah (1887–93), and her more recent teaching at the Laura Sunderland School in the North Carolina Piedmont, they held classes at the three nearest schoolhouses, established a kindergarten, a day nursery, and three Sunday schools, and made arrangements to send several girls to school in Harlan and several boys to college at Berea. Stoically coping with travel on foot or by horseback, mud, rain, heat, and fleas, they helped care for the sick and bury the dead.

The Sassafras encampment was longer than the earlier ones (1 July to 1 October), and the women were pleased with what they accomplished. They reported to the federation that they had done "more truly settlement work than has been done [in the mountains] before, in the sense that we have been able to help and cheer more people in more varied ways." But "to do lasting good," they argued, "the settlement must be permanent." They recommended sending "a woman to live the entire year in one community." "Send a good Christian woman with industrial training into a thickly settled place," they said, "and in the course of time a permanent Social Settlement may be started there, which may prove a great power for good in the mountains of Kentucky."[27]

As early as the previous summer, in fact, there had been moves in several quarters to establish a permanent settlement at Hindman. Cora Smith of New York had visited Camp Industrial, looking for a site for an "industrial school," and there was a later visit from a gentleman who was interested in "getting the settlement work in all of the mountain counties." Two weeks before their departure, the women met with Hindman lawyer John E. Baker, who made "an earnest appeal for a good school" and urged Smith to locate her school there.[28] Pettit's diary for the next summer records another meeting in Hindman with some men who were "very anxious for us to establish a school there" and had already obtained local pledges of eight hundred dollars toward a permanent school.[29] Several times during the summers of 1900 and 1901, the women were visited by local octogenarian Solomon Everidge, who implored them to start a school.[30]

Pettit and Stone apparently left Hindman in the fall of 1901 committed to starting a settlement-type industrial school, for the following February found them in Boston at a meeting of the Eastern Kindergarten Association, outlining their plans and (apparently) seeking support. They reported that the Kentucky WCTU proposed "to start a Christian Social Settlement in connection with a first-class school and kindergarten, normal and industrial departments. To live among people in a model home, to show them by example the advantages of cleanness, neatness and order, and to inspire them to use pure language and to lead pure, Christian lives will be our effort, hoping thereby to elevate and uplift them."[31] The association voted to contribute "reading matter" but (apparently) no money. Three months later, however, the *Commons* reported that the women, "by a series of talks given in the east this winter," had raised enough money to buy land.[32]

Since virtually all early records of the school that Pettit and Stone established were destroyed in fires in 1905 and 1910, details of its actual founding are scarce. Fragmentary evidence suggests that by early in 1902 they had raised about twenty-six hundred dollars, bought one existing building, rented another, and accepted a three-acre strip of land bought by local citizens. Several small buildings were soon erected, and the "Log Cabin Social Settlement" opened with 190 students in the autumn of 1902.[33]

The number of boarding and day pupils rose quickly, and buildings were built steadily (and rebuilt after fires).[34] By the time the "WCTU Settlement School" became the independent Hindman Settlement School in 1916, there were fourteen buildings, including a powerhouse and a hospital, and three hundred students, one hundred of whom boarded.[35] By 1927 the plant comprised 345 acres of land and twenty buildings, including dormitories and offices, a workshop, a hospital, a twenty-eight room settlement house, a library, and a powerhouse that supplied electricity for both the school and the town of Hindman using coal from a mine located on school property. The institution's annual budget was nearly seventy thousand dollars, and its net worth was more than double that amount.

In the most obvious respects, the school was a success from the beginning. For a county in which the illiteracy rate among voting-age males had been nearly 33 percent in 1900, a school of any type was a boon, and the settlement school's annual waiting list of several hundred students suggested that it was recognized as such locally.[36] Each time fire destroyed

FIGURE I-4
Local men helping to move stones for construction of settlement school buildings,
ca. 1902
(Hindman Settlement School Archive).

buildings, local citizens rallied to rebuild, pledging money, materials, their labor and that of their horses and mules, and vast goodwill. Buildings were quickly rebuilt after fires in 1905, even though hauling each three-quarter-ton wagon load of building materials from the railroad took five wintry days.[37]

By 1910, however, there were signs of strain within the school. After another fire that year that wiped out several buildings, Pettit seriously debated whether to rebuild. She decided to do so, however, and she and Stone went once again to New York to raise money.[38]

But Pettit's time with the rebuilt school was short. As early as the spring of 1910 she was contemplating a new school at another location. By the following spring she had decided to build it at Pine Mountain in neighboring Letcher County. A year later she left Hindman and established Pine Mountain Settlement School.[39]

Officially, the explanation for the split was that Pettit had long ago promised Pine Mountain resident Uncle William Creech that she would someday come and open a school there; she was simply keeping a solemn promise. But it was apparently more complicated than that. In a letter to

FIGURE I-5
Hauling supplies by wagon for settlement school
(Hindman Settlement School Archive).

his Russell Sage Foundation superior John Glenn, John C. Campbell spoke of troubles between May Stone and staff member Marguerite Butler, who had been "a partisan of Miss Pettit during the differences that led to the separation of Miss Stone and Miss Pettit and the founding of Pine Mountain Settlement School." Campbell felt that he had been able to be instrumental "in preventing that separation from being viewed as a rupture of friendly relations and causing it to be regarded somewhat as an outgrowth of the work at Hindman." It would be unfortunate, Campbell observed, "to have an open break between two such prominent leaders" of mountain work.[40]

In 1918, Stone herself seriously considered leaving Hindman and giving the school free of charge to "any board or group of individuals" who would take it over entirely. Citing the difficulty of keeping teachers and maintaining the plant (coal for heating was—oddly enough—hard to get), she said she wanted such a transaction completed before the 1919 school year began.[41] But it turned out that Stone remained, and at least until the late 1920s Hindman continued to flourish in most of the directions originally contemplated. It was running a progressive farm, orchard, and dairy of sufficient size to provide most of the food for the school; its work with Lexington physician Dr. Joseph Stucky in 1910–11 had virtually eliminated trachoma, which had been rampant among local people.[42] By 1922 the academic program, with a staff of twelve teachers, included all grades from kindergarten through high school, and a large percentage of the school's graduates were continuing their educations at Berea College, the University of Kentucky, Wellesley, and elsewhere.

Despite the success of the school as an academic institution, however, there were substantial unresolved tensions and contradictions within its agenda: It was a boarding school which aimed to provide a comprehensive (in some senses, rehabilitative) environment for its students, but many day students (an increasing percentage as the years passed) returned every afternoon to the same homes whose perceived educational and cultural lacks had first called the school into being. The school professed to educate its students "back to their homes, rather than away from them," but provided in fact the most reliable means for many a mountain boy and girl to leave. It was a private, independently financed institution drawn by inexorable social change into partnership with a secular public school system based upon quite different educational theories and assumptions. It was an advocate for cultural values and expressive forms that were being repudiated in practice by most of the community as relentlessly as they were being celebrated formally.[43]

Thus Hindman solved in short order the problem of providing a "first class education." But relating itself to local culture proved a much more vexing dilemma. Central to that task was the problem of finding some way to relate traditional culture to the dramatic social change that accompanied the industrialization and commercialization of the area. In the first letter she wrote to John C. Campbell on her new Pine Mountain Settlement School stationery, Pettit posed two questions that went straight to the core of the matter: "What value do you put upon the old civilization of the mountains, and do you think there is anything in [it] that should be preserved?" and "Are the companies who own the mining towns organizing them with any view for the welfare of the mountain people?"[44]

Pettit's own struggle with those questions by then had stretched nearly twenty years to her first week's stay in a Hazard hotel in 1895. To follow that struggle—which she shared with many another woman of her social and cultural background, her values and perspectives, who cast her lot more or less permanently with the "fotched-on" women in the mountains—is to encounter a host of difficult questions: Where did the women *come from*, intellectually, socially, and culturally? How did they apprehend the social and cultural system they encountered in the mountains? To what extent did they wish to preserve it, or to change it? Through what mechanisms or programs did they seek to preserve or change? What was the impact of what they did? And what does the history of their efforts reveal about the way disparate cultural systems interact under highly stressed conditions?

Fotched-On Women in the Mountains

In the more than seventy years between the Seneca Falls convention of 1848 and the passage of the Nineteenth Amendment in 1920, American women sought in a variety of ways not only to gain their constitutional rights as citizens but also to find work that was worthy of the energy of the educated, competent professionals an increasing number of them were becoming. Before Seneca Falls, there was only one women's college in the country (Mt. Holyoke, founded in 1837). But three years later the Female Medical College of Pennsylvania opened, and after mid-century the "Seven Sisters" women's colleges began to open: Vassar in 1861, Smith and Wellesley in 1875, Radcliffe in 1879, Bryn Mawr in 1885, and Barnard in 1889.

There was a lag, however, between social acceptance of the idea of higher education for women and the opening of business and the professions to them. As a result, there were one or two generations of women who, as Allen Davis has pointed out, had to create professionally challenging and socially useful work to do. Some became foreign missionaries; some joined with other socially concerned (but not necessarily educated) women to found the Women's Christian Temperance Union in 1874; some blended the efforts of their local women's clubs into the General Federation of Women's Clubs, founded in 1890. Others—many others—found places in the emerging social settlement movement. In 1887 four Smith College alumnae, following a discussion of the beginnings of Toynbee Hall, decided to start a settlement house. It opened at 95 Rivington Street in New York City two years later. The move led to the formation of the College Settlements Association (CSA), based in the Seven Sisters colleges, all of which quickly formed chapters. Upon the founding of the CSA, one New York newspaper reported that "seven lilies have been dropped in the mud, and the mud does not seem particularly pleased."[45]

How Katherine Pettit and May Stone came to think of urban settlement houses as a model for their work in the mountains is difficult to reconstruct, despite what is known in a broad sense about the general movement of the idea to rural areas and to the South. Information on Pettit's early life is scarce; she guarded her privacy with a success that is most frustrating for the historian. She was born in 1868, into a "pioneer central Kentucky family"—a descendant of John Bradford, who reportedly brought the first printing press into Kentucky and published the first newspaper west of the Alleghenies. Pettit's father (Benjamin F.) owned a farm on Tate's Creek Road near Lexington, and the family's financial situation was apparently quite comfortable. Of a trip to Lexington and Louisville in late 1911 with Pettit and Stone, Elizabeth Watts said that "all through the Blue-grass region . . . we had such fun over who lived where and what kin they are to Miss Pettit, for practically all the fine old homes belong to someone who was in some way connected to her." [46]

Pettit attended Lexington's private Sayre Female Institute for about two years (1885–87), where she was a slightly above average student, but appears not to have graduated.[47] Little is known of her life between 1887, when she left Sayre, and 1895, when she took the first trip to eastern Kentucky. She was reportedly an active worker in the WCTU during this period.[48]

Scarcely more is known about Pettit's co-worker May Stone. She was born 1 May 1867 in Owingsville, Kentucky, to Henry L. and Pamela Bourne Stone. Henry Stone (1842–1922) was a Bath County native who served in the Kentucky Cavalry in the Civil War, at the close of which he established a law practice in Owingsville. The family moved to Mt. Sterling in 1878, when May was eleven years old, and to Louisville in 1885. Stone served four terms in the Kentucky legislature beginning in 1873, and was later city attorney of Louisville (1896–1904). He sent his daughter to private schools in Owingsville and Mt. Sterling (Harris Institute) and then to recently opened Wellesley in 1884. She departed one year before she would have graduated in 1888, however.[49]

Although settlement work had been under way in May Stone's hometown of Louisville since 1896, the two women turned instead toward eastern Kentucky.[50] By all accounts, Pettit was an energetic, strong-willed person who probably would not have relished working in someone else's settlement. Among women drawn to settlement work, there also appears to have been something of a pattern of seeking out new "needy" areas— both urban and rural—where settlements could be started. Moreover, from the 1880s to the turn of the century, as a result of the opening of the coalfields and the notorious family and clan feuds that occurred simultaneously, the violent and brutal social unrest and dislocations of eastern Kentucky had been much in the news.[51] And by no means least, the socially conscious members of Bluegrass Kentucky families were beginning

FIGURE 1-6
Katherine Pettit (Hindman Settlement School Archive).

FIGURE I-7
May Stone (Hindman Settlement School Archive).

to consider it their social and moral responsibility to lift their benighted brethren in the mountains.

One of the earliest important influences on Pettit (and perhaps on Stone as well) appears to have been the pioneer eastern Kentucky missionary work of the Reverend Edward O. Guerrant.[52] Guerrant (1838–1916) was born at Sharpsburg, near Lexington. His father was a doctor who was left with eight children when his wife (Mary Howe Owings Guerrant) died in 1850. In 1856, Guerrant entered Centre College in Danville, where he distinguished himself as a student and experienced a powerful religious conversion. His subsequent seminary study was terminated by the Civil War, in which he served on the staffs of Generals Humphrey Marshall, William Preston, and John S. Williams (1862–65). His unit saw action throughout southwest Virginia and eastern Tennessee, and to a lesser extent in eastern Kentucky, giving him his first acquaintance with the mountain area and mountain people. After the war, Guerrant studied medicine at Jefferson Medical College (Philadelphia) and Bellevue Hospital Medical College (New York), from which he graduated in 1867. For six years he practiced medicine in Mt. Sterling, but gave it up to study theology again. After two years (1873–75) at Union Theological Seminary (Richmond, Virginia), he returned to a pastorate in Mt. Sterling.

In 1877, Guerrant was appointed to the Committee on Home Missions of the Synod of Kentucky. His report urging special work in the mountains angered some of his fellow Presbyterians, but brought the Reverend Stuart Robinson—a man of strong convictions and great personal force—to his defense.[53] By 1881, Guerrant had convinced the Presbyterians to appoint him evangelist of the synod for the eastern half of Kentucky. For the next thirty-five years he conducted what can only be called a prodigious missionary work in the mountains.[54]

In the 1880s and early 1890s, while pastor of churches at Troy and Wilmore near Mt. Sterling, Guerrant made (generally during the summers) frequent tours of eastern Kentucky—mostly to Wolfe, Breathitt, Clay, Leslie, and Carter counties, but including others as well—where he organized scores of Presbyterian churches and Sunday schools. In 1897, he founded the Society of Soul Winners to carry on and extend his missionary work in the mountains. Within four years the society had dispatched sixty-seven evangelists to eastern Kentucky. Their work was regularly chronicled in the society's publication, *The Soul Winner* (1902ff.). By 1910 the society's budget was in the neighborhood of thirteen thousand dollars per year. After about 1910, Guerrant and the society focused on starting schools and colleges in the mountains, the last of which was Stuart

Robinson School at Blackey (1913). When the society's assets were turned over to the Presbyterian church in 1913, they included seventeen schools and mission stations, an orphanage, thirty-four buildings valued (probably conservatively) at fifty thousand dollars, and a staff of fifty missionaries.[55]

Guerrant's home base at Mt. Sterling lay on the border between the mountains and the Bluegrass, and his work seems to have been an important mediator between the social and economic orders and self-concepts of the two areas. More particularly, Guerrant served as a Christian mediator of the claims of social conscience which the former laid on the latter. After an 1884 preaching tour he described the little community of Bear Creek on the border of Lee and Breathitt counties as lying in the "regions beyond . . . the blue grass and brick houses." "Let the people of Kentucky be . . . admonished of their duty to these perishing people," he declared in 1892. "The curse of poverty and the desolation of sin are over them all. Without our help they must perish."

Guerrant recognized eastern Kentucky as a troubled region on the brink of major industrial development. "We saw coal veins all along the road, just sticking out of the mountains," his daughter recorded after a tour in 1894. "Sometimes we rode over solid coal beds; and the biggest trees I ever saw grew along the creeks and rivers." Someone on Lost Cove, she said, "told Papa that they were poor, but their souls were worth as much as rich people's."[56]

Guerrant's message also had a secular counterpart in the contemporary novels of John Fox, Jr., which regularly suggested that there was a "blood" kinship between mountaineers and the Bluegrass aristocracy. During the half-dozen years in which Pettit and Stone began their work in the mountains, Fox published four widely read novels in which the theme was prominent: *A Mountain Europa* (1894), *A Cumberland Vendetta* (1895), *Hell-for-Sartain* (1897), and *The Kentuckians* (1898). In those novels—as in those by Fox's successors Charles Neville Buck and Lucy Furman—the "blood kinship" between mountaineers and the Bluegrass aristocracy is the basis for everything from clichéd mistaken identities, to marriages, to individual and organizational uplift efforts in the mountains.[57]

Providing Katherine Pettit with money, further reinforcement for the idea of Bluegrass obligation to the mountains, and both theoretical and practical access to the settlement house model were three women members of the prominent Breckinridge family: Sophonisba, her younger sister Curry, and their sister-in-law Madeline McDowell Breckinridge.[58]

As the oldest of the three, Sophonisba Breckinridge (1866–1948) seems to have provided the most direct link to Jane Addams and Hull House.

Sophonisba graduated from Wellesley in 1888 (May Stone's class). In 1892, Wellesley professor Vida Scudder invited her to apply for a newly established fellowship being offered by the College Settlements Association for a year's work in a New York or Philadelphia settlement.[59] Three years later she began graduate studies in social work at the University of Chicago. While working part-time as a dean's assistant and fellow (1898ff.), Sophonisba lived at Hull House, as she continued to do for part of each year for many years. Her early stay there coincided with the summer settlement encampments in the Kentucky mountains.

Sophonisba was at the forefront of the most progressive social dynamics of the day—as writer, teacher, and administrator. She was the first woman admitted to the Kentucky bar (1895), and she became a professor of public welfare at the University of Chicago. She wrote and lectured extensively on delinquent children, juvenile court legislation, and related topics. And although she was away from Kentucky at the university for most of the years immediately prior to the founding of Hindman, her letters show that what she was learning at both the university and Hull House was regularly communicated to her family. A few months after Pettit and Stone established their settlement in the mountains, they wrote to thank Sophonisba "for all you did for us."[60]

A more present and thus perhaps more powerful influence was Sophonisba's sister-in-law Madeline McDowell Breckinridge (1872–1920), whose social involvements were similar to Sophonisba's, but all of whose work was done in Kentucky.[61] Educated in private schools in Lexington and Farmington, Connecticut, and at the State College [University] of Kentucky (1890–94), Madeline married Desha Breckinridge, who was editor of the *Lexington Herald*. She was a dynamic woman who—like her older sister-in-law Sophonisba—became a leader in a wide range of progressive movements.[62]

Madeline Breckinridge and Katherine Pettit were friends and close associates during the gestation period (1895–1902) for Hindman Settlement School. Just before she set up Camp Cedar Grove on 1 August 1899, Pettit went with Breckinridge and a group of friends on "a month-long trip through the mountains of Kentucky, Virginia, and Tennessee."[63] Indeed, at the same time, Madeline was setting up her own social settlement-type industrial school in the mountains—at Proctor, near Beattyville, about thirty miles west of Hindman. Opened in May 1899 (more than three years before Hindman itself), the settlement occupied an Episcopal mission house that had earlier been a tavern serving boat traffic on the Kentucky River. In addition to a kindergarten, classes were organized in sewing, cooking, carpentry, basket making, and (later) weaving. A group of young people ("The Proctor League") worked on neighborhood improvement projects.[64]

Pettit's involvement with Curry Desha Breckinridge was relatively brief, but close. Named for her grandfather Desha, a medical doctor, Curry was drawn early in life to social service and medicine. Her independence and social concern manifested themselves while she was still quite young. "You have brain enough to succeed in any profession," her father wrote to her while she was traveling in Europe with Sophonisba in 1891, "I have never doubted that you'd come out all right; that you would make something of life and yourself . . . . You have an unusual intellect and a pure, upright, noble nature; and God has some work for you. . . . [That you are in Europe] is proof that the work requires a preparation somewhat unlike that most usual and natural for Kentucky girls in our station of life." In a later letter to Sophonisba her father said Curry "is so high-principled, her desire to do her duty is so great and her love so genuine." She was, he said, "always in a hurry, never at rest, and . . . very much interested in her various works."[65]

Although formally in favor of her getting preparation for the medical career she preferred, her father apparently opposed it initially. As an alternative way to prepare herself for socially useful work—"Sister thinks I am dreadful and talk people blue in the face about politics," Curry wrote to her father in 1896—she took a "course in kindergarten" and became one of the first kindergarten teachers in Lexington.[66]

During a summer vacation from kindergarten teaching in 1900, Curry went with Pettit and Stone to set up Camp Industrial in the mountains. "Curry got off yesterday with her party," her father wrote to Sophonisba in mid-June. "[She] took tent, cot, hammock, croquet, books, lunch and cccc [etc.]; and ought to be comfortable." She remained in the mountains until the end of August, working with the kindergarten children at the camp. Just after her return, her father wrote to Sophonisba that

> the first fruits of [Curry's] missionary enterprise was gathered last
> evening; just at dark as she and I were sitting at the front door, a
> mountain boy twelve years old came up. He believed that Miss Pet-
> tit had agreed to meet him at the depot and he had come up from
> Frankfort and waited around the depot for nearly two hours and
> then had got a negro to guide him to our house; he was very man-
> nerly and entirely self-composed and had no doubt of his welcome;
> . . . Curry took him for a streetcar ride and a visit to Madge

[Madeline], put him up in her room and has him on her hands this morning.[67]

Thus the impulse behind Katherine Pettit's work in the mountains appears to have been a multistranded blend drawn from a variety of sources: her own intelligence and personal dynamism; the evangelical and social concern of the Presbyterian church—probably as mediated by Guerrant; some recurrent themes in certain popular fiction of the day; the liberal social concern of the WCTU and the Federation of Women's Clubs; the progressive social work undertaken by other women at the time (especially the Breckinridges); and the example of settlement work in northern cities, into which a few of her Bluegrass friends were being drawn.

And running through and beneath it all was a more or less vague sense that the mountains and the Bluegrass had something to offer each other. "We . . . feel the most important question for us," Pettit wrote in her Camp Industrial diary in 1900, "is how to bring the strong, healthy and learned Kentuckians into healthful touch with the poorest, most ignorant and humblest mountaineer and at the same time make the one appreciate the vitalizing strengthening influence of the other,—How can we make the people of the Blue Grass feel and see the need of the people in the lowliest cabin on the mountainsides!"[68]

As an abstract social and ethical impulse, such a position was appealing. But in fact, the genteel, Christian, Victorian Bluegrass women who started conducting summer social settlements among real flesh and blood mountaineers in 1899 experienced considerable culture shock. They found it difficult at times to retain confidence in the social and cultural worth and attractiveness they were convinced lay beneath what they judged to be some perfectly shocking ways of living, thinking, and behaving. If they regarded mountaineers as "their kinsmen, unjustly deprived of their rights"—as Lucy Furman noted years later—*some* of those kinsmen were at least temporarily a blot on the family escutcheon.[69]

On page after page of early diaries and newsletters, one may watch the settlement women trying to come to terms with a most troublesome cognitive dissonance. They are too intelligent and humane to be snobbish or condescending, and too Christian to judge or ridicule. But they nevertheless struggle with, on the one hand, their *conviction* that their new neighbors are descended from "hardy pioneers . . . of strong intellect and great force of character . . . will power, good hard sense in abundance . . . and good judgment" and, on the other hand, their *observation* that many of them eat little but bacon, coffee, and cornbread; go barefoot; sleep (in their clothes) all together in one room; drink moonshine, swear, and fight; and indulge (one hears) in shocking immorality.[70]

Even the religion of mountaineers they judged to have degenerated. A long account, "A Funeral Meeting in the Mountains," in an early (ca. 1908) newsletter depicts the three long sermons and the protracted shouting and crying of the day-long meeting. Confessing "a great ache for this tragedy of soul before us," the writer concluded that "they have no religion, and no opportunity to get any from their preachers." Such meetings "are their diversion and social intercourse, but as to food for the soul and a religion in which to live and die, it is not theirs."[71]

In New Englander Elizabeth Watts's career at Hindman may be seen, in fact, a good deal of the culturally based stress induced in the women who guided one early settlement school in the mountains. Born in 1890 in Medford, Massachusetts, Watts was the oldest of five children of cultivated (but not affluent) parents. When her mother remarried in 1898, the family moved to Bristol, Rhode Island, and Elizabeth soon entered Abbot Academy, a strict finishing school for women in Andover, Massachusetts.

Watts grew up in an urbane environment. Her stepfather, Henry W. Boynton (1869–1947), headed the English Department at Phillips Academy at Andover (1892–1901) before becoming chief book reviewer for *Atlantic Monthly* (1901–4). He edited and wrote more than a dozen books on English and American literature (including one co-edited with Thomas Wentworth Higginson) and contributed articles to *Nation, Bookman, Outlook*, and other magazines.[72] The Boynton household was filled with books, talk of books, and visits by eminent literary people of the day. It was not, however, a home in which either parental politics (moderate Republican) or social involvements tended to direct the attention of the eldest daughter to a social settlement in the Kentucky mountains.

Then how did it happen? The possible influence of Abbot Academy upon her decision is difficult to assess. Abbot principal Emily Means had a "passion for order," considered that "decorum and cultivation were synonymous," and mounted, it is said, an "almost fanatical defense of traditional behavior against modernistic incursions." The elocution teacher she hired admonished many an Abbot girl to "lift up your torso!" But on the other hand, Abbot students at the turn of the century heard lectures on Jewish immigrants and the Irish in South Boston. They also had a gym teacher (Rebekah Chickering) who was a progressive and a suffragist and who coached both the basketball team and Shakespeare plays.[73]

Although Katherine Pettit reportedly visited Abbot on her fund-raising trips and spoke to students about Hindman, Elizabeth Watts seems not to have heard her. Her going to Hindman happened, Watts said seventy years later, by "mere chance."

But it was not entirely chance. Having graduated from Abbot in 1908, Watts was at home, rather at loose ends, and looking for interesting work. A younger sister of her mother's best school friend from Medford was Olive Dame Campbell, wife of John C. Campbell, who had recently undertaken an extensive social survey of the southern mountains under the aegis of the Russell Sage Foundation. As a dinner guest in the Boynton home, Mrs. Campbell talked of her work and of the many new "church and independent" schools she had visited in the mountains.

Watts—whose interest in Kentucky had first been piqued by having read the "Little Colonel" series of children's books, which were set in a romanticized Bluegrass Kentucky—told Mrs. Campbell rather casually to let her know if she heard of interesting work she might do in the mountains. A few weeks later a letter arrived inviting her to come to Hindman, and one week later she boarded a train for Kentucky. A two-day trip by horseback (her first) brought her to Hindman, where she intended to spend perhaps a year. She stayed forty-seven years, first as a teacher (of eighty pupils in one room), and later as assistant director (1924) and director (1946).[74]

And yet from a cultured, literary, finishing school environment in New England to Hindman, Kentucky, was at the deepest levels a difficult move to negotiate. "Last night I dreamed," Watts wrote to her mother after she had been in the mountains two and a half years, "that you arrived in a new kind of automobile and told me that you could easily take me home in two hours to spend the day. . . . It made me terribly homesick to wake up and find it wasn't true." But fifteen months later she wrote, "I love this place and everyone in it and I'd like to settle down and enjoy life here always. I wasn't built for the outside world and I *was* for this."[75]

Elizabeth Watts's nocturnal dream of a joyful flight homeward and her daytime wish to "settle down and enjoy life here always" suggest quite succinctly the cultural tension that underlay the Hindman experiment: mountaineers as hopelessly degenerate or merely temporarily wayward kinsmen of the "best stock"; local culture as beautiful and life-affirming or perverted and moribund; settlement women as bearers of modernity and enlightenment or seekers of primal authenticity amid modern alienation and anomie. Neither Watts nor any of her colleagues appear to have located themselves at either extreme, but available evidence suggests that

FIGURE 1-8
Elizabeth Watts (Hindman Settlement School Archive).

they all felt the tension at some level. It is clear in any case that culture was the touchstone at both origin and destination; culture was the key—to perceived difference, to energizing motive, to rescue and rejuvenation.

All Very Christmasy and Nice: Hindman Settlement School as Cultural Change Agent

Every Saturday night all the "bad uns" around here "hev a gathering" where they pick the banjo, dance, drink moonshine, swear and fight. . . . Ever since we heard of the "gatherins" . . . we have been wondering what we can do to show them how the young people can meet in a social way and have a good time, without doing the dreadful things they do.
Katherine Pettit, Diary of 1901, pp. 23–27

Precedents for making culture both a conceptual and a practical base for settlement work were well established long before Katherine Pettit began her work in the mountains. Allen Davis has pointed out that university men in the early London settlements wanted to "make their settlement in the slums an outpost of education and culture." That they came close to doing so was not lost on an American observer who found Toynbee Hall "essentially a transplant of university life. . . . The quadrangle, the gables, the diamond-paned windows . . . the dining room with its brilliant frieze of college shields, all make the place seem not so distant from the dreamy walks by the Isis or the Cam." The parallel survived transplantation to America. Gregory Weinstein, a Russian Jew who went to Stanton Coit's Neighborhood Guild in the late 1880s, noted a similarity between the guild and educated Russians who "sometimes went to live in the villages to bring peasants culture and education."[76]

Culture became the basis for many an urban settlement program: classes in ethnic handicrafts for men, women, and children; instruction in native drama, poetry, and language; craft shops; music programs; festivals; art galleries; and dance classes. As Jane Addams phrased it, the aim was, on the one hand, "to preserve and keep whatever of value [the immigrants' lives] contained" and, on the other, "to bring them into contact with a better type of Americans." The perceived danger was that immigrants—especially older ones—would "lose the amenities of European life without sharing those of America."[77] Hence the contradictory agenda of preservation and assimilation.

In some respects the history of urban settlements can be read as a tug-of-war between those which pressed on *beyond* cultural programs to social action, as it became clear that such programs—however appealing—were of limited social use, and those which turned more and more *toward* cultural programs, as the hazards and frustrations of direct social action emerged.

The implicitly conservative politics of the latter choice were noted repeatedly by a number of observers of the contemporary urban scene. Thorstein Veblen judged that "the solicitude of settlements . . . is in part directed to enhance the industrial efficiency of the poor and to teach them the more adequate utilization of the means at hand; but is also no less consistently directed at the incubation, by precept and example, of certain punctilios of upper-class propriety in manners and customs." A character in a Sinclair Lewis novel castigated settlements more bluntly as "cultural comfort stations, rearing their brick Gothic among the speakeasies . . . and upholding a standard of tight-smiling prissiness." And an observer of settlement work among Lower East Side Jewish youth in New York complained that the settlements were replacing the healthy street life of children with "sit-up-straight-and-be-good social rooms, literature clubs, civics clubs, basket-weaving and scroll-iron work."[78]

Much later, in a scholarly study of the so-called music settlements, Nicholas John Cords confirmed many of the impressions of these contemporary observers. Cords found that the music settlements, for all their formal veneration of immigrant culture, were concerned primarily with the preprofessional training of students destined to be classical musicians in the western European tradition. They were less interested in music as a socializing or recreational mechanism or as a means of continuity with the old country—and least of all with its possible usefulness in social action. Music at Chicago Commons, Cords noted, was designed to supplement "the street songs and lower class of music." And settlement leader Albert J. Kennedy feared that "strongly rhythmic" music such as jazz would "set free the lower centers." [79]

The cultural tensions and ironies were in no way attenuated when the settlement model moved from the cities into the southern mountains. More than seventy years after she rode into Hindman on horseback, Elizabeth Watts recalled "no feeling of condescension" toward local culture on the part of any of the settlement school teachers and workers. Asked why there seemed to be none, she said, "I liked the people," and quoted Cecil Sharp as having said that mountain people were "the most cultured people in the United States." [80]

Pettit's diaries and other early documents reveal, however, that the perception of cultural *difference* was great on both sides and that the differences easily translated into a hierarchy of cultural values. "The thing that strikes me so," Pettit said, "is the utter lack of self-control the children have. They do absolutely as they please and the parents do not know how to control . . . them. They are so rough and brutal in their treatment of them." [81] On a visit up Pershing's Branch to the home of the Collins family, Pettit found, on the other hand, a neat and clean one-room log cabin inhabited by Mr. and Mrs. Collins and their eight pretty, well-mannered daughters. "They were so far away and seldom saw anyone," Pettit remarked, "that it was quite remarkable to see something like culture." But of the visit of Mr. Combs from Sassafras to their camp a few days earlier, she recorded: "He told us of his only child a boy five years old that he was trying to bring up right and how hard it was. He said that he was nothing but an awkward plain man and didn't know what to do in company, but that he sought every opportunity to go where cultured people were." Ten years later, when Watts showed some Hindman children pictures of her family's new home in Rhode Island, they exclaimed, "[You] must be rich. Look at all those books." [82]

Contradictions notwithstanding, it seems reasonable to conclude that, to Pettit and her co-workers, "culture" was not the full range of attitudes, beliefs, practices, customs, and lifeways of a group, marked by both beauty and ugliness, consistency and contradiction, but rather a select *few* items (such as "manners," dress and "carriage," eating habits, home decoration, and "breeding") *certified* as culture by a late-nineteenth-century, upper-middle-class, Victorian consensus—items which were in short supply in eastern Kentucky. The women therefore disapproved of those who did not recognize or accept the consensus, and wrote approvingly of those who, like the "plain man," "didn't know what to do in company" but knew real culture when he saw it.

What was the actual culture of Knott County like at the turn of the century? Pettit's diaries preserve some clues. On a visit to Uncle Rob Cornett's home the settlement women saw a bed covered with beautiful handwoven coverlets and heard Cornett play "meeting house songs" on a dulcimer he had made forty years earlier. At Mrs. Enoch Combs's house on Red Oak Branch they saw homemade baskets and homespun blankets, coverlets, linsey, and jeans. They watched people raising log houses, attending funeral meetings, working at a homemade turning lathe, boiling sorghum, dyeing cloth with vegetable dyes. They saw quilting patterns like *Waves of Ocean, Sun Flower, Catch Me If You Can,* and *Democratic Banner* sewn from solid yellow, green, and red calico put together with white. Rhoda Combs sang old ballads for them, and from another they heard of a ballad that Basil Beverly had recently written about Granville Stacy robbing the local post office. They heard the Baptists line out hymns in "the old way" and sat on porches and sang ballads, play-party songs, and hymns out of *The Sweet Songster.*[83]

But the appearance of cultural stability conveyed by these old-time ways was largely an illusion. If lined-out hymns, unaccompanied ballads, and dulcimer and fiddle tunes were the musical background, the banjo was coming to dominate the foreground, and a host of mail-order instruments would soon be on their way. A minister's wife warned Pettit against having banjo music at Camp Industrial, since "nobody but wicked folks" would allow banjo picking around them. Another man told them of a "no-good" preacher who would "horse-swap [and] listen to the banjo"—both morally and socially reprehensible activities, one judges. As late as 1912, Elizabeth Watts was able to hear an old woman play "Long [Flop] Eared Mule" on a gourd fiddle, but surer signs of the times were the mandolin and guitar she heard at a "pounding" for newlyweds and the Mill Creek Brass Band playing on its mail-order instruments. After being entertained by "the Maggard boys" playing on cornet, "harp" (mouth harp?), and tambourine one evening as early as 1901, Pettit asked where the instruments had come from. Harrison Maggard told her they "saw them advertised in a book, sent off for them and, just as soon as they came, went to playing . . . and had been playing ever since."[84]

Thus the culture around the fotched-on women was—like every live culture—characterized by both continuity and discontinuity, stability and change, indigenous and borrowed elements. Its energies were divided between drawing upon a usable past and divining a mysterious future; enduring and adapting; fearing and resisting change and welcoming and embracing it. It was old quilt patterns cut from new store-bought goods; old (and new) songs played on mail-order instruments; new realities (coal mines and coal camps and post offices) cast in old ballad meter or parlor-song style. This was, on the whole, a cultural situation incomprehensible within the concept of culture employed by Pettit, Stone, and their co-workers.

Paradoxically, for all their professed reverence for traditional culture and their wish to forestall the cultural effects of impending industrialization, the settlement school women were themselves powerful instigators of cultural change. As early as the "Camp Industrial" summer of 1900, boys and girls in cooking classes were taught to make cakes with chocolate icing, "how to dress a chicken properly," to cook beans without lard ("They think our way very nice"), and to wash and put away dishes. In between times, children were taught to sing temperance songs to the accompaniment of a portable reed organ.[85]

Similar patterns were repeated and elaborated the following summer. Knott County women and girls were taught to fry apples and to make cottage cheese, "light bread," beaten biscuits, and candy. They were given lessons in ironing, sewing, and crocheting and helped to "weave picture frames out of rafia" ("When the frames were finished they put in pictures of George Washington and they went home very proud of their morning's work"). They attended their first Sunday school classes and music classes, heard for the first time about Fourth of July celebrations and Christmas trees, and gazed at stereoscopic slides of far-off places. Children in kindergarten made pin wheels and played with their first paper dolls, and families attended genteel "socials" designed to replace the boisterous "gatherins" the young people were accustomed to. And as many as possible were induced to sign the temperance pledge.[86] In sum, much of the indigenous culture of the area was being intentionally replaced by genteel turn-of-the-century mass culture: light bread, pump organs, "socials," Fletcherized food, and napkins on the left, please.

A particularly graphic example of the process was the settlement's transformation of local Christmas celebrations. Before the turn of the century, many mountain people still celebrated "Old Christmas," the family and religious holiday on 6 January, the birthday of Christ as depicted in the ancient "Cherry Tree Carol":

On the sixth day of January
my birth-day will be;
When the stars in the elements
shall tremble with glee.

In the late 1880s, folklorist James Mooney reported from his collecting in the North Carolina mountains that Old Christmas was being celebrated, that children were hanging stockings by the chimney on Christmas Eve, and that the Christmas tree was still unknown.[87]

Some evidence suggests that for many in the mountains the usual Christmas season stretched from New Christmas on 25 December to Old Christmas and involved religious observances, parties, dances, and gift giving. Traces of such a pattern linger, for example, in the fiddle tune "Breaking Up Christmas." As late as the 1970s, fiddler Lawrence Bolt (b. 1894) of the Galax, Virginia, area recalled the social context in which he heard the tune as a child: "Through this country here, they'd . . . have a dance at one house, then go off to the next one the following night and all such as that. The week before Christmas and the week after, that's when the big time was. About a two-week period, usually winding up about New Year. . . . They'd play a tune called 'Breaking Up Christmas,' that was the last dance they'd have on Christmas. . . ."[88]

Christmas customs in the mountains were gradually shifting in the 1890s, however, under a variety of influences. In Asheville, one of the more important metropolitan areas in the southern mountains, there had been central-station electricity and electric streetcars by 1890. The city's population was growing dramatically (from just over twenty-five hundred in 1880 to over ten thousand in 1890), and mainstream ways and values were gaining in prominence. Thus the 24 December 1894 issue of the *Asheville Daily Citizen* carried a picture of Santa Claus on the front page, and the 26 December issue noted that Christmas Eve "as regards fireworks, was tame as compared to the old way of celebrating" a half-dozen years earlier. On the other hand, local merchants ran advertisements for "Christmas presents" through 5 January (the eve of Old Christmas), suggesting that Christmas was still thought of not as the one-day event of the "new way" but as the twelve-day celebration of old.

Instead of encouraging established local practice, Hindman Settlement School reinforced the drift toward a new style of celebration. Prior to the arrival of the school, local people seem to have been accustomed to two Christmas celebrations: a rowdy one on 25 December, favored by the young people for its somewhat saturnalian aspect; and a quieter religious observance on 6 January. The settlement women, wary of saturnalian revels but convinced that both the date and the popular forms of the Christmas celebration in mass society were "correct," sought to replace local custom with Christmas trees, stockings by the fireside, and Victorian carols. The import of the change was not lost on one mountaineer, who recalled later to a teacher at a neighboring school, "Well, Christmas, hit used to be the rambangin'est, shootin'est, killin'est, chair-flingin'est day in the year till the school come."[89]

Thus at the settlement 25 December became the official Christmas Day, celebrated according to popular conventions. To the carols locally favored on Old Christmas—the ancient "Cherry Tree Carol" (Child 54) and the more recent but venerable "Brightest and Best" (composed 1811)—were appended such current popular favorites as "We Three Kings" (1857) and "Good King Wenceslas" by J. M. Neale (1818–66). A school newsletter of 1912 describes Christmas as it came to be celebrated every year at the settlement: a Christmas tree decorated with popcorn and paper chains, stockings hung by the chimney, dolls for the girls and tops for the boys. Fifty-five children marched in behind four marshals carrying pine limbs trimmed with holly and red ribbons, and arranged themselves in a "Christmas carol tableau." It was, the newsletter said, "all very Christmasy and nice." For the outlying districts, there were trees and celebrations in local schoolhouses. "And just think," a visitor reported after one such celebration, "this past Christmas is the first *real* Christmas they have ever known."[90]

The settlement women also introduced other secular (or secularized) popular holidays, including the Fourth of July, St. Patrick's Day, May Day, and St. Valentine's Day.[91] By contrast, Elizabeth Watts reported that an attempted "Mountain Day" celebration in 1912 was marred by so much rowdiness, shooting, and fighting that it would not be repeated.[92]

How did local people react or accommodate to such changes? Little concrete evidence is available beyond Katherine Pettit's early diaries, but those suggest that the response was quite positive. Although school trustees at George's Branch at first refused during the summer of 1901 to let the women use the schoolhouse for Sunday school classes (to which some church members were opposed), they later relented. Similarly, opposition to their sending girls away to school in Lexington and Louisville was both infrequent and temporary.

For the most part, local people appear to have welcomed the new world presented to them. "The stereoscopic pictures," Pettit reported, "are quite the most wonderful things many of them have ever seen and it is hard to convince them that such beautiful things are in the world." Local girls were "enthusiastic" at their cooking lessons and "fascinated" with making hem-stitched table cloths. Local people proved especially fond of the new portable organ and the music that came with it. "The children are learning the songs so well," Pettit recorded in her diary, and the girls are "setting the table just like they do in the pictures." Ida Combs told them that her folks "like the [new] way she cooks," and one young woman asked to come to live at the settlement because she liked "clean living and pretty fixings." [93]

One family, Mrs. Stacy and her daughter Rhoda, proved to be especially apt pupils. After a visit to Camp Industrial, Mrs. Stacy had returned home and transformed her small house to look as much like the camp as possible, with magazine pictures on the walls and other decorative touches favored by the settlement women. The next summer, she asked Pettit "how to cook everything and how to set the table," learned to play some hymns on the organ, and was excited to hear for the first time about decorating Christmas trees. "When we reached home," Pettit wrote after one day spent visiting in mountain homes, "Rhoda and Mrs. Stacy were sitting in the doorway with hymn books, singing Miss McNab's songs 'yourn way—not ourn.'" On another evening, Pettit sat before her Camp Industrial tent and listened to a local woman hunt for her cow, singing not the old songs of the mountains but "On the Safe Side of Temperance I'll Soon Take My Stand."

Thus the professed (and at some levels, real) veneration of the settlement women for local culture was *selective*, and the mechanism of selectivity was the colored lens of their own culture, which was for all practical purposes the genteel popular culture of the turn of the century. The full cultural significance of the settlement is to be found less in its tentative, initial contact with local culture, however, than in its long-term, organized, institutionalized cultural programs: its work with traditional ballads and handicrafts.

Ballads and Handicrafts:
Hindman's Organized Cultural Programs

The Civil War had not long been over when word began to trickle out that "old ballads" were to be found in the southern Appalachians. Attention was focused primarily upon the type of ballad that Francis J. Child can-

FIGURE I-9
Christmas gifts for settlement school children, Hillside House
(Hindman Settlement School Archive).

FIGURE I-10
Settlement students in July 4th pageant
(Hindman Settlement School Archive).

FIGURE I-11
Settlement youngsters dancing around Maypole, Mouth of Combs' Branch
(Hindman Settlement School Archive).

onized in his *English and Scottish Popular Ballads* (1882–98).[94] The *Journal of American Folklore* published its first scholarly article on music in the Appalachians near the turn of the century; the first state folklore societies (North Carolina and Kentucky in 1912; Virginia in 1913; and West Virginia in 1915) were established primarily to collect ballads; and by 1913, U.S. Commissioner of Education P. P. Claxton, at the suggestion of folklorist C. Alphonso Smith at the University of Virginia, had issued a circular urging that the public collect "English and Scottish popular ballads," which he called "valuable treasures which otherwise would be lost." Professor Smith's statement, included in the circular, quoted poet Sidney Lanier's estimate of the moral and social value of such ballads. "I know," said Lanier, "that he who walks in the way these . . . ballads point will be manful in necessary fight, fair in trade, loyal in love, generous to the poor, tender in the household, prudent in living, plain in speech, merry upon occasion, simple in behavior, and honest in all things."[95]

The settlement schools quickly became focal points for ballad collecting. They encouraged ballad singing among students and their families, made their own collections, used ballads and photographs of ballad singers in their promotional literature, and served as headquarters for collectors who made sojourns to the mountains.

From their first summers in eastern Kentucky, the settlement women had been aware of the ballad tradition—both the singing of old ballads and the making of new ones. Pettit recorded in her journal in 1901 that "Mrs. Stacy and Rhoda sang old ballads while they carded and spun" and that "Basil Beverly says he will write a ballad 'about you'ns and the tent.'"[96] Preserved among the Camp Industrial papers at Hindman is a scrapbook with the words of many songs and ballads—presumably collected during the summer's sojourn. The collection—which includes Child ballads ("Pretty Polly," "Massey Groves," and "Barbara Allen"), at least one nineteenth-century English ballad ("The Drunkard's Dream"), native American ballads ("Poor Ellen Smith" and "Omie Wise"), and several lyric songs ("Come All You Young and Tender Ladies")—suggests that the ballad tradition in the area was both lively and eclectic.

By 1907, Pettit had submitted a collection of ballads from Hindman to a scholarly journal. Edited by Harvard scholar George Lyman Kittredge, the collection included about two dozen items, including in about equal numbers Child ballads, broadside and stall ballads, native American ballads, and play-party songs.[97] Thus the word was out that there were ballads to be collected from settlement school children.

A half-dozen or so years later, New Yorker Josephine McGill spent a summer collecting ballads in Knott and Letcher counties, partly among Hindman students and their families and friends.[98] "To hear the children of Hindman Settlement School lustily carolling 'Susie in the Parlor' and 'Down Among the Daisies,'" she wrote, "is to be assured that the founts of joy and an inherited feeling for rhythm and melody are not exhausted."[99]

Apparently, McGill had gotten interested in ballads by reading some of the many ballad studies then being published and by hearing the concert interpretations of ballads that were gaining in popularity. Her attention was drawn to the Kentucky mountains by Lucy Furman's fictional accounts of Hindman Settlement School (1910ff.) and by an invitation from May Stone—perhaps on one of Stone's fund-raising trips to New York.[100]

The "picturesque wild land" that McGill sketched in her strongly romanticized account of her trip was obviously experiencing rapid cultural change. She recalled riding her horse into "a clearing where Beauty fairly smote the vision," and stopping in "a lonely spot at the head of a narrow creek in a world of green and silver." Listening to mountain singers of "Lord Randal," "The Gypsy Laddie," and "The Twa Sisters," she felt "the rapture of the gold-washer when the ore begins to gleam." But along with ballads and the primitive mouth bow, she also found banjos, reed organs, and "feud songs." The banjo she passed quickly by, seeking a "richer melodious booty," and the feud songs—although treasured by a few as proof that the art of ballad making still survived—she judged to have "tedious" narratives, "cheap" meters, and "tawdry" tunes.

Like many another collector of the time, McGill was of two minds about mountaineers and their culture. On the one hand, they sometimes held to the charming old musical ways, but on the other, they too often lapsed into picking the banjo, wheezing out a Sunday school song on the reed organ, or composing tawdry feud songs like "The Rowan County Crew." On the one hand, their nobility was sometimes evident ("a veritable mountain Madonna," she called one singer), but on the other, that nobility itself seemed out of place and uncharacteristic. "While the mother sang," she wrote of one gold-collecting session, "her beautiful dark-eyed daughter came and stood in the doorway; she might have been a highland sister to Jeanne d'Arc or some other peasant girl of history who 'born better than her place, still lent grace to the lowliness she knew.'"

McGill was followed to Hindman two years later by fellow New Yorkers Loraine Wyman and Howard Brockway, who had been invited by Pine Mountain Settlement School codirector Ethel DeLong.[101] Arriving in mid-May 1916, they made both Hindman and Pine Mountain their base of operations, collecting in Knott, Harlan, Letcher, Estill, Pulaski, Magoffin, and Jackson counties. A portion of their collection was published a few months later as *Lonesome Tunes: Folksongs of the Kentucky Mountains*, and in late October they presented some of their materials in concert.[102]

Like McGill before him, Brockway (1870–1941) viewed mountain people and their culture rather ambivalently.[103] Having studied and performed in Germany in the 1890s and taught at Peabody Conservatory (1903–8), Mannes School of Music, and Julliard, he found the southern mountains alien indeed. Thus his preparations for the expedition "took the form," he said, "of riding lessons, . . . of innoculation, of vaccination, and of the purchase of suitable equipment for outdoor life." He judged the people of the mountains to be "absolutely innocent of any knowledge of the progress of the world at large," marveled that one singer did not know where New York was, found corn bread and razorback hogs arrestingly exotic, and winced to see a woman spit tobacco juice into the fire. Yet mountaineers seemed to him to have "[a] poise and innate dignity . . . a culture all their own . . . thinking minds and a philosophy of life both broad and trenchant."

Brockway's definition of what was culturally "significant" also mirrored McGill's: Child ballads and dulcimers were good; banjos and the newer music to be heard at the railheads and the county seats were not. Banjo and guitar pickers "were never conversant with the object of our quest," Brockway said. "They played a type of song which had for us no interest whatever." The "outer world" and its "trivial and commonplace music" were a "killing blight"; the impending social and economic changes within the mountains would bring only "contamination." Before both, the ballad collector must move quickly.

At length the ballad-collecting process turned out to be circular: Hindman (and more especially Pine Mountain) were predisposed by a variety of factors toward the older cultural survivals. That predisposition led them to prefer certain aspects of the total cultural system of the area. Their doing so brought them to the attention of scholars and collectors who were similarly disposed. By their activities and principles of selection, and particularly the publication and publicizing of their findings, the collectors reinforced the schools' preexisiting cultural theories and judgments.

In retrospect, it appears that Hindman's best chance to do cultural work whose effect would be positive over the long term would have been to ground their cultural programs in the complex dynamics of both traditional culture and cultural change in the area. Such an emphasis might have allowed them to see the composition of feud songs or the playing of new instruments, for example, as evidence of the continued vitality and creativity of the culture, rather than of its woeful degeneration.

But they chose otherwise. Hindman publicity materials uniformly emphasized cultural *survivals*—marvelous but essentially anachronistic artifacts: ballads and baskets, archaic speech and manners, dulcimers and play-party songs. Over and over again, the word went forth from the settlement schools that mountain culture was "Elizabethan." Hindman's 1910 newletter reported that "our children come to us from pioneer homes, where the language of Shakespeare is spoken." In an extended popular exploration of "Shakespearean speech" in the mountains for *Harper's Magazine* in 1915, William Aspenwall Bradley reported that "when the mountaineer begins to read at all, he displays so marked a preference for Shakespeare that it is invariably [his] works . . . that have most frequently to be rebound in any library to which he has access." Hindman made at least one attempt to allow settlement children to employ their supposedly natural "Elizabethan" speech patterns by acting in a Shakespearean play. The results were not entirely satisfactory. The seven year old who played Puck in the school's 1914 production of *Midsummer Night's Dream* complained that if his part "were only in our own language, I could learn it better." [104]

More attention was given to old ballads from across the water than to Elizabethan speech, however. Hindman students were taken to perform ballads before "outside" audiences in the 1920s, and as late as 1933—when the coal industry had been careening along at full tilt in eastern Kentucky for two decades—a newsletter announced that Hindman students were being encouraged to sing ballads "so that these old folk songs will not be forgotten as the victrola and radio creep gradually into the hills." "Now as the little girls scrub the floors," it concluded, "they sing about Lord Bateman and the Turkish Lady." [105]

As late as 1938 the theme was repeated. A generation ago, reported the January 1938 newsletter, Hindman had almost no mining-camp children. Now there were several, "bringing with them the 'Ways of the World' and the problems thereof." It is easy enough, the newsletter continued,

> to wash off the cheap paint and powder, but can we show the girls
> . . . the difference between cheap tawdry things and the beauty of
> simplicity? . . .
>
> A child with a genuine love for music expressing itself in raucous
> singing of so-called "hill-billy" songs, learns at our Saturday night

gatherings beautiful *lasting* melodies, and the true mountain ballads that are a heritage from English forbears. Her keen ambition to take piano lessons is fulfilled.

The distinctions being made were *class* distinctions; the progression was from cheap paint and powder to piano lessons. And, appropriately, the newsletter statement concluded by recalling that Sharp commented during his visit to Hindman that "if I didn't know where I was, I should think your children came from an English school of the better class." [106]

Hindman's other major cultural endeavor during its early years was its handicrafts program, called "Fireside Industries." The rationale for that program was similar to that for revitalizing the ballad tradition, but also larger in one important sense. In addition to honoring and preserving local traditions for whatever they might contribute to individual identity, family and social stability, and cultural continuity, the handicrafts program was considered to offer mountain boys and girls and their parents manual skills that would be useful personally, domestically, and economically, and to generate income for the school itself.

The link between settlement work and the revival of handicrafts was as old as the settlement movement itself. The earliest London settlements sought to incorporate into their buildings and programs the theories of Carlyle, Ruskin, Morris and others who were arguing for a revival of handicrafts as a counter to dehumanized and dehumanizing industrial production. As early as 1877, Morris lectured to the Trades Guild of Learning on decorative arts, and during the ensuing years he elaborated his thought in a series of essays and lectures. [107] In an essay of 1888, Morris argued that the destruction of handicrafts leads to a degradation of life, that production by machinery results in "utilitarian ugliness," that the division of labor robs the workman of joy in his work, and that life removed from the realities of production by hand is vicarious life only. [108] The vision as projected by Morris was noble indeed: "Let us educate ourselves to be good workmen at all events, which will give us real sympathy with all that is worth doing in art . . . and prepare us for that which is surely coming, the new cooperative art of life, in which there will be no slaves, no vessels of dishonor. . . ." [109]

The settlements found particularly attractive Morris's contention that "the complete work of applied art, the true unit of the art, is a building with all its due ornament and furniture." [110] The new or converted buildings of the settlements offered opportunities to apply Morris's idea holistically, as an expression of a coherent social ideal and program: The set-

FIGURE I-I2
Settlement students in Shakespeare production
(Hindman Settlement School Archive).

tlement house itself could be "the complete work of applied art." In 1859–60, Morris himself had sought to embody his ideas in the building and furnishing of his Red House outside London.[111]

The arts and crafts movement in England was primarily an urban phenomenon. C. R. Ashbee's Guild and School of Handicraft appeared in London in 1880, and eight years later London artists and craftsmen who were refused recognition by the Royal Academy organized the Arts and Crafts Exhibition Society.[112] A corollary of the argument that modern industry was dehumanizing workers, however, was the contention that traditional handicrafts should be fostered and preserved where they still existed among not yet industrialized people in rural areas. Still another corollary was that handicrafts might be revitalized (or even reintroduced) among rural people who were being enticed into urban centers by declining handicraft markets or the wages offered by industries. Thus efforts to reinstigate weaving at Westmoreland and on the Isle of Man led to the founding of the Home Arts and Industries Association.[113]

In the United States as in England, many of the early efforts to preserve or revive handicrafts took place in urban areas. Philadelphia had its Society of Art Needlework as early as 1877. Maria Storer founded Cincinnati's Rookwood workshop in 1880. Many other such organizations followed in the closing years of the century, including the Indiana Keramic Association (1897), the Boston Society of Arts and Crafts (1897), Chicago's Industrial Arts League (1899), and the Arts and Crafts Society of Dayton, Ohio (1902).[114]

Other important centers for handicrafts work were of course the settlement houses. Hull House opened its "labor museum" of handicraft artifacts, tools, and processes in 1900, and many other settlement houses instituted crafts programs.[115]

In the United States several conditions combined to cause the handicrafts movement to flourish more rapidly in rural areas that it had in England—predating in some cases its appearance in urban areas. In the first place, the more rural character of the country made handicraft survivals more obvious and the apparent possibilities for preserving them more numerous. In addition, the Reconstruction-era movement to provide manual training for blacks in the South suggested aspects of a model: Hampton Institute opened in 1868, and Booker T. Washington founded Tuskegee Normal and Industrial Institute in 1881.

Indeed, the arts and crafts revival movement was carried to the South (and especially to the mountains) first not by urban arts and crafts societies but by rural social settlements, "industrial" schools, and what John C. Campbell called the "church and independent" schools.[116] Perhaps the earliest work in the mountains began at Vassar graduate Susan Chester's Log Cabin Settlement near Asheville, in the mid-nineties. At about the same time, Frances L. Goodrich, a social worker for the Presbyterian Women's Board of Home Missions in western North Carolina's Buncombe and Madison counties, began the work that led to the opening of the Allanstand craft sales room in Asheville. By 1896, Berea College President William G. Frost, Eaton reported, "encouraged the holding of homespun fairs during commencement week." By 1900 a Berea College coverlet had won a medal at the Paris Exposition.[117]

During the next two decades the crafts revival swung into full operation in the mountains, leading to national and international recognition for those aspects of local tradition that the revival chose to encourage and represent. Before World War I commenced in Europe, important craft revival enterprises were begun at Biltmore Industries (Asheville, 1901), the Berry School (Rome, Georgia, 1903), the Tallulah Falls Industrial School (Tallulah Falls, Georgia, 1909), the Pi Beta Phi School (Gatlinburg, Tennessee, 1912), and the Pine Mountain Settlement School (1913). On the eve of World War I mountain women were weaving fabrics for Mrs. Woodrow Wilson's planned "Mountain Room" in the White House.[118]

Hindman Settlement School thus began its handicrafts work at a pivotal juncture. As early as the summer settlement at Sassafras in 1901, Katherine Pettit recorded in her diary, one of her co-workers was learning to make willow baskets from a local lady "so that she could teach the women at Sassafras." Soon a basket-weaving class was started, and the settlement women were trying to learn to weave from local women.[119] By 1904 a local temperance newspaper reported that the school had started woodworking classes the previous year.[120] A half-dozen years later the school's own newsletter described classes for girls in basketry and weaving (in addition to the usual domestic skills of cooking and sewing) and for boys in furniture making, blacksmithing, and carpentry. Local men and women were encouraged to bring their handmade baskets, brooms, quilts, coverlets, chairs, and other items to the school for marketing by Fireside Industries, the school's production and marketing organization. The January 1914 newsletter spoke of a "widening circle of weavers of baskets, blankets, and coverlets" and noted that the younger generation appreciated "this chance to secure a little income by keeping alive these disappearing arts."[121]

For six decades Fireside Industries brochures offered to the public handicraft items produced by both Hindman students in its own shops and their parents and neighbors in nearby mountain homes. Many a city dweller must have breathed a bit easier amidst the pressures of modernity while looking at Fireside Industries brochures showing "Aunt Cord" Ritchie and her husband walking a mountain path carrying with them their latest batch of new-made baskets.[122]

Thus at one level the handicrafts enterprise was simple, direct, and reassuring. But at others it was so convoluted as to be nearly impossible to decipher from this historical distance. At the very least, it is clear that Hindman's Fireside Industries was not simply preserving and revitalizing local handicraft traditions—if only because so many of its handicraft instructors came from far outside the region and appear to have had no prior contact with its cultural traditions. The woodworking teacher in 1911–13, for example, was Ruth Huntington, a Smith College graduate (1897). She was followed by Raymond Smith, a graduate of Hackley Manual Training School in Muskegon, Michigan. Indeed, although records of the period are too scanty to furnish a full roster of instructors, it appears that a large percentage—like the academic faculty—were from outside the region and that their ideas about handicraft were drawn primarily from urban revival contexts, such as settlement houses, arts and crafts societies, manual training schools, and universities.[123]

Taking Fireside Industries brochures, photographs, and a few surviving

FIGURE I-13
Settlement girls in cooking class
(Hindman Settlement School Archive).

FIGURE I-14
Settlement students in woodworking shop, Fireside Industries
(Hindman Settlement School Archive).

FIGURE I-15
Local women delivering baskets to Fireside Industries
(Hindman Settlement School Archive).

artifacts at Hindman and in the surrounding community as evidence, it appears that the handicrafts produced at Hindman ranged from the strictly traditional (willow and split baskets, dolls, split-bottomed chairs, perhaps some weaving patterns), to quasi traditional (other weaving patterns), to frankly imported (furniture case goods). Some of the furniture was traditional, but much was of the Roycroft-William Morris design associated with Elbert Hubbard's Roycroft Shops in East Aurora, New York, and as such had little to do with local esthetics or craft traditions. A letter from an early teacher depicted the resulting stylistic mix: "I don't believe many mountain schools are so homelike," Ethel DeLong wrote four years after the school opened, "or preserve so well the fine simplicity of mountain arts and crafts, for the [settlement] house is furnished with

FIGURE 1-16
Aunt Cord Ritchie and husband bringing baskets to Fireside Industries
(Hindman Settlement School Archive).

home-made white oak split-bottomed chairs . . . [and] with tables, desks, dressers . . . of wax-finished walnut made [here] in the mountains in plain William Morris fashion." [124]

If the baskets and split-bottomed chairs were clearly local, and the Morris furniture was clearly not, the weaving enterprise straddled the line. Although some efforts to employ local weavers (and their own traditional patterns) were made, there were other influences. A 1918 brochure recalled the return three years earlier of former pupil Inez Sloan from a weaving course at Berea College to take charge of weaving for Fireside Industries.

Although Berea was becoming known widely for its production of supposedly authentic mountain crafts, its weaving reflected many nonlocal influences. Berea began to develop its own "fireside industries" work shortly after President Frost came to the college in 1892. Berea's first commence-

FIGURE I-17
Aunt Cord Ritchie (Hindman Settlement School Archive).

ment-day "homespun fair" was held in 1896, and by 1902 two buildings had been adapted for use by the handicrafts program. Berea's earliest weavers and weaving instructors were local people, but the situation changed in 1911 when Anna Ernberg, a native of Sweden, came to direct the weaving enterprise. Although she apparently recovered and reused some traditional patterns, Ernberg also introduced a new lightweight loom and lighter fabrics.

By the time Hindman's Inez Sloan studied weaving at Berea, those changes—in addition to the "Swedish designs" Eaton also noted—were already much in evidence. And early letters from Pettit to President Frost remaining in Berea's library suggest that ties between Hindman's handicraft program and Berea's were close. During the spring of 1903 she wrote several times to ask Frost to send a manual-training teacher—"a good mountain boy that has been trained at Berea." [125]

To the extent that Hindman's handicrafts program was oriented toward reinforcing individual identity, family cohesion, and community stability by fostering traditional designs and skills, it presented no dilemma. Older local people could be sought out to teach young people, and both could use the products of their hands to create a beautiful environment at the school and in their homes.

But when the enterprise became linked to the handicrafts revival movement and transformed into an economic venture named Fireside Industries, dilemmas and contradictions followed, as they did for many a mountain handicrafts revival effort of the period. At Hindman some of the contradictions flowed from the effort simply to produce a "home-like" environment at the school itself: the juxtaposition of split-bottomed chairs and Roycroft bookcases, for example. Others flowed from perceptions of, and efforts to respond to, the handicrafts market.

For reasons of their own, middle- and upper-class people outside the region were acquiring a taste for traditional handicrafts. Mountaineers were among those who had the skills to satisfy that acquired taste and who were economically hard-pressed enough to find the modest potential market attractive. Unfortunately, those who constituted the market were much less attracted to mountaineers' *way of life* (to which the actual products of mountain craft had long been matched) than they were to the crafts' abstract design features: "old timey" design motifs, natural materials, handwork processes, and so on. Mountain craft workers were thus obliged to change their designs in order to match their products to the lifestyles of their potential customers.

The changes, though slight or negligible in some areas (baskets, for ex-

ample), were dramatic in others. In weaving the transformation was sufficient to produce what was in fact a hybrid style one might call "traditional
chic": a combination of some traditional colors, processes, and designs
blended with alien (Swedish, for example) design features and materials,
the whole applied to the making of new products rarely if ever seen in
mountain homes, such as cloth napkins, table runners, and place mats.

Both the dynamic itself and the perspective that encouraged it are evident in a statement by Jennie Lister Hill, who came to manage the handicraft enterprise at Berea in 1903. "What is the future of these fireside industries?" she asked, "Will they die out as the mountain region is opened
to trade, and machine-made products take the place of homespun? So far
as the uses of the mountaineers themselves are concerned, this will probably be the case. But for really well-made homespun products there is an
ever-growing demand." Assessing that demand, Hill laid bare the differences in class and taste that were reshaping the traditions:

> Nothing is more artistic for furnishing country houses or for country
> wear. The mountain girl may choose the flashy, shoddy goods at the
> country store in preference to her mother's homespun, for it is new
> to her, but the golf girl will not. There is a work here, then for the
> friends of the mountain people to do. They must help them find a
> market for these products of their skill and they must teach them
> . . . to turn [that skill] into new channels adapted to modern meth-
> ods of living. The woman who can weave a coverlid, can weave por-
> tieres and table draperies when she is shown what they are. Instead
> of linsey and blankets for her own use, she can weave golf skirtings
> and homespun suitings.

Hill was confident that "an increased knowledge of the world, its wants
and achievements, together with their own inherited skill, will fit out
mountain women for a new creative period. . . ."[126]

The "new creative period" envisioned for mountain people who were
drawn into the cultural programs and activities offered by Hindman, Berea, and similar institutions thus was to prove problematic. The cultural
message was in fact a dual one, structured for conflict and ambivalence:
Cherish your traditions, but mind your new manners; affirm what you are,
but groom yourself for social mobility; life in the mountains is wonderful,
but its wonders must be shaped according to the vision of the great stereoscopic world beyond. To resolve the conflict, scores of Mrs. Stacys and
Rhodas simply affirmed the *dominant, functional* cultural message of the
settlement, which was—the formalities of ballad clubs and Fireside Indus-

tries notwithstanding—that in any real contest between "yourn" and "ourn," the former is to be preferred.

It was the cultural analogue of a message being communicated more powerfully by the emerging economics and politics of eastern Kentucky. Others had lately discovered those veins of coal that Guerrant saw along the trails and creek banks, and their discovery would transform eastern Kentucky in a generation. The settlement women might wash the cheap makeup from the face of the coal-camp girl, but the shape of her life would nevertheless be determined henceforth more completely by the coal industry than it ever would again (or perhaps ever had been) by ballads and handicrafts.

Hindman always prided itself on educating its students "back to their homes, rather than away from them," but it was clear that those homes, in any meaningful emotional or spiritual (or even practical or economic) sense, were threatened at a level beyond the capacity of strictly cultural programs to alter. Unless the school could address itself to the profound economic and political inequalities and dislocations that were wrenching life in the mountains from its traditional moorings, the only real chance young people would have for a decent life would lie in the world outside.

Hindman and Social Change in the Mountains

"We stayed out of politics for seventy-five years."
Elizabeth Watts, 1980

In March 1913, a few months after the railroad had reached Hazard in neighboring Perry County, Hindman Settlement School children staged a debate on the topic "Resolved that the railroad should come to Hindman." [127] The negative side won, but the railroad came nevertheless. Its coming had been assured at least since an agent for a group of investors headquartered in Abingdon, Virginia, bought the first coal rights in the county for fifty cents an acre in 1885. [128] How did Hindman—the most important social settlement in the mountains—relate to the ensuing social, economic, political, and cultural dislocations?

Pettit and Stone conceived of Hindman Settlement School as a new type of mountain school, one that would differ markedly from the "mission schools" that had preceded it by more than a half-century in the mountains. [129] Yet the difference was in many respects not very great. The reasons why it was not are to some extent obscure, but it is clear that Pettit and Stone's particular interpretation and adaptation of currently available models had a good deal to do with it. The settlement house model comprised both conservative and progressive strains; Pettit and Stone inclined toward the former. The "industrial school" model, upon which they also drew considerably, was rather thoroughly conservative—in some respects even reactionary.

Precedents for serious attempts to moderate or reverse the impact of rapid industrialization and unrestrained commercial activity were abundant among the urban settlements upon which Hindman had been partially modeled. As early as 1897, settlement worker Alzina Stevens—who had started to work in textile mills at the age of thirteen and had a missing finger to prove it—proclaimed that "settlement workers soon learn that economic conditions control the social structure, and if they fail to see this they do not make very valuable settlement workers."[130]

Although some critics charged that settlement workers were merely "young ladies with weak eyes and young men with weak chins flittering confused among heterogeneous foreigners, offering cocoa and sponge cakes as a sort of dessert to the factory system," the work of many settlements ranged beyond such irrelevant confections.[131] Some settlements were, as Davis says, "ardent [defenders] of labor unions at a time when they had few defenders." Settlement workers were involved in municipal reform movements in Pittsburgh, Boston, New York (against the Tammany Hall machine), Philadelphia, and Rochester, where settlement school centers became so politically and socially active that the legislature blocked their appropriation in 1910.[132]

In a variety of places settlements agitated on behalf of working women and children, made surveys of social conditions, wrote exposés, lobbied for progressive state and federal legislation, and helped to organize women into labor unions.[133] The efforts of the Allegheny Society for the Improvement of the Poor after 1895 led to the founding of the Wood's Run Industrial Settlement in Pittsburgh in 1908, which worked among steel and foundry workers. The Heights Settlement Association in Wilkes-Barre, founded in 1908, worked mainly among Irish and Welsh miners.[134]

Such involvements were particularly evident at Hull House. The Hull House fight in the 1890s against Johnny Powers, the feudal boss of the Nineteenth Ward, was one of the most significant of its type among all the settlements.[135] In *Twenty Years at Hull House*, Jane Addams detailed the organization's social and political engagement on many fronts: child labor legislation, housing reform, educational reform, sanitation, and the like.[136] As early as 1895, Addams and her co-workers published *Hull House Maps and Papers*, which included Florence Kelly's essay "The Sweating System," Alzina Stevens's "Wage Earning Children," and Addams's "The Settlement as a Factor in the Labor Movement." In 1896 Hull House workers defended striking garment workers who lived nearby, holding mass meetings, collecting money, and sheltering harassed leaders (as they had Eugene Debs earlier during the Pullman strike of 1894).

Addams herself made thousands of prolabor speeches, including some during both the Pullman strike and the Building Trades Council strike of 1900—both high points of antilabor sentiment in Chicago.[137] In 1898, Addams wrote that labor organizations "probably . . . come nearer to expressing moral striving in political action than any other portion of the community." More than a decade later she contended that for a settlement to be "drawn into the labor issues of its city" would seem improper "only to those who fail to realize that so far as the present industrial system thwarts our demands, not only for social righteousness but for social order, the Settlement is committed to an effort to understand and, as far as possible, to alleviate it. That in this effort it should be drawn into fellowship with . . . trades-unions is most obvious."[138]

Besides aiding the causes of practical municipal reform and "industrial democracy," Addams and her co-workers stayed in touch with progressive and radical thought of the day and offered Hull House as a forum for free political discussion. Christian Socialists held their annual meeting at Hull House, and for seven years a "Working People's Social Science Club" met to discuss topics ranging from trade unionism to socialism and anarchism. As Addams spoke of it in *Twenty Years at Hull House*, a settlement was "above all a place for enthusiasms, a spot to which those who have a passion for the equalization of human joys and opportunities are easily attracted. It is this type of mind which is . . . so often obnoxious to the men of conquering business faculty, to whom the practical world of affairs seems so supremely rational that he would never vote to change the type of it even if he could" (p. 184).

Thus within the history of urban settlements there were many examples of an aggressive and politically sophisticated approach to social reconstruction and social change. But as much as the Hindman women espoused the settlement approach formally, the school they actually built owed much more—especially in its relation to social change—to the "industrial" schools that dotted many another corner of the southern landscape. In the main, those schools were deeply conservative.

The concept of an industrial school had a number of partial antecedents. The "manual labor movement" of the early nineteenth century led An-

dover Seminary to add courses in gardening and wood chopping to its curriculum as early as 1820. Later, there were the mechanics' institutes, the
agricultural and mechanical colleges set up under the Land Grant Act of
1862, and the movement for public vocational education after the Civil
War. A central figure in the industrial school movement was Calvin Woodward, who established the Manual Training School in St. Louis in 1879
and crusaded widely to incorporate the concept into public education. The
concept proved particularly attractive to northern reformers working
among blacks and poor whites in the South.[139]

The Reverend A. D. Mayo, who conducted a survey of southern industrial schools for the U.S. Department of Labor in the late 1880s, commented upon the "vast realms of our Southland yet untilled" and the "in-
competence of our labor system to deal with the . . . development of this
new world."[140] "[The] industrial demand of the day," Mayo continued, "is
intelligence in the masses and skill in the leadership of labor." And although the immediate object of industrial education was "the fit training
of the operative classes in the new manufacturing centres," deeper levels
in the agenda were evident in Mayo's report. "Every Southern state," he
said, "is now making great efforts to attract the only sort of immigration of
real value. Nothing would so complicate the Southern situation as the
swarming in of large bodies of ignorant European people, whose hatred of
the Negro would precipitate labor difficulties, with impending peril of social war" (p. 16).

That peril was played up strongly in Katherine Pettit's hometown newspapers at the turn of the century. Kentuckians were being treated almost
daily to stories of racial lynchings, hangings, "race wars," and the like in
the Midwest and eastern United States. The toll for one two-month period
in 1901 in the *Lexington Morning Herald* was twenty-six blacks dead in seventeen incidents, including one in which six thousand whites watched a
black burned at the stake in Winchester, Tennessee.[141]

Thus Mayo's analysis reflected several of the dominant anxieties of the
period, both regional and national: the potential for racial conflict, the instability of the class system ("operative classes" is a normative as well
as descriptive phrase), and the threat of foreign (that is to say, politically
radical) ideology. Against all of that, industrial education was seen as a
bulwark.

The great antecedent for industrial education in the mountains was of
course the scores of institutions like Hampton (1868) and Tuskegee (1881)
which had been opened for southern blacks. In them the conservative politics of industrial education were quite plain. Its most celebrated statement

was probably Booker T. Washington's controversial 1895 speech in Atlanta, in which he argued that blacks should not agitate for social equality before they attained economic equality. But such sentiments were also widespread among other advocates of industrial education. Mayo explained that the black man had made such progress in so short a time because "he learned the three fundamental conditions of modern life—steady and persistent work, and the language and religion of the foremost people of Christendom" (p. 14).

A dozen years later, George Winston, the son of a former slaveholder, wrote in the *Southern Workman* that since "the Negro is not far enough from nature to live in cities and towns," he should be trained for agricultural work by the industrial schools, and should "let alone political matters, leaving them to be settled by the whites, whose sense of justice and self-interest will . . . protect the Negro in his rights." In 1913, C. Vann Woodward notes, southern educator Thomas P. Bailey put the matter quite bluntly in his "racial creed" for Southerners. "Let there be," Bailey said, "such industrial education of the Negro as will best fit him to serve the white man."[142]

But the industrial education scheme was not confined solely to blacks. The *Southern Workman* frequently carried articles on experiments in industrial education among other socially and economically exploited racial and cultural groups, including American Indians and Puerto Ricans. And Winston urged that "the industrial education of Southern whites is no less important than that of the blacks."[143] During the year before Pettit established her school at Hindman, her hometown newspaper frequently carried articles on industrial education for blacks, and ever since the 1880s church missionary magazines had been suggesting that liberal concern for southern blacks should be shifted to mountain whites.[144]

By any reasonable measure, industrial education was education in a deeply conservative mode. It became no less so when it moved into the mountains of eastern Kentucky. By choosing it as a partial model, and blending it with the more conservative aspects of the urban social settlement experience, the fotched-on women eventually were left with little more than a "cultural gospel" that led Hindman and its successors into a socially and politically blind alley of romantic cultural revivalism.

Eastern Kentucky *was* in some ways still a beautiful and romantic "world of green and silver" when the settlement women held their summer "industrial" camps there at the turn of the century. But it was also a world beginning to collapse around them, and they heard it falling. In her diary for the summer of 1901, Pettit wrote of the "great crash of the trees falling on the mountain near by, where men [are] getting out poplar timber." A few weeks later, the *Lexington Morning Herald* reported that a deal had been closed to ship nearly a million dollars worth of eastern Kentucky white oak to Austria to be made into barrel staves.[145] Even so conservative a commentator as University of Chicago sociologist S. S. MacClintock, who followed Berea College president William H. Frost and others in seeing the mountains romantically as a "Rip Van Winkle . . . region [which] went to sleep while life flowed around it and beyond," was writing at the same time about the "passing of so much land into the hands of outside capitalists" in eastern Kentucky and of coal company stores that forced people to buy from them at "exorbitant prices." During the summer of 1901, while Pettit ran her camp in the mountains and listened to the trees fall, the *Lexington Morning Herald* carried story after front-page story on the oil industry boom in Bath, Wayne, and Rowan counties, which bordered the mountain counties on the west.[146]

The years immediately following the school's founding were years during which the railroad was pushing its last miles into the heart of the mountains. Hindman's 1913 newsletter announced that it was only twenty miles from the school's door and that "the long isolation of the mountains is past." There is "grave danger," the newsletter continued, "that the new type of civilization may lack something of the solid values for humanity of the old." The settlement women viewed themselves as "trying to build up a form of education that shall mean growth, and not retrogression, as the type of mountain civilization changes with the incoming railroads. We believe we have chosen wisely." Wrestling with the inevitable trade-offs, they quoted James A. Burns (founder of a nearby mission school): "Bring us your Northern culture, but leave us our civilization." Even as the Hindman newsletter was being mailed, however, John C. Campbell was writing to John Glenn of the Russell Sage Foundation that "a recent letter from Miss Katherine Pettit brings the information that Miss Newman, their secretary, has secured toward the endowment of the school . . . $25,000 in preferred stock of the Elkhorn Fuel Company, stock which is non-taxable in the state of Kentucky and said to yield a net income yearly of $1,250.00." The gift, Campbell noted, brought the school's total endowment to thirty-three thousand dollars. Thus a decade after its founding, at least 76 percent of the school's small endowment was in coal company money.[147]

The plea to "leave us our civilization" was thus plaintive but futile. The great Hazard, Harlan, and Elkhorn fields of eastern Kentucky were fully mapped, and competition for their valuable seams (which ranged up to eighty inches thick) was keen. The G. S. Beckwith Company of Cleveland had bought eighty thousand acres of coal land in Knott and Letcher counties by 1907; by 1911 operators from Pennsylvania had put together 175,000 acres in Knott, Letcher, and Magoffin. And a year earlier, Maryland-based Consolidation Coal Company bought 100,000 acres in Knott, Letcher, and Pike. "Many an acre of this valuable fuel was sold for as low as $1 an acre," reported an industry publication in mid-1918, and more than forty mines had opened in the past four years. A three-thousand kilowatt steam electric plant at Lothair (a mile above Hazard) was supplying electricity to nearby mines, and more than three hundred carloads of coal a day were leaving the Hazard field—from the Racoon mine of Columbus Coal (the oldest in the field), from Kenmont Coal Company on Buckeye Creek, from Blue Diamond on First Creek, and from the new mines of many another company with names like Daniel Boone Coal, Solar Coal, and Kentucky Block Coal. Thus coal production in Kentucky, which had been only 300,000 tons in 1873, rose to 2.7 million by 1890. Production in Knott County in 1900, on the eve of the school's founding, was only about 1,200 tons. But by 1922 it was 214,000 tons, and by 1928 it had risen to 569,000 tons.[148]

The scraps of documentary evidence that remain from the settlement's attempt to comprehend the meaning of the advance of the railroads and coal industries suggest that, for all their undeniable selflessness and energy and goodwill, the settlement women—unlike their model Jane Addams— lacked the political and social sophistication that might have allowed them to make sense of the dynamic of change and respond to it with more than a plea to the corporations to "leave us our civilization."

The lack is painfully evident in the school's 1920 newsletter account of the coming of the new order. A stranger appears at a nearby house, and is invited to share a meal:

> As the meal progressed the stranger was asked his age, whether he was married . . . and various other questions the true mountaineer puts in making acquaintances.
>
> Inquisitiveness, however, even in the mountains, has its limitations and the stranger was not asked his business. It was well known that he would broach this himself in due season, which he did. The men folk had repaired to the yard, when the stranger very tactfully suggested his mission. This was in reference to the coal rights he had bought the day before over on another creek. Of course old Smith had been hard to deal with and had made him pay the enor-

mous price of two dollars and a half per acre for his thousand acres of worthless mineral . . . but the men he worked for were just rich fools. He knew they would go broke at it, but it was their business; he was only carrying out orders. All of this was said with cunning glances askance to note the effect on his host.

Now, be it said to the credit of the mountaineer that he is no fool when it comes to ordinary barter. They are sharks at horse jockeying and perfectly at home in the small traffic of their section, but this mineral game was beyond their ken. . . . Of course [coal] was worthless here, for nearly everybody burned wood anyhow, but the "furriners" seemed to want it, so why not make them pay the most for it—which most at that time was about five dollars per acre. This was the price named by our native . . . . The stranger was horrified. Robbery! The native was obdurate. . . . [The] banter and bicker of the deal . . . lasted an hour and ended in a compromise. It was sold for three and a half dollars an acre!—two hundred acres, we'll say, worth now, if the railroad has reached it, . . . fifty thousand dollars.

While, of course, the above suggested scheme was not the universal method by which the astute speculators possessed themselves of the natural wealth of these mountains, it is representative. For lack of a milder term, it will have to be called commercial exploitation. It is a certainty that the rich mineral holdings of this section passed out of the hands of the original owners for the merest fraction of their real value.

However, this is not being written merely as commercial history. I am leading up to a new problem that develops and about which, I believe, you have not been told before. The coal now [being] in [the] possession of capital[ists], railroads were required to develop it; so Hindman, which, until several years after our school was established, was forty-five miles from a railroad, is now only sixteen miles from the C & O, and about the same distance from the L & N. We are closer, almost face to face, with the problems that sudden developments bring to a people not ready for them. The mineral, the only real material wealth the people possessed, is no longer theirs. Many of the late owners are now numbered among the miners and laborers at the new operations.

This is commercialism. These people shut in here for a century and a quarter are not prepared to cope with it. They must be trained to meet the changing order of things rather than be picked up in its vortex and swept on—or destroyed. Far be it from us, however, to give the impression that the coal operators are ruthless. Many of them fully appreciate the problems to be met. A number of them realize their obligations to this section and at least a dozen companies contribute to Hindman Settlement School. With their gifts come the most sympathetic letters. One of the operators wrote us a short time ago . . . that our school had been put on his books indefinitely for an annual contribution. We need such encouragement.

It is the abrupt change, the rushing-in of the aggressive commercial world on a people so unprepared both by training and experience that adds to the problem. Their wealth has passed into other hands, but they still have their splendid possibilities of personal development.

Thus the essential facts of the case were well enough known to the settlement women to enable them to outline the entire scenario for their newsletter audience of friends and contributors: the overarching intent of the corporations to possess the wealth of the mountains; their use of glib, ingratiating agents to manipulate mountaineer landowners; the vast disparity between value and purchase price; the symbiosis between coal and railroads; and the socioeconomic results of the transfer for mountaineers ("many of the late owners are now . . . miners and laborers").

Showing through the otherwise tough-minded account of a "representative" transaction in one mountain dooryard, however, are unmistakable signs that temperamentally and politically, the women were unprepared to respond as Addams and her co-workers were doing in Chicago. "For lack of a milder term," they said almost apologetically, the scheme "will have to be called commercial exploitation." They are most reluctant ("Far be it from us . . . to give the impression . . .") to say that the new owners are what they are: ruthless. And besides, they concluded, many owners are humane contributors to Hindman who accompany their contributions with "the most sympathetic letters."

The school also had a close tie to one of the most powerful and socially reactionary corporations in Kentucky through May Stone's father, who was an official of the Louisville and Nashville Railroad and a member (one of six) of Hindman's advisory board. The L & N was formed by Milton H. Smith in the 1880s, at a time when major southern industries (especially steel, tobacco, and railroads) were coming under the absentee, monopolistic control of such financiers as J. P. Morgan.[149] Smith's social philosophy was simple: "Society," he said, "[is] created . . . for the purpose of one man's getting what the other fellow has, if he can, and keep out of the penitentiary."[150] On the basis of such a philosophy, Smith managed to gather control of a third of all the rail mileage in Kentucky by 1889.[151]

Opposing the L & N in Kentucky took great courage. In what Woodward called the "first southern reform movement to make a determined fight for power," Kentucky state senator William Goebel in the 1890s worked to limit corporate power and increase corporate taxes. In his turn-of-the-century campaign for the governorship, he focused much of his effort on making the L & N "the servant instead of the master of Kentucky."[152] Narrowly defeated in the governor's race, Goebel was assassinated by a killer who was never apprehended. The significance of the L & N's power for mountain people was apparent to the head of at least one nearby mountain school at the time. In her journal for 18 January 1909, during a visit to several schools near Hindman, Olive Dame Campbell recorded the assertion of the head of Oneida Institute that the L & N was the "regular robber of the poor man."[153]

Also important in predisposing the settlement women to increasingly ineffectual programs for dealing with "the rushing-in of the aggressive commercial world" was their conviction that personal improvement through education could be the key to coping with rapid and radical structural change in the mountains of eastern Kentucky: Mountaineers' wealth "has passed into other hands," they observed, "but they still have their splendid possibilities of personal development."

How unequal the contest really was—because of both the new owners' power and the disorientation that flowed from some of the women's own cultural and social values—may be glimpsed in a letter that Elizabeth Watts wrote to her mother in 1912 after two Hindman teachers visited the new mansion of local (Paintsville) coal baron John C. C. Mayo. Mayo, a Pike County native (b. 1848), had bought thousands of acres of eastern Kentucky coal land for fifty cents to one dollar an acre, both for himself and for eastern and midwestern interests for whom he served as agent. In 1901 he joined with other investors and formed Northern Coal and Coke to develop four hundred thousand acres of coal land; the company was sold to Baltimore-based Consolidation Coal the next year. By 1907, Mayo owned or controlled seven hundred thousand acres, and he had used his legal training to help get new state land and tax laws to solidify titles to mountain lands on which he owned mineral rights. At his death, Mayo was worth $20 million.[154]

But the significant aspects of Mayo's career were—in Watts's view—not his self-serving manipulation of the entire social, economic, and cultural system but the style of life that resulted. "[The settlement school teachers] had a glorious time," she wrote to her mother, "staying at the home of John C. C. Mayo, a self-made multi-millionaire, a coal company being the cause of it. They have just moved into a $500,000 house that has taken seven years to build and is perfectly wonderful. They had sense enough to have interior decorators who knew [their] job and both Miss Rue and Miss DeLong say it was wonderful. They had beauteous things to eat with three butlers to wait on them." [155]

Indeed, in the surviving records of Hindman Settlement School I discovered no indication that the school ever attempted to serve as a community forum for the kind of social and political ideas Goebel so courageously espoused, or that it envisioned or instituted any program or initiative designed to challenge the new order or redress any of the abusive social, economic, or political circumstances that paid for John C. C. Mayo's house and his butlers, and undergirded the eastern Kentucky empire of Consol.[156] As a result, the school was left with a conventional academic program—taken over increasingly by the public schools—and finally with a set of cultural endeavors that can only be called romantic and contrived.[157]

With the public schools providing basic education, and with the determination of both social and economic structure and the pace and direction of social change relinquished to the coal industry, Hindman had to be content with a narrowly defined "culture" as its ambit. By the mid-1930s "recreation" was claiming a major share of its attention and resources. In 1936 it acquired its first full-time recreational director and erected a recreational building.[158] Children were taught singing and dancing games, and "community sings" were held "to learn some new songs, revive . . . old mountain hymns, and linger over the much-loved ballads to which [local people] inevitably turn as their own." [159]

Although the school had attempted to make local culture a part of its program since the beginning, the effort of the late thirties was on a different scale. With the coming of Ruth White of Knoxville, Tennessee, in 1940, the *Hindman News* reported on the school's fiftieth anniversary, "folk dance and ballads came into their own at Hindman." [160]

During World War II, Pauline Ritchie described the school's recreation house as "a brown, solid, and friendly structure resting high on a hillside in a nest of honeysuckle vines. . . . It is a happy house well loved by all who have ever climbed the winding trail of stone steps. . . . From the front porch . . . [one can] see the curving track of Troublesome Creek . . . [and hear] the girls singing as they pin white blowing things to a clothesline in the sun." Ritchie reported that dancing (local "play-party" games,

English and Danish country dances, morris dances) was "the chief form of recreation" of settlement children and that there were hopes for a sword-dance team.[161]

By the late 1940s Hindman was holding "Recreational Leadership Workshops" under the auspices of the University of Kentucky's Extension Department and the Council of the Southern Mountains.[162] In 1954, Raymond McLain joined the staff as recreation director. "He has been brought up in the Folk Arts type of Recreation," the newsletter reported, "and has a wonderful fund of music, stories, and folk dances to share with us." Two years later, Elizabeth Watts retired, McLain was named to head the school, and the "cultural" program became effectively its only program.[163]

Certainly the most arresting image in the new emphasis—and perhaps its most revealing component—was morris dancing, which was gaining considerable popularity in certain quarters in the mountains at the time, largely through the influence of Berea College and the settlement and folk schools, which had gotten them originally from ballad collector Cecil Sharp.

Sharp had first seen a morris "side" at Headington, England, during the Christmas season of 1899. The Headington side, disbanded in 1887, had recently been revived by dancer William Kimber. Kimber learned the dances from his father, who had danced as early as 1847. Sharp, preoccupied with ballad collecting at the time, did not pursue his interest in morris dancing until 1905, when the head of the Esperance Working Girls' Club asked him to teach the dances to club members.

By 1907, Sharp had published the first volume of *The Morris Book*, and two years later he persuaded the Board of Education to give morris dance a place in the official physical education syllabus. Through his recently organized School of Morris Dancing, Sharp endeavored to supply trained teachers and promoters of the form. In 1910 he witnessed his first sword dance, performed by a group of men he coaxed to relearn the dance they had last performed in 1886. Until the advent of World War I much of Sharp's effort was directed toward reviving traditional dance in England. His research convinced him that English morris dance was one surviving form of ancient pan-European seasonal pagan observances associated in some way with fertility. As such, its roots reached deep into the British cultural past, and were eminently worth reviving.

In England, Sharp's efforts did indeed produce such a revival. Morris and sword-dance teams soon proliferated. Teams of six male dancers clad in hats decked with ribbons and flowers, with pleated linen shirts and boots and pads of bells attached to their right legs, danced the ancient figures to the music of pipe and tabor (or fiddle and concertina). "[We] felt assured," Sharp wrote, "that we were helping to restore a means and method of self-expression in movement, native and sincere, such as is offered by no other form of dancing known to us." [164]

When, at the urging of Olive Dame Campbell, Sharp came to the southern mountains to collect in 1916, he was overwhelmed at the rich store of traditional British ballads to be found there, but he specifically noted his failure to find "songs of a ritual nature . . . and others of religious origin, such as those associated with the Morris and Sword-dance ceremonies." [165] What did survive in the mountains, however, were variants of some of the morris dance tunes and some social-dance figures that Sharp believed to be derived from morris dance figures. [166]

Almost as soon as he arrived in the mountains, however, Sharp began to teach mountain people the English dances he had been reviving at home. As early as March 1916, John C. Campbell wrote to John Glenn of the Russell Sage Foundation that Sharp, only a day or so after he arrived in the mountains, "gave a most delightful talk to the girls at the [Presbyterian] mountain school here and taught them several folk dances which captivated all of them." [167] Later, at both Hindman and Pine Mountain Settlement School, Sharp again taught morris and sword dances to teachers and local children. Many photographs in Hindman's archive show Hindman morris and sword dancers in full regalia—white shirts and pants, sashes, bells at the knees, and swords interlocked in artistic patterns. At Pine Mountain especially, the dances took hold, and the school's morris and sword-dance teams practiced and performed for years thereafter. A Pine Mountain morris team performed at the White Top Folk Festival in the 1930s. [168]

In light of the most recent and rigorous scholarship, the story of morris dancing in the southern mountains becomes even more ironic. If one accepts Sharp's own scholarship (or even that as late as the 1960s), one might reasonably question "reviving" a dance form which—though never actually known in the mountains—was at least rooted deeply in English history. A meticulous recent study by John A. Forrest shows, however, that even *those* roots are open to question. From a study of the Cotswold morris, Forrest concludes that "the fertility-ritual theory of origin of the morris dance . . . is false," and that "the morris dance is not indigenous to the British Isles. . . . [Instead], the contemporary Cotswold morris dance developed out of a sixteenth-century [upper-class] European dancing fad, the matachin" and, in the form in which Sharp studied it, is less than two hundred years old. [169]

Thus, having focused on a romantic cultural "world of green and silver," having declined to involve itself in the major economic and political realities that were shaping life in the mountains, having judged that the cultural forms (feud songs, railroad and mining ballads, and mail-order musical instruments) that the people themselves were developing to comprehend and assimilate those realities were beneath serious consideration, and having chosen to lay the norms of genteel Victorian popular culture upon mountain people, the settlement had at best neutered itself and become a subtle agent and facilitator of the changes it formally opposed. In the image of economically dispossessed mountain boys, attired in an antique garb borrowed from a tradition impossibly remote from any cultural reality that they (or their parents or grandparents) were familiar with, wooden swords woven artfully into a star above their heads, one encounters the deepest ironies of the settlement.

Image and Icon: Uncle Sol and His Delineators

The other half of the story of Hindman—besides the record of what it *did* in the mountains—is what those outside the mountains were led to believe was going on at the Forks of Troublesome. Their opinions were for the most part formed not as a result of direct experience or observation but through images and explanations disseminated by the school itself—in its newsletters, in hundreds of fund-raising speeches by Pettit and Stone, and (perhaps most important) the novels of Lucy Furman.

In the surviving record, one image is preeminent: that of white-haired, eighty-year-old Uncle Solomon Everidge, who appears in most accounts of the settlement school as the mountain patriarch who walked barefoot twenty-two miles to Hindman to implore the "quare women" to start a school for his "grands and greats." Although it appeared in many forms during the school's early years, the most accessible version was probably that in William Aspenwall Bradley's *Scribner's Magazine* article of 1918, "The Women on Troublesome":

> He wore homespun trousers and a white home-woven shirt of flax, and he was both bareheaded and barefooted—peculiarities of attire that he explained on the ground that "the Lord had given him plenty h'ar, so he didn't need no hat," while his heels were so hard he could crush chestnuts out of the burr without feeling it.
>
> For the rest, his aspect was patriarchal and imposing. He was tall, straight, and still strong-looking. He had a massive head, with thick

FIGURE I-18
Sword-dance team of Hindman Settlement School students, 1940s
(Hindman Settlement School Archive).

white hair and heavy eyebrows, under which his fine dark eyes shone out with an expression of remarkable intelligence and nobility.

"When I was jest a chunk of a boy . . . ," he said, "and hoein' corn on the steep mountainside, I'd look up Troublesome and down Troublesome, and wonder if anybody'd ever come in and larn us anything. But nobody ever come in, and nobody ever went out, and we jest growed up and never knowed nothin'. I never had a chanst to larn anything myself, but I got chillern and grandchillern jest as bright as other folkses', and I want 'em to have a chanst.". . .

"Times is a-gittin' wuss and wuss," he continued. "When I was a boy I was purty bad. The next gineration was wusser." Then, pointing to a baby whose mother . . . was fanning it with a white turkey wing, he asked, "What will this gineration be unless you women come to Hindman and help us?" [170]

Once spread abroad, the image proved remarkably attractive and durable. Uncle Sol's picture—sitting in a split-bottomed chair in an open door-

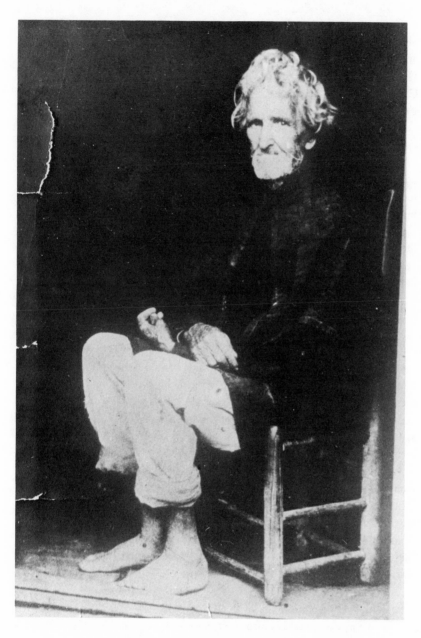

FIGURE I-19
Uncle Sol Everidge (Hindman Settlement School Archive).

way, barefoot, with rolled-up trouser legs—graced scores of Hindman Settlement School brochures, appeared in countless newspaper articles and magazine stories, and was reproduced on a brochure announcing a Hindman benefit performance of Lula Vollmer's mountain play *Sun-Up* in Chicago in 1923. Uncle Sol appeared as "Uncle Ephraim Kent" in Lucy Furman's novel *The Quare Women* (1923), and the Uncle Sol story was repeated in Pauline Ritchie Kermiet's memorial article "May Stone: The Ladyest" (1946), in a Bryn Mawr College social work thesis of 1975, and in the Appalachian Regional Commission's public relations magazine in 1981. Uncle Sol's cabin was long ago moved to the school grounds and reconstructed, where it remains as a memorial more than eighty years after his fabled barefoot walk to Hindman.[171]

Although the story varies slightly from one account to another (Berenice Stevens repeats a version of the "local legend"—reported by Bradley sixty years earlier—to the effect that Uncle Sol "could crack a chestnut with his bare, hardened heels"), it has the shape of a myth whose essential features have long since been agreed upon. The consensus was and is that Uncle Sol was—as one of his "greats," Pauline Ritchie Kermiet, called him—the "visionary founder" of the school.

From Bradley's account of the founding one may extract the essential mythic elements: Katherine Pettit, he said, first came to eastern Kentucky out of "pure curiosity" stirred by reports of the mountain feuds that were quite unaccountably raging amongst "Americans of unimpeachable pedigree, descendents of pioneer woodsmen and Revolutionary soldiers speaking the language of Shakespeare and singing old ballads straight from the pages of Percy's *Reliques*. . . ." On their visit, he said, the "women of the rich and aristocratic Blue Grass" heard the Damascus call from Uncle Sol. "It had never occurred to them before," he reported, "that they might do anything to alleviate the poverty and suffering that so appalled them." Their "idle curiosity" was "suddenly transformed" into a desire to help. Having heeded Uncle Sol's request, the women went about their task protected from violence by a dozen armed men who "accompanied them everywhere."[172]

Why did the image of Uncle Sol prove so marketable and durable, in view of the actual complexity of the school's history? Uncle Sol was first of all at once a recognizable cultural archetype and stereotype. He was a regional and national patriarch, hallowed ancestor *redivivus*, redemptive apparition from our mythic past. He was a biblical Moses who crossed the mountains and saw a Promised Land a-borning for his children at the Forks of Troublesome. He was—wondrously—an idealistic and progressive hillbilly, barefoot and ignorant himself, of course, but properly ambitious for his multigenerational progeny. And probably most important, he bore the simple message that a convulsed region and an increasingly uncertain nation wanted to hear: The ills attending rapid economic and social change could be healed by "education"—conventionally conceived and individually administered. Finally, one comes to understand this truth not as a result of painstaking historical, economic, social, or cultural analysis but in the midst of one's essential innocence, guided and transformed by a miraculous vision. Thus in Uncle Sol were blended classic elements of American values, social and political views, and regional prejudices. He promised a solution that entailed no social cost, that confirmed rather than challenged the status quo.

These elements of the Uncle Sol legend—together with other aspects of the school—were explored at length in the short stories and novels that Lucy Furman wrote about Hindman. A native of Henderson, on the Ohio River in extreme northwestern Kentucky, Furman was orphaned while young. Later she attended Sayre Female Institute in Lexington, where she was Katherine Pettit's classmate. After a year at the University of Cincinnati she began working as a court reporter and secretary for a law firm. While nursing an invalid aunt, she began to write short stories; her first collection, *Stories of a Sanctified Town*, appeared in 1896. Following the death of a beloved relative, Furman went to Hindman in 1907 to become a housemother for young boys and superintendent of the gardens, grounds, and dairy.[173]

During the next two decades, Furman wrote several stories and four novels about the settlement: *Mothering on Perilous*, serialized in *Century Magazine* in 1910–11 and published by Macmillan in 1913; "Hard-Hearted Barbara Allen," in the March 1912 issue of *Century*; *Sight to the Blind* (1914); *The Quare Women* (1923); and *The Glass Window* (1925).[174]

Furman's novels sold steadily into the late 1930s. *Mothering on Perilous* went through at least three editions (1913, 1915, 1927); *The Quare Women* appeared in at least four editions (1923, 1924, 1929, 1930); and *The Glass Window* saw four editions in twelve years (1925, 1926, 1929, 1937).[175]

Though published second in Furman's series of three novels about Hindman, *The Quare Women* takes up the story at the earliest point—the summer encampments that preceded the school's founding. Rather sketchily it presents themes more fully developed in the other two novels. Into a mountain region racked by feuding (one local hard drinker and feudist is four years old) come the "fotched-on" Bluegrass ladies who, when asked why they came, echo Katherine Pettit's journal: "to learn all we can, and teach all we can, and make friends, and give the young folks something pleasant to do and think about" (19). In the process, they put an end to the feuds and teach mountain people "the right way to set a table" with flowers and cloth napkins (8); to wear corsets, celebrate the Fourth of July, and sing "The Star Spangled Banner" to the accompaniment of a portable reed organ (4); and to yearn for the dazzling three-dimensional beauties pictured on stereopticon slides (13).

Although Aunt Ailsie ends up being ashamed of her checked tablecloth and quilts (she has no sheets), Uncle Ephraim (counterpart of Uncle Sol) says contentedly that "all hands is a-larning civility and God-fearingness" (21). "We wa'nt able to help ourselves," he says, "We needed outside help" (57). "This here summer," he tells the ladies, "has been the ridge-top of my life" (207). Having now seen the promised land, Uncle Ephraim implores the ladies to stay and start a school. "I hain't seed a single thing but good come from [your] being with us," he says. "Times is bettered, peace has lit like a dove upon us" (213).

As warrant of that peace, a final "entertainment" is staged at the end of the summer, featuring tableaus from "Sleeping Beauty" and staged scenes from Child ballads, with rehabilitated feudist Fighting Fult Fallon in "the velvet clothes and plumed hat of Lord Lovel" (204). The ironic symbolism of pairing the Sleeping Beauty and Lord Lovel productions (not pursued in the novel) is striking. Sleeping Beauty (the mountains?, the female principle or essence) awakens to her (Bluegrass/reformed mountaineer) lover. But Lord Lovel, who in the ballad is "going a far journey / Some strange [Bluegrass? stereoptical?] countrey to see," returns to find his (mountain?) lady Nanciebel (Sleeping Beauty?) dead. "Lady Nancie died," says the ballad, "for pure, pure love," but "Lord Lovel died for sorrow."

In *Mothering on Perilous* (*MP*) and *The Glass Window* (*GW*) one encounters more complex statements of some of the same themes, focusing on life in and around the settlement school. Both novels elaborate upon the essential pathology of mountain life. The primary symbol of that pathology in *Mothering on Perilous* is the ubiquitous and interminable feuds. In Furman's short novel *Sight to the Blind* (1914), based upon the school's efforts to eliminate trachoma among mountain people, the pathology is explored through another symbol Furman came to use repeatedly: the physical sickness of mountain people. In the novel a settlement school nurse finds a woman (Aunt Delmanthy) with cataracts and sends her to the Bluegrass for treatment, which leads not only to a physical cure but also to a spiritual transformation. Formerly full of rage at God for her condition, Aunt Delmanthy enters—says muckraker Ida Tarbell in her introduction—the "new world which the settlement opens to the mountaineers, one ruled by cleanliness, thrift, knowledge, and goodwill" (p. 21).[176]

In *The Glass Window* the pathology is developed at greater length by little Lowizy, terminally ill with tuberculosis but precociously intelligent, and passionately committed to teaching her neighbors' children. Little Lowizy's tragedy is highlighted by continual assertions that mountain people derive from "better stock" and carry vestiges of a higher culture than one might assume from their currently debased condition. That they do so is evidenced by repeated reminders that they are related by blood and underlying cultural affinity to old England, young America, and contemporary Bluegrass. "There is a fine, old-fashioned dignity in their manners, and great gentleness in their voices," the settlement teacher records in her journal (*MP*, 10). "[Shut] away here in these mountains, some of the purest and best Anglo-Saxon blood in the nation is to be found." "[Before] the Marrses came to America," she says, "they were brave and gentle folk for five hundred years in Old England" (*MP*, 109). A mountain girl who comes to the settlement "has the look of the ideal woman . . . and judging from her perfect manners, might have been reared in marble halls instead of a two-room house on the head of Wace. She has distinctly the look of race—and her name, how it carries one back through centuries of English history!"(*MP*, 249). More tangible warrants of the culture of old England include ballads (*MP*, 125) and archaic speech (*hit, holped, sarch, larnt, pyore*).

As it was in old England, so it is in New England. Mountaineer Giles Kent returns from college in the "level land" convinced that in comparison with most of their contemporaries, mountain people "have been freer from temptation, better able to keep the faith of our fathers" (*GW*, 36). He tells his compatriots they are "more like the founders of this nation, the old Pilgrim Fathers, than anybody else now in it" (*GW*, 36). Carrying the New England vision and heritage tangibly into the settlement is redhaired nurse Christine Potter.

But the most proximate reservoir of the still *active* (as opposed to dormant, submerged, or latent) virtue, taste, refinement, decency, and order of Old/New England is the Kentucky Bluegrass. In its more concrete forms, Bluegrass virtue is embodied in the doctors and surgeons who are repeatedly summoned from there to the mountains to save Aunt Delmanthy's sight, patch up a wounded feudist (*MP*, 208), or extract a ruptured appendix (*GW*, 255) at the point of a frightened mountaineer's gun ("if you kill Florindy, a-cyarving on her, you [will] die straight-away"). Less frequent but equally symbolic is the discovery of actual blood ties between

Bluegrass ladies and moutaineers, as when settlement teacher Susannah Reeves discovers her long-lost cousin Cory—descended from a branch of the family that tarried in the mountains and was lost (*GW*, 72ff.).

The central symbol of the light brought to the mountains by the settlement ladies from Old/New England-Bluegrass is the glass windows they haul in by wagon. Mountain people have heretofore lived in a physical, social, and spiritual darkness darker than the dank interiors of their windowless cabins. "There's hundreds of creeks and branches," says Lowizy, "and all along 'em young'uns sitting in darkness" (*GW*, 153). Mountain people's *resistance* to light is dramatized in Hardshell Baptist Uncle Lot's refusal to look up from "Scripter" long enough to understand that Aunt Ailsie needs more light at her loom, but their *hunger* for it is made poignant by little Lowizy's deathbed vision: "What a pretty light," she exclaims, "a-coming in strong, through my glass window. . . . Come on . . . everybody—let's all go out and see the spring!" (*GW*, 280). In the end, even Uncle Lot dons his black silk tie (previously rejected as unscriptural) and puts in his glass window. At the Forks of Troublesome, light has entered and fighting has ceased. "Never anywhere," says a teacher when she looks at her boys dressed for Sunday school, "have I observed such an aristocratic looking set of boys" (*MP*, 50).

Focusing primarily upon the social and cultural interaction between mountaineers and Bluegrass ladies, neither novel attends signficantly to the settlement school itself, which is referred to only fleetingly. Pettit and Stone ("Amy" and "Virginia") remain shadowy background figures.

Thus Furman's books, while inspired by her experience at Hindman, do not provide a comprehensive account of the settlement's actual operation. They nevertheless reflect much of the drama of cultural interaction that was central to the effort. That drama is worked out through a complex set of interrelated oppositions: darkness versus light, privilege versus duty, ignorance versus knowledge, passivity versus action, irrationality versus rationality, conservatism versus progressivism.[177]

Thus, as a representation of the social and political dynamics of the mountains, and the place of the settlement in it, Furman's novels can only be called seriously deficient. One could read them all and never know that the timber cutters and coal operators even knew where Knott County was—as in fact they had known most intimately for nearly a half-century. Indeed, the diaries of Presbyterian missionary E. O. Guerrant of forty years earlier afford a more sophisticated view of those aspects of the area's history.

But reviewers outside the mountains seem not to have sensed the deficiency. Of *The Glass Window* the *New York Herald-Tribune* said, "If Miss Furman's purpose was to give a picture of life in the Kentucky mountains and of the light let into it by the quare women's glass window . . . she has given such a picture." Those "who do not know the primitive customs and ancient turns of speech in the Kentucky mountains should make their acquaintance here," said R. D. Townsend in *Outlook*. In a comment that centered precisely but unconsciously on the problem, Walter Yost wrote in the *Literary Review* that "a life that would torment most of us to bitterness and resentment, under Miss Furman's sure and sympathetic hand, is lifted into its actual beauty." [178]

Such bitterness and resentment as there was in Furman's novels was occasioned by trivial and childish interfamily animosities that led to mindless feuds, not by the profound social changes and shifts of economic and political power that were altering the very ground of individual identity, cultural continuity, and family and community life in eastern Kentucky. Those shifts and changes were commented upon frequently by Furman's contemporaries—even some who were quite as conservative as she. Even in John Fox, Jr.'s sentimental novel *The Heart of the Hills* (1913), which focuses partly upon the women of the settlement, the coming of land surveyors, railroad men, and coal speculators—and the consequent exploitation of local people—is a central concern. Protagonist Jason Hawn goes to the settlement partly to gain the skills he needs to recover coal lands stolen from him by the likes of Colonel Pendleton (from the Bluegrass), "an intermediary between buried coal and open millions [of eastern capital]." And even William Aspenwall Bradley, as early as his 1918 article on Hindman, noted the "ruthless exploitation of [Knott County's] natural resources by the outsider" and described local people as "victims of circumstances rather than their own undisciplined passions, which were the result, not a cause, of their economic condition." [179]

Whether such an analysis was or was not undreamt of in Furman's philosophy, it was not communicated to the larger public through her novels. The message she sent forth was embodied in Uncle Sol, and Little Lowizy, and Fighting Fult Fallon, tamed and outfitted in purple velvet knee britches.

Grands and Greats: Cultural Legacy
from the Forks of Troublesome

Clearly Hindman Settlement School did not substantially alter the social, economic or political dynamics of Knott County or eastern Kentucky. Measured against the contemporary standard of the urban settlements that it advertised as its main inspiration and model, its ambit was narrow, its achievement quite limited. What it did do for a time—very well indeed—was to provide a superior basic education for hundreds of Knott County youngsters, along with food, clothing, shelter, and medical care for many of them. That was no mean accomplishment by any standard. The treks of parents and children on foot or horseback to the Forks of Troublesome—and the school's perennial waiting list—were evidence that the settlement was perceived as "a good thing" by a majority of local residents. It offered an opportunity for their children to "better themselves"—an attraction understood by most parents in most times and places.

But what was the effect of the settlement's cultural endeavors—its commitment to use local traditional culture in order to educate children "back to their homes, rather than away from them"? To support or revive local culture as a basis for personal identity and growth, and community stability and continuity? To answer these questions conclusively is impossible, since so many of the school's graduates from the years before it merged its academic programs with those of the public schools (that is, before 1928) are no longer living, and no systematic studies were undertaken at the time.[180] Yet some useful evidence upon this point was left by two eastern Kentucky natives who were directly influenced by the settlement and who spent most of their later lives studying, collecting, and interpreting the traditional culture of the area.

Josiah H. Combs (1886–1960) was Hindman's first graduate. Katherine Pettit reportedly told of having found sixteen-year-old Combs, who had never been to school, sitting barefoot beside the road, reading a "history book." Appealing as the image is, it does not accord with the facts as Combs himself reported them later.[181] Although D. K. Wilgus said Combs was born in Hazard, Combs himself says he moved to Hindman from outlying Carr's Fork at age seven (1893) and attended a "village school" for nine years—that is, until the settlement opened in 1902, when he was sixteen.

Combs spent three years at the settlement, where his teachers soon recognized him as an excellent informant concerning the traditional music of the area, which they were eager to revive among their students. Shortly after his departure, Pettit sent Harvard ballad scholar George Lyman Kittredge a small collection of ballads from eastern Kentucky, some of which Combs had given her.[182]

Upon his graduation from Hindman, Combs walked forty miles to Jackson, where he took the train to Lexington to attend Transylvania University. Acutely homesick for the mountains, he stayed only a few weeks.[183] He returned later, however, and under the tutelage of Professor Hubert G. Shearin began serious scholarly inquiries into ballads and folk songs. Together they published *A Syllabus of Kentucky Folk-Songs* (1911). After graduating from Transylvania, Combs taught in high schools and colleges in Kentucky, Tennessee, Virginia, and Oklahoma (1911–18), served in the U.S. Army during World War I and in the Czechoslovakian Army (1920–21), and returned to be a professor of English and Spanish at West Virginia University (1921–24) while working for his doctorate at the Sorbonne. His doctoral thesis, *Folk Songs du Midi des Etats Unis* (1925), was the most extensive early scholarly study of traditional music in the southern mountains.

Although Combs was trained primarily as a linguist and spent most of his life as a university professor of modern languages, he remained throughout his life a strong partisan and interpreter of the traditional culture of his native region, which he wrote about in scholarly journals and presented through lecture tours and folk-song recitals.[184]

Reflecting upon his development as a scholar and partisan of traditional culture, Combs recalled his years at the settlement with great fondness and gratitude. "I owe most of [my] intellectual curiosity to those early years at Hindman," he told the *Hindman News*. In an earlier letter to Pettit, he said, "I have constantly kept you in mind, as a sort of inspiration, always wondering, whenever I get in the mood to write something, what Miss Pettit would think of it. . . . For me, that epoch at Hindman was a sort of Utopia . . . which I relished with more than a fierce joy. Books! intelligent, cultured people. . . . I felt all the enthusiasm of those old Renaissance writers when they broke through the thick crust of medievalism. . . ." A few months later he wrote to Lucy Furman that "those days were a sort of paradise."[185] In *The Kentucky Highlanders from a Native Mountaineer's Viewpoint*, written a few years after he left the settlement, Combs called the school "the most valuable [educational institution] of its kind, not only in the Kentucky mountains but in America" and spoke of "the great work those noble, self-sacrificing women from all parts of the Union are doing."[186]

Combs's views of mountain people and mountain society, as he expressed them in his early published work, were congruent with those prev-

alent among the settlement women and educated "outlanders" during the
pre–World War I period. To him, the customs, language, names, and general culture of mountain people bespoke their "Anglo-Saxon" origins. He
took note, as did many a contemporary commentator, of their "reticent,
undemonstrative nature," their hospitality, the hard lot of their women,
the absence of "social castes," and the survival of "old English customs
and superstitions" among them.

To a surprising degree, Combs seems to have shared also the essentially
racist and nativist views that were being used by so many to justify "mountain work." "Anglo-Saxon blood" and "Teutonic instincts" were to him
not mere mental constructs but concrete characteristics which determined
individual behavior and social structure and development. The "question
for the south to work out," he said, quoting a well-known educator of the
time, "is not that of the negroes so much as that of the whites of the Southern Alleghenies." Combs lamented that more money was being spent to
educate the "thousands of foreigners that pour into our country monthly
by way of New York harbor" than the "virile and sturdy" Anglo-Saxon
stock of the mountains. An opportunity was being lost, he said, "to invest
capital for the preservation and enlightenment of America's manhood." [187]

In several respects, however, Combs's analysis of problems in the mountains was more sophisticated than that of his settlement teachers. He felt
that mountaineers were not only threatened from without by national policies biased against them but also endangered from within by avaricious
entrepreneurs. "Capitalists and speculators [are] buying up thousands of
acres of mountain lands," he said, noting that Consolidation Coal Company owned more than 100,000 acres in four eastern Kentucky counties
(including Knott) and that the "mountain millionaire" John C. C. Mayo's
Northern Coal and Coke Company of Paintsville owned thousands of
acres. Combs called the Mayo-like entrepreneurs "jackals of civilization"
who "are abusing the confidence of the hillsmen . . . and possessing their
lumber, coal and mineral wealth, without according them the right to
share in the development of the resources of their own native hills." [188]

Thus in the two decades after he left the settlement, Combs outgrew
some of his teachers' views. They had seen the same things he saw, but
could not bring themselves to call a jackal a jackal, and were more easily
impressed by John C. C. Mayo's butlers and taste in furnishings than they
were outraged by the havoc he and his like were wreaking in the mountains.

In one additional sense Combs's views of culture outstripped those of
the settlement teachers. Like them, he perceived the multifaceted threat
to the old culture: phonographs and modern science, public schools and

Primitive Baptist churches, banjos and pianos, newspapers and singing schools, jazz and ragtime. He lamented the renowned mountain fiddler who entered the baptismal waters saying "Good-bye, Sourwood Mountain" and emerged singing "Been a long time travelling here below," and he regretted that "the damsel with the dulcimore is retreating before the boy with the banjo." With some approval he quoted a mountain judge's charge to his jury: "Gentlemen! Whenever you see a great big overgrown buck sitting at the mouth of some holler . . . with a big slouch hat on, a blue, celluloid collar, a celluloid, artificial, red rose in his coat lapel, a banjo strung across his breast, and a-pickin' 'Sourwood Mountain,' fine that man, gentlemen!, fine him! For if he hasn't already done something, he's a-going' to!" [189]

As Uncle Sol and the "damsel with the dulcimore" were icons of the old culture, so the dandified banjo picker was of the new: aimlessness and rootlessness, bad taste in clothes and music, indolence and vulgarity, an offense to public decency, and a potential threat to the social order. Thus far Combs walked with his teachers.

And yet he also knew that the new culture was producing its own music, much of it as meaningful and functional as the old. He decried the long hegemony of the ballad canon established by Francis James Child, praised the more inclusive definition of folk song employed by a few modern collectors, and noted that the same impulses and methods of composition used by the originators of the Child ballads were producing current ballads on local crimes, train wrecks, and similar dramatic events. It was a view of culture and culture change that the settlement women could never bring themselves to accept, from the summer they first climbed a hill near Hindman and saw the "ugly new frame houses" dotting the valley. Basil Beverly's ballad about the robbing of the local post office and his promise to write another about "you'ns and the tent" were cultural messages of great import. But the significance of those messages was lost upon the settlement women.

A more complex example of the settlement's effect as a mediator between local people and their own culture is provided by the Ritchie family, who were in fact some of Uncle Sol's "grands and greats" and most of whose fourteen sons and daughters attended both Hindman and Pine Mountain Settlement schools.[190] From the family seat on Elk Branch, near Viper (in neighboring Perry County), the Ritchies sent their children to the settlements until the public high school opened at Viper—to the great disappointment of the youngest child, Jean.

Like the Combses, the Ritchies were a "singing family"—one of whom

FIGURE I-20
Boy with a banjo (Hindman Settlement School Archive).

later served as an informant for the Library of Congress folk-song archiving project and several of whom had part- or full-time careers as performing musicians—and they valued the cultural emphasis of the settlements.[191] Many years later, in her preface to *Folk Songs of the Southern Appalachians as Sung by Jean Ritchie*, Jean said "one of the many good things" about Hindman was its music program, which "gave young Kentucky mountaineers a tremendous sense of pride in their inherited music, and an incentive to sing, enjoy and preserve it that many of them would not otherwise have had." Commenting on the effect of the settlement, *Louisville Courier-Journal* writer Rena Niles said that the Ritchies' education in the settlements made them "more aware of traditional values rather than [alienating] them from their native culture."[192]

But the story is not as simple as these comments suggest. The Ritchies *were* a singing family who loved the old songs and whose great-grandfather was the very Uncle Sol whose image was so central to the Hindman myth.[193] But they were also apparently a progressive family, in touch with and enticed by the new ways. Jean's father, Balis, had only an eighth-grade education, but he was a school teacher for a time and published the first newspaper in Hindman. Her uncle Jason—the source for many of the most traditional songs she learned and later published—was a lawyer and self-taught historian.[194] Jean's grandmother may have been a pillar of the Old Regular Baptist church and her mother a devoted listener to selections from *The Sweet Songster*, but when Balis used his printing press to publish *Lover's Melodies: A Choice Collection of Old Sentimental Songs Our Grandmothers Sang and Other Popular Airs*, Child's "The Brown Girl" appeared alongside "Casey Jones" and "Kitty Wells"—both perhaps learned from the record player the family bought from Sears and Roebuck as early as 1905.[195]

In *Singing Family of the Cumberlands*, Jean Ritchie presents the settlements as a sort of cultural breakwater, standing against the new values and esthetics carried by the radio, the railroad, the phonograph, and the automobile. "The big things the settlement schools did," she recalls, "was to bring in level-country people . . . whose ways of doing things . . . helped us to see that there was a different kind of life than the hard one we knew." When her sister Una first visited Hindman, she said, "It was like the whole world was opening up like a blossom."

Her own first introduction to the ways of the settlement produced a different reaction, however, which suggested both the underlying cultural conflict and the relationship between such conflict and personal identity. Rebuked for her bad table manners by her settlement-habituated sisters

("If you were to ask for the bread that way at Pine Mountain, you'd get sent right home"), Jean replied, "This ain't Pine Mountain, and you all ain't my bosses." But her later summary judgment of the settlements was wholly positive: "If it hadn't been for the settlement schools, many of the old mountain songs would have died out when the ways of the world came in on us. But the Women loved our music and plays, so that they became a regular part of the life around the two schools." [196]

One cannot know, of course, whether the "if . . . then" logic is justified or not. At the very least, it can be demonstrated that the culture of the settlement was a selective, reinterpreted sample of local culture, blended with Bluegrass and New England versions of mainstream genteel culture. Beyond that, all one can do with the Ritchie story—which is the most complete available record of the interaction between a local family and the settlements—is to use the interpretation placed upon the settlement experience by one of its most articulate commentators to add a few other dimensions to the history.

It can be established, at least, that however strongly the settlements educated them "back to their homes" in their heads and their affections, most of the Ritchie daughters in fact passed *through* the settlements on their way *out* of the mountains. Kitty and Edna went from Pine Mountain to Berea; Una and Pauline went from Hindman to Science Hill Academy and then to Wellesley, and Una subsequently married a Harvard student, Thomas Takhub, and made her home in New England. [197]

Paradoxically, the best key to understanding the cultural significance of Hindman for the Ritchies may be the fourteenth and last child, Jean, who was born too late to attend the settlements herself. She was born in 1922, a decade after the first flower-bedecked locomotive reached Hazard, two years after the first commercial radio stations crackled onto the air, and on the brink of the Twenties boom, the Jazz Age, and the Grand Old Opry. Having heard exciting tales of the settlements all her young life—of Jason leading collectors Josephine McGill and Loraine Wyman to the best singers in the country, of sister Una and cousin Sabrina singing for Cecil Sharp—it fell her lot to attend the prosaic public high school in Viper before going on, not to Wellesley, but to Cumberland College (Williamsburg, Kentucky), where "the thing to do was to sing in the glee club and the choirs, take voice and piano lessons, and try to imitate opera stars." Chided by her father for her "new voice," she soon stopped taking lessons. Standing at the very boundary between the old culture of her grandparents, parents, and older siblings, and the new culture of the radio and her college classmates, she felt a profound confusion. "And so in my mind," she recalled later, "the songs got all mixed and tangled until I came to think on the hillbilly songs and the old songs as the same kind of thing, got ashamed to be caught singing either kind, got to liking the slick city music on the radio best." [198]

Following her graduation from college (in social work), Jean went to New York as a group worker at the Henry Street Settlement (her Hindman and Pine Mountain?). Initially drawing upon her family's culture only informally in her work with Henry Street children, she gave her first public performance of traditional music at a New York University alumni tea in 1947. The next year she met folklorist Alan Lomax, who recorded some of her traditional repertoire for the Library of Congress. Lomax asked her to perform later at NYU festivals, and in 1950 she produced her first record on the new Elektra label, *Jean Ritchie, Singing Traditional Songs of Her Kentucky Mountain Family*. A Fulbright fellowship in 1952 led to a year of collecting in the British Isles. With her filmmaker husband George Pickow she later produced several documentary films on folklore. Performances at the Berkeley and Newport festivals in the late 1950s brought her to the attention of a much wider audience. [199]

Josiah Combs and Jean Ritchie were born a generation apart, one at the beginning of the settlement era in the mountains, the other at its effective (if not formal) close. Their lives (and those of most of the other Ritchie daughters) paralleled each other in at least one important respect, however: both left the mountains, but spent the rest of their lives as public exponents of the received culture. The critical point, of course, is that although changing social and economic conditions in the mountains had forever doomed that culture as a functional basis for individual identity or family and community life, in the urban, middle-class world into which its professional carriers moved there was space, leisure, and money to promote, acquire, and "appreciate" it as a cultural icon or possession—as one would a Navajo drum or a Wedgwood plate.

A revealing long-term result of the settlement's projecting a selective version of local culture—and the dovetailing of that version with the impulse of middle-class people beyond the mountains to collect cultural artifacts from picturesque mountaineers—is its promotion of the three-stringed dulcimer as the "real" or official mountain musical instrument.

At the time the settlement school opened, the most prevalent instruments in the area were fiddles (which had been prominent in most parts of the mountains since earliest settlement) and banjos (which were coming in through mail-order catalogs, along with many other new instruments). Indeed, when Olive Dame Campbell heard her first ballads at Hindman in late 1908, they were accompanied on banjo rather than dulcimer. Katherine Pettit showed her a dulcimer, but no one at the settlement knew how to play it.[200]

How prevalent the dulcimer was in the area at the time, and how long it had been there, is not clear. The most comprehensive recent study concludes that "the established record of [the J. E. Thomas] type of dulcimer [concentrated in southeastern Kentucky] does not predate the early 1870s." That date is corroborated by Allen Eaton's earlier interviews with Thomas, a Letcher County native, who was the area's outstanding dulcimer maker.[201]

At least two factors account for the settlement women's choice of "the girl with the dulcimer" over the "boy with the banjo." In the first place, the banjo appears to have indeed been associated with new and somewhat rowdy music and ways—as one judges from both Combs's anecdote and the historical record. To the extent that it was, it was a liability for a new school which needed the goodwill of the church and the pillars of the local community. Probably more important as a factor in the choice, however, were the settlement women's own genteel Bluegrass acculturation and their Bradley-Furman view of mountain culture. Within that view, the shadowy and presumably ancient origin of the dulcimer was appealing; its plaintive, simple sound was congruent with prevalent assumptions about "Elizabethan" culture in the mountains; and perhaps best of all, the instrument was physically unsuited to playing the lively banjo tunes that were insinuating themselves into more and more mountain households.

Thus Bradley and Furman—and the settlement itself, through its public-relations and fundraising efforts—paved the way for the dulcimer to become established in the popular mind as the "real" instrument of mountain people. But at least some of the evidence suggested otherwise: Uncle Ed Thomas told Allen Eaton that most of the fifteen hundred or so instruments he had made had been sold in New York, rather than among his eastern Kentucky neighbors. How many were sold to Bradley and Furman's readers is unknown.[202]

The settlement's institutionalization of the dulcimer received a major impetus from former Hindman student Jethro Amburgey, who returned to the school in the early 1930s as its woodworking teacher. Amburgey was a descendant of Ambrose Amburgey, who came to Knott County from Virginia in 1825 and settled on ten thousand acres on Carr Creek, which he bought for six cents an acre.[203] Jethro was born in the closing years of the nineteenth century and attended Hindman Settlement School as a young

FIGURE I-21
*Uncle Ed Thomas, dulcimer maker from whom Jethro Amburgey learned his
craft
(Hindman Settlement School Archive).*

boy. After receiving his elementary-school teaching certificate from Berea Normal School in 1924, he returned to Knott County and became (ca. 1931) manager of the school's woodworking shop.

For approximately four decades, until his death in 1971, Amburgey concentrated almost exclusively on making dulcimers. Although some of his dulcimer-making contemporaries experimented with the instrument's design, Amburgey held religiously to the pattern he got from Uncle Ed Thomas.[204] Thus, in the midst of dramatic cultural change, Amburgey continued to produce romantic cultural artifacts for a selected public predisposed by the settlements to a certain view of culture in the mountains. That was the ultimately ironic meaning of being "educated back to [one's] home" as that home had been defined in cultural terms by the settlement.

One larger, long-term result of Amburgey's choice came about—oddly enough—partially through Jean Ritchie, whose Uncle Jason taught her to play dulcimer when she was a child. Ritchie chose to feature the dulcimer in her later concerts and recordings—perhaps because it seemed to fit that portion of mountain music she characteristically presented. And since her growing popularity as a performer coincided with the urban folk revival of the late 1950s and early 1960s, demand for the dulcimer rose sharply and Amburgey's fame as a maker spread widely. Of the scores of orders for dulcimers remaining in Amburgey's papers, most date from the 1960s, most are from outside the mountains (frequently from the urban and academic centers, where the folk-song revival was most pronounced), and many mention having seen Amburgey's name in Ritchie's *Dulcimer Book*.[205] By the mid-1970s, Ritchie could sketch a virtually worldwide network of "dulcimer people" who were playing the instrument—a sort of pan-cultural community of devotees of the settlement version of mountain music.[206]

Indeed, one of the paradoxes of intervention-induced cultural change is its very durability and the degree to which imported forms and styles are accepted and defended by local people whose actual cultural traditions they altered or displaced. At one level, amid the new social circumstances of the post–World War II period, Hindman cast about (along with many other independent mountain schools) for a new role for itself. It offered its facilities (no longer needed for many of their original purposes) for conferences; donated land for a community building and swimming pool; housed and fed a few students from remote areas who attended public school in town; provided supplementary teachers for the public-school system in such areas as art, music, and recreation; offered classes in pottery and piano.[207] And throughout, it continued to advertise itself as providing—as the historical marker near its entrance says—an opportunity for mountain children to remain "mindful of their heritage."

But the situation was a good deal more complicated than such an assertion suggests. It should by now be more than clear that Hindman's cultural program was and was not related to the "heritage" of the surrounding area. Instead of winnowing the authentic from the artificially laid-on, the passing of the years merely confirmed the complicated mix. Thus Hindman's 1981 "Family Folk Week" featured performances by Jean Ritchie and Edna Ritchie Baker, the [Raymond] McLain Family Band, and dulcimer-maker Morris Amburgey (son of Jethro). Knott County native Colleen Messer represented the Quicksand Crafts Center, an early Hindman outpost which in recent years had turned to producing a variety of "traditional" woven goods derived principally from the Scandinavian-influenced patterns and methods introduced by Berea College shortly after the turn of the century.

In her 1981 article on Hindman, Mercy Coogan concluded with an imaginary conversation between Uncle Sol and the school's present director (Knott County native Michael Mullins), who brings Uncle Sol up to date on the school's history. "I reckon," Uncle Sol judges, "hit was worth the walk." If one pushes beyond the historical myth to confront the full and complicated historical record, however, one might also reasonably reckon that, *culturally* speaking, Uncle Sol might nearly as well have saved himself the walk.

Jean Ritchie recalled in the mid-1950s that after a period of cultural disorientation induced by the radio and other innovations in which the family "didn't near sing our own songs like we used to," there was a memorable family reunion. After dinner, family members drifted out to the front porch as of yore, and someone started singing "The Cuckoo, She's a Pretty Bird." Soon everyone joined in, and "we sang back all the happy days and ways of our growing up." [208]

Like the Ritchies on that magic evening, Hindman Settlement School tried to "sing back all the happy days and ways," but it couldn't. A mountain family—brought together from now far-scattered homes—might sing them back in a brief moment of luminous memory, but schools—even settlement schools—and families are vastly different institutions.

2

All that is native and fine

The Cultural Work of Olive Dame Campbell,

1908–1948

[The] folk movement in the mountains . . . seeks the
recognition and preservation of all that is native and fine. . . .
We would like to have the people recognize the worth and
beauty of their songs; we would like to have the singing of
these songs encouraged in all the mountain schools and centers;
we would like to have them displace the inferior music that is
now being sung there. . . . The people have already begun to
be somewhat ashamed of their songs; they need to have them
appreciated by outsiders. . . .

Olive Dame Campbell to Cecil Sharp, 20 December 1916

Do you know Miss Jackson? She is a wonder for a
mountaineer. A mountain girl, who graduated at Holyoke, and
has been teaching at Bryn Mawr for a long time. She is now
back at her home in Laurel County and is buying up mountain
land as an investment. She got interested in these ballads while
she was at Bryn Mawr.

Katherine Pettit to Olive Dame Campbell, 23 March 1911

OF THE SCORES of "cultural workers" who collected, recorded, photographed, wrote, published, and founded organizations in the "Southern highlands" in the half-century between 1890 and 1940, Olive Dame Campbell was one of the more sophisticated and humane.[1] From the time she heard her first ballad at Hindman Settlement School late in 1907—as a recently married twenty-five-year-old New England native—until she retired nearly forty years later as head of a school she founded in the mountains, she worked to comprehend the connection between culture and the intricacies of politics, economics, and social structure in the Appalachian region. It was a connection sought by few of her culture-worker contemporaries.

Like many progressive and socially active women of her era, Campbell was prodigiously productive. By wagon, foot, and horseback, she traveled hundreds of miles with her husband through the mountains, helping with the social survey he was conducting for the Russell Sage Foundation, and in fact eventually wrote most of the study herself.[2] She undertook some of the earliest and best scientific ballad collecting in the region and collaborated with English ballad collector Cecil Sharp on the pathbreaking *English Folk Songs of the Southern Appalachians* (1917). She traveled to Scandinavia, studied the "folk high school" movement, wrote a book about it, worked to adapt the concept to mountain conditions, and founded the John C. Campbell Folk School and directed it for more than twenty years. She helped guide the early work of the Conference of Southern Mountain Workers and was one of the founders of the Southern Highland Handicraft Guild. And along the way, she buried her husband and two infant daughters.

And yet it was Olive Dame Campbell's quite human lot to see through a glass darkly—to know in part and to prophesy in part. To seek to preserve "all that is native and fine"—and to reinforce the natives' own confidence and pride in its fineness—is one thing, but to understand the convoluted cultural and ethical odyssey of a bright mountain girl from Laurel County to Mt. Holyoke and Bryn Mawr and back to Laurel County to collect ballads in the morning and speculate in the mountain lands of her neighbors in the afternoons is another. Transplanting the economic and social idea of cooperatives from Denmark to agricultural Cherokee County, North Carolina, was enlightened and progressive; but teaching mountaineers Danish gymnastics and dances proved problematic at best. And as the years passed, other ironies, paradoxes, contradictions, and unanticipated negative results emerged. Thus Campbell's work not only invites admiration, but also demands the sober reflection and analysis made possible by historical distance.

A Prevailing Smell of Stale Tobacco Juice:
Olive Dame Campbell Goes South

After a day on the train between Fredericksburg and Charlottesville, Virginia, in October 1908, Campbell wrote in her journal, "There were many nice looking Southerners on the train—the type is unmistakable. . . . They wear soft collars, & large ties and black felt hats. . . ." But, she continued, "so many of them chew! Spitoons are everywhere. . . . The coaches have a prevailing smell of stale tobacco juice."[3] Although it was not her first trip south, the physical and cultural landscapes were still unfamiliar enough to provoke perplexity over "nice looking" Southerners with uncouth habits. It was a long way from New England even to rural middle Virginia, and would be further still to the back country of the Blue Ridge, the Smokies and the Cumberlands.

Born in Medford, Massachusetts, in 1882, Olive Dame graduated from local Tufts College in 1903 and had spent several years as a school teacher by the time she met John C. Campbell on a trip to Scotland during the summer of 1906. The two returned to Boston "practically engaged" and were married the following spring.[4] Letters that Mrs. Campbell wrote to her family during the nine-month wedding trip to Europe and the Mediterranean (much of which was spent at Taormina in Sicily) contained almost no hints of the work that lay ahead for them. Her comments on local people were sensitive, but hardly rose above what might have been expected from any thoughtful tourist.[5]

While they were abroad, however, John Campbell read of the formation of the Russell Sage Foundation in New York.[6] Although the days of widespread grantsmanship lay far in the future (there were only eight foundations in the United States at the time), Campbell saw a possible opportunity to extend work he had begun in the southern mountains nearly a decade earlier.

Born in Indiana in 1867 to a Scottish immigrant who rose from railroad machinist to general superintendent of the Chicago and Northern Pacific Railroad, Campbell spent much of his youth in Stevens Point, Wisconsin, before going east to Phillips Academy ('88), Williams College ('92), and Andover Seminary ('95). Learning from "home missionaries" of distressed social conditions in the southern mountains, he decided to go there to work after graduating from the seminary.[7]

Campbell began his own work in the mountains (which he had first visited on business for his father) as principal of an American Missionary Association school at Joppa, Alabama. He taught one year back in Wisconsin (1898–99), but returned to the mountains to head a school at Pleasant Hill, Tennessee, before going to Piedmont College at Demorest, Georgia, of which he later became president. The death of his first wife in 1904 and the pressure of his job led him to resign from Piedmont College early in 1907. Shortly thereafter he married Olive Dame.[8]

The Russell Sage Foundaton, incorporated only a week before the Campbells were married, had been formed to disburse part of the $65 million that Russell Sage left to his wife upon his death in 1906.[9] Several factors, it turned out, predisposed the foundation to favor both Campbell's broad proposal for southern mountain work and the more specifically cultural endeavors of his wife. Board member Robert C. Ogden was interested in educational work among southern blacks and whites; director John M. Glenn had earlier been president of both the National Conference of Charities and Corrections (NCCC) and the Board of Supervisors of City Charities in Baltimore. Glenn steered the foundation toward "the development of social work" as its major focus and organized its earliest endeavors into departments of recreation, education, "child-helping," and "women's [industrial] work." To head the Department of Child Hygiene at the Sage Foundation, Glenn chose Luther H. Gulick, an early exponent of using folk dances in community recreation and physical training programs; the head of its Recreation Department was William Chauncy Langdon, who worked extensively with "community pageants" popular at the time.[10]

The foundation's initial link to the Campbells came through Glenn's wife, then serving as chairman of the NCCC's section on needy families, a vast number of which were generally thought to reside in the southern mountains (where Mrs. Glenn's parents had sometimes vacationed). For the May 1908 meeting of the NCCC in Richmond, Virginia, Mrs. Glenn scheduled a discussion of social and economic conditions in the mountains. John Campbell was invited to attend, along with numerous other "mountain workers." After talking with the Glenns in Richmond, Campbell proposed that the foundation fund a social survey of the southern mountains. On 20 June 1908 the foundation gave Campbell three thousand dollars "to secure a report on what is being done in the mountains and what the needs are for further work; what are the best methods of work, and how cooperation among the various agencies now working in the mountains can be secured." [11]

For Campbell, the grant led to more than ten years of research, travel, organizing, and writing in and about the southern mountains; the opening of the foundation's Southern Highlands Division office in Asheville, North Carolina; the organization of the Conference of Southern Mountain Workers in 1913; and the posthumous publication of *The Southern Highlander and His Homeland* in 1921. He studied population statistics, natural resources, education, conditions in mill villages, churches, and health and sanitation. But for Mrs. Campbell, the focus was primarily cultural. As she traveled with her husband in the mountains, Mrs. Campbell began to pay particular attention to the music she heard in people's homes and churches, the quilts and coverlets on their beds, the baskets and tools they made and used. Within a relatively few months, her interest met with a sympathetic hearing inside the foundation.

In their sympathy to such matters, Glenn, Gulick, Langdon, and other foundation officers reflected some of the larger movements and preoccupations of the period. The Playgound Association of America had been organized in 1906, and the first national Play Congress had occurred in Chicago in 1907. Both owed their existence partly to the urban settlement houses of the 1890s, which had experimented with a variety of culturally based recreational programs (dance, song, pageants, festivals, handicrafts). Activities of the Playground Association also overlapped those of a growing company of folk-dance enthusiasts: at the 1908 Play Congress in New York, children from playgrounds in the city's "foreign" neighborhoods presented folk and national dances. [12]

John Campbell's work in the mountains was cut short by his death in 1919 at the age of fity-one, but Olive Dame Campbell's stretched over nearly a half-century. And although in some ways it meshed naturally with (and found support in) broader national trends in culture studies—trends reflected in the Sage Foundation's programs—it was a work of a pioneering sort, undertaken in alien territory by a young New England woman who had almost no technical or professional training for what lay ahead.

The journals that Mrs. Campbell kept on one of her earliest trips south reveal her puzzlement over a land where people lived, thought, spoke, dressed, and behaved so differently from her New England neighbors. "The rural aspect of the south strikes one immediately," she wrote a few months after her marriage, "no large cities and stretches and stretches of woodland and cornfield."

Recalling romantic images of the plantation South, she found that "the fertility and beauty of the Virginia countryside [around Charlottesville] is a constant joy, and gives one a better idea of the old days than any other part of the South I have yet seen. We met constantly people on horseback and driving blooded horses." Discomforted by uncertain train schedules further south, however, she concluded that "they don't seem to have any idea how to manage things down here. I don't know exactly why." [13] A train ride from Bristol to Knoxville convinced her that "nothing could have been more different from New England. The towns are small and struggling—unattractive mostly, and the men unkempt." Local people she found "like children—and chewing gum! Everyone chews—the men tobacco, I suppose—but the women and children gum. . . . It is not an alluring performance. Such conditions must make a woman of Miss de Graffenreid's culture sigh for her poor South. . . . Miss de Graffenreid was one of the first I have met, of the old stock, and I found her charming. She appears to be in touch with all the old Southern aristocracy." [14] Counterposed with Miss de Graffenreid were the gun-toting mountaineer sitting on a railway station platform holding a live possum by the tail, and the grubbiness of Jackson, Kentucky, where the "streets [are] fearfully irregular—houses at all angles." "No pigs are loose," Mrs. Campbell observed, "but stys are in evidence and sad-looking cows . . . lumber along the narrow irregular plank walks." [15]

Reality was being tested against both the myth of the Old South and the tidy New England norms. Neither test yielded reassuring results. But the tests were only temporarily useful, and as Campbell's travels in the mountains continued, invidious comparison gave way increasingly to detailed nonjudgmental observation. Riding in a wagon toward Young Harris, in the Georgia mountains, she said, "The cabins looked very attractive tucked in along the roadside, tho' I can't help thinking that in spite of their picturesqueness . . . they must be desperately lonely in winter. . . . Hard on the women and children. We passed a sorghum mill where the cane was heaped high and the horse was going round the tread mill. There were lots of children about and there was an air of festivity and cheer." Later on in the Kentucky mountains she found some houses "dirty and careless beyond mention," but she refrained from New England or Old South comparisons. [16]

Throughout the fall and winter of 1908–9, the Campbells traveled through the mountains by foot, horseback, wagon, and train—through north Georgia and east Tennessee, eastern Kentucky and western North Carolina. They stayed in the homes of both missionaries and mountaineers, and visited mission and settlement schools old and new: the Berry schools and Pleasant Hill, Berea College and Lincoln Memorial University, Oneida Institute and Hazel Green Academy, Hindman Settlement School and Asheville Farm School.[17] As her views of life in the mountains became better grounded, the full range of social conditions emerged in her journals: bountiful tables in some homes and hunger-distended bellies in others; handwoven coverlets and quilts on some beds, torn and dirty linens on others; good farms and bad; healthy communities and long-standing feuds; good schools and poor.

Within a fairly short time, Campbell was able to set aside most of the irrelevant norms and obfuscating myths that continued to distort the vision and judgment of many another "fotched-on" mountain worker—especially those who chose culture as their primary domain. Distortions and dislocations emerged later in her work, as will be seen, but at the outset she approached the culture of the region with a balance, sophistication, and respect unmatched by most of her contemporaries. Asked by a teacher at the Asheville Farm School in March 1909 if she did not "find it depressing to study these peculiar people," she replied that she would, perhaps, "if at bottom they were not pretty much like the rest of us."[18]

It was a judgment not widely shared. Popular understanding of the Appalachian South at the time reflected virtually every shade of opinion. While for some, mountain people were "backward," unhealthy, unchurched, ignorant, violent, and morally degenerate social misfits who were a national liability, for others they were pure, uncorrupted 100 percent American, picturesque, and photogenic pre-moderns who were a great untapped national treasure. Much of the argument was conducted in cultural terms, and Olive Dame Campbell played a major role in the debate.

Absolutely Minor and Fascinating: Ballads and the Argument Over Culture in the Mountains

"In the evening," Campbell wrote in her journal after a visit to Hindman Settlement School early in December 1908, "all the children came in like a family to sit for an hour over the open fire. Miss Breck got them to singing old ballads, the Swapping Song, Barbara Allen, Brown Girl . . . and Bailiff of Islington. The tunes were as old as the hills—the real old plaintive folk tunes handed down from mother to daughter—absolutely minor and fascinating."[19]

How early in her life Campbell heard ballads is not known. She could well have heard them before she came south, since theater pieces and pageants using ballads began to be produced in northeastern women's colleges soon after the turn of the century.[20] But for whatever reasons, from her first day in the mountains Campbell began—apparently instinctively—to collect ballads.

In so doing, she placed herself near the head of a long column that was to follow. Although as early as 1905, Tennessee writer Emma Bell Miles had included remarks on "some real American music" in *The Spirit of the Mountains*, scholars were tardy in taking the hint. In 1889 the first article on Carolina mountain folklore appeared in the *Journal of American Folklore*, but dealt with music almost not at all. Four years later, Lila Edmonds published one ballad and two songs she had collected in the Roan Mountain section of North Carolina. As late as 1907, however, Haywood Parker, in a long article on the folklore of North Carolina mountaineers, asserted his belief that "remnants of old English and Scottish ballads still linger in some isolated coves," but reported that he had encountered none.[21]

In the ten days before Christmas of 1908, however, Campbell prevailed upon Hindman Settlement School children to give her words and music to a score of ballads: "Lord Daniel's Wife" and "The Turkish Lady," "Young Edward" and "William Hall," "Loving Hanner" and "The Brown Girl," "The Lonesome Valley" and "The Old Salt Sea," "Jackaro" and "Pretty Polly."[22]

Unlike most of her ballad-hunting contemporaries of the next decade, Campbell did not confine herself initially to English ballads of the type canonized in Francis J. Child's *English and Scottish Popular Ballads* (1882–98). She recorded the nineteenth-century North Carolina murder ballad "Omie Wise" in her journal, and on New Year's Eve of 1908 persuaded two Hindman girls to teach her "Guide Me O Thou Great Jehovah." Three weeks later, riding out of Hazard on horseback, she passed a mountain cabin, "heard a banjo going," and regretted that she had no time to stop.[23]

By mid-summer of 1909 her collecting was far enough advanced for her to confer with John Glenn of the Sage Foundation about possible publication.[24] Her work progressed rapidly as she rode with her husband on his rounds in the mountains. By early in 1910 she had collected from singers in Kentucky's Knott, Perry, and Clay counties; Rabun, Habersham and Walker counties in north Georgia; and Flag Pond, Tennessee. Her first assembled collection was in Glenn's hands early in 1910.[25]

Glenn explored possibilities for getting the collection into print, talking to friends and associates in commercial publishing (G. Schirmer judged the ballads to have little commercial merit), universities (Tufts College professor L. R. Lewis found them "a substantial and unique contribution to the literature of what might be called American Aboriginal Music"), and foundations.[26] He also approached Harvard ballad scholar George Lyman Kittredge, who had helped Katherine Pettit publish the first Hindman-collected ballads in the *Journal of American Folklore* in 1907. Kittredge found the Campbell ballads "a remarkable collection . . . of real interest and importance . . . [which] ought to be printed" and told Glenn that Harvard had recently given money to former Harvard student John Lomax for collecting such material in Texas and the Southwest.[27]

Although Glenn apparently offered to subsidize publication through the Sage Foundation, Campbell's ballads were not to reach an audience for another half-dozen years. World War I was partly responsible for the delay, but a more immediate cause was the theoretical and territorial ballad "wars" then being carried on among scholars and collectors interested in southern mountain ballads. Ballads were viewed as a scarce and endangered species, and collectors sought them (and guarded their sources) as jealously as an antiques collector on the trail of the last John Townsend blockfront.[28]

Campbell apparently confided to Katherine Pettit that she was encountering some of the territorial jealousies, for Pettit wrote to her in March 1911: "[We] have always expected you to publish our ballads, and shall be glad to have you do it. I think it was absurd for Joshua to take that attitude. . . . He and Professor Sharon . . . at Transylvania University are planning to publish them, and I suppose that is why he did it. I advise you to get yours out as soon as you can. . . . Miss Jackson and Dr. Frost at Berea are planning to get some published right away."[29]

Although Campbell's own ballad collection was not to be published "right away," public and scholarly interest in southern mountain ballads was growing at a great rate and would eventually spur their publication. State ballad and folklore societies were formed in Kentucky and North Carolina in 1912 and in Virginia in 1913, and University of Virginia professor C. Alphonso Smith was collecting avidly. In November 1913 the U.S. Bureau of Education, partly at Smith's suggestion, issued a bulletin urging that a "national ballad search" be undertaken before all the surviving ballads were swept away by currents of modernity.

Help in getting Campbell's collection published eventually came—like many of the ballads themselves—from England, where the formation of the Folk Song Society in 1898 had brought the old music to public attention. In 1903, Cecil Sharp began collecting ancient ballads, songs, and dances among the old people in the rural districts of England.[30]

Sharp (1859–1924), the son of a slate merchant, had taken a degree in music from Cambridge in 1882. He went to Australia and washed hansom cabs and worked as a bank clerk before becoming an associate to the chief justice of Australia. After a period as codirector of Adelaide College of Music, Sharp returned to England in 1892 to continue his work as a composer. He encountered his first traditional music and dance in 1899 and by 1903 was collecting seriously.[31] For the next decade, he collected assiduously, wrote, helped found the English Folk Dance Society (1911), and endeavored to awaken the public to the value of the older ballads, songs, and dances. The coming of war in Europe made it impossible for him to continue his work, however, and late in 1914 he accepted an invitation to come to New York to help with a production of *Midsummer Night's Dream*. But he did not meet Campbell until his second trip the following summer.

Her first meeting with Sharp came after the Sage Foundation's William Chauncy Langdon met a brother-sister quartet of singers from England (the Fullers) who were concertizing in the United States. After hearing them perform some English ballads on one of their programs, Langdon showed them some of Campbell's southern mountain ballads, which he said "they were inclined to think . . . were purer and older, many of them, than their own Dorset and Somerset versions."[32] Rosalind Fuller sent some of the ballads to Sharp (her former teacher), who looked at them and quickly asked to see Campbell. Sometime late in June the two met and talked in Lincoln, Massachusetts.[33]

Within a few days, Sharp became convinced that investigating southern mountain ballads "would be particularly congenial for me . . . because it would in a sense complete the work upon which I have been engaged so long in England." But there could be difficulties, he said, because he was both "a very busy man" and "a very poor man."[34]

But Campbell's description of the waiting harvest was irresistible, even to a busy and poor man. "There is a great amount of material untouched here," she told Sharp, "'ballets,' as they call them, of all sorts new and old singing games, . . . and some carols. There are also old-fashioned dances, much frowned upon by the people because of their strict religious ideas concerning such amusements. . . . There has been some collecting done . . . [but] almost nothing [has been done] with the music."[35]

Intrigued by the possibilities, Sharp took Campbell's collection back to England with him, and soon wrote to suggest that they "form a partner-

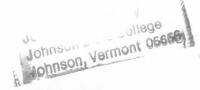

ship" to explore the field her work had opened up. She replied that she would be "only too happy to cooperate."[36]

In the midst of an activity then generally characterized by personal ambition, territorial exclusivity, and condescension toward the bearers of such cultural treasures, this remarkably simple agreement set Sharp and Campbell far above their contemporaries.[37] "I in no way have a special right in collecting from this region," Campbell told Sharp. "In collecting the songs, I was not considering any possible financial gain nor literary prestige. I liked them, knew they were valuable from a scientific point of view, and hoped that if I could get them published they would be a real contribution to folk-lore. . . ."[38]

But Campbell's position was broader yet. She knew the lurid newspaper tales of violence, ignorance, and depravity in the mountains, and she knew of other ballad collectors who—virtually in the same breath—extolled their most recent find as a cultural treasure, clucked their tongues over the singer's dress or speech or housekeeping habits, and paraded their own superior taste, knowledge, and sophistication. And so, she continued,

> I hoped that through the ballads, attention might be drawn to the mountain situation in such a way as to help the mountain people. One cannot help these people by exploiting their weaknesses and peculiarities. . . . [My] object has been two-fold: to preserve the ballads and to help the people. I have always felt that these people were my friends, and I believe that the ballad singers from whom I have gathered materials have always felt that I was their friend. I should not be willing to have their confidence violated.[39]

Although hoped-for financial aid from the Carnegie Trust had not materialized, Sharp had become convinced that "the work must be done somehow or other at all hazards." He thus laid plans to return to America, and arrived back in New York in late February 1916.[40] Warning them ahead of time that he ate no "animal food" and was a heavy smoker, he spent several days with the Campbells in Asheville late in March, going through Mrs. Campbell's collection.

The necessity to support himself by lecturing, consulting, and teaching classes ("selling myself for a week at a time to various cities," Karpeles says he called it) prevented Sharp from beginning the projected enterprise immediately, but after surveying the collection again on the train to St. Louis, he told Mrs. Campbell he was "really amazed at the richness of the material." He could foresee, he said, "a jolly patch of work ahead to do."[41] And in a long letter to John Glenn he confided that the value of the material [Mrs. Campbell] has already harvested is even higher than I had estimated. To me it is quite wonderful that anyone so far away from, and so little in touch with, any work of the kind that has been done elsewhere should have set herself such a high standard, and in effect reached it. She has just the combination of scientific and artistic spirit which work of this kind needs if it is to be of any use to posterity. . . . What she has so far accomplished is of great value but . . . [is] only the beginning. The field that has yielded what she has harvested must be a very rich one.[42]

Thus even before the actual collecting enterprise began, it was clear that theirs would be no Wyman-Brockway self-congratulatory excursion into a romantic "world of green and silver," using mountain people and their culture as grist for the cultural mills that ground nightly upon New York concert stages. Sharp anticipated that he would have "little difficulty in getting on with [mountain people] and persuading them to sing," although his New York and Boston acquaintances—steeped in the mountain lore purveyed by the newspapers—warned him the mountains were "wild, and dangerous," and told him he should go armed.[43] After his first visit to Asheville, the Campbells concluded that indeed he was "not the kind to queer things by coming into a community," and that he knew "how to deal with country people."[44]

One of Sharp's potential liabilities as a collector in the mountains can hardly be charged to him personally, since it was almost universal among ballad collectors at the time: a preference for the ballads canonized by Francis J. Child and a consequent disinterest in other materials occurring in profusion in the same "field"—religious music, popular music, instrumental music, and recently composed ballads and songs.

The possible import of another of Sharp's attitudes is difficult to assess at this historical distance. "I look upon it as a great privilege," he wrote to Mrs. Campbell from England in the autumn of 1915, "to have been able to do work of this kind, because . . . posterity will need the primitive songs and ballads to keep their two arts of music and dance real, sincere and pure." So far, so good: If one overlooks for a moment the problematic connotations of "real" and "pure," it is a normal statement of the importance of the past, concern for the future, and the possible utility of cultural artifacts in preserving continuity. Elsewhere, however, there were hints of more limited cultural horizons—of a narrow cultural nationalism. After helping to train dancers for dramatist Percy MacKaye's production of the *Masque of Caliban* in New York, Sharp said he "felt more proud of being an Englishman" than he had ever felt before, and that the participants had "[become] English, every Jew, German, French, Italian, Slav one of them."[45] Although held in check by Sharp's intelligence and scientific rigor, the destructive potential of such sentiments was real indeed, as was to become clear in the cultural work of John Powell with the White Top, Virginia, folk festival fifteen years later.[46]

Delayed by teaching obligations, illness, and the great Asheville flood of 1916, Sharp finally reached western North Carolina to begin his collecting near the end of July.[47] He left almost immediately for the outlying districts, and from Allanstand (a small community forty miles from Asheville) he wrote to Mrs. Campbell on 1 August that he had taken down twenty-five tunes, of which "the average quality is very high." "I found the singers very easy to handle," he told her. "[They] are just English peasant folk [who] do not seem to me to have taken on any distinctive American traits. They talk English, sing English, behave English!" A week later, Sharp was in the "Laurel country" northwest of Asheville, which he found "the richest field" he had ever entered. Sharp's informants, John Campbell judged, were "taking pride in having conserved something that he thinks is eminently worthwhile."[48]

In mid-August, Sharp reported from White Rock, North Carolina that he had ninety-one ballads and variants. Toward the end of the month, John Campbell told Glenn that Sharp was "highly elated" by his expedition into the North Carolina-Tennessee border country, having secured thirty ballads from one woman singer in Hot Springs. A year's collecting in England had never yielded more than three hundred ballads, but one month in the southern mountains had produced more than half that many.[49]

Sharp's letters from his earliest days of collecting in the mountains show that he was serious and industrious and uniformly gracious to and respectful of local people. Leaving North Carolina and Tennessee in mid-September for the Charlottesville, Virginia, area, however, he encountered a collector with a rather different style. University of Virginia professor C. Alphonso Smith had been collecting for some years, and had urged the Bureau of Education to issue its "national ballad search" entreaty in 1913. After a day in the country with Smith, however, Sharp reported that the professor "treated the singers just as a University Professor is accustomed to treat his students, and it was amusing to see the faces of blank amazement that his questions and talk produced. He is not what you would call a 'born collector.'"[50]

His visit with Smith concluded, Sharp's first collecting in the mountains was over. It had netted him nearly four hundred ballads and variants. He had shown himself not only aggressive in his pursuit of fugitive cultural treasures but also sensitive to their hereditary conservators. His sensitivity both allowed him to see the deficiencies of an august professor's treatment of mountain people and led him to pay out of his own pocket for clothes for Alleghany County, North Carolina singer Reuben Hensley's thirteen-year-old daughter to attend a mission school at Hot Springs. Emma Hensley found her new surroundings and prospects uncongenial, and almost immediately caught a ferry across the river and ran away home. Sharp applauded her spirit. "A scion of such a natural singing family," he said, "could not be expected to fit any Presbyterian mould; better that she kept her liberty." [51]

Out of Mrs. Campbell's earlier collecting and Sharp's 1916 expedition came their joint publication, *English Folk Songs of the Southern Appalachians* (1917). Although Campbell had cautioned Sharp against generalizing about a region that was in fact quite diverse, she told him he was free to "go ahead and say what you think" in the introduction. [52] His remarks turned out to be warm and positive. To him, mountaineers were "leisurely and cheery people, . . . in whom the social instinct is very highly developed"—curious, hospitable, gracious people with "an easy unaffected bearing and the unselfconscious manners of the well-bred." Mountaineers have, he said, the "elemental wisdom, abundant knowledge and intuitive understanding which only those who live in constant touch with Nature and face to face with reality seem able to acquire." Newspaper and magazine stereotypes of the time frequently depicted mountain people as unhealthy and unattractive physically, but Sharp saw them as "cleancut and often handsome." "They carry themselves superbly," he said, with "an easy, swinging gait." Of moonshining he said he "saw nothing and heard but little," and he reported that feuds "had long since been discontinued." Admitting that illiteracy was widespread, he observed that the fact "that the illiterate may nevertheless reach a high level of culture will surprise those only who imagine that education and cultivation are convertible terms." [53]

Sharp found music in the mountains to be as resonant and vital as the social order was healthy. Having been accustomed to finding ballads in England only among scattered older singers, he said he found himself "for the first time in my life in a community in which singing was as common and almost as universal a practice as speaking." Music was "interwoven with the ordinary avocation of everyday life," and people had a "delightful habit of making beautiful music at all times and in all places."

Having been so far spared seeing the burgeoning development and consequent social dislocations of the central Appalachian coalfields, Sharp was probably more disposed to perceive and record "all that is native and fine" in mountain culture than any collector who preceded him. His collaboration with Campbell had indeed produced a remarkable document: the first major, carefully documented collection of music that could be heard among mountain people, presented in a dignified way, with the integrity of text and tune preserved.[54] Where other collectors, such as Josephine McGill and Howard Brockway had found it paradoxical that such good music could survive among such a benighted people, Sharp perceived the essential harmony of their cultivated lifeways and their fine music. "I am so glad of your genuine appreciation of the mountain people," John Campbell wrote Sharp late in 1916, "for I grow weary of the many who come to the mountains simply to exploit the mountaineer. Miss Wyman and Mr. Brockhurst [sic; Brockway, presumably] are unfortunate in the people who write up their work . . . and are even more unfortunate if the newspaper accounts at all represent their attitude toward mountain people."[55]

Of Campbell's dual hope that their work would "preserve the ballads and help the people," however, the former turned out to be much simpler to realize than the latter. The old notions of mountain people were deeply ingrained among those who set themselves up as official arbiters of cultural norms. In February 1917, while the book was being readied for the printers, the Nation reported on Sharp's collecting in "America's Arcady," among "Americans whom time has forgotten, and Progress never hustled."[56] Arcady or not, ballad singers or no, mountaineers, because of their isolation and recent involvement in "the blood feud," still seemed to the Nation writer to have "a manner of life [that] might be called Albanian."

Avoiding such comparisons, New York Times music critic Richard Aldrich (who had befriended Sharp when he first arrived in the United States and had helped him try to get money for his work from the Carnegie Corporation) called the book "the most important collection that has ever been made to this special phase of folk song." Reviewing it in tandem with Wyman and Brockway's Lonesome Tunes (1916) and Josephine McGill's Folk Songs of the Kentucky Mountains (1917), Missouri ballad scholar H. M. Belden said it was "the most noteworthy publication dealing with folk-song in America that has yet appeared."[57]

But for all its excellences, the Campbell-Sharp collection was not a completely satisfactory document. Although he noted in his introduction that he was speaking "only with respect to that part of the mountain district into which I penetrated" (p. iii), Sharp nevertheless generalized rather broadly. A more serious problem, however, was his excluding of whole categories of music known even then to be prevalent in the areas he visited: instrumental music, popular songs, and especially religious music. Back in England sorting through the songs collected on his first trip in 1916, he wrote Campbell that he was omitting sixteen of hers, including two hymns. "Personally I am rather weak on hymnology," he said, adding that an English authority judged them to be Negro spirituals that were "not brought out from England . . . [but] somehow or other trickled into the mountains from outside negro-Methodist sources." The record is not entirely clear on the point, but most evidence suggests that Sharp's exclusion of religious music was not doctrinaire, but based upon his admitted lack of expertise and his preference for materials of provable English origin. Indeed, on his next trip to the mountains, he wrote to Campbell of his personal excitement over hearing a woman in eastern Kentucky sing a Holiness hymn.[58]

There were also two theoretical and conceptual problems: Sharp's essential neglect of social context and his concept of a "racial heritage." "The region is from its inaccessibility a very secluded one," he said in his introduction to the published collection. "There are but few roads . . . and practically no railroads. Indeed, so remote and shut off from outside influence were, until quite recently, these sequestered mountain valleys that the inhabitants have for a hundred years or more been completely isolated and cut off from all traffic with the rest of the world." Some of the places in which he collected were in fact rather isolated—especially portions of western North Carolina's Madison County. But others were not. Indeed, almost half of the more than three hundred items he collected were gathered near Asheville and Charlottesville. The former was a major metropolitan center of more than twenty thousand (which by then had had central station electric power and electric streetcars for twenty-five years); the latter was the seat of the University of Virginia.[59] Hot Springs, one of Sharp's major collecting points in Madison County, had been a tourist spa for a half-century, and the county itself was dotted with Presbyterian mission schools. Allanstand had been the seat of a social settlement and handicrafts revival effort for more than twenty years.

Thus whatever the mountains were, they were not an isolated and stable repository of old songs brought from across the water ever so many years ago. Had Sharp been more aware of the actual interplay between old songs and new social and economic conditions, he would probably have altered the image of the mountains he presented in his initial volume.

Possibly such an awareness could also have carried him safely beyond the treacherous "racial heritage" notions prevalent at the time.[60] Without it, however, those notions seemed tenable. "That the illiterate may . . . reach a high level of culture" is due partly to the leisure they have to give to cultural development, he said, "but chiefly to the fact that they have one and all entered at birth into the full enjoyment of their racial heritage. Their language, wisdom, manners, and the many graces of life that are theirs, are merely racial attributes which have been gradually acquired and accumulated in past centuries and handed down generation to generation. . . ."

But the "racial heritage" explanation was no more than a tautology which in fact obscured more than it explained, as Sharp found when he returned to a different section of the mountains for more collecting in the spring of 1917.[61] In mid-April he found himself in Sevierville, Tennessee. It was, he said, "the most American place I have yet struck. . . . It reminds me of some of Dickens' sketches of American life." He took down two tunes from an old fiddler who had just won a fiddlers' contest in Knoxville, apparently planning to build a collection of such tunes to add to the ballads.[62] To Mrs. Campbell he wrote that singers were providing some "quite new stuff but nothing of any importance." Anxious to "sample the songs and singers of Kentucky," he and his assistant, Maud Karpeles, headed north from Knoxville toward Cumberland Gap.

After a disappointing few days at Lincoln Memorial Institute at Harrogate, Sharp checked in to the Continental Hotel at Pineville, Kentucky, near the end of the month.[63] A six-week stint of collecting in Harlan, Bell, and Knox counties yielded more than two hundred songs, but the field proved most uneven. "Drawn a blank at Harlan," he telegraphed the Campbells early in May, before moving on to Barbourville, which yielded sixty-five ballads in less than two weeks.[64] Plagued by ill health and a depression that came over him from time to time, Sharp moved west of the mountains to Berea. Although Karpeles wrote later that Berea was "not very good" as a collecting field, Sharp nevertheless took down eighty-one songs and ballads there.[65] John Campbell went to Berea to check on Sharp and reported to John Glenn that he was "up and down mentally." He had never seen anyone, he said, "who was so utterly hopeless when he is down." Early in June, Sharp returned to the Campbells' home in Asheville and then left the mountains to take care of some teaching and lecturing obligations in New York.[66]

At the end of July, Sharp returned for more collecting in western North Carolina, but shortly moved back into Kentucky for the late summer and early fall. He went home to England toward the end of 1917 and did not return to his collecting in the mountains until April 1918. Most of his third trip was taken up with collecting in Virginia (thirteen out of nineteen weeks); he did not return to Kentucky or Tennessee at all, but spent another six weeks in North Carolina (mostly in McDowell and Yancey counties). In all, as Karpeles reckoned it later, Sharp worked for forty-six weeks in the mountains, collecting more than sixteen hundred tunes to about five hundred songs from 281 singers.[67]

Of the two trips he made after the initial nine-week foray of 1916 which led to the volume he coauthored with Campbell, the first (of 1917) affords the best insight into the ballad collecting enterprise as cultural intervention—not only because his letters from the trip are some of the most revealing he wrote, but also because he spent some of his time at Hindman and Pine Mountain settlement schools.[68]

Approaching eastern Kentucky through the Cumberland Gap early in August 1917, Sharp found the field at first disappointing. "We have been into scores of cabins," he wrote to John Campbell, "only to be told that they used to sing [ballads] but no one had done so for 25 years or more. Obviously folk-singing is not nearly so vital as it was in the Laurel section, and it is difficult to explain why, unless it is the influence of the County Seat—it cannot be the railroad for that is too recent. . . . Collecting is therefore rather a slow process as one has to wait until singers have studied and recalled what they used to sing." Five days later, in a letter from Oneida Institute, Sharp reported a similar frustration. On 27 August he wrote to Mrs. Campbell that at Manchester "money-making is the preeminent passion, and the desire to be genteel and behave like city people pretty general amongst all classes."[69]

Clearly Sharp was encountering conditions that were forcing him to change the image of the mountains reflected in his first book, even before the book went on sale. As he wrote to Glenn:

> This trip is causing me to modify the opinion that I first formed
> that the singing of folk-songs was universal in the mountains. It was
> undoubtedly true in North Carolina, but I have as yet found no
> district elsewhere of which this is true. Primitiveness in custom and
> outlook is not, I am finding, so much the result of remoteness as
> bad economic conditions. When there is coal and good wages to be
> earned, the families soon drop their old-fashioned ways and begin to
> ape town manners. I found . . . that Clay County despite its remoteness
> was quite sophisticated. Frame houses were the rule along

many of the creeks . . . and here the inhabitants received my remarks about the old songs with a superiority of air that was almost
contemptuous.[70]

Obviously no concept of a "racial heritage" could explain what Sharp
was meeting up with in eastern Kentucky: money-grubbing, social disor-
der, old songs dropped from memory, and the ascendancy of town ways.
"Really one carries one's life in one's own hands in this country," he wrote
to Olive Campbell from a hotel in Manchester. "The people who frequent
this hotel—all men—are a very rough, unkempt lot with whom it is a real
trial to sit down at table. Except for the fact that they don't grunt when
they eat, they might be hogs. . . . They are not mountain people but travelling business men of a very low order." A month later, Sharp described
Hazard as "a second Harlan—a hurly-burly of dollar-hunters, dirty,
unkempt, unsanitary, slipshod."[71] And whereas in North Carolina he
had found good music and good manners to occur side by side, in Kentucky "dirt and good music are the usual bedfellows, or cleanliness and
ragtime!"[72]

Eastern Kentucky reality was grating rather harshly against several
things in Sharp: his prior experience in England and the less socially dis-
traught areas of western North Carolina, his theory of how and why people
reach or retain "a high level of culture," and—not least—his genteel sen-
sibilities. Thus the places in eastern Kentucky he found most to his liking—where he felt most comfortable, most rewarded for his efforts, most
confirmed in his theories and estimates of mountain culture and its origins—were the settlement schools at Hindman and Pine Mountain. It is
no coincidence that those were also the two places where more or less successful (though ultimately temporary) efforts had been made to set aside
current social and economic realities, to revive the old culture, and to confirm the more naive current theories concerning its nature, origins, and
use in individual and community life.

Six months before Sharp's first trip to the mountains, Katherine Pettit
wrote to John Campbell from Pine Mountain Settlement School, "I am so
glad to know of Mr. Sharp's proposed visit to the mountains. You will not
fail to bring him to us, will you?" Eighteen months later, Hindman's May
Stone begged him not to omit a visit to her school.[73] Since Sharp's usual
practice (suggested by the Campbells) was to stay at one of the many
mountain missionary settlements and visit singers within walking distance, he had met many of the missionary women early on and formed
some reservations about their impact on mountain people and their ways.

"Some of the women [missionaries] I have met are very nice and broad-minded," he wrote after he had been in the mountains about two months, "but I don't think any of them realize that the people they are here to improve are in many respects far more cultivated than their would-be instructors, even if they cannot read or write. . . . For my part, I would leave them as they are and not meddle. They are happy, contented, and live simply and healthily, and I am not sure that any of us can introduce them to anything better than this."[74]

Nevertheless, Sharp found Hindman and (especially) Pine Mountain greatly to his liking. He arrived at Pine Mountain at the end of August and was immediately taken with it. A letter he wrote to the Campbells soon after his arrival revealed how deeply his theories about culture in the mountains were based in his own socialization:

> Pine Mountain proved a most pleasant business. There is a mountain school—if you can call it a school—after my heart! I never met more delightful children. They behave just like the well brought up children of gentle-folk, quite well-mannered . . . not the least bit assertive, and evidently thoroughly happy. Their good manners and general bearing are of course in their blood. What Pine Mountain has done for them is to teach them an added ideal, e.g., cleanliness, how to eat and behave at table, to be useful and work, as well as no doubt a certain amount of schooling. Miss Pettit and Miss deLong . . . quite realize the type they are dealing with, and see what they can give them and what is already theirs by inheritance. Everything is beautiful. The houses are well-built, commodious, and nice to look upon. The food is first-rate and plentiful. The dining hall . . . is a beautiful room and the meals are served and eaten as they would be in the houses of gentlefolk. . . . [Dinner] napkins are used by everyone. . . . They sing very prettily, ballads and graces before meals, and are singing all over the grounds. . . . [Pine Mountain teachers] appreciate the qualities of mountain children and know how to handle them.[75]

Sharp found the Pine Mountain area a "prime case for songs" and collected three dozen in less than a week. He considered his major find, however, to be the so-called "running set," which he first saw on the lawn at Pine Mountain. As early as the autumn of 1915, Olive Campbell had told him little attention had been paid to the kind of mountain dancing one could see at "frolics," " 'lasses bilings," and the like. Pine Mountain Settlement School was somewhat removed, to say the least, from a 'lasses biling or a log rolling, but what he called the "running set" dance was an authentic form in the mountains, and Sharp found it most interesting. "It is a quite wonderful dance," he said, "and I shall not rest until I have mastered it and got all its many technical details onto paper." [76]

Sharp found Hindman Settlement School slightly less appealing than Pine Mountain, but the music was to his liking. "The girls here are bubbling over with [songs]," he told the Campbells, "and I really ought to stay here longer than I intended." He collected more than sixty items in the week or so he was at the school. [77]

Except for about five months he spent, mostly in Virginia, on his final collecting trip to the mountains in 1918, Sharp's Appalachian work was over. Virginia proved a disappointing field. Shenandoah County he found "too Dutch and German to yield songs," but Buena Vista was "as prolific as North Carolina." [78] A brief foray into southern West Virginia was unproductive, as were visits to other communities in the south central counties of Virginia. Expecting Shooting Creek in Franklin County to be a good place to collect, he found "a thoroughly respectable community living in comfortable farm houses, owning, many of them, their own motor cars while the women we saw going to a week-end 'preaching' wore low-necked dresses, high-heeled shoes, talk[ed] in loud raucous voices and used face powder lavishly." Moving on to the Meadows of Dan area in neighboring Patrick County, he encountered "a most fertile agricultural district inhabited by thoroughly prosperous farmers" who, when they could be induced to sing at all, "had to lug out the songs from the back recesses of their memories." [79]

One comes away from the record of Sharp's collecting in the mountains—from his initial collaboration with Olive Dame Campbell through his later more independent work—with two impressions. On the one hand, he was by all odds the best-trained, most humane and open-minded collector working in the area at the time. He was a conscientious and productive worker, and it may indeed be that his Appalachian collection is— as Bertrand Bronson has asserted—the best regional collection we are likely to get. On the other hand, Sharp was obliged by personal and financial considerations to move too fast and to try to cover too much territory. Both those circumstances and his predisposition to favor certain types of material frequently caused him to look in the wrong places and ask the wrong questions.

A letter to his early American benefactor, written shortly after he got home from his final collecting trip, reveals Sharp's own awareness of the problems deriving from his perspective, expectations, and unconscious norms. "I would," he told her, "that I had visited America twenty years ago before my character and habits had been so fixed." [80] Even more pointedly, he wrote to Glenn from Winston-Salem, North Carolina, about his first encounter with a large black population:

They are wonderful people, especially when they have a lot of money to spend on their dress. The negress who did my room yesterday was got up in her Sunday best—a black satin skirt and a pink . . . chiffon blouse, quite transparent! It looked most odd to see the pink over an ebony background, and it gave me quite a shock when I realized she was black all over! I suppose my ideas of the negro were orginally formed from seeing the nigger minstrel. . . . [81]

Even where a minstrel-derived stereotype of blacks did not distort his vision, however, there were problems in perspective. Both Shooting Creek and the Meadows of Dan, where Sharp found high heels, low-cut dresses, raucous voices, face-powder, motor cars, and prosperous farmers in profusion—but few songs—had quite lively musical traditions at the time, the existence of which could still be documented more than fifty years later. [82]

Franklin, Henry, and Patrick counties were, at the time Sharp was there, the scene for a rich blending of the southern West Virginia and Virginia Blue Ridge fiddle traditions. In the Franklin-Floyd border area, such fiddlers as Maxey Ferrum, "Peg" Hatcher, N. H. Mills, and Norman Wimmer were known by all their neighbors, though opinion was divided upon whether Frank Kingrea or Norman Wimmer's father, Mark, was the best of the lot. There was also a strong fiddle-banjo tradition in the area. In Patrick County many excellent fiddlers, such as John Chilly, Pett Gilbert, and Uncle Dick Scott, paid homage to the greatest of them all, Wallace Spangler (1851–1926), of the Meadows of Dan area where Sharp tried more or less unsuccessfully to coax the "prosperous farmers" to lug out the old songs from memory's depths. Had he spent more time, or asked different questions, he might have produced the volume of fiddle tunes that the *Times Literary Supplement* promised its readers in January 1918. [83]

How then does the collaboration of Olive Dame Campbell and Cecil Sharp look after more than a half-century? In the narrowest terms—the quantity and quality of the preferred material they assembled and the skill of its presentation—their work remains a landmark in the history of an enterprise that witnessed more than its share of greed, pettiness, and misrepresentation.

The most difficult question to resolve concerning the Campbell-Sharp collaboration is its implicit cultural politics. Clearly, the work of a "mere" ballad collector has inescapably political dimensions. It involves presuppositions and judgments about the relative worth of disparate cultural systems; the selection of certain cultural items in preference to others—frequently in accordance with an unspoken theory of culture; the education (not to say manipulation or indoctrination) of a public regarding the worth (or worthlessness) of unfamiliar cultural forms or expressions; and the feeding back of approval-disapproval into the "subject" culture so as to affect the collective image and self-images (and therefore the survival potential) of its members.

Thus when a scholar such as Shapiro depicts Sharp as a culturally and politically naive, self-aggrandizing promoter of myths of Merrie Olde England and "the inherent value of the naif culture of Appalachia," the judgment lies within the domain of the politics of culture and cultural intervention. As I have shown, however, it is a view which the available documentary evidence will not support. Nor can such an interpretation be squared with Sharp's known activities and political sympathies in England, as Archie Green has recently argued.[84]

Green's contention that Sharp's politics made him most understanding of the relationship between cultural continuity and the movement into a capitalist industrial economy is reinforced by a letter that Sharp wrote to the Sage Foundation's John Glenn late in 1920 concerning a strike by Welsh coal miners. As he saw it, the strike had arisen because of "[the miners'] distrust, deep and complete, both of the mine owners and the Government under whose control they still are; and the determination not to work for anybody's profit. . . . Capital they say should be well rewarded but no more, and should not make surplus profits. Moreover they contend that their interest in the industry is quite as great as that of the capitalist and . . . consumer, but as things are, neither consumer nor worker get proper consideration." So far as he was personally concerned, Sharp continued, "I feel that the organization of industry has somewhere or other to be radically changed. Men won't any longer work like slaves with the fear of unemployment constantly before their eyes." Warehouses stocked with goods that people have no money to buy, he said, show that "the economical principle upon which the world is run at the present moment is fundamentally unsound." In England, Sharp concluded, there was "enough discontent to lead a dozen revolutions."[85] On the whole it was not a statement which could have come from a politically naive cultural hustler.

On the other hand, Sharp's work in the mountains had been highly selective in its enthusiasms, and in its selections and representations to the public. For a number of reasons, including both the character of his earlier work in England and the advice of the Campbells, he had chosen to visit (and praise) those mountain people who lived far enough outside the areas of the most turbulent social and economic change—in the more isolated counties, the more placid coves, on hills there was no coal under—to have the space, tranquility, and leisure to sing the old songs. He viewed those who worked in the mines or mills and drove their motorcars back home to frame houses where they listened to ragtime on the phonograph as inse-cure in their cultural identity, deficient in cultural judgment, and cor-rupted by modern ways. Had the kind of sensitivity Sharp displayed to social and economic dislocations in his homeland in 1920 guided his earlier encounter with southern mountaineers more surely, his itinerary would undoubtedly have shifted in important respects. And a different itinerary might have produced a substantially different collection—one more con-gruent, in fact, with both his own broader politics and the cultural past and present of mountain people.

Although Olive Campbell continued to correspond with Sharp through the early 1920s and visited him as late as 1923 in England, her work di-verged rather sharply from his as the years passed. After she finished writ-ing *The Southern Highlander and His Homeland*, her attention turned al-most entirely to the Danish folk school movement and her efforts to start such a school in the southern mountains.

Keep On till You Come to Green Fields: The John C. Campbell Folk School

Early in October 1908, the Campbells left the middle Virginia countryside around Charlottesville, with its lingering echoes of the Old South, and headed toward the Great Smokies, the Blue Ridge, and the Alleghenies. Some of the work that lay ahead—the ballad collecting, the social survey, the Southern Highlands Division—began immediately and flowered early. But a major part of Mrs. Campbell's work—the John C. Campbell Folk School at Brasstown, North Carolina—did not take form until more than fifteen years later, a half-dozen years after Mr. Campbell's death.

In her journal for 7 October 1908, Campbell recorded parts of a conver-sation she had in Knoxville with Philander P. Claxton, executive secretary of the Conference for Southern Education. "He feels the time for the church school is almost past," she wrote. "Three ideas to emphasize: (1) Adapt school's curriculum to life of people. . . . (2) establish schools for grown-ups—; cites grown-up schools of Denmark and Sweden. (3) Sage fund as mediator."[86]

The Campbells had sought out Claxton on the advice of Dr. Wallace Buttrick of the Rockefeller-funded General Education Board (GEB), which was using mass-media advertising, revival-like meetings, and state-by-state crusades to spread a limited and conservative educational gospel in the South.[87] The germ of the idea Claxton gave them—"the grown-up schools of Denmark and Sweden"—had been growing in his own mind since he attended a meeting of the Pan-Scandinavian Education Association at Askov Folk School more than ten years earlier.[88]

For a decade after he first talked with them in Knoxville, Claxton continued to urge the Campbells to investigate Scandinavian folk schools as a possible model for an updated educational venture which might supplant the earlier mission schools in the mountains.[89]

The idea behind the Scandinavian folk schools, which originated in Denmark in the 1840s, was conceived by Bishop Nikolai Grundtvig (1783–1872) as a response to the problem of educating and "enlivening" Danish farmers and rural people, only recently freed from centuries of subjugation and abuse under a feudal agricultural, economic, and legal system. Grundtvig's own plan for a "Royal School for Life" was never realized, but his ideas were embodied in the school that a shoemaker's son—Kristen Kold (1816–70)—started at Rödding in 1844. Ten more schools were founded in Denmark during the next twenty years, thirty more in the five years after the nation lost one-third of its territory to Prussia and Austria in the war of 1864–65, and sixty-five more between 1870 and 1900. The idea spread to Germany almost immediately after the school at Rödding opened, to Norway and Sweden twenty years later, and to England at the turn of the century.[90]

Shortly after Claxton left Tennessee to become U.S. Commissioner of Education in July 1911, he sent two men to Denmark to investigate and report on the folk schools. Their reports were published by the bureau in 1914.[91] Investigator L. L. Friend, who was state supervisor of high schools in West Virginia and who subtitled his report "with some suggestions as to possible application of the folk high-school idea in mountain and Piedmont sections of the United States," found that there were about eighty such schools in Denmark, serving about ten thousand students. "More than anything else," he said, "the folk high school seeks to awaken the intellectual life of its students, to start new forces operating in their lives, to make them want to live more efficiently and nobly." Friend concluded that the schools had improved agriculture, raised the intellectual level of rural people, heightened their political sophistication, and cultivated a patriotism that emphasized "lives of service in times of peace" rather than fighting in times of war.

Like rural Denmark, Friend said, the mountain and piedmont regions of the South were inhabited by "rugged and unspoiled people" possessing "many homely virtues" not found in "regions in closer touch with trolley cars and towns and cities." Such people, he said, are "still poor when they might be rich"; they need to be "aroused to the realization of their real worth and of the greatness of their possibilities." He suggested a "modified form" of the folk school for mountain people, combining intellectual and industrial instruction.

Bureau investigator H. W. Foght's more extensive report attended closely to the role of the folk schools in democratizing a previously class-biased social order. "The schools pointed the way," he argued, to important social changes ranging from land reform, to low interest loans for farmers, to (ultimately) control of the government by the "radical or left party" (composed of "small and middle-class farmers"), which was responsible for most of the recent "progressive and social legislation."

But the Campbells were at work on a folk school for the mountains long before Claxton's activities at the bureau attracted enough attention to merit a major article in the Sunday New York Times.[92] As early as April 1909, John Campbell wrote to the American Consular Service in Copenhagen and to heads of some of the folk schools themselves.[93] He also began to talk with Glenn about visiting Denmark to study the schools.[94] The Sage Foundation actually made arrangements for his trip in mid-1913, but canceled them. A year later, Campbell renewed his request, arguing that denominational groups were getting interested in folk schools and that he lacked sufficient knowledge to help them. Glenn again agreed to finance the trip, but before Campbell could depart, war broke out in Europe, and plans were again canceled.[95]

Campbell pushed ahead, nevertheless, urged on by Glenn's judgment that "you and Claxton and a few others know enough to start a good school and adapt it to American conditions without waiting to see Denmark."[96] In mid-1916 the supervisor of Presbyterian "country church work" at White Rock, North Carolina, told Campbell that he was ready to start a folk school as soon as money could be found, and a few months later Lincoln Memorial Institute officials were considering Campbell's suggestion that they convert the institution into Lincoln Memorial Folk School.[97]

Although he urged the folk school idea in every possible quarter, Campbell did not live to see it actually attempted in the mountains. He died in May 1919, and Olive Dame Campbell continued the work alone.[98]

Soon after her husband's death, Mrs. Campbell went to her family's home on Nantucket to finish the writing of *The Southern Highlander and His Homeland*. In the chapter on education she developed a brief rationale for folk schools in the mountains.[99] Sketching quickly the rather well known mountain problems of illiteracy, poor public school facilities and teachers, and county school superintendents concerned more with local politics than education, she noted recent state and federal efforts to improve education, but argued that those efforts were insufficient to meet "the present emergency."

Nor could the two hundred-odd "church and independent" schools meet that emergency, as she judged from extensive firsthand observation. The former suffered from "long distance control" by church boards, and the latter were too dependent on their individual founder-leaders. And the much-touted "industrial" schools too often offered young men little more than badly planned work on poorly managed school farms and young women, ill-conceived "domestic science" courses.[100]

The need, she argued, was for "greater emphasis . . . upon the various phases of work that fit for life in the mountains." Mountain schools have usually trained students "away from the country rather than . . . for leadership in the country." It was thus incumbent upon the church and independent schools—most of which were searching for a new role for themselves—to "find through experiment and to inspire by example a new type of school which will serve the country."

For such a purpose, she found "suggestion and inspiration" in the Danish folk schools, which she sketched in very attractive terms. Folk school emphasis is "largely on the cultural" and "all that tends to stimulate idealism and patriotism." Books are not important and there are no exams; students live "as a large family" and learn from a teacher who inspires them through "the alchemy of personality." Moreover, a crucial link between education and economic improvement is forged by the school's ties with the cooperative movement. "In such a school," Campbell concluded, "the beauty of the Highland country, its part in the pioneer life of the nation . . . its native culture . . . and its folk-song in particular, would all be given expression. . . . The folk schools . . . might be adapted readily to meet the changing and varied needs of this land."

Soon after completing *The Southern Highlander and His Homeland*, Campbell received an American-Scandinavian Foundation fellowship to study Danish folk schools firsthand. With her sister Daisy and Marguerite

Butler of Pine Mountain Settlement School she arrived in Copenhagen in August 1922. For about fourteen months she traveled, observed, and talked with folk school teachers and students.[101] By April 1923 she wrote to her American friends that she was "more and more keen over the whole thing . . . and its possibilities for the mountains." She commented enthusiastically on the friendly atmosphere of the schools, the singing, the "whir of spinning wheels, looms, and sewing machines, lathes and saws—stacks of costumes, dresses and handmade furniture." She was particularly moved to see a "primitive" Karelian wedding ceremony acted out at one school by three dozen folk school students who were political refugees from the Russian-Finnish border "[When] you see what can be done in six months with such a group," she wrote, "just think what it could mean to our mountains."[102]

The journals that Campbell kept on her trip—and the book she later drew from them—show that her study of the schools ranged considerably beyond bedazzlement over whirring looms and colorful national costumes.[103] She was in fact a careful, systematic, and thoughtful observer who studied Danish history and language, tax and land reform laws, agricultural statistics, and political organization. She talked with public officials, and visited dozens of folk schools old and new—from the rather aristocratic Askov to the smaller, humbler, and more ascetic Vestbirk; from the more doctrinaire Grundtvigian schools to the more practical ones attuned to the specific needs of farmers and industrial workers.

The features of the folk school that she found most attractive were most apparent at Askov: the beneficent and energizing presence of the principal and his teachers; the order apparent in all things; the reliable *assent* of the mature young adult students and the mutual regard between them and their teachers; the civilized daily rituals and small social observances; the singing before classes; the dancing and gymnastics; the underlying idealism of the curriculum and the simultaneous grounding of the lectures in everyday events and local surroundings. "We are melted into the group," Campbell wrote after five weeks at Askov. "We become really a part of it, are for the nonce, Danes and rural Danes" (p. 123).

Moving beyond the best-known rural folk high schools, she visited Neils Bukh's Gymnastic Folk School (p. 169), Johann Borup's school for industrial workers in Copenhagen (p. 172), the Workers' Folk School at Esbjerg (p. 177), and several agricultural schools, including Ladelund, Dalum, and the "Husmandsskole" at Odense (pp. 184ff.).

Proceeding (as the folk schools themselves had) to Norway, Sweden, and Finland, Campbell studied the adaptation of the folk school to other

FIGURE 2-1
*Olive Dame Campbell and Marguerite Butler in Copenhagen
(Southern Historical Collection, University of North Carolina
at Chapel Hill).*

environments. "The silent Norwegian, stern in his rugged honesty," was using—paradoxically—the Danish folk school idea to recover a national identity submerged under centuries of Danish cultural and political domination (p. 213). Of the thirty-two Norwegian folk schools—all "purely Grundtvigian"—she visited Voss, Hardanger, and Fana (pp. 216ff.).

The folk schools in Sweden (pp. 228ff.) were "a practical method of educating the peasantry," rather than a "response to . . . national aspiration" as in Denmark. The seven schools visited ranged from the older Hvilan (founded 1868) and Tärna (1876), which resembled their Danish models, and the more recently founded but traditional Sigtuna—where rooms in the monasterylike buildings were "decorated in the fashion of bygone ages"—to the more urban and politically oriented schools": Brunnsvik, where "the emphasis was on political and national economy" and "most of the students . . . were social democrats, communists and bolshevists"; a school near Stockholm linked to the cooperative movement; and the Birkagården school for Stockholm's industrial workers.

The "deep snow country" of Finland offered still other examples of adaptation. Long dominated by Sweden, and only recently delivered from a brutal interval of "Russification" (1901–5), Finns had adopted folk schools as instruments of national renewal. The complexity of the social, economic, and cultural situation—a Swedish-speaking aristocracy whose financial holdings, accustomed privileges, and social standing had been sharply reduced by recent reforms, on the one hand, and a newly enfranchised, Finnish-speaking lower class, on the other—was reflected in both the number and the orientation of the folk schools: thirty-three were Finnish speaking, and fifteen were Swedish speaking (p. 276).

In her journals and letters from Scandinavia, and even more systematically in her book on the Danish schools, Campbell revealed her personal predispositions and philosophical preferences, her concept of social change, and her judgments about the most acceptable instruments for bringing it about. Thus the outlines of her own folk school experiment could be discerned long before she ever returned to the United States.

The "living center" of the folk school, she said, was "a deeply religious motive and a purely democratic base; or, if you will, a real love for the people which is the purest kind of democracy and religion." Growth, she maintained, was "the burden of the folk-school teaching." But beyond these still relatively vague pieties, there were more specific indicators.

Personally, she was drawn to the scores of simple, gracious, daily rituals of folk school life and to the sense of order that underlay them: the formal greetings and leave-takings, the songs before class, the morning chocolate and cakes, the "tranquil sweetness" of it all (as she remarked following a Christmas service at Vestbirk). Life *could* be orderly and humane; people *could* arrange their days both artfully and meaningfully. The world might be coming apart most places, but its disintegration could be forestalled in a few special places.

Campbell's preference for the tranquilly sweet rituals was linked to her overarching belief that, for preserving continuity in human affairs, culture was *primary*. "If we learned anything at all in Denmark," she said, "we learned the deep foundations of that culture we saw flowering about us" (p. 13). That culture was—had to be—the ground for every choice in the present, every projection in the future: personal, communal, national. Indeed it was shared, ancient culture that was the sole warrant for the state. "*Human, natural, national* are the words he used again and again," Campbell said of Bishop Grundtvig (p. 64).

As she employed the term, *national* had several gradations of meaning. She quoted approvingly a folk school principal who distinguished between "national" (which implied inward development) and "nationalistic" (which implied outward expansion) (p. 164). And yet she also approved the poet Æ's statement that "a national purpose is the most unconquerable and victorious of all things on earth" (p. 225) and judged that the preponderance of fairhaired and blue-eyed people in Sweden's Dalecarlia province "appeals to the imagination and seems to point toward a powerful future state" (pp. 229ff.).

In her affection for Bishop Grundtvig, one sees above all the idealism that was central to Campbell's character. The life of the "living word" of the Grundtvigian school had its source in "a lofty idealism . . . a deep belief in nation and humanity" (p. 62). She was not ignorant of the dark, greedy, cynical, manipulative, power-driven side of human history (indeed she sketched portions of it in her brief background account of Scandinavian history), but she was nevertheless a thoroughgoing idealist: People can and *will* commit themselves to ideals and remain faithful to them through the temptations and confusions of life; society *can* be shaped by such individuals, such noble ideals.

Thus in contrast to the Hindman Settlement School women, who decried the frame houses rising in the valley, she maintained that in comparing modern development with ancient ways, "one [is] obliged to hold before one always human values." The new houses, "built on harder lines and with composition instead of thatched roofs," were less picturesque than the old, and yet "in a few years when vines and trees are trained against the walls, when gardens and hedges have grown," they will present a different aspect. And in any event, they are homes for people who previously had none and who now own and farm small plots carved by the state out of the great feudal estates of the past (p. 210).

And what were the proper, acceptable *instruments* of social change? First, an "enlightened and enlivened" citizenry, aware of their shared cultural heritage, skilled in the tasks required by their chosen work, and tolerant of their mutual interdependence. For such purposes, the Grundtvigian folk high school was a marvelous—probably the best—instrument. Its revered principals carried and interpreted the national culture, in which students participated through countless small daily observances; dancing, singing, and handicrafts instruction; and lectures on Danish history and literature. Daily gymnastics built strong and graceful bodies; lectures imparted necessary technical information on animal husbandry or chemistry or hygiene or cooperative principles.[104]

As central to the folk school concept as its underlying idealism, in Campbell's view, was a commitment to the stewardship of limited resources. Necessitated by the situation of a small, far northern country not particularly rich in natural resources, that commitment had been formalized and institutionalized in the cooperative movement. Farmers at Hjedding formed their first cooperative creamery in 1882, and many others in all phases of agriculture followed (p. 46). Indeed the folk schools and the co-ops were complementary: the former engendered the enlightened sense of interdependence and continuity that the latter required, and the latter was crucial to the economic viability of rural communities from which most folk schools drew their students.[105]

A corollary of Campbell's idealistic commitment to cultural continuity and culture-based nationalism, her confidence that the old and the new could coexist peacefully, and her belief in folk schools and co-ops as instruments of social change was a vague unease with "pure" politics, a distrust of radical political parties and movements as such. Her comments on the more radical political currents abroad in Scandinavia at the time conceal her essential distrust of them but poorly. While she understood (and deplored) the historical abuses visited upon Denmark's peasants by the landlords and the nobility, she clearly distrusted radical political ideology. Thus she passed lightly over the folk school at Helsingör, whose students were mostly industrial workers who belonged to a union "allied . . . with the extreme socialist wing" (p. 167), and judged that the Workers' Folk School at Esbjerg, built by working people "in the interest of advancing socialism," had in fact "no real right to the name" (p. 179). Indeed her hero Grundtvig was himself a political conservative who was "never interested in politics as such" (p. 55).

Thus it developed that Campbell studied most intently—and at length tried to replicate—not *the* Danish folk school, but one among the many *types* of Danish folk schools, which ranged from the most romantic, nostalgic, and rural to the most urban and politically radical.[106] The one she chose proved to resemble the former far more closely than the latter. Even though she visited the urban, industrial worker-oriented schools—including especially that of Johann Borup, 90 percent of whose students were trade-union men, and at which she reported having "one of my most stimulating experiences"—she decided upon her return to the mountains to focus on "a new type of education in relation to the rural problem." We tend to think of opportunities as lying in the city, she wrote to Lee Hanmer of the Russell Sage Foundation, but perhaps it might be possible to "make able young people love the country and be willing to throw in their lot with the soil."[107] Thus Campbell's trip to Scandinavia had strengthened her conviction, expressed earlier in *The Southern Highlander and His Homeland*, that the folk school could be adapted to conditions in the United States, and especially to rural areas in the southern mountains.

How aware Campbell was of previous attempts to transplant Danish folk schools in the United States is uncertain, but some of the evidence was not encouraging. Prior to the political upheavals in Denmark in the mid-1860s, there had been little emigration to the United States, but from then until the early 1890s, more than 120,000 Danes came.[108] As early as 1878, folk schools were beginning to be established among the immigrants. Partly under the guidance of F. L. Grundtvig (1854–1903), son of the bishop, seven had been established among them by 1902.[109]

Even before the turn of the century, however, the schools were in trouble, as John H. Bille reported as early as 1897. Writing in the *Transactions of the Wisconsin Academy*, Bille said that support from Danes for the first folk school at Elkhorn, Iowa, was so low that after only two years the school's organizers turned it over to the church, which continued to operate it as a Grundtvigian school, but never with more than forty students a year.[110] Undaunted, the Grundtvigians established four more schools, one of which failed immediately; the others never averaged three dozen students per year. As Bille saw it, the support that Danes in America gave the folk schools was "exceedingly small," and the schools' influence upon them was "still smaller."

Indeed the fate of the schools among immigrant Danes was evidence of the unbalanced split among them regarding assimilation versus maintaining their Danish culture. The Grundtvigians allied themselves with the Dansk Folkesamfund, which favored cultural preservation. But they numbered only 3,500, and were thus overwhelmingly outnumbered by the more than 128,000 other Danes in the United States who favored assimilation. Indeed, when the Elkhorn, Iowa, folk high school was reorganized in 1890 to give more prominence to the "English branches" of the curriculum (that is, to English language study), attendance tripled.[111]

More than fifteen years after Bille's investigation, H. W. Foght also reported in his Bureau of Education study that none of the folk schools in the United States had succeeded "as well as their friends had hoped," because money was scarce, the Danish population was widely scattered, and folk school leaders found it difficult to adapt to new conditions. Nevertheless, he argued, the "South Atlantic Highland" area would be a good place to try a new folk school experiment. "The folk school," Foght argued, "would cause 'the breaking through of slumbering souls' and remove prejudices and give a national outlook, both of which are needed in the mountains."[112]

Immediately upon returning to the United States, Campbell took up the argument that Foght and the bureau had more or less left off a decade earlier. "The problem of building an enlivened, enlightened rural population is fundamentally the same everywhere," she argued. "Is it better for our rural civilization," she asked, "to . . . train thoroughly a few . . . [or to] help to stimulate a movement of the people, the whole host of farmers advancing together, and the leaders to be found in all ranks?"[113]

At the April 1924 meeting of the Conference of Southern Mountain Workers in Knoxville, Campbell laid out her argument. Past educational efforts in the mountains had mostly hastened the migration of "stronger stock" to the city, as had happened in Denmark, where discouraged and jobless rural young people drifted to the cities or to America. Luckily, Denmark's earlier land reforms and its inward-turning regeneration sparked by military and political defeat helped bring forth the people's colleges (folk high schools), which—unlike conventional schools—served rural people's real needs and helped them move "toward freedom." Eventually, Danish rural people came to control not only their own lives and work but Parliament as well.

Like Denmark, the southern mountains contained a "more or less homogeneous people," possessing a somewhat common history and representing a rather definite culture. Mountain people have been "defrauded of much of their timber, mineral and water-power wealth"; the land is passing out of the mountaineers' hands. But it was "unthinkable," Campbell asserted, "that he should be allowed . . . to become a permanent tenant on the land of his fathers, to be driven from it, or to become the industrial servant of those who took the land from him."

The main need, she argued, was for mountain people "to be encouraged *to want*. If they are awakened and enlivened, they will act for themselves." Thus people's colleges could "help the larger group march forward, slowly but together—the solid rural foundation on which the nation rests." [114]

There was then no question in her mind whether she would start a folk school. The only unresolved point was where. A young teacher in eastern Kentucky's Leslie County wanted it there, but Asheville or Hot Springs, North Carolina, also seemed attractive. The abandoned buildings of Grand View, the old American Missionary Association academy at Harriman, Tennessee, were also available. Hindman Settlement School's May Stone wanted to establish a folk school in connection with Hindman's new community center at Quicksand. Campbell herself also traveled widely in western North Carolina and West Virginia looking at various sites. [115]

At a deeper level, the search for a physical location was the first stage of trying to adapt Danish ideas and models to local conditions and to sort through the ideas and models themselves. Probably several folk schools should be started, Campbell thought, but there was a special need for "a carefully supervised central experiment where some of the first necessary adjustments of the Danish theory and practice to our conditions can be made." [116]

Backed by a small grant from the Sage Foundation that allowed her to travel and plan, Campbell continued her search. Tazewell County, Virginia, she found "rather too wealthy and touched by outside influences." "We are awfully puzzled about our plans," she confided to one correspondent early in 1925. "This balancing of points is rather wearying!" [117] But an experimental folk school short course at Berea, in which two dozen men and women (all but two from Kentucky) attended lectures and gymnastics classes and sang and danced in Danish folk school fashion, further convinced her of "the soundness of several basic principles of the Danish folk schools." There could be no turning back. [118]

By April 1925 Campbell had decided that "our hearts turn most" to an area on the border of western North Carolina's Clay and Cherokee counties, near the Brasstown and Peachtree communities and a half-dozen miles from the town of Murphy. Ann Ruth Metcalf, Marguerite Butler's former colleague at Pine Mountain Settlement School, was working in Cherokee County and urged her to bring the school there. [119]

To what extent the school was actually located at Brasstown in response to a felt and expressed local need is not clear. In what has come to be the official version of the story, there is little ambiguity. An invitation came from local people after Campbell had "all but decided" to build the school in West Virginia, trustee Fred Brownlee reported years later. Responding to that invitation, Marguerite Butler visited the community in September 1925, and "Uncle Luce" Scroggs came to beg her for a school "which will help the county, not just make preachers and teachers." After being shown around the community by Uncle Luce's son Fred, Butler presented her ideas at a meeting in a local church. Visiting the community shortly thereafter, Campbell found a warm response and decided to locate the school at Brasstown. A local campaign for support was begun, and Uncle Luce gave twenty-five acres of land; the two county agents promised to cooperate; and the Congregational, Episcopalian, and Northern Presbyterian churches offered money. Plans were laid to get a Dane to manage a demonstration farm planned in connection with the school. "The people of the community were jubilant" at the announcement in the Brasstown church, the *Cherokee Scout* reported, and "the entire group sang one verse of 'America' before being dismissed." Two weeks later the Carnegie Corporation committed four thousand dollars to the enterprise.[120]

The articles of incorporation of the John C. Campbell Folk School, which were shortly drawn up, said the plan was to establish "a Folk School on the order of the Danish Folk Schools, with such changes and adaptations as may be found necessary or desirable." The object was "to enrich the whole content of rural life," to build up an "enlightened and enlivened citizenship, which will . . . realize of its own initiative, a full and satisfactory rural life," and "to inspire a community life . . . satisfying to the young people of the county."[121]

Although this version of the story appears true in its essentials, the situation was somewhat more complicated than the story suggests. A letter from Campbell to John Glenn a full year before Uncle Luce's legendary call, for example, hinted at the shadowy boundary between local initiative and the agendas of self-confident reformers. "One cannot establish a school of [this] type," she said, "unless one is thinking pretty definitely of the people one is trying to reach. One has got to know them; care for them; and then try to give them the thing that they unconsciously are asking for."[122]

The image of Uncle Luce also obscured as much as (or more than) it explained. Like Hindman Settlement School's Uncle Sol Everidge and Pine Mountain's Uncle William Creech, Uncle Luce was projected as he

FIGURE 2-2
*View of Brasstown community, as seen from folk school grounds
(Southern Historical Collection, University of North Carolina
at Chapel Hill).*

was because he was useful to the new school—an "old man of the mountains," an embodiment of traditional values, a tie to older wisdom, a quasi-sacred link to the progressive secular world. A request from Uncle Luce could therefore not be taken lightly, and actions taken in response to it could not easily be questioned locally.

And yet it was in fact Uncle Luce's *wife's* land which was given, and mainly his son Fred who worked to get the school. Born about 1892 (and therefore a *young* man), Fred O. Scroggs was an avid reader all his life ("Law, that's all he ever done," his wife recalled a half-century later), an early graduate of Young Harris College in Georgia (and therefore not an illiterate mountain man), and a former school teacher. He was thoughtful enough to assemble a collection of Cherokee Indian relics eventually acquired by the Wachovia Museum and progressive enough to run successfully later as a Democratic candidate for county commissioner (in 1932).[123]

The relatively scanty records of the school's early months suggest that, however uncertain its local warrant, Campbell's program got under way

FIGURE 2-3
*Uncle Luce Scroggs, legendary donor of land for the
John C. Campbell Folk School
(John C. Campbell Folk School Archive).*

FIGURE 2-4
Mill house under construction
(Southern Historical Collection, University of North Carolina
at Chapel Hill).

quickly. By the fall of 1926 the existing farmhouse had been cleaned and painted and a museum building erected. The farm (increased to eighty acres) was being revitalized by Georg Bidstrup (who was also teaching Danish gymnastics on Saturday afternoons); a model chicken house had been built; a young engineer-forester (Leon Deschamps, who had married Pine Mountain Settlement School student May Ritchie) was working on the school's woodlands and plans for new buildings. The community, for its part, had donated more than eight hundred days of labor. A community meeting room opened during the summer of 1927, and a formal dedication was held in the fall, with speeches by local leaders and by Jakob Lange, head of the Smallholder's School at Odense, Denmark.[124]

Folk school courses themselves were longer in coming. The first one was planned for December 1927. During the following winter, Campbell reported that there were five "steady students"; she was teaching them history, Marguerite Butler was giving classes in geography, and Georg Bidstrup was teaching agricultural skills and Danish gymnastics. Admitting that young people's natural shyness and home responsibilities made drawing steady students difficult, Campbell nevertheless went to New York to raise money for a "community building" to house boarding students.[125] By the spring of 1929 the building was completed and work had begun on a dam for a school water supply. The farm had grown to more than two hundred acres, and offers of volunteer help were flooding in.[126]

What had Campbell wrought in four years? The "spirit of the school," she said, was "quite in keeping with the Danish schools. . . . [I am] astonished at how closely we have been able to follow the general Danish practice." But she judged that it would take many such schools many years to "revolutionize the life of this section," and thus found "an experimental rather than a propagandist frame of mind" appropriate. Nevertheless, to her old mentor Philander P. Claxton she wrote that she believed "more thoroughly than ever in the whole program as it is working out." It was going to be "a long slow pull," she said, "but the general method I believe is sound."

The program of the school had developed in four areas: "short courses" and the regular Danish-type four-month winter folk school course; a model farm and related agricultural courses; farm-related cooperatives; and handicrafts. Thus it blended the three major institutions Campbell had studied in Scandinavia: folk schools, agricultural schools, and cooperatives.

Paradoxically, the standard winter folk school residential course seems to have remained relatively small: in 1926, Campbell had envisioned a "small boarding family" of about one hundred, but there were still only sixteen students for the term of 1931—attending classes in basic academic subjects as well as agriculture, domestic skills, handicrafts, and gymnastics. Short courses on handicrafts, singing games, gymnastics, and the like, were apparently better attended.[127]

The model farm and its associated agricultural courses took shape rather quickly, even though lime for the fields had to be hauled by wagon from the railroad in Murphy. The farm "keeps us with our feet in the soil and does not allow us to fly too high," Campbell wrote to a benefactor.[128] The registered Jersey herd was the "best foundation herd" in the area, according to a state dairy specialist; a registered bull and stallion were made available to the community for breeding purposes, and there were efforts to improve seed stocks. Annual reports from the early 1930s show that considerable scientific farming was being done on the school's land and that the effort was linked to a teaching program for young farmers.[129]

How good a decision was it, in fact, to orient so much of the school's program toward agriculture in Clay and Cherokee counties? Did Clay and Cherokee counties offer—as Campbell said in 1930—"reasonable hope for the development of a wholesome and satisfying life on the basis of agriculture"?[130]

FIGURE 2-5
Oscar Cantrell with folk school students in forge
(Southern Historical Collection, University of North Carolina
at Chapel Hill).

Agricultural statistics for the first two decades of the century offer some clues.[131] National agricultural trends of the period are of course well known. In 1880 slightly less than half the nation's people lived on farms, but by 1920 less than a third did. Average farm size was rising as farm lands were gathered into fewer hands. But North Carolina, although it had substantial industry and a half-dozen sizable metropolitan areas, was still a heavily agricultural state: farm population *increased* by almost 20 percent (to 1.5 million) from 1900 to 1920. The number of farms also increased (225,000 to 270,000), but farms were getting markedly *smaller* instead of larger as in the country as a whole (reduced from 101 to 74 acres on the average).

Farming in Cherokee and Clay counties, where the folk school was, was a relatively small operation. Although 245,000 acres were being farmed (60 percent of the total area), farm property in 1920 was valued at less than $6 million and crops at only $1.7 million. The percentage of land in farms had also declined in the past two decades (from 71 percent to 57 percent). In contrast, two larger western North Carolina counties (Buncombe and Haywood) which were also heavily agricultural but which also had consid-

FIGURE 2-6
*Leon Deschamps teaching surveying to folk school students
(Southern Historical Collection, University of North Carolina
at Chapel Hill).*

erable industry and a large urban population, produced $4.5 million worth
of crops on 438,000 acres valued at $30.5 million. Cherokee-Clay pro-
duced only $158,000 worth of dairy products; Buncombe-Haywood's pro-
duction was nearly three times as large.

Cherokee-Clay farms were also relatively poor. The value of land and
buildings per farm was about $2000—less than half the value of Bun-
combe-Haywood farms, or of the average in the state. The value of farm
property per acre was only $19.20, compared to $72.18 in Buncombe-

Haywood. With 56 percent as much farmland as Buncombe-Haywood, the value of Cherokee-Clay farms was only 19 percent as high.

The poorer farms were also less productive. Again, with 56 percent as much land, Cherokee-Clay produced crops valued at only 38 percent of those in Buncombe-Haywood. The value of dairy products per acre was only $0.64, compared to $1.17 in the other two counties. And the lower rates of production required nearly 50 percent more fertilizer.

There were some factors, however, which made agricultural *prospects* look better in Cherokee-Clay. In Buncombe-Haywood the number of farm owner-operators had increased only 7.4 percent in twenty years; but in Cherokee-Clay, the increase was 44 percent (from just over 1,000 to nearly 1,500). Cherokee-Clay also had a larger percentage of owner-operators (75 percent as opposed to 66 percent)—and therefore a smaller proportion of tenant farmers, and there was a slightly greater tendency for Cherokee-Clay farms to be debt-free (80 percent to 77 percent). In addition, farm population was declining at a slower rate (the 1900–1920 loss in Buncombe-Haywood was from 79 percent to 58 percent; in Clay-Cherokee it was from 71 percent to 57 percent), and farms were a bit larger on the average (ninety acres as opposed to seventy-six acres, which was approximately the average in the state).

Statistics for the two counties thus generally confirm Campbell's impressions and appear to justify her projections: two small, relatively unproductive agricultural counties, remote from industrial-urban centers, had a substantial (and growing) number of both farms and farmers, *some* of whose circumstances suggested that they might be successfully aided to remain on the land and make decent lives for themselves. In Campbell's view it was "a section poor, but capable of agricultural development. . . . Its greatest asset is . . . a small group of farmers with a high reputation for integrity." [132]

Campbell was convinced that the most promising means for developing agriculture in the two counties was cooperatives, the history of which in Scandinavia she had found "a thrilling tale." After studying co-ops in Denmark, she had also gone on to Ireland to meet the great cooperator Sir Horace Plunkett and survey the co-ops of the Irish Agricultural Organisation Society (IAOS). [133]

The first of the folk school-backed co-ops in Cherokee County was a credit union, which was organized in April 1926, with headquarters in Fred Scroggs's store. By late 1928 the Brasstown Savings and Loan Association had seventy-five members; four years later it had one hundred fifty members and depositors, with assets of about fifteen hundred dollars. Al-

FIGURE 2-7
*Folk school credit union members in front of Fred O. Scroggs's store, May 1926
(Southern Historical Collection, University of North Carolina
at Chapel Hill).*

though some smaller local credit unions had also been started in outlying areas, the growth of all was very slow because of depression conditions.[134]

But the agricultural co-ops at Brasstown grew more quickly and steadily. By about 1915—the year North Carolina *Progressive Farmer* editor Clarence Poe published *How Farmers Co-operate and Double Profits*—the cooperative movement in the South was, according to Saloutos, "on the threshold of its greatest expansion." Enabling legislation was enacted in most states in the early 1920s, along with important federal legislation such as the Cooper-Volstead Act of 1922.[135]

Co-ops were most prominent, however, in areas where major cash crops, such as cotton and tobacco, predominated. Thus the co-ops tended to be large and to orient their policies and services toward the large-scale financing, storage, marketing, subsidy, tax, transportation, interregional rivalry, and tariff problems associated with those crops. Relatively little was being done with co-ops among marginal, subsistence farmers.

In addition, early organizations that had addressed the problems of "dirt farmers"—such as the Granger movement (1867ff.), the Brothers of

Freedom and the Agricultural Wheel (both founded in 1882), and the Farmer's Alliance (1875)—had hardly touched such farmers in the mountains, and had in any case long since disappeared. The Granger movement was mostly midwestern; a state grange organized in North Carolina in 1873 declined rapidly after 1877, and disappeared in the 1890s. The Brothers of Freedom and the Agricultural Wheel were both born in Arkansas; only the latter ever reached much outside the state (mostly to the western portions of Kentucky and Tennessee). The alliance, larger than any previous such organization, peaked in the 1890s. Its members in Virginia were mostly of the better-off sort. Thus in the early 1920s, there was no strong farmer's organization in or near western North Carolina.[136]

It was indeed an open field, and Campbell proceeded quickly. A cooperative purchasing association and hatchery were in operation by early 1928, and by November of that year the Brasstown Farmers' Association had sixty-three members and had installed a corn mill and placed its first $500 order for feed and fertilizer.[137] New Jersey businessman J. R. Pitman loaned the school $1,000 to start the association (later called Mountain Valley Commercial Agency) "to buy and sell feeds, fertilizers, and all kinds of farm products and farm supplies." Profits were to go to a co-op creamery. Although sales reached above $10,000 per year in the early 1930s, profits remained low (less than $1,000 for the 1931–32 fiscal year).[138]

In December 1928 the Mountain Valley Creamery began operation, started partly with an $800 personal loan from Mrs. Campbell. It was managed by Danish immigrant Sigurd Nielsen.[139] By mid-1931 it had more than $6,000 in assets, and during that year it paid nearly $17,000 to farmers for eggs and cream and produced 50,000 pounds of butter. Receipts climbed to about $20,000 in 1932, and the next year butter production rose to 94,000 pounds—close to the 100,000 pounds the state Department of Agriculture predicted would be necessary to make the operation pay. Although production continued to rise (to 103,000 pounds in 1934), prices were falling steadily because of the Depression—from 45 cents per pound in 1929 to less than 20 cents in 1932—so that receipts, which should have climbed from just under $1,000 to over $45,000, actually reached only a little above $20,000. After the Depression the situation improved; a $20,000 loan from TVA's Tennessee Valley Associated Cooperatives allowed the co-op to expand quickly. Total business volume climbed to $137,000 in 1942, to over a quarter of a million dollars four years later, and to about a half-million by the late 1940s.[140] For an area in which the total value of farm production in two counties was only $1.7 million in 1920, the co-op was thus making a substantial economic impact.

FIGURE 2-8
Mountain Valley Cooperative and creamery
(Southern Historical Collection, University of North Carolina
at Chapel Hill).

The later history of the co-op is unclear. A report from a November 1949 board meeting lists 1949 sales at $528,000 and projects three-quarters of a million dollars in the near future. But the 3 May 1952 report said the co-op "is, and has been, insolvent for a number of years," and that the Coble Dairy's offer to buy it for $45,000 was being considered. By late May, Coble was operating it under lease.

In the late 1930s still another strategy was added to the school's agricultural ventures. "It seems a sad waste," Campbell wrote to *Progressive Farmer* editor Poe, "for these boys who had had some preparation and who could contribute to the building of a better life here [to] be sucked into Canton or Akron, Ohio, . . . where after many years they may perhaps . . . accumulate enough to buy a farm." Could money be found, she asked, to buy or lease land for such young men?[141]

By February 1938 a Sears, Roebuck executive had given $5,000 as a "revolving fund for helping students to become established as land owners . . . in the region of the school."[142] Local farmers Will Brendle and Arthur Ford helped get the program established, and loans of from a few hundred to several thousand dollars were made available to help young men buy houses or farms or improve buildings or equipment.[143]

Despite its auspicious beginning and rapid growth in some areas, however, the school's agricultural program was actually vital for only about fifteen years (1928–43). The school farm lost almost $5,000 in 1951, and by mid-1952 the farm and herds were run down and the co-op was leased to a private operator.[144] What had happened?

Most important, the Depression had taken its toll. For years individual donors had supplemented the major backing that the school received from churches, the Keith Fund in New York, and an endowment that totaled only $20,000 by 1932, when expenses were running slightly above $30,000 a year. But in the spring of 1931, Campbell wrote to Ralph Rounds of the Keith Fund that "almost no contributions are coming in." The *Cherokee Scout* had reported several months earlier that the Bank of Murphy was closed, and Cherokee Bank officials were trying to reassure anxious depositors.[145] Campbell and Marguerite Butler began contributing most of their own very modest salaries toward operating expenses for the school.[146] Photographer Doris Ullman, who had spent some time at the school with ballad collector John Jacob Niles in late 1933, photographing local craftspeople (including some folk school students) for Allen Eaton's Russell Sage-sponsored study *Handicrafts of the Southern Highlands* (1937), died in 1934 and left some $350,000 in trust for the school, but meeting day-to-day expenses remained a problem.[147] Nor did the waning of the Depression improve things much. By the fall of 1940, continually declining income was a "cause for serious concern," and the situation did not improve in the postwar period.[148]

The coming of the Depression-born Tennessee Valley Authority in 1933 increased some of the school's problems as well. To major benefactor Ralph Rounds of the Keith Fund, Campbell confessed herself "considerably stirred up" by some of TVA's plans. Relocation of families from reservoir areas drove up land prices in the two counties, and in the early 1940s the building of three dams nearby pulled young men off the farms in favor of construction work at high wages. There were also reports that a large aluminum plant was to be built at Andrews.[149] Thus, as the years passed, the number of local students at the folk school dwindled steadily, and the ones who came were younger.

The school's agricultural program had grown out of Campbell's conviction—born of her travels through the mountains with her husband, and later through Scandinavia—that mountain people need not have to choose between poverty on the homeplace and migrating to the piedmont cotton mills, which lured them with promises and then ruined them both physically and economically. As early as 1908 she had seen the dire effects of that process.[150] She also knew the limits of the "mission-barrel schemes" that salved the social consciences of middle-class benefactors—some of whom snipped the buttons off shirts before dispatching them to children in the mountains.[151] Such niggardly beneficence was in some respects even less attractive than the forthright hostility of General DuPont, who told Hindman Settlement School's Katherine Pettit in 1912 that he "did not want to spend any money on the Kentucky mountains, did not believe in the people, did not take any interest in them in any way, and thought all of the mountain people ought to be washed off the face of the earth."[152]

Had helping poor mountain farmers to defy General DuPont and stay on their land been its sole agenda, the John C. Campbell Folk School would probably have closed its doors in the 1940s—a victim of changing economic and social circumstances: new money, new jobs, new horizons and aspirations, and the consequent waning of old social patterns and values. And yet it *did* survive, physically at least, into the 1950s, '60s, '70s and '80s. How did it survive the departure of the young men to TVA or the aluminum plants, the sale of the creamery to Coble Dairy, the yielding of green fields to cedar and scrub pine?

The most arresting clues lie in the images of folk school students that Doris Ullman preserved on film in the early 1930s: not farmers and creamery workers, but weavers and woodcarvers. The photographs, which found their widest currency in Eaton's *Handicrafts of the Southern Highlands*, are soft-focused and sepia-toned: dark-eyed weaver Virginia Howard at her loom (p. 87); whittler Floyd Laney, tilted against a fence in a split-bottomed chair (p. 134); whittler W. J. Martin against the rough interior of a cabin (p. 11); a young Haden Hensley, knife and carving block in hand (p. 126).[153] The images are romantic and nostalgic—period recreations, some of them, such as those of Pine Mountain Settlement School benefactor Uncle William Creech's granddaughters dressed in bonnets and granny dresses hauled out of musty trunks for the occasion.[154] The implicit message of the photographs was that the school's primary agenda was not agricultural but cultural.

Campbell had her romantic and idealistic side, but she was on the whole much tougher minded than Ullman. And from her earliest days in the mountains, her conviction grew that indigenous culture might be a possible base for social reconstruction. "[The] children need culture—[a] love of [the] beautiful," a local woman told her in Harlan, Kentucky, in 1909.[155] Her early work with ballads and her collaboration with Cecil Sharp

FIGURE 2-9
*Hayden Hensley (Doris Ullman photo; used with special permission from
Berea College and the Doris Ullman Foundation).*

strengthened her conviction that "all that is native and fine" in the mountains should be not only preserved but also reinforced in the people themselves as a resource for coping with the challenges that were already upon them and the changes that lay ahead. "There is such a chance for self-support in these old industries," she noted in her journal after buying "three lovely mountain baskets" at the Pleasant Hill Academy in Tennessee in the fall of 1908.[156] Two weeks later, in company with Berea College president William Frost's wife, she saw a woman spinning wool, and another showed her "a great heap of quilts" with names like Seven-Diamond and Dove-in-the-Window. With Katherine Pettit she sought out other weavers, spinners, and quilters in eastern Kentucky and bought an indigo-dyed "Queen's Victory" coverlet from a woman near the settlement school.[157] Later she visited the site of the renowned Allanstand weaving industry begun by Frances Goodrich in 1895 and found it nearly deserted, its former activity marked only by a few rolls of wool and baskets left in the weaving room, and only three or four women weaving for Goodrich in their nearby homes.[158]

Believing that "a chance for self support" might indeed lie in craft revival efforts, Campbell was nevertheless aware that such activities were fraught with hazards. A large percentage were directed by wealthy (or at least well-to-do) women whose exalted self-image caused their condescension toward mountain people to outstrip by far their admiration for them, and whose unquestioning confidence in their own esthetic judgment allowed them to tamper with local taste and design in a high-handed manner.

George Vanderbilt's wife, for example, had started "Biltmore Industries" in 1901 on the 130,000-acre mountain estate her husband had bought for $2.25 an acre in the 1890s.[159] In the shadow of Vanderbilt's 780-foot-long Richard Morris Hunt-designed French Renaissance chateau, Eleanor Vance and Charlotte Yale spent nearly fifteen years teaching mountain people craft work. Desiring especially to revive weaving, Mrs. Vanderbilt sent Yale and Vance to England to study methods, materials, and patterns. An old loom was imported from Scotland, Allen Eaton reported, so that cloth could be made "somewhat after the homespun" of Scotland and Ireland.[160]

During a 1909 visit with Dr. Swope, the rector of the Episcopal church in Vanderbilt's red-tiled and half-timbered English village of Biltmore, Campbell came face to face with some of the ironies of the enterprise. As she wrote in her journal:

FIGURE 2-10
Students singing behind Keith House
(Southern Historical Collection, University of North Carolina
at Chapel Hill).

[We were] ushered into a modern inartistic tho' luxurious room much besprinkled with rolls of wallpaper. Shortly Mrs. Swope rolled in in elegant silk gown & exchanged a few condescending words before sailing out again. Next followed the worthy Dr. much impressed with his relation to Vanderbilt. Without much greeting he sunk into a chair and with a [fou-fou?] air, asked, "Do you want to interview me?" I stated my business and asked a few questions—whereat he gave me an account of the Industrial Club of Biltmore & work at Arden [Episcopal school for boys]. The former is in Mrs. Vanderbilt's care. She rides around in her kerridge and gets the women to weave, sells for them & rolls around to pay again. Woodwork, weaving, and baskets are taught on the estate—almost 150 being employed. . . . [Dr. Swope] warmed up a little at the last, but I was glad to get away.[161]

There had to be a better way. The eastern Kentucky settlement schools had craft and music programs, but had used culture mostly to insulate

FIGURE 2-11
Folk school students performing Danish dance, "Anders He Was a Lively Lad"
(Southern Historical Collection, University of North Carolina
at Chapel Hill).

themselves from the hard economic facts of life around them. Fortunately, the Scandinavian folk schools offered another model—a blending of idealism and realism, culture and economics, tradition and change.

In 1945, while Denmark was still under Nazi control, Campbell's sister Ruth Coolidge wrote that "the vibrations of Danish culture are ringing across the southern mountains" from a bell at the folk school presented by Danish friends. The symbolism was both powerful and appropriate. In twenty years, Campbell had appropriated for her folk school not only the culture-oriented aspects of the Danish folk schools as models, but—oddly enough—sizable portions of Danish culture itself. The result was a cultural program that was—though for very different reasons—as conflicted and bizarre as that of Hindman Settlement School.

The earliest cultural activities of the school were singing and dancing. To what extent music traditional to the area was used—as folk school theory predicted it should be—is not clear. The Campbell papers contain many photographs of local fiddlers, banjo players, and guitar pickers at the school (a number of them came to each of the school's "creamery

FIGURE 2-12
Weaving room and students
(Southern Historical Collection, University of North Carolina
at Chapel Hill).

days," for example), but also many of the Danish dances and recorder consorts. Campbell's sister reported in the 1940s that popular songs such as
"When You and I Were Young, Maggie" were sung, but in "good old
Danish folk school fashion." And Marguerite Butler's various accounts of
music and dance at the school refer to both Danish and local traditions.[162]

It is nevertheless clear that Campbell herself turned for materials not
primarily to the work she had done earlier with Sharp on music traditional
in the mountains but to what she had heard and seen more recently in
Denmark—the songs that opened folk school classes (many of them composed by Bishop Grundtvig) and the Danish dances. Thus all but two of
the thirty-three tunes and related dances or games she published from
among those used in the early years were from Scandinavia. They had
names like "Danish March," "Lotte Walked," "Anders He Was a Lively
Lad," and "Gustaf's Toast," and they employed steps such as the "double
Tyrolean" and the "Anders Hop." The school's own residential students,
as well as the hundreds who came to "recreation" short courses, thus
learned Danish songs and danced Danish dances in the name of preserving
"all that is native and fine" in Cherokee County, North Carolina.[163]

Along with her enthusiasm for Danish folk school songs and dances, Campbell had returned from her Scandinavian trip convinced that the craft skills she had observed during her earliest trips through the mountains could contribute to social and economic reconstruction in western North Carolina, as similar skills had in tiny Denmark. The coverlets and baskets she had bought from mountain women fifteen years earlier were tangible reminders of the creativity of mountain people. Thus by late 1929 she was able to report that nearly a score of local people had been working at various crafts at the folk school during the past year and that a craft shop was under construction. Weaving was also introduced, and by the summer of 1931 six girls were weaving regularly in the school's weaving room.

Although a variety of crafts were practiced at the school (brooms, furniture, baskets), the main ones were weaving and the carving of small wooden animals. Handicraft teacher Jane Chase was experimenting with natural dyes for weaving, and woodworking teacher Park Fisher was teaching local boys to make wooden boxes and other simple objects. A school craft guild, organized early in 1929, had had nearly $1,200 in sales its first year, and by the fall of 1932 sales were running $125–200 per month. "Someday," Marguerite Butler wrote to Ralph Rounds, "I hope we will be able to compete with the Swiss carvers." A year or so later, Campbell told him "we can see ourselves a carving community one of these days."[164] By 1934 one student was supporting himself and his family entirely by carving, the guild had nearly fifty members, and two former students had opened a woodworking shop on the strength of their folk school training and a loan from the school's credit union.[165]

The craft enterprise continued to thrive in the years that followed. Sales that amounted to only $1,400 per year in 1934 grew to over $10,000 by 1942, and there were ninety local craftspeople involved. A sawmill and kiln had been installed, and the shop was also turning out beds, chairs, tables, and church pews. Even after many of the men left to go to war, the craft endeavor held its own with seventy-five workers; fifty-one carvers had nearly $5,000 in sales during 1946, and the school sawmill reported that 48,000 board feet of lumber was ready for their use.[166]

But figures on the number of weavers and carvers and their annual sales tell but little, actually, about the school's cultural endeavors. How were those endeavors linked—if they were—to the local traditions they purportedly represented, preserved, and encouraged? And how did it interpret those traditions and its own role in their preservation to the world beyond Clay and Cherokee counties?

FIGURE 2-13
Mr. Massey carving with young boy
(Southern Historical Collection, University of North Carolina
at Chapel Hill).

Evidence was abundant, of course, that the southern mountains (like many other regions of the country) harbored a tradition of blending manual skill with an esthetic sense to produce useful objects which were also beautiful: buildings, furniture, tools, pottery, textiles, firearms, baskets, vehicles, fences, grave markers, musical instruments, and the like. As in any relatively isolated, preindustrial, premercantile society, mountain people had had to supply most of their own needs and had made what they needed as well and as beautifully as time, materials, leisure, and taste would allow.

By 1925, however, even rural Cherokee and Clay counties were neither preindustrial nor premercantile. The local weekly newspaper regularly cataloged the arrival of mass culture in the late 1920s: a traveling tent show was competing for an audience with "The Thief of Baghdad" (starring Douglas Fairbanks) at the Bonita Theater; an eight-story hotel was rising on Murphy's main street; Parker's Drug Store was installing a jukebox; private power companies were damming the Hiwasee River to run the

FIGURE 2-14
Folk school boys carving in front of fireplace, Keith House
(Southern Historical Collection, University of North Carolina at Chapel Hill).

electric refrigerators advertised alongside Fords, Whippetts, and Hup-mobiles. At the time the folk school opened, the other big news stories locally were the opening of the Appalachia Scenic Highway from Atlanta to Asheville (via Murphy) and early plans for the formation of the Great Smoky Mountains National Park. By the spring of 1927 an automobile raced to Asheville in two hours, thirty-nine minutes—nearly fifty miles an hour. The annual Cherokee County Singing Convention, organized in 1894, was still drawing as many as fifteen hundred people in 1925, but the old ways were clearly dying.[167]

It was therefore no easy matter to say what cultural forms were (or ever had been) indigenous to the area, or what the local "cultural traditions" were, even with respect to physical objects, to say nothing of such intangibles as values, beliefs, and the like.

From the incomplete evidence now available, it appears that the folk school crafts had at best a marginal grounding in local tradition. The school's earliest woodworking teacher, Park Fisher, was from the Georgia mountains, but his successor, Muriel Martin, was from outside the region.

Louise Pitman, who directed handicraft work at the school from the late 1920s until 1951, was a Columbia University graduate from South Orange, New Jersey, who learned about vegetable dyeing (for example) from Wilma Stone Viner, a Vassar graduate who had grown up in well-to-do circumstances on a Louisiana plantation and summered at Saluda in the North Carolina mountains before spending six years at Pine Mountain Settlement School, where she in turn had learned what she knew about dyeing from Katherine Pettit and others around the school.[168]

The carving enterprise may have had a slightly closer connection to local tradition. According to the oft-repeated official version of the story, Campbell noticed men whittling in front of Fred Scroggs's store, "gouging deep into the loungers' bench," and tentatively "began to direct this activity into simple carving."[169] Actual designs for the farm animals and other wooden items the carvers produced seem to have derived from some by now unchartable combination of the students' own taste, that of their folk school teachers, and market considerations. During his visits to the school in the early 1930s, Allen Eaton concluded that the designs owed more to students' own tastes than to any other factor, but it is not clear that that was the case. Indeed a school newsletter of the late 1940s reported that "most of the carvings are designed by the teacher, but if the student shows any imagination he is encouraged to use it."[170]

Even in the relatively few cases in which the teacher was native to the area, that did not necessarily guarantee that designs would reflect local tradition. Herman Estes, who claimed to be a fifth-generation descendant of Daniel Boone and whose grandfather was a maker of long rifles, taught woodworking (mostly lathe work) from 1939 to 1952. He had learned his lathe work, however, at Berea College (1911–13) and during a cabinet-making apprenticeship in upstate New York.[171]

One of the students who showed the most imagination, and whose career was invoked over and over again as proof that a folk school could work in the North Carolina mountains, was carver Hayden Hensley—"our first boy," as he was called in a school report. Hensley was one of five children in a local farming family of modest circumstances. He disliked school and dropped out in the seventh grade. But he found the folk school to his liking, entered with the first students in 1927, and stayed three years. He danced the Danish dances, played the singing games, and along the way became the school's star carver. Later, having met and married a local Brasstown girl who was working at the school, Hensley asked for a loan from the school to buy some land, built a house on it, and "whittled out every dime" it took to pay off the loan (twenty-five dollars every six months for ten years at 2 percent interest). After hitchhiking to the school to sell his finished pieces, he would bring back a sackful of wood and start again, glad to be making two or three dollars a day while his friends who were lucky enough to have jobs at all were making half that or less. Of the five Hensley sons and daughters, Hayden was the only one who stayed in the area; the others left for factory jobs in the big cities.[172]

If the actual product of the folk school handicraft workers was only tentatively related to local traditions, and if there were in fact precious few Hayden Hensleys among its students, the public image of the enterprise was nevertheless marketed proudly and widely. It began to achieve wide currency and credibility no more than a half-dozen years after the school opened. As early as 1932 sales of folk school handicrafts were being arranged in Boston and New York, and three years later an exhibit of southern mountain handicrafts at Rockefeller Center included John C. Campbell Folk School items.[173]

The primary mechanism for promoting the folk school version of mountain crafts, however, was the Southern Highland Handicraft Guild, which Mrs. Campbell helped to found in the late 1920s. She got the idea, apparently, from a cooperative craft sales shop in Finland, and soon after her return to the mountains in 1923 she began to think seriously about the "mountain [handicraft] industries problem." She suggested that "some sort of loose federation ought to be worked out" among the schools and other crafts "producing centers" to maintain standards, help with marketing, and so forth.[174]

Just after Christmas, 1928, Campbell and others from mountain craft centers met at Penland School in western North Carolina and laid plans to form the guild; to her it seemed "a forward [step], with large possibilities."[175] From the beginning, the discussions were guided by Campbell and other craft-center leaders who had been instrumental in blending traditional mountain design and materials with ideas drawn from other cultures (especially that of Scandinavia) and frequently filtered through university or arts-and-crafts movement training: President Frost of Berea College, Allen Eaton, Mary Martin Sloop of Crossnore, Clementine Douglas of the Spinning Wheel in Asheville, Lucy Morgan of Penland, and others.

The early history of the guild shows clearly that it was tied primarily to the folk school, settlement school, and crafts revival "producing center" version of handicrafts in the mountains; that it was able to establish itself quickly as the major arbiter of design in mountain crafts; and that it became a more forceful *change agent* than conservator of local traditions.

The first president of the guild was Marguerite Butler of the John C. Campbell Folk School, and its first board of directors was made up of Butler, May Stone of Hindman Settlement School, Clementine Douglas, Lucy Morgan, and O. J. Mattil of the Gatlinburg (Tennessee) Woodcarvers and Carvers.[176] The first by-laws placed voting rights in the hands of the producing centers and required approval by an "admissions committee" for all those who wished to join after an initial charter period. Most of the guild's annual meetings during its first six or seven years took place at Berea College, the folk and settlement schools, and the producing centers, or in conjunction with meetings of the Conference of Southern Mountain Workers (which in turn was dominated by folk, mission, and settlement school people).[177]

Prior to the formation of the guild there had been almost no systematic effort to inform the general public about southern mountain craft traditions, except for some early efforts by Berea College and several of the settlement and mission schools. But the guild quickly filled the void, staging exhibits at each of its meetings and forming alliances with those in the crafts revival movement outside the mountains and with public and private agencies. By doing so, it placed itself in a position to approve or forestall most major public and private efforts in the area of mountain crafts. At its spring 1931 meeting, for example, Emile Bernat, editor of the crafts revival-oriented *Handicrafter*, brought a weaving exhibit from the St. Louis Handicrafts Guild, and Frances Goodrich announced her plan to turn over her Allanstand craft sales room in Asheville to the guild.[178] The American Federation of Arts, the Country Life Association, and the Russell Sage Foundation cooperated with the guild on an exhibition of mountain crafts that toured the country, stopping at such prestigious museums as Washington's Corcoran Gallery, the Brooklyn Museum, and the Milwaukee Arts Institute.[179]

By 1934 the guild was consulting with both the U.S. Department of Labor and the Tennessee Valley Authority concerning the economic aspects of crafts work in the mountains.[180] In 1935, Clementine Douglas and several other guild members became the directors of TVA's new Southern Highlanders handicrafts cooperative, and the guild began consulting with newly created state and federal parks in the region concerning exhibits and sales of craft items in the parks.[181] Having achieved the credibility implied by these working relationships, the guild had gained considerable power to certify or discredit any mountain craftsperson through its admissions committee. That power could by no means be taken lightly by native craftspeople.

It also became clear quite early that—in the name of preserving tradition—the guild would actually function as a major change agent. Its first major exhibit (1930) included—as Eaton noted—pieces of "mountain design and construction," but also "carefully styled pieces from some of the schools and better workshops of the region." Indeed, at the 1928 exploratory meeting, much of the discussion (as reported by Eaton) adumbrated the guild's later role as change agent: the organizers talked of tradition and the value of the "old ways," but also of "standards," "disposing of work not up to standard," "protection of [individual] designs," "creation of new objects and new designs to meet market requirements," "partial use of machinery in handmade articles," and the like.[182]

By 1935, when the guild was in the early stages of its cooperation with TVA, it was already clear how far things had moved from the old ways—not only from older esthetics but also from old notions of limited production for use. At the autumn 1935 meeting, Eaton reported, "the need for determining the requirements of a new consuming public was discussed, and the advisability of engaging a designer and production manager to assist in solving the . . . problems growing out of the demands of this public."[183] The language was bureaucratic, corporate, and market-oriented, and between it and old ways in the mountains yawned a chasm the guild had helped to create—in the name of tradition.

During the 1940s, Campbell and the folk school continued as central participants in the guild. Her crafts director, Louise Pitman, was on the guild board by the early 1940s, and Campbell in 1943 became chairman of a committee to chart the guild's future.[184] Through the committee, she managed to secure money from the General Education Board to begin a major survey of mountain crafts and "crafts education." Directed by Professor Marion Heard of the University of Tennessee's School of Home Economics, the GEB-funded study helped to further legitimize the guild, and place it on a firmer organizational footing. In May 1945 it was formally incorporated, and soon opened its first office in Gatlinburg.[185]

Campbell withdrew from active involvement with the guild at the end of the 1940s, but folk school influence continued through former John C. Campbell Folk School crafts director Louise Pitman, who came to head the guild in 1951. Pitman was succeeded in 1961 by Robert Gray, formerly of the Worcester (Massachusetts) Craft Center, who further strenghtened guild ties with the professional crafts orientation of the American Crafts Council.[186]

A useful index to the guild and craft-school influenced handicrafts situation in southern Appalachia in the mid-1960s was poet Jonathan Williams's 1966 survey for *Craft Horizons*, which called the guild "the key [crafts] organization in the mountains." Williams reported (without detectable irony) Blenko Glass Company art-glass designer Joel Myers's elitist observation that in his "short residence in West Virginia" he had found "a lack of anything really recognizable as crafts," and art-potter Marguerite Wildenhain's judgment that local potters at the 150-year-old Bybee pottery in Kentucky were "artistically and creatively quite dried up. All their shapes are old seventeenth-century ones, and they have never developed since that time. *In my shop you would learn why some forms are good and alive and why some are not.*" In their certitude, the sentiments were eerily reminiscent of the judgments of pioneer ballad hunters of sixty years earlier.[187]

At one level, of course, the influence of the folk school interpretation of mountain crafts perpetuated itself through individual lives, like second generation carver Jack Hall, who as late as the mid-1960s said his interest stemmed from his childhood, when he watched his father carve the wooden blocks brought home from the John C. Campbell Folk School.[188] More important, however, the influence persisted through the school itself as an institution, and through the guild, which by the early 1980s was firmly entrenched and credible enough to be selected by the National Park Service to manage and operate a new multi-million-dollar crafts center at the Asheville entrance to the Blue Ridge Parkway. Through the center every year file hundreds of thousands of tourists who accept as authentic and traditional "mountain handicrafts" the guild-produced items whose lineage leads far more often to the craft-design programs of major universities (and to the folk and settlement schools) than to mountain-bred potters, metal workers, or chair-makers and the patterns handed down to them from the past.[189]

The ascendancy of the guild—provoked by the vast social and economic changes of the post-Depression and post–World War II periods—was one side of the coin so far as the John C. Campbell Folk School was concerned. The other side—the rise in industrial employment in the mountains, the advent of mass media and attendant new values and social relationships, the decline in agriculture—had already made its impact on the school.

As World War II drew to a close, it became impossible to ignore the fact that the folk school was in a serious crisis. In 1946, Campbell retired as director, and was replaced by Dr. D. F. Folger, former dean of West Georgia College. Born in 1894 in the northwestern South Carolina foothills, Folger held degrees in engineering (Clemson), sociology (Vanderbilt), and education (Yale) and had spent five years as an administrator in the Farm Security Administration's rural resettlement communities at Cumberland Homesteads (Tennessee) and Tygart Valley (West Virginia).[190]

In his letter of appointment, Folger was directed to recommend "a policy . . . in respect to the proposed rental or sale of any parts of the school lands." Such a move could never have been contemplated except as a last resort, and Folger apparently tried to meet the crisis head-on. Casting about for new programs for the school that might match new conditions, he cooperated with Western Carolina Teachers College and the University of North Carolina to offer a six-week summer course for public school teachers, and he expanded vocational courses for returning war veterans.

But Folger's efforts ran into opposition from the school's staff quite early. By early 1949, board member Fred Brownlee was complaining to Campbell (who was by then living on Nantucket) that the vocational courses for veterans were "taking [the school] away from its moorings." The main issue, he argued, was "whether we want to have a folk school or some other kind of school." He had never seen, he said, "an educator produced by regular schools whose whole personality is alive with the fire that must have burned in the soul of Grundtvig."[191] Staff members upset by Folger's attempt to find new directions were holding caucuses and drafting statements of position. By the spring of 1949, the board had asked Folger for a "critical appraisal" of the school and its possible future, to be considered by the board in executive session at its spring meeting.[192]

Folger's response was straightforward.[193] He noted the impact of major social and economic changes in Cherokee and Clay counties (and in the larger society) upon the school's original aims and programs. He located three-quarters of the two hundred former students and asked them about their experiences at the school. Nearly a hundred did not even reply to his inquiry. The nearly sixty who did, did not present an encouraging picture—at least insofar as the agriculture program was concerned. They had by and large remained neither on the land nor in the local area. They were scattered in fourteen states, and only five were full-time farmers. Thirty-five lived in cities and towns.[194] Although they spoke of their folk school experience as "a unique educational opportunity that is greatly prized," they were not able to say precisely what it had meant to them. Folger admitted that the school had had a major impact on farming in the area (mainly through the Mountain Valley Cooperative), but its demonstration farm had been supplanted by TVA and other state and federal programs, as had its early efforts to provide a small library and a public health nurse for local people. The situation resembled that of the urban settlement houses

FIGURE 2-15
*Olive Dame Campbell (Southern Historical Collection,
University of North Carolina
at Chapel Hill).*

after services they had provided were "municipalized," and of Hindman
Settlement School after 1928, when its students began attending public
schools.

Folger noted that there were also other problems: hostility or indif-
ference from the surrounding community, dissatisfaction with the co-op,
the emphasis upon English and Danish songs and dances rather than those
native to the area, and failure to work with the public schools.[195]

What could the school do under the circumstances? Much impressed
with Dr. Arthur E. Morgan's work on small communities, Folger suggested that certain features of the old school be retained and revitalized
(the co-op, the carving, the recreational program), but that it be reoriented
in the main toward small community development of the type suggested
by Morgan. "It is in the small community," he argued, "that we have op-
timum conditions for the transmission of culture and for the development
of well-adjusted personalities." The folk school could help to stimulate "a
finely designed community with a vital community spirit" if it was willing
to consider setting aside some of its internal pieties and accustomed func-

tions, and "discover what interests people [actually] have." But if that were to be done, he admitted, every program and function would have to be evaluated dispassionately in the light of actual current circumstances in the local area. "If we [are] willing to compromise with custom and adapt our program to our culture," he concluded, "I think we might stand a better chance of attracting students."

Overall, it was a commonsensical statement of obvious fact: to survive, the school had to change to meet new circumstances. It was also perfectly in line with the school's formal philosophy. The board's response was to ask for Folger's resignation and begin a search for a new director. As Campbell noted in her letter to one of the first new prospects, the board "wished to hold to the general plan of the old school." [196]

Next in line was the Reverend Howard Kester, a Martinsville, Virginia, native who recently had been directing a displaced persons program for the Congregational church, but who had been involved for more than twenty years in religious organizations working for social justice. Kester had served as a director of European Student Relief (1923–25); secretary of the Fellowship of Reconciliation (1927–34); executive secretary of the Committee on Economic and Racial Justice (1934–40); executive secretary of the Fellowship of Southern Churchmen (1940–42), which he had helped to found in 1934; and principal of the Penn School on St. Helena Island, South Carolina (1944–48). He had been involved in some of the most forthright challenges to exploitative systems and conditions in the South, such as sharecropping, farm tenantry, racism, and lynching. [197]

Kester arrived in the midst of turbulent times at the school. Woodworking teacher Herman Estes was warning that the school had been "25 years ahead of the community" in the beginning, but was now 25 years behind. Most of the staff had come to see themselves in conventional bureaucratic terms as "department heads," and as such they were demanding not a powerful Grundtvigian leader but an executive who would leave them "power to carry on" the work of their departments. [198]

From his first days at the school in July 1950, Kester appears to have been clear, humane, and aboveboard in his dealings with the staff and forceful and articulate about his plan to rebuild the school as an instrument which would "help people help themselves." He lasted eighteen months, and resigned in late 1951. [199]

Upon Kester's departure, the ghost of Grundtvig rose again to stalk Cherokee County. Georg Bidstrup—who had come from Denmark to the school a quarter-century earlier—took charge and announced his plan to "build up [an] old folk school type of student body." But the situation was not promising. The farm lay mostly idle, and equipment was deteriorating; only the crafts program was making money, and almost the only students were veterans taking vocational courses under the G.I. Bill.[200]

But Bidstrup was undaunted. Summer short-course students played recorders, watched puppet shows, and danced Danish dances amid what Bidstrup called "daily discussion of what the John C. Campbell Folk School is all about." Folk school carvers at the Southern Highland Handicraft Guild fair "delighted the public," he reported, as they whittled "mad mules and horses." In Bidstrup's account, they were "all happy students and workers together—the school farmer and dairyman, chicken man, carpenter, blacksmith, crafts teachers, hostess, dietician . . . director and students."[201]

A few months later there was a "Little Folk School" session in which children were taught to do the Flamborough sword dance, and plans were laid for "hobby nights," "nature study" courses, and "advanced dancing" ("the more difficult folk dances") classes. To use the facilities (they were in fact unused most of the time), "folk school vacations for families" were projected, and there was even talk of allowing people to build permanent or vacation homes on the farm property.[202]

As late as 1955, Bidstrup was still assuring folk school partisans that the school was "facing the challenges of a changing time." In a world, he said, "marked by indecision, suspicion, and fear, when the search for security often leads to personal and national destruction, and when the values and meanings of our ways of life are constantly challenged, *there is more need for folk schools than ever before*."[203]

But in fact the situation was not promising. The Scandinavian model that fascinated the Campbells in the pre–World War I era was complex, flexible, and multistranded. But changing circumstances, the passing of time, and romantic personal visions such as Bidstrup's at length selected the folk cultural strand as most attractive, and hung the entire destiny of the school upon it. Had the folk school version of culture been spun from native fibers, it might have been strong enough to bind the school to the community through decades of change. But it was instead what is known in the textile industry as a blend—and one in which native fibers were difficult to detect.

Bidstrup was nevertheless confident that the blend was serviceable. "While these [Danish and English dances] were brought in mainly to serve as a bridge to the traditions of the people," he said, "they have become . . . traditions of the people. . . . They have become . . . traditions in their own right; and they are on their way to being incorporated into the

Southern mountain dance form." Luckily Bidstrup overstated the case. In scores of local dances that still take place every weekend in the mountains, there is scarcely a hint of folk school influence.[204] But in one sense, Bidstrup was correct: in certain quarters, the folk school has been able to establish its version of mountain culture as the legitimate one. Indeed, among the culture-conscious middle and upper classes both within and beyond the region, it is more often than not the settlement school/Berea College/folk school/Southern Highland Handicraft Guild version of "authentic" mountain culture that predominates: dulcimers and Country Dance Society dances, Richard Chase folk tales and Jean Ritchie ballads, "designer-craftsman" pottery, Churchill Weavers [Berea] place mats, and enameled copper.[205]

There can finally be no doubt that the effects of systematic cultural intervention can be both pronounced and remarkably durable. From the record it is clear that Campbell recognized that potential from the beginning and considered the attendant responsibilities and risks acceptable. To a young eastern Kentucky teacher who wrote to her as early as 1924 about the wisdom of introducing new Christmas customs among local people, she replied that "it is certainly . . . desirable to . . . enrich the life of the community by introducing [such] customs. . . . After all the early church did . . . [so] with the old heathen festivals. We can learn from them. If we are going to take away objectionable things we must fill their place." Indeed, she continued, "[if] we insist upon our way being the right way, then there is no logical halfway point to stop in preparing [mountain people] to compete with the outside." Her sense of risk was muted by comparison. "Is there not some way," she quietly mused, "by which the community can be helped to be more alive, more self-determining, more fulfilled . . . than by establishing an *outside* force in every community?"[206]

Although she conceived of the folk school as rooted deeply in local culture, it was in fact—and remained through all the years—an "outside force." As early as the first winter, Campbell wrote to her family back in Massachusetts about "a nice old man here in Murphy who makes good furniture reasonably and can copy anything." But it was not local designs she wished him to copy for the projected folk school crafts enterprise. "If you can lay your hands on any pictures of good old-fashioned bureaus or little tables," she wrote, "please send [them to] me at once. We may as well have good lines."[207] Although two months later Campbell's sister (who had come to help get the school started) excitedly bought locally made cupboards, beds, spinning wheels, and coverlets from a family that was selling out and moving away,[208] the dominant patterns of the folk school's work with culture emerged quite early and remained remarkably stable for a half-century: Danish traditions in music and dance were freely introduced, frequently in direct conflict with (and in preference to) local traditions; genteel esthetics were preferred and genteel standards of performance were enforced; and middle-class craftspeople who accommodated "folk" forms and idioms to the fine-arts esthetic of university crafts training programs were imported as teachers and models for folk school students. In sum, the school set itself up unapologetically as the arbiter of important cultural questions and sought to extend and normalize its hybrid version of mountain culture.

The influence of university-trained musicians and craftspeople appeared early and persisted. As early as mid-1929, Campbell wrote to benefactor Ralph Rounds of the Keith Fund that "a very delightful sculptress is now eager to join us"; and in the mid-1930s New York-born ballad singer and collector John Jacob Niles spent a year at the school. Later art-potter Lynn Gault took up residence.[209]

Evidence of the school's willingness to serve as cultural arbiter is not difficult to find. Writing to her old mentor Philander P. Claxton in 1931, Campbell spoke of the school's course on singing games as giving mountain teachers "a new point of view as to preserving what is best in the native culture," and a few years later a newsletter reported that a recreation course led by Frank Smith had helped "extend to neighboring communities the Folk School standard of excellence in communal folk games." In 1949, Georg Bidstrup wrote confidently to Campbell that he had been asked to judge a square dance contest at nearby Waynesville's Tobacco Festival and had taken the opportunity to discourage the "'jitterbug' type" of square dancing.[210]

Except for Southern Highland Handicraft Guild handicrafts, the clearest example of the dissemination and larger public acceptance of folk school mountain culture is probably the singing (or "play party") games that the school promoted through all its years. Writing to Helen Dingman of Berea College in 1939, Campbell—drawing upon arguments common in the urban settlement house-based recreation movements since the turn of the century—sketched a vision of renewal in the mountains through socials and singing games. People in the country, she said, have

> little opportunity . . . to come together in a natural, wholesome fashion; . . . little chance to express themselves; to satisfy the creative spirit. Here it seems to me, are rather obvious causes of . . . anti-social attitudes . . . excesses, fanaticism, individualism, suspi-

cion of all new, conservatism—even . . . poverty. . . . [Playing] together, creating together often accomplish . . . what is almost
impossible to accomplish through intellectual conviction. . . . [F]olk
music, drama, folk dancing, crafts, arts, hobbies [carried] out into
the country . . . will prove one of the best bases on which to build a
new life.[211]

It was a beguiling argument: the personal, social, and even economic
problems people faced when economic systems collapsed and old ways of
life and schemes of value were eclipsed could be solved through "healthy
recreation." Even the school's own program was broader and more realis-
tic than that, but it was nevertheless singing games and healthy recreation—rather than cooperatives and credit unions—which the school promoted, spreading them across the mountains and beyond.

In 1933, Campbell published her *Singing Games Old and New*, and
Georg Bidstrup made trip after trip to teach and promote the folk school
version of recreation: to the Pi Beta Phi settlement school in Gatlinburg,
to Berea ("where they have taken the college by storm"), to Blue Ridge
Industrial School, to the Dorland-Bell school, and even to the Young
Friends' Conference in the Midwest. A Danish teacher was employed to
carry the games especially into Presbyterian schools in the mountains, and
Helen Dingman reported that "Berea is thoroughly innoculated now."
Students were doing the games in such large numbers, she said, that "they
may yet become one of the traditions of the mountains."[212]

By the mid-1940s the folk school recreation program was sufficiently developed to draw a grant from the General Education Board to spread it and
its underlying philosophy in the public schools.[213] Converts multiplied.
After a workshop led by Campbell at Hiwassee, Georgia, in 1945, a school
principal (newly arrived from central Georgia) started regular sessions
at his school. And a series of festivals at Rabun Gap, Georgia, in the
mid-1940s became a stage for folk school culture: folk games, songs, recorder consorts, and puppet shows. Campbell and Marguerite Butler (now
married to Georg Bidstrup) led countless sessions for schools and clubs,
and most short courses at the school drew students from a dozen or more
states: teachers, ministers, librarians, YMCA workers, and others. "So . . .
the School and its philosophy of rural life and its belief in creative recreation," said the 1945 annual report, "is spreading . . . through . . . the
whole Southern Highlands and beyond."[214]

And spread it did. Berea College still promotes the folk school version of
mountain culture through its annual Christmas country dance sessions,

and many an urban group of folk-club dancers gathers weekly to learn what they understand to be "southern mountain" dances from their Berea- or folk school–trained teachers.[215]

The ripples appear to move forever: Danish singing games and sword dances; puppet shows and recorders; designer-craftsman pots and enam- eled copper ashtrays. Meanwhile, we are given to understand, moun- taineers sit placidly in some magical living sepia-toned photograph, carv- ing an infinite series of ducks and mad mules, oblivious to and untouched by the periodic expansions and contractions of a Rube Goldberg economic system. Culture has become not the deeply textured expression of the to- tality of one's life situation—hopes, fears, values, beliefs, practices, ways of living and working, degrees of freedom and constraint—but a timeless, soft-focused, unidimensional refuge from the harsher aspects of reality.

Even in the Hayden Hensley story, some of the contradictions surfaced as the years passed. After ten years of full-time carving, "our first boy" found that he was bored by it, that it was "just like going to a job"—"the same old grind every day" he called it forty years later. So he quit carving altogether in 1941, took a job firing a boiler for a local veneer plant, and didn't carve another piece for twenty-five years. Only after retirement did he begin again, and then at the local community college instead of at the folk school. His students are not the local young people that Olive Dame Campbell hoped to keep on the land, but mostly retirees looking for a way to occupy their leisure.

What is at issue, finally—as it was with Hindman Settlement School earlier and the contemporary White Top festival—is the politics of cul- ture. Why and how did Campbell, who understood the transformation of Denmark from a feudal to a democratic society and who put so much of her energy into organizing cooperatives—which at least had some poten- tial for improving the economic facts of life in Clay and Cherokee coun- ties—allow herself to be boxed at last into the corner of Southern High- land Handicraft Guild and folk school culture? And how did she allow such a romantic concept of "culture" to divert her from her larger social concerns?

Of her *knowledge* of certain of the economic and political facts of life in the mountains—and in Denmark—there can be no doubt. In *The South- ern Highlander and His Homeland* she wrote of the "commercial short- sightedness and greed" that had destroyed mountain forests (p. 231), the "lumber syndicates," and the control of hydroelectric power in North Car- olina by a few corporations (p. 235). In her book on Danish folk schools she returned again and again to the abuses of the country's feudal past, and the struggles of farmers to reform its legal, economic, and political system. In her more than ten years of travel in the mountains with her husband, she had seen more than most people of the corruption of local and state political systems and social institutions, the social costs of shortsighted laissez-faire economic policies.

Although she left no summary of her political and economic philosophy, some of its central elements are fairly clear. Despite her initial distaste for the "prevailing smell of stale tobacco juice" that hung over the back country of the South, she came to hold a highly romantic view of rural life. It was apparent in her response to Scandinavia; it was clear in her design for the folk school at Brasstown, the motto for which was "I Sing behind the Plow." Correspondingly, she distrusted urban, industrial society and the politics of organized industrial workers—as was obvious in her response to the worker-oriented urban folk school of Borup.

Part of her distrust of "pure" politics—that is, politics which she judged to lack a religious or cultural base—apparently derived from her response to Bolshevist hostilities against Finland. "I'm afraid I never could be a consistent pacifist here," she wrote from Finland in 1923, "when I see what she has suffered and what the Bolshevists have done." [216] As for the folk schools, she said after she returned, "schools which seek to bring out the best in man are naturally religious" in the sense that religion stands basically for "the equality of human souls." Thus, she reported, "socialistic and communistic labor groups" were suspicious of the folk schools. [217]

Thus at one level, Campbell seems (like her mentor Grundtvig) to have considered politics essentially irrelevant if daily life was orderly, attractive, and comfortable. Visiting the U.S. Steel Company coal camp of Lynch, Kentucky, shortly after her return from Denmark, she admitted to a friend that "the town is *owned*, votes and all, by the company." But it was also, she said, "really awfully well kept whatever one thinks of the system." [218] It was a contradiction she was content to leave unresolved.

And there were other contradictions. On the one hand—to take a major one—she understood and commented upon the basic structural changes that had been prerequisites to the transformation of Danish society (including the expropriation of large estates and the consequent disestablishment of the upper class), and she knew from her early work in the mountains that many of the facts of social and (especially) economic life were set by large-scale economic forces such as corporations. On the other hand, she herself took a gradualist, meliorist approach to social change, directing her work at the folk school toward the small-scale economics of family farms and cooperatives, and assuming that individuals could find adequate room for mobility within an essentially unaltered system.

Finally, it appears never to have occurred to Campbell to question whether the larger national social, economic, and political system was in fact democratic and equitable, and therefore whether it could be accepted as a hospitable context for humane change in any local area such as the southern mountains. The hard-won reforms of recent Danish history were, she was confident, built into the very fabric of American society as first principles. Her criticisms of structural defects in the system did not even extend as far as those of the more politically conscious urban settlement house workers of a generation earlier, to say nothing of the even more stringent analyses common in the late 1920s and the Depression era.[219]

The fairest judgment of Campbell's work must be rendered, finally, according to the standards of her own times—the social, political, and cultural efforts of her contemporaries. In comparison with other ballad collectors of the 1910–25 period, her early work was exemplary, as has been shown. Taken as a whole, her work was at least more complex than that of the settlement school women of Hindman and Pine Mountain, and the weaving-revivers of Allanstand, Crossnore, Biltmore, and Penland. And she did more with cooperatives in the mountains than anyone else of the period except the Farmers Federation's James G. K. McClure.

But when one moves beyond these limited and local examples, the comparisons become less favorable. A vast number of strategies and organizations in the South in the 1920s and 1930s worked to improve the lot of common people and help them organize and struggle against a variety of oppressors: landlords, corporations, banks, racism and lynching, and economic policies (such as onerous mortgage, credit, and tax laws). The mid-1930s especially saw the birth of the Southern Tenant Farmers Union (1934) and a variety of analogous organizations.[220]

So far as experimental, social change-oriented schools and communities are concerned (and there were a number of them in the mountains), the Campbell Folk School may perhaps best be understood as falling somewhere near the midpoint of a spectrum that stretches from the Ozarks' Commonwealth College (1925–40) and north Georgia's Macedonia Cooperative Community (1937–58), on the one hand, to nearby Black Mountain College (1933–56), on the other. All were idealistic and admirably motivated; all were directed by energetic and imaginative people; all were in some ways at odds with mainstream values, assumptions, and processes. But for a variety of reasons all failed, if failure is to be judged by their ability to work substantial and durable changes within their chosen local contexts.

Black Mountain College, though promoted as a bold alternative to conventional educational institutions (which in many ways it was), was the least effective in guiding or promoting social change locally—primarily because it never really attempted to do so.[221] Founded in 1933 by Floridian John Anders Rice, Black Mountain was from the first tied to a free-floating national and international avant-garde of writers, dancers, musicians, architects, and others who clearly felt no allegiance to the mountains in which they set up their school—and apparently little to any other *place* or indigenous cultural tradition. A roster of former students and teachers reads like a *Who's Who* of fringe thought of the period: John Cage, Eric Bentley, Merce Cunningham, Buckminster Fuller, Jonathan Williams, Charles Olson, and many others.

If Black Mountain people shared any estimate of local people and culture, it appears to have been contempt. Students were mostly from the Northeast and seem in the main to have shared Peggy Bennet Cole's feeling that coming across Black Mountain teacher Josef Albers in "[a] hillbilly setting, in the Southern Baptist convention country of the Tarheel state was a little like finding the remnants of an advanced civilization in the midst of a jungle."[222]

The college never attempted to relate to local problems—agricultural, industrial, racial, or otherwise. Its faculty and student body remained lily-white until the mid-1940s. And while the Campbell Folk School's motto "I Sing behind the Plow" was romantic, it at least recognized that the school was located in a predominantly agricultural area. Black Mountain's Rice declared loftily, on the other hand, that "untoiling poets may sing of the dignity of toil, [but] others know there is degradation in obligatory sweat."[223]

As for local tastes and traditions, Albers's wife Anni, who was a weaver, found local weaving uninteresting because it "simply reproduced set patterns from the past." Her romantic approach emphasized individual creativity and innovation.

Local people, for their part, reciprocated the unconcern and neglect. Few local students ever attended the college, and there were the usual rumors about godlessness, nudity, "free love," and other "goings on" among faculty and students.

One might argue about the larger cultural or intellectual significance of artistic collaboration between John Cage and Merce Cunningham at Black Mountain, but its *local* significance can easily be assessed. It was nil.

At the opposite end of the scale was Commonwealth College. Born in Louisiana's Newllano Cooperative Colony in 1923, the college found its permanent home in agricultural Polk County, Arkansas in 1925. "We wanted," recalled a former student and teacher many years later, "a free marketplace of ideas for sons and daughters of workers."[224]

Commonwealth's first leader was former University of Illinois labor and economics professor William Zeuch, who sought no particularly close alliances with the labor movement or other social-change organizations. Following Zeuch's departure in 1930, however, the school—by then made up of working-class students, disaffected upper-middle-class intellectuals and professionals, social activists of various political persuasions, and radical teachers and writers—forged a close link with many southern and national groups such as labor unions, radical student and political alliances, cooperatives, agricultural reform organizations such as the Southern Tenant Farmers Union (STFU), the American Civil Liberties Union, the League against War and Facism, and others.

As a result of such connections, Commonwealth became for a short while an important center for social reform thought and movements in the South. It paid a price for that progressivism, however, after a trumped-up charge of sedition was brought against it by the state in 1940. The school's 360 acres and 22 buildings were auctioned off at a sheriff's sale for $4,610. Its large labor library brought $360 and was never seen again. Its records were impounded in the Polk County courthouse and disappeared several years later.

Some aspects of Commonwealth's history and local situation could have justified setting up a folk school not unlike Campbell's: Polk was a rural, agricultural county (on the Arkansas-Oklahoma border 125 miles from the nearest sizable town) inhabited mostly by a poor, culturally homogeneous population which could have benefited from cooperatives and other self-help enterprises, presumably including cultural "support" and "reinforcement." But the prior experience (and resulting politics) of Commonwealth's founders, teachers, and students led in other directions.

Paradoxically, Commonwealth—despite its serious political aspirations—apparently related in some respects to the culture of the local area better than the Campbell Folk School did. They staged talent shows, held square dances with music by a local fiddler, and visited local ballad singer

Emma Dusenberry, whose ballads were committed to paper by a Commonwealth teacher before they were collected "officially" by Alan Lomax for the Library of Congress. And Ozark folklorist Vance Randolph visited the school many times and wrote an admiring account of it.[225]

Instead of filling a "folk" museum with old-timey things from an era long since mostly disappeared (Emma Dusenberry's spinning wheel, for example), Commonwealth established a "museum of social change," to be filled with such things as lynch ropes, photographs of the idle rich at Atlantic City, strike relics, and a "plush [Episcopalian] collection bag with gilt pole" promised by H. L. Mencken.[226] Instead of the Victorian Christmas play produced at the folk school each year, playwright Lee Hays (a later organizer of the politically radical Almanac Singers) formed the Commonwealth Players to produce labor-oriented plays such as *One Bread, One Body* (1937). Meanwhile, Campbell Folk School students were writing and producing short "folk" plays. *Get Up and Bar the Door* (1935) was set in a one-room mountain cabin and featured Sal and Hickory Perkins ("By cracky, Sal, we had better roll the punkins under the bed, for they'll shore freeze in the hen-roost afore mornin'").[227]

It is also true, however, as Denisoff points out in his study of folk music and the American left, that some Commonwealth students and teachers tried as hard to get local people to learn and sing the more doctrinaire labor songs of the period (including the "Internationale") as Campbell did to teach North Carolina mountaineers "Anders Was a Lively Lad." Indeed the contrast between Commonwealth's dramatic demise at a politically inspired sheriff's sale and the Campbell Folk School's slow yielding to scrub cedar in the green fields should not obscure some more fundamental similarities between the two institutions. For at one level at least, the two failed for the same reason: they attempted to impose an essentially alien ideology and social program which ultimately could not be successfully integrated with local ideas, customs, mores, and institutions. In the final analysis, the hard-line Communists who came to dominate Commonwealth were no more intractable than the soft-headed (but paradoxically no less doctrinaire) Grundtvigians who ultimately held sway along little Brasstown Creek.

Gentler and less overtly radical than Commonwealth, far more locally engaged than Black Mountain (or even Commonwealth itself for that matter), and similar to the folk school in its attempt to relate to and build upon the local small-farm agricultural system was the Macedonia Cooperative Community.[228]

Macedonia arose out of the Quaker social idealism of Morris Mitchell, who had become excited by experiments in progressive education and decentralized grass-roots community building in the late 1920s and early 1930s. In 1937, Mitchell bought one thousand acres in north Georgia's rural Habersham County, an area inhabited by 93 percent native born, 94 percent white, mostly poor mountain dirt farmers. He started Macedonia with several mountain families and operated it with modest success as a cooperative community until the early 1940s.

Mitchell's pacifism and other problems (including a rumored wartime FBI investigation) led to a period of instability and decline until Macedonia found new energy and direction as a pacifist community (1948–52). With the arrival of pacifists and political activists Staughton Lynd and his wife, Macedonia was linked to the national and international radical pacifist movement.

Thus although the community was closely tied to larger currents of thought, which included a tough structural analysis of why Habersham County mountaineers were so poor, it had lost its grounding in the local community—as had the folk school, though for far different reasons. Most of the Macedonia people had either left or united with the religious Bruderhof community by 1957, and the land and buildings of the Macedonia enterprise were sold at public auction in 1958.

Comparative judgments do not entirely set aside, however, the nagging question of why Campbell made the choices she made in the place where she found herself. Partly it was temperament, of course, and socialization. The quiver in Campbell's nostrils at the "prevailing smell of stale tobacco juice" was not only a sign of her New England middle-class socialization but also a forewarning that she would be unable to see, touch, and conceive of certain things in her chosen part of the South. It turned out to be a fairly reliable sign: except for her work with cooperatives, she remained almost completely out of touch with the more vigorous movements for social change in the 1920s and 1930s.

Moreover, circumstances in the place where she chose to build her school tended to reflect and confirm her predispositions: except for the small black Texana community in Murphy, there were virtually no blacks in Cherokee and Clay counties to remind her of the racial struggles of the Piedmont and Deep South. There were no large farms, landlords, or beaten-down tenant class to urge her toward an alliance with the STFU. There were no major corporations exploiting hundreds of Gastonia millworkers or Harlan miners.

Had there been, she might have developed a more sophisticated political analysis. And her folk school might have resonated less to vibrations from a Danish bell and more to the seismic rumbles that were unsettling the domestic social and political order—rumbles which even Katherine Pettit had recorded as the virgin tulip poplars crashed down at the Forks of Troublesome at the turn of the century.

3

'This Folk Work' and the 'Holy Folk'

The White Top Folk Festival, 1931–1939

A town and a county like this should have a spring festival,
. . . not in stuffy halls but out of doors.

To the top of Walker Mountain on Sunday evening. O, that
I had been a singer there. . . . [Banks] of dark clouds rose
above Whitetop . . . in the distance.

Sherwood Anderson, *Marion* (Virginia) *Democrat*, 11 and 18 April 1929

[Our] only hope for a nation in America lies in grafting the
stock of our culture on the Anglo-Saxon root. . . . [The]
beauty of Anglo-Saxon music surpasses any other in the whole
world. . . . Here, at last, we have a basic idiom competent to
express our national psychology.

John Powell, "How America Can Develop a National Music,"
The Etude, May 1927, p. 350

BY THE LATE 1880s, the tri-state area where Virginia, North Carolina, and Tennessee meet—like much of the southern Appalachian region— was in the early stages of a transformation that would soon alter every aspect of the social, economic, and cultural life of its people. Lumber companies had discovered vast stands of virgin timber, built logging camps, and begun clear-cutting the mountainsides. A few years later textile plants and furniture factories moved in, lured by rivers that could be dammed for hydroelectric power and an abundance of workers who could be hired at low wages. The older towns, like Wytheville, Marion, Abingdon, and Bristol, were growing, and by 1905 a new planned industrial center at Kingsport was on the drawing boards.[1] The generally agricultural pattern of life that had prevailed for generations was being pushed aside by a new urban-industrial order.

Soon after the turn of the century, concern arose in some quarters over the cultural (especially musical) changes the new order would bring about, and during the next several decades (as has been noted in the preceding chapter), collectors and preservers of the supposedly imperiled traditional music of the southern mountains crisscrossed the region in large numbers. The music that the scholars and collectors attended to and valued was for the most part archaic—usually the unaccompanied ballads from the old country stalked by Wyman, Brockway, Sharp, and so many others. To savor such music was not only respectable; it was an esoteric activity valued highly by an intellectual elite.

But academic folklorists and private scholars were not alone in their zeal. In the mid-1920s scouts for commercial recording companies also uncovered a storehouse of exciting traditional musicians, whom they recorded, packaged to fit a surprisingly salable "hillbilly" image, and marketed nationwide: Al Hopkins and his Hillbillies, the Carter family, Dock Boggs, G. B. Grayson, Henry Whitter, Fields Ward, Ernest "Pop" Stoneman, Frank Blevins, and Jack Reedy from southwest Virginia; an entire constellation of musicians from around Galax, Virginia; and countless others.[2]

In the late 1920s and early 1930s, OKeh, Vocalion, Victor, and Brunswick were decking their fiddlers and string bands in ever more outrageous hayseed garb for promotional photos. Eager to expand their markets, they attempted somewhat ambivalently both to purge the music of the very archaisms valued by the scholars (they recorded almost no unaccompanied ballads, for example) and to appeal—through carefully shaped images of rusticity—to the nostalgic longings of a public caught in the midst of the rapid social transformations of the late 1920s.

It proved to be a most effective strategy. Sales of hillbilly records multi-plied dramatically by 1929, and the image the records purveyed came to be accepted by a large segment of the public as an authentic representation of southern mountain music.[3]

But not everyone was pleased. Those who considered themselves "seri-ously" interested in traditional music (that is, those collectors, academic folklorists, and composers who considered it their mission to conserve and use traditional music for "higher" purposes) perceived the growing com-mercial popularity of mountain music to be part of a grave cultural prob-lem. On the one hand, the forces of industrial (and musical) modernity were undermining the rural and agricultural base of the traditional music that such people valued; the machine had entered the folk garden, and was wreaking havoc. On the other hand, they judged, the burgeoning popular interest in southern mountain music stimulated by commercial recordings was misdirected: the offerings of Vocalion and the rest were cheap and tawdry; they were vulgarizing an ancient cultural treasure. Such an analy-sis of the cultural dynamics of the late 1920s implied that a fight had to be waged against both the sweep of modernity and the very popularity of a warped version of traditional culture.[4]

What was needed—as best one may recover the logic—was a way at once to moderate the destructive impact of modernity upon the lives of traditional musicians themselves and to correct the misleading images of their music being foisted upon a credulous public by commercial record companies and the radio barn dances which were proliferating throughout the 1920s. Introduced first in 1923 by WBAP in Fort Worth, Texas, other radio barn dances followed in quick succession: Chicago's WLS (later, Na-tional) Barn Dance in 1924, and—eventually the most popular of all—WSM's barn dance (later, the Grand Ole Opry) in 1925. By the late 1920s local and regional radio stations throughout the Southeast—such as Ashe-ville's WWNC and Atlanta's WSB—were regularly broadcasting "hillbilly" music to growing audiences.[5]

Something had to be done, obviously, if "pure" tradition was not to be swept aside. Traditional musicians needed to be reinforced in their pre-sumed struggle to hold on to their culture in the face of both the pressures of modernization and the blandishments of radio and recording com-panies. At the same time, a mechanism had to be constructed to bridge the gap between the esoteric concerns of the scholar-collector and the more popular concerns of the public arena in which both taste and conceptions of traditional culture were formed and nurtured. Obviously, conventional academic collecting, archiving, and publication were unequal to the task.

The means chosen by several lay advocates of traditional music on the eve of the Depression was the "folk festival," which seemed to offer advantages that books and scholarly archives did not. Scholars had collected tunes from the most traditional ballad singers and banjo pickers in the isolated privacy of their homes, and had filed them away in academic archives. At most, a book might eventually be published for a coterie of cognoscenti. But the singers and pickers themselves were unlikely to have their spirits bolstered by reading the reviews, and no throngs came to their doors to tell them that they and their culture were valued. Meanwhile, their potential audience was huddled around the Victrola listening to Vernon Dalhart's citified rendition of "The Wreck of Old 97," or assembled in a neighbor's parlor on Saturday night to hear Dr. Humphrey Bate and the Possum Hunters over WSM's Grand Ole Opry.

A public festival, on the other hand, would bring the performers out of their isolated surroundings and place them before an appreciative audience. That approval would heighten the performers' sense of self-worth and pride in their imperiled culture. Confronted by the beauty and authenticity of the "real thing," the audience would be moved to forsake vulgar commercial imitations. If such an event were repeated enough times, the public would be reeducated and its taste refined and elevated.[6]

Apparently upon the basis of approximately this sort of reasoning, four large festivals of traditional music were inaugurated in the half-dozen years between 1928 and 1934, and quickly claimed national attention: Bascom Lamar Lunsford's Mountain Dance and Folk Festival in Asheville, North Carolina (1928), Jean Thomas's American Folk Song Festival in Ashland, Kentucky (1930), Annabel Morris Buchanan's White Top Folk Festival in southwest Virginia (1931), and Sarah Gertrude Knott's National Folk Festival (1934).[7]

Although the shortest lived of the four, the White Top Folk Festival (1931–39) was in some ways the most interesting. From its somewhat tentative beginning in 1931, through 1933 when Eleanor Roosevelt's visit helped draw upwards of twenty thousand people and a host of newspaper reporters and newsreel cameramen to the mountaintop, to its demise when the 1940 festival was canceled because of heavy rains and flooding, a variety of personal, social, cultural, and political circumstances combined to produce a drama of surpassing complexity. To comprehend that drama— even in outline—is to gain insight into major aspects of traditional culture in the southern mountains: the relationship between elite and traditional music and musicians; the impact of modernity upon traditional culture; the dynamics of interaction between traditional musicians and academics and intellectuals embarked upon a cultural mission; the intersection of racial and cultural politics in the 1930s; and the projection of images of traditional culture and their reception by mainstream audiences. Partly because its origin, growth, and demise were packed into less than a decade, the White Top festival offers a conveniently concentrated example of the origins, assumptions, processes, and results of systematic cultural intervention.

A Festival on the Mountaintop

Local legend has it that the Indians held White Top sacred. Too perfect to be lived upon, it was dedicated to the Great Spirit. Lying at more than fifty-five hundred feet above sea level, its summit was covered with snow or frost much of the year, and signal fires lighted there could be seen for fifty miles. An Indian story told how the hair of an Indian goddess whose lover was killed in battle turned white with grief, and how after that the Great Spirit sent the snow each year as a permanent bridal veil.[8]

Many Indian tribes used the mountain in peace for generations as a common hunting ground, but when the white men came and began drawing their jealous territorial lines upon maps, it merely helped define the corner of Smyth, Washington, and Grayson counties in the Commonwealth of Virginia.

For a variety of historical reasons (the absence of coal, for example, and the traumatic social dislocations its exploitation brought to the mountains seventy-five miles further west), these counties and a few nearby soon became some of the richest culturally in the southern Appalachian region. By the turn of the twentieth century, when modernity had already brought mass culture to much of the rest of the country, the hills and valleys of southwest Virginia were still alive with ballad singers, fiddlers, banjo pickers, and dancers. They were in evidence at every level from the fireside to local community gatherings to—after 1923—the commercial phonograph recordings that found an unexpectedly wide market.

As early as 1924, only a year after the first "hillbilly" commercial recording went on sale, Galax native Ernest Stoneman journeyed to New York to record his first sides for OKeh. Nearby Mountain City, Tennessee, was the site of a large and well-publicized fiddlers' convention the next year, and in 1926 Grayson County's own Fields Ward (b. 1911) recorded eight sides for OKeh in Winston-Salem.[9] Slightly to the west of White Top were the coalfields homes of banjo player Dock Boggs, who began to record for Brunswick in 1927, and the Carter family, discovered by Victor Talking Machine Company scout Ralph Peer the same year. North Carolina's bordering Ashe and Alleghany counties were also strongholds of mountain music.

Indeed, if one had looked for the "center of gravity" of southern mountain music in the late 1920s, one might well have located it on the lofty meadows of White Top. And although the mountain had been in private ownership for all of its recent history, until the end of the 1920s it was nevertheless used freely by local people, who climbed its slopes by foot, horseback, or wagon to picnic, hike, and play music together in the summertime.[10]

Early in 1931, U. V. (Ike) Sturgill of nearby Konnarock approached Abingdon attorney John A. Blakemore (a principal of the White Top Company, which owned most of the mountain) to ask if a fiddlers' contest might be held on White Top on July Fourth.[11] Blakemore mentioned the idea to his cousin John P. Buchanan, whose wife, Annabel Morris Buchanan, had long been interested in traditional music.

As early as 1923, Mrs. Buchanan had prepared a "Costume Recital of Folk Music" and a program of "American Folk Music" for Marion, Virginia's Monday Afternoon Music Club (which she had organized). The programs included club members (and their costumed daughters) performing "Indian dances" and Virginia reels, Negro spirituals, and ballads from the southern mountains accompanied by dulcimer. On one of the programs, Mrs. Buchanan played American composer David Guion's piano transcription of "Turkey in the Straw" while Mrs. Charles Jennings clog danced.[12]

In the late 1920s, Mrs. Buchanan became acquainted with Richmond composer-pianist John Powell, who had long used traditional musical materials in his classical compositions, and North Carolina composer Lamar Stringfield, whose suite "From the Southern Mountains" had won the Pulitzer Prize for music in 1928.

Mrs. Buchanan liked Sturgill's idea, discussed it with Powell (with whom she had already presented traditional musicians at the Virginia Choral Festival in Charlottesville), and began to lay plans for a musical event on the mountain.[13] "It seems that they want to make it . . . a contest of old fashion music, folk music, I believe they call it," Blakemore wrote to one correspondent.[14]

Since the weather on the mountain was frequently bad in July, Saturday, 15 August was selected instead of July Fourth. Quite early in his promotional efforts, Blakemore—who took charge of the business aspects of the event—began to think in more than purely local terms. The festival was advertised as the Interstate [Virginia, Tennessee, North Carolina] Folk Music Festival, and ten thousand flyers were printed for distribution locally, through Southwest Virginia, Inc. (the regional Chamber of Commerce), and by Norfolk and Western Railroad station agents. Blakemore also sent notices to local and regional newspapers and to press wire services.[15]

The flyers announced that the festival would commence at 10:00 A.M., and prizes were offered in harmonica playing ($2.50), dulcimer ($5.00), singing ($5.00), fiddling ($10.00), banjo playing ($10.00), "group" ($10.00), clog dancing ($5.00), and "highland fling" ($5.00). "Only old-time music considered in contests," entrants were cautioned, "No modern songs, tunes, or dances."

It is not clear what models, if any, Mrs. Buchanan had in mind for the festival. The fiddlers' contest idea was implicit from the beginning, of course. John A. Burrison has established that there were fiddlers' conventions in Atlanta as early as 1899 and that an annual one was established in 1913. Bill C. Malone says fiddlers' contests "have been held in the South at least since the 1740s." Mrs. Buchanan was apparently unaware of Lunsford's Mountain Dance and Folk Festival, held annually in Asheville since 1928, or of Jean Thomas's American Folk Song Festival, founded a year earlier than White Top. In July 1931 she mentioned having talked with John Murray Gibbon, "who gets up the wonderful Canadian folk festivals." Gibbon's festivals, held at Winnipeg, Regina, Banff, Calgary, Vancouver, and Toronto in the 1920s, were designed to help assimilate Canada's many immigrant groups, promote interracial and interethnic harmony, and demonstrate the cultural riches of a multicultural nation.[16]

Local musicians (and some not so local) responded to the White Top announcements in considerable numbers. Oscar Osborne wrote from Mouth of Wilson, "We Osborne brothers wish to enter. . . . We play violin, banjo, guitar, and harmonica." R. W. Gose of Castlewood, Virginia, registered as a fiddler and square-dance caller; R. E. Jones of Warrensville, North Carolina, entered as a harmonica player; Harve G. Sheets and his daughter Josie of Konnarock wanted to compete as clog dancers. From Fountain City, Tennessee, Lee Irwin registered as an old-time fiddler. From Jonesboro, Tennessee, J. W. Milhorn [?] wrote: "Deair friend i saw your ad in the paper where you all was going to have a big music Festival So we have a band of 4 would like to bee with you all if so you can raing [arrange?] the matter that if we dident win you will pay our gas faire But

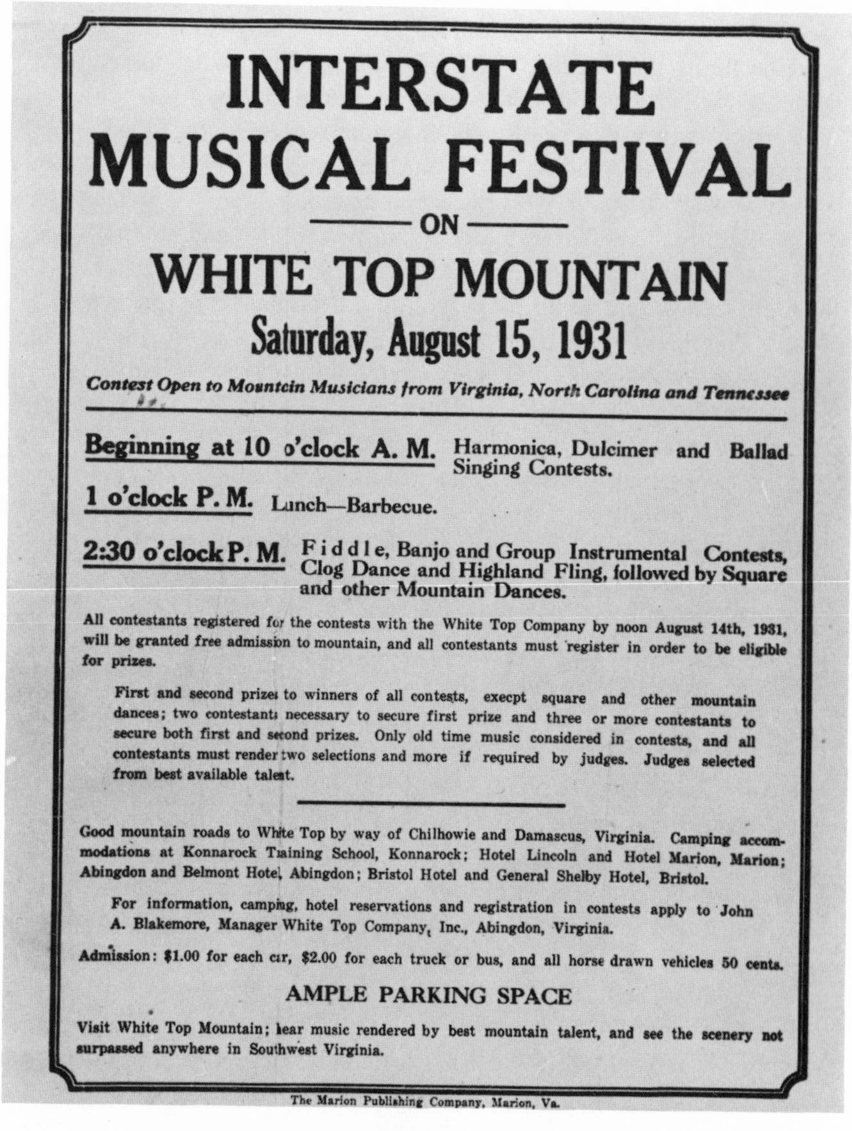

INTERSTATE MUSICAL FESTIVAL

— ON —

WHITE TOP MOUNTAIN
Saturday, August 15, 1931

Contest Open to Mountain Musicians from Virginia, North Carolina and Tennessee

Beginning at 10 o'clock A. M. Harmonica, Dulcimer and Ballad Singing Contests.

1 o'clock P. M. Lunch—Barbecue.

2:30 o'clock P. M. F i d d l e, Banjo and Group Instrumental Contests, Clog Dance and Highland Fling, followed by Square and other Mountain Dances.

All contestants registered for the contests with the White Top Company by noon August 14th, 1931, will be granted free admission to mountain, and all contestants must register in order to be eligible for prizes.

First and second prizes to winners of all contests, execpt square and other mountain dances; two contestants necessary to secure first prize and three or more contestants to secure both first and second prizes. Only old time music considered in contests, and all contestants must render two selections and more if required by judges. Judges selected from best available talent.

Good mountain roads to White Top by way of Chilhowie and Damascus, Virginia. Camping accommodations at Konnarock Training School, Konnarock; Hotel Lincoln and Hotel Marion, Marion; Abingdon and Belmont Hotel, Abingdon; Bristol Hotel and General Shelby Hotel, Bristol.

For information, camping, hotel reservations and registration in contests apply to John A. Blakemore, Manager White Top Company, Inc., Abingdon, Virginia.

Admission: $1.00 for each car, $2.00 for each truck or bus, and all horse drawn vehicles 50 cents.

AMPLE PARKING SPACE

Visit White Top Mountain; hear music rendered by best mountain talent, and see the scenery not surpassed anywhere in Southwest Virginia.

The Marion Publishing Company, Marion, Va.

FIGURE 3-1
*Advertising poster for first White Top Folk Festival, 1931
(Appalachian Collection, Appalachian State University).*

we will try our Best to Win for you rite me as soon as you get this and tell me How far from Abingdon." [17] Although Mrs. Buchanan had reservations about string bands ("I'm not so keen on group playing," she wrote to Blakemore and Powell), nearly a dozen groups registered: the "Dixie Serenaders" from East Radford, the "White Top Jiggers," a group led by Jake Rosenbaum of Bristol ("We will name our group later," he wrote), the "Moonlight Ramblers" from Lansing, North Carolina, and others. [18]

As the date approached, Mrs. Buchanan confided to Powell that the festival "has grown out of all proportion to our original conception of it." And to Powell's wife she wrote that Blakemore "thought at first of having only an old fiddlers' contest for a few around this locality . . . and I wished all this on him." [19]

Even by contemporary standards, however, the first White Top festival was not elaborate; some fiddlers' contests were as large or larger. Blakemore rented a forty-by-sixty-foot tent from Knoxville for forty dollars, built a simple platform and some rough benches for spectators, and arranged for a barbecue lunch to be served by some local ladies from Konnarock. About a hundred contestants registered, and their competition was witnessed by about three thousand spectators. Expenses and receipts ran to between four and five hundred dollars. [20]

Of the three dozen or so groups and individuals who competed, about three-fifths were from nearby Virginia counties and towns. A few came from east Tennessee, fewer from North Carolina, and one from West Virginia. Judges (in addition to Stringfield, Powell, and Buchanan) were George Pullen Jackson, an authority on white spirituals from Vanderbilt University, and Arthur Knecht, director of the Cincinnati Symphony. In the competition there were eight fiddlers, a half-dozen banjo and guitar players, seven clog dancers, six string bands, four ballad singers, two harmonica players, and one or two dulcimer players. [21]

Lamar Stringfield presented prizes to the winners—many of whom were to become part of a regular "stable" of White Top performers in years to come: Frank Blevins and O. C. Roark tied for first in fiddle; C. B. Wohlford was judged best on banjo; John Cruise of Damascus took the ballad prize; Harve Sheets was the champion clog dancer; R. E. Jones was the best harmonica player; "the Peakes" of Bristol were named best in the group category; and Francis N. Atkins of Marion won the dulcimer competition.

Thus in one sense the first White Top festival had fulfilled its organizers' intentions: it had attracted local musicians and a large and appreciative audience and had rewarded the musicians for holding to tradition rather than being swept along (and away) by popular musical fads. But already there were hints of irony and manipulation, which were to grow in later years.

The prize that Atkins won for his dulcimer playing is a case in point. As has already been noted in the discussion of Hindman Settlement School, the status of the dulcimer in traditional music is not at all clear. Nearly fifty years after the winner's ribbon was pinned to his coat on White Top, Francis Atkins recalled that there had been no traditional music in his family at all and that he had never heard of or seen a dulcimer until his uncle bought one from a family in Roanoke. He himself had started to play in the mid-1920s, and, while a student at Emory and Henry College in 1929–30, had put on an early-morning radio program using the dulcimer. But since his main musical experience beforehand had been playing in a marching band in Marion, Virginia (the one pictured in Sherwood Anderson's *Hello Towns* of 1929), he was playing strictly popular tunes on the dulcimer. Persuaded by Buchanan (who was choir director at his church) to play at the festival, he had to be coached to play the kind of tunes they wanted.[22]

The 1932 White Top festival was a slightly expanded replay of the first festival. "Times are very hard and money is scarce with us, but we wish to attend the festival," one contestant wrote to Blakemore. A slightly larger tent was rented, modest handicraft exhibits were added ("Those New York and Richmond people . . . will snap up mountain handicraft if it is any good, you know," Mrs. Buchanan told Blakemore), and the event extended to two days (12–13 August).[23] An informal program and square dance were held on Friday evening, preliminary contests on Saturday morning, final contests in the afternoon, followed by a program by the winners, and a dance in the evening. An audience of nearly four thousand listened to more than seventy-five individuals and groups perform.

"It's about to swallow us, isn't it?" Buchanan confided to Blakemore after it was over. But two weeks later she wrote ecstatically to Powell, "Oh, it gets me thrilled, every time I think of it. And I wake up in the night, happy and thrilled again . . . at being a part of this folk work. O, Mr. Powell, don't you feel that we are pioneers in something that may be really making American musical history?"[24]

Coincidentally, developments on the national political scene caused the 1933 festival to grow beyond even Mrs. Buchanan's wildest nocturnal imaginings. In November 1932, Franklin D. Roosevelt was elected president. His wife's interest in working people, minorities, and the dispossessed was already well known, and as early as March 1933 she wrote to Mrs. Buchanan that she would like to attend the White Top festival.[25]

FIGURE 3-2
Group of fiddle contestants
(Virginia State Chamber of Commerce and Southern Historical Collection,
University of North Carolina at Chapel Hill).

News that Mrs. Roosevelt might attend galvanized the White Top festival planners. Blakemore widened roads and had an architect design a rustic festival pavilion. The Lester brothers of nearby Glade Spring cut the shingles, erected the building, and fitted the chestnut siding. Local mason Abram Stamper built a massive stone fireplace.[26] As word of the impending royal visit reached the newspapers, Blakemore was besieged with propositions from commercial promoters and entertainers. During early July alone he declined offers from a merry-go-round operator, a seller of "music playing cards," an acrobat, a team of parachutists, and a hot-air balloonist.

They met her at the railroad station in Abingdon, and she motored to White Top through throngs of local folks who lined the highways to see the president's lady who had come to see them and hear their music. On the mountain (where estimates of the crowd swelled by her presence ranged from twelve thousand to twenty thousand) she was provided with a cottage and two black cooks. At a special musical program she heard six-year-old Muriel Dockery play the mandolin and octogenarian S. F. Russell play "Waterbound" on the dulcimer. Jack Reedy and C. B. Wohlford played "Cluck Old Hen" and "Jenny Put the Kettle On" on their banjos;

Horton Barker sang "The Farmer's Curst Wife," and Texas Gladden and Nancy Baldwin sang "Three Little Babes" and "Pretty Saro." Mountain people presented Mrs. Roosevelt a handwoven bedspread and canes carved from local dogwood and maple; mountain musicians posed with her for pictures on the pavilion steps. An evening tale-telling session was led by dramatist Percy MacKaye. "While the dry beech logs were crackling in the great fireplace on the stage," George Pullen Jackson reported, "Mr. MacKaye told his story of The Hickory Picktooth. Other 'whoppers' followed, stories told by the mountain people in their quaint, direct, and picturesque English."[27]

Commenting on Mrs. Roosevelt's visit a few months later, Powell said that "a lovely dignity was lent to the . . . festival by the presence of the First Lady of the Land."[28] But the visit was a more complex event than Powell's elegant and innocuous language could convey. When Powell went on to note that Mrs. Roosevelt came "not as a stranger, but as one who had been known and loved in the White Top region since the days when her father lived there," he hinted at historical connections between her family and southwest Virginia that made her presence at White Top somewhat ironic.

Mrs. Roosevelt's father, Elliott (a brother of Teddy Roosevelt), had spent about two years in southwest Virginia before the turn of the century (1892–94). Although he went there ostensibly to calm his nerves and regain his health, he accepted his brother-in-law Douglas Robinson's offer of a job helping to oversee the extensive land holdings of the Douglas Land Company, one of many companies responsible for altering the social, economic, and cultural organization of the area.

Incorporated in 1890, the company was authorized to purchase up to 250,000 acres of land in Smyth, Washington, and Grayson counties, to manufacture "articles of any kind" and "lumber in any shape;" to erect blast furnaces, forges, and mills; to keep inns, stores, hotels, and shops; and to mine ore and build railroads. Its home offices were in New York.[29]

Elliott Roosevelt apparently had responded ambivalently to southwest Virginia. On the one hand, he loved the landscape and local people. Long after his death in 1894, stories lingered of his giving five-dollar bills to farm boys who opened gates for him, distributing hundreds of turkeys to families at Christmas, attending local dances, staying all night in the homes of mountain people, and helping to finance and build St. Paul's Episcopal Church in Damascus.[30] To daughter Eleanor he wrote of listening delightedly to the children of the local Trigg family (his black ser-

FIGURE 3-3
White Top Folk Festival grounds, mid-1930s
(Virginia State Chamber of Commerce and Southern Historical Collection,
University of North Carolina at Chapel Hill).

vants), who "have made a practice of coming outside my door with a quartette . . . (in which I have taken much interest) and singing the sweetest, softest, old-time songs to me—those . . . my Mother used to sing."[31]

On the other hand, Roosevelt was an agent of those forces that were altering southwest Virginia forever—in a way that dozens of White Top festivals forty years later could never stay or turn back. Besides working for his brother-in-law's land company, Roosevelt helped supervise the development of Coeburn, Virginia (a coalfield town), and became a major stockholder in an Abingdon bank. It was therefore as if the Trigg children sang their own requiem to an audience composed solely of the most proximate agent of their own demise, who heard the melody as "the sweetest, softest old-time song."

Thus from our historical perspective Elliott Roosevelt's sojourn in southwest Virginia lends at least an ironic cast to his daughter's return forty years later to honor traditional culture on White Top, and suggests some of the limits of direct efforts to "preserve" traditional culture in the face of induced structural change in an entire social and economic order.

Both Powell and Buchanan expressed confidence, nevertheless, in the usefulness of the festival to help achieve that and several other cultural desiderata. During a course of lectures on "the origin, structure, modality, and recording of English-American folk tunes and their place in American

FIGURE 3-4
Black cooks employed for Mrs. Roosevelt's visit, 1933
(Southern Historical Collection, University of North Carolina
at Chapel Hill).

FIGURE 3-5
*Festival musicians posing with Mrs. Roosevelt: Frank Blevins (fiddle), Jack
Reedy (banjo), Ed Blevins (guitar), Muriel Dockery (mandolin)*
(Norfolk and Western Magazine *and Southern Historical Collection,
University of North Carolina at Chapel Hill*).

composition," presented to about three dozen folklorists, composers, and others prior to the festival, Powell stressed "the wholesome influence exerted by the festival appearances on the mountain people themselves, giving them, along with greater confidence in the worthwhileness of their culture, an added self-respect and dignity." Buchanan spoke of collecting and preserving the artistic traditions of the area so that they would both "become available in the realm of creative art" and "enrich the esthetic life of those who experience [them]." George Pullen Jackson wrote effusively of "a musical tradition which goes back beyond Sumer Is Icumen In and disappears in the cultural mists of the Angles, Saxons, and Celts." In Jackson's judgment, "it was one of the revelations of the festival that this 'keeping alive' of the old arts was no artificial process . . . no blood transfusion." [32]

But Buchanan had moments of uncertainty. Even though the crowds had grown larger, the list of participants longer, and the program more elaborate, she wrote to Powell three months before the 1933 event, "[For] two cents I'd throw up the whole thing. . . . I believe we are doing more harm than good."[33]

And to Bruce Crawford, radical editor of *Crawford's Weekly* in Norton, Virginia, the festival seemed something of an anachronistic fantasy. Crawford's newspaper reported regularly on life in the conflicted Virginia and Kentucky coalfields a few miles to the west of White Top. He had recently worked with Theodore Dreiser, John Dos Passos, and other writers who held hearings on terrorism in the coalfields, and had been attacked and shot by "gun thugs." Watching "fantastic hillbillies with fiddles under their arms" perform in the "immense pavilion constructed of freshly sawed timbers," Crawford was thus poignantly aware that "modernity has all but engulfed these musicians of the hills. . . . The new generation sings more of the 'Tin Henry' and less of 'The Flop-eared Mule.'" The present generation, he said, though cut off from tradition by moves to coal camps and mill towns, was nevertheless making its own songs. "Textile workers have songs to express sorrow and revolt. Coal miners are beginning to sing 'blues' of their own making."[34]

The festival was nevertheless rather firmly established, and there was apparently little serious thought of not continuing it. The fourth festival was held 17–18 August 1934.[35] Although heavy rains hampered the performances, many of the regular performers were there (S. F. Russell, a group of sacred singers brought from Galax by W. E. Alderman, Sailor Dad Hunt, fiddler Howard Wyatt, banjo player C. B. Wohlford, clog dancer Harve Sheets, and ballad singer Horton Barker). George Pullen Jackson reported that instead of the one or two reluctant ballad singers of the first year, there were twenty-two.

The increasing number of ballad singers was part of a growing body of evidence that the White Top organizers were urging local musicians in directions which they considered desirable, but which were not necessarily in accord with the musicians' own wishes. Some of the twenty string bands in 1934 were "quickly eliminated," Jackson reported, "by reason of their evident leaning toward what radio listeners now know as 'hill-billy' music, in which the folk tradition is caricatured."[36]

At a conference held during the festival, the numerous folklorists, composers, and other notables who attended (Buchanan, Powell, R. W. Gordon, Mellinger Henry, Jackson, and others) agreed that the festival was having a most salutary effect upon "folk tradition" and helping to offset the impact of popular culture and commercial derivatives of folk culture. "In the crowd of performers," the *New York Times* reported, "were many

FIGURE 3-6
Sailor Dad Hunt
(Virginia State Chamber of Commerce and Southern Historical Collection,
University of North Carolina at Chapel Hill).

with snow-white hair and long beards who pointed with pride to the fact that their folk music is still alive." [37] Powell became rather lyrical—almost mystical—as he described what he conceived to be the festival's immediate effect upon those who attended:

> The gathering seems wholly spontaneous, as indeed it may be said to be. For two days music and dancing take possession of the great mountain. Every visitor becomes instantly part of all that goes on, and his own traditional heritage pours into the general stream. . . . Thoughts fly back to Pioneer days, to sailing ships bearing immigrants from England to the New World, to Elizabethan merrymaking, to Chaucer and the Canterbury pilgrims, and at times to a remote period which the mind of the race has long ago forgotten, but which persists in a creeping thrill up and down the spine. . . . Through the music . . . we are put into contact with our own lives in a mysterious and electrifying fashion. . . . There is a sense that we are a folk and that in that fact lies some of the secret of the Golden Age. [38]

In such convictions, and in more temperate versions of them held by others among the White Top coterie, lay most of the momentum that was to carry the festival to the end of the decade, despite the momentary doubts of its director.

Several aspects of the 1935 festival adumbrated tendencies, however, that were eventually to transform the event rather substantially. The contestants for the first festival in 1931 had come on their own—sending their names to John Blakemore on postcards or scraps of paper torn from their children's school tablets. But as the producers invested more money, energy, and time, and as the event grew larger, Buchanan and Blakemore came to feel that the presence of certain star performers was essential. Thus fiddler Jess Johnson of Wolf Pen, West Virginia, was offered a payment of about twenty-five dollars to appear in 1935, and "special prizes" were made available to Sailor Dad Hunt, dulcimer player S. F. Russell, banjo player C. B. Wohlford, George Pullen Jackson's Old Harp singers, and Bob Mast's dancers. [39] More and more notables from around the nation were attending (academic folklorists such as John Lomax and Arthur Palmer Hudson; WLS radio personality John Lair; music critics from prestigious magazines and newspapers; heads of such national organizations as the American Folklore Society and the American Folk Dance Society); the local, regional, and national press was carrying regular stories on the fes-

FIGURE 3-7
George Pullen Jackson's Old Harp Singers
(Southern Historical Collection, University of North Carolina
at Chapel Hill).

tival; and Blakemore was trying to persuade a national radio network to broadcast the final contest.[40]

Another innovation in 1935 was a performance of sword and morris dances. Powerfully moved as he was by any possible link between mountain music and what he called "Anglo-Saxon culture," Powell had been drawn first to the dance tunes—generally considered at the time to be Elizabethan (hence, vaguely Anglo-Saxon) in origin. As such, they were of inestimable value. "Those who are not familiar with our [Virginia] dance-tune tradition," wrote Virginia violinist Winston Wilkinson, who worked closely with him on the festival, "are liable to underestimate the extremely fine quality of many of the [morris-derived] dance tunes, confusing them perhaps with the boisterous, uncouth, and unmusical concoctions called 'Mountain Music,' 'Hill-billy,' etc."[41]

The problem was that sword and morris *dances* (unlike some at least latter-day versions of the tunes) had not been in evidence in the United States for three centuries, if ever, and had certainly never been recovered from

FIGURE 3-8
*Old Virginia Band of Harrisonburg: Mark Rittenour (banjo), Bill Michael
(fiddle), Emory Stroop (guitar),
(Virginia State Chamber of Commerce and
Southern Historical Collection, University of North Carolina
at Chapel Hill).*

tradition in the southern mountains. But two circumstances combined to render them available in revival versions for the White Top festival. One was (as has already been explained) that Cecil Sharp taught them to Hindman and Pine Mountain Settlement School children before 1920, and the settlements—because of their romantic perspective on local culture—continued to develop them in an organized way. Another was that morris dance was experiencing some popularity beyond the mountains, largely through the efforts of British-born May Gadd (b. 1894), who had seen her first revival performance of morris dance in England in 1915, joined the staff of the English Folk-Dance Society in 1924, and arrived in the United States in 1925 to help establish an American branch of the society.[42]

Thus it became possible in 1935 for wooden-sword-wielding Kentucky coalfields children from Pine Mountain Settlement School to dress in bells, flowers, and ribbons and dance for White Top audiences dances that had been extinct even in England since before the turn of the century. Powell was delighted, and a few months later Mrs. Buchanan told Blake-

more that "many persons (including myself) considered the Pine Mountain dancers the best thing on the program."[43] But Paul Rosenfeld, who
witnessed a similar performance at White Top several years later (and who
was by all odds the most sophisticated critic ever to comment publicly on
the festival), was more moved by the fiddling of West Virginia's "Fiddling
Fool," Jess Johnson. "A bunch of lads advanced and started a morris-
dance," he reported. "Skillfully enough they wound their bodies beneath
wooden swords held chain-wise between them and with the aid of the in-
dispensable hobby-horse enacted a little fertility-rite. The whole was a
piece of archaism—an emissary of the Richmond English Folk-Dance Society had coached the group."[44]

The emissary appears to have been Richard Chase, one of the more au-
dacious of the folk-revival entrepreneurs of the 1930s.[45] Chase (1904–), the
son of a nurseryman of New England extraction who established his business in Huntsville, Alabama, had apparently lacked direction in his life
until he stumbled upon the burgeoning folk movement of the early 1920s.
He had attended a private school in middle Tennessee, studied at Vanderbilt University for a year and at Harvard for a year, worked in his father's
nursery a year, returned to Harvard for a short spell, and then worked a
few weeks as a probation officer for a juvenile court in Boston. At a tea at
Harvard's Longfellow House he heard of "a school in Kentucky" (Pine
Mountain) that sounded interesting. Hitchhiking there in 1924, he heard
mountain children sing ballads (as Olive Dame Campbell had in 1907 and
Cecil Sharp had a decade later), and was captivated. It was, he recalled
more than fifty years later, "something vital." Taking a job as a country
schoolteacher in Alabama, he used one of Sharp's books to teach ballads to
his students. A short while later, he learned his first morris dances (from
Sharp's associate Charles Rabold) at a private school in Connecticut.[46]

Chase subsequently returned to college long enough to get a degree
from Antioch College and taught for a while at New York's progressive
Manumet School. But the "vital" cultural lode of the southern mountains
soon claimed his full attention, and he was to spend the rest of his life as a
professional folk entrepreneur. Shortly after 1930, he met John Powell,
and was soon able to attach himself to the White Top festival. In 1936 he
became associate director.[47] Just prior to the 1939 festival that Paul Rosenfeld found so perplexing, a Richmond newspaper reported that Chase was
training Richmond dancers for White Top, and quoted Powell as saying
that "children trained by [Chase] will . . . show the audiences how the
children of 'Merrie England' some 500 years ago played and danced on the
village green."[48]

FIGURE 3-9
*Pine Mountain Settlement School sword-dance team at White Top Folk
Festival, 1935
(Virginia State Library and Blue Ridge Institute,
Ferrum College).*

In early 1939, Chase posed and answered the rhetorical question "How can we keep these [dance] traditions alive?" by suggesting that White Top was "the one festival in America that sets forth in its integrity the musical culture of our people." But any "general restoration" of the dances, he cautioned, "will require skillful social engineering." Despite his own audacity as an engineer, Chase nevertheless maintained that the dances "must always come from an inherent social situation."[49]

An additional feature that Chase urged upon the festival was folk drama, a form which flourished in academic centers from World War I onward, but which had no recognizable counterpart in the traditional culture of the southern mountains. Although his initial urgings in 1934 were resisted, in later years there were some excursions into folk drama at White Top. The Carolina Playmakers' Lula Vollmer (1898–1955) presented one of her own plays, and there were several performances by actors from the Barter Theater in Abingdon. Folk drama nevertheless remained a subordinate aspect of the festival.[50]

There was some question about whether the White Top festival would be continued after the "morris dance year" of 1935. Her marriage disintegrating, and complaining that work on the festival was too exhausting, Mrs. Buchanan moved to Richmond to work for the Federal Music Project (being directed in Virginia by Powell). Blakemore leased the mountain to an associate, fretted about financial losses on the festival, and insisted that if it were done again the budget would have to be very spare. At length he agreed to go ahead ("it looks like we can have a Festival this year," he wrote to Buchanan in May), but continued to fear that crowds would not match those in former years.[51]

Crowds were in fact smaller (about three thousand on Friday and five thousand on Saturday), but newspapers reported more than two hundred contestants, and the festival even turned a small profit.[52]

Probably the most important feature of the 1936 festival was not the public event itself but the White Top Folk Conference held at Marion College for the ten days before the festival opened (2–13 August).[53] Since 1933, when Buchanan and Powell had arranged a small, informal conference during the festival and Powell had given a class in folk music and a recital prior to the festival's public opening, the conference had grown steadily in importance.[54] Both it and the festival itself had come to be cosponsored by the Southeastern Folklore Society, and were drawing not only major music critics and luminaries from the world of classical music but also such people as Ralph Borsodi of the School for Living; an array of officials from both the English Folksong and Dance Society and the English Folk-Dance Society of America; Carleton Smith, chief of the New York Public Library's music division; and a number of academic folklorists and collectors (Amos Abrams, Frank C. Brown, R. W. Gordon, Mellinger Henry, Arthur Palmer Hudson, George Pullen Jackson, Alton C. Morris, Reed Smith, and others).

The 1936 conference combined theoretical and tactical discussions of the White Top enterprise with concert performances by Powell; instruction in morris dancing and country dancing by Richard Chase; and a folk music course in which Powell explored the background and history of "Anglo-Saxon folk music," its "emotional and technical" qualities, and its modal characteristics. Powell's wife presented examples of drama "from ancient Robin Hood plays, mummer's plays, medieval and Elizabethan drama." Professor Abrams gave "an entertaining account" of his work with Elizabethan plays, sword dances, and mummer's plays at Appalachian State Teachers College in North Carolina. Richard Chase presented a Punch and Judy show "from ancient script in the British Museum," it was reported, with "clever additions of his own."[55] In addition to an address by the Russell Sage Foundation's Allen Eaton, conference participants heard R. W. Gordon of the Library of Congress lecture on ballads, the WPA's Ella Agnew talk about women's handicraft projects in the WPA, and Borsodi lecture on "The Economics of Home Production."[56] The Barter Theater presented an Elizabethan play, and there were recitals of folk-song interpretations by classical musicians.

Although the rhetoric of the 1936 conference was rather elevated and the festival itself appeared successful and stable, the harmonious and celebratory public image masked some conceptual and ideological problems, as well as interpersonal conflicts, that would soon prove insurmountable.

Signs of conflict were apparent to musicologist Charles Seeger (then working for the Resettlement Administration), who visited several festivals in the mountains during the summer of 1936. Although he found Bascom Lunsford's Mountain Dance and Folk Festival in Asheville a "very worthwhile affair," he stringently criticized White Top and its "well-meaning, self-advertising city cultivators of the 'folk.'" "While the small coterie who manage the affair do not entirely agree," he wrote to his superior Adrian Dornbush, "there is sufficient unanimity to warrant the general charge that they are self-contradictory to a degree and that possibly instead of furthering their aim they are destroying the possibility of its realization."

In his long letter to Dornbush, Seeger encapsulated the social, political, and cultural perspectives (as well as the logic) of the conference participants and festival organizers:

> The thesis runs as follows . . . : The folk is a holy thing. It knows what is best for itself. We city people must not try to interfere or influence it. Its music and dance and lore is finer than any "art" product of the city. It is the true, pure art. It is universal among the American people and the greatest folk art in the world. It is alive. . . . All classes in America know it. It is not mountain music; it is not rural music. Why, do you know from whom the only example of "Lord Randall" . . . ever found in this country came from? From a Virginia Tucker. How many ballads did he know? Three. Many of the people who have the best tradition know only two or three. They do not sing them for any old intruder. No. They keep them to themselves. . . . Do the majority of the populations of the large cities know the American traditional music? What? Those beasts? Why, New York, Philadelphia, Chicago—they are not America. . . . They are . . . beneath contempt. Yes, they do make up the majority of America. And worse too, they contaminate the country around them. I tell you, you have to go to the greatest lengths to find the true tradition. Here even, on White Top, we have to be very careful. That banjo player uses steel picks on his fingers. We do not even allow him to compete. That girl there was refused as an entry for the clog because she does not dance a pure clog. . . . You have to keep a tight rein on things or else you hear nothing but jazz. Yes, the dancing has not developed this year. This evening's dance, oh, there will be just one big set with simple figures—they don't practice enough to learn the complicated ones—and that alternates with jazz. . . .
>
> One looks at the audience. One paid a dollar a car to get on the mountain. The roped in auditorium would seat 1,000 at 40 cents apiece. "Holy folk" settin' [there]? Not a bit of it. The holy folk are standing around the outside of the ropes while a handful . . . of city people sit, while the contestants play to an approximately 9/10s empty house, *all day*. . . . There is some fine music. . . . But there is very little of it. The girl who won in her class learns the ballads especially for the festival. Her mother vouchsafed her daughter never sings them at home—except to practice for the festival and never sang them before the festival's first year. The father made the

[tune]. The dance orchestra makes the best—and very fine—showing. The dancing is a flop. Only one almost dumb set, taught by
Richard Chase during the two weeks preceding to the students at
the Folk Conference, even tries to dance—unofficially. . . .

Altogether a feast of paradox. . . . [Such] preposterous self-
sufficiency I have never seen at other festivals. . . .

And add to this protestation and the one about the "holiness, self-
sufficiency, and artistic supremacy" of the folk the statement (. . . by
a noted student) to the effect that (1) the folk-song is not the property of the public; (2) it is not the property of the singer, for it is
wrong to offer him money for singing it to the collector or for recording; (3) it is the absolute property of the collector . . . ; and
(4) collectors must keep off each other's preserves (that is, you must
not poach on mine), and one wonders if he is in a lunatic asylum
or what.

White Top, Seeger concluded, was "reactionary to the core." "Under a
smoke-screen of pseudo-scholarship," he said, "it is really sinister." [57]
The "feast of paradox" Seeger observed during his visit to White Top
did not arise merely from his personal point of view. The images and
phrases he relayed somewhat telegraphically to his Washington superi-
ors—the "holy folk" roped off from their own music for lack of forty
cents; city people held in cultural contempt for their sin of not living in
southwest Virginia; a banjo picker banished for using steel picks; a mother's confidential admission that her daughter learned ballads for White
Top, but never sang them otherwise; snobbish collectors guarding their
preserves jealously against folkloric claim jumpers—were both prescient
and prophetic. White Top, was in many respects a jerry-built cultural
wonderland that was bound to topple. It was indeed ridden with paradox;
principal members of its coterie (there *was* a coterie) cordially despised
one another; there were agendas layered upon conflicting agendas; respect
and reverence for the folk mingled quite indiscriminantly with contempt,
condescension, and manipulation.

So deep were the conflicts, in fact, that the festival expired after only
two additional years. There was no festival at all in 1937, for reasons that
are not entirely clear, but Mrs. Buchanan's marital difficulties, which she
had been having for several years, may have contributed substantially. She
had married John Buchanan, a lawyer from an old southwest Virginia family, in 1912. After about 1930, his drinking and other irrational behavior
are referred to with increasing frequency in her letters (and some unpub-

lished short stories she wrote under a pseudonym). As early as 1933, in a letter to Powell, she spoke of being "heartsick over family affairs in general." John Buchanan was hospitalized several times during the next few years, and the couple apparently separated about the time of the 1936 festival.[58]

Nevertheless, Buchanan wrote repeatedly to Powell and Blakemore in early 1937, trying to persuade them to do the festival again. But there were other barriers (to be discussed subsequently), and no commitment was forthcoming. To Powell she wrote early in June, "I am heartbroken at not going on this year. . . . I can't fight any more. The difficulty is to care any more. . . . [To] be a middle-aged woman and a failure is something I cannot endure. . . . The White Top work was mine to do and I have failed in that. Failed, apparently, as a wife and as a home-builder. . . . Failed in any kind of public enterprise. . . . There is no room anywhere for a failure." A few days later she wrote to Powell again, speaking of personal difficulties, fear, and "paralyzing despondency." She concluded rather dramatically that "I, Annabel Morris Buchanan, was called into this world to do a certain work. When it is done, I leave this world—not for 'a better'—for oblivion. But my work must live on, as the only immortal part of myself."[59]

Mrs. Buchanan effectively withdrew (or was pushed aside) from White Top after 1937. To support herself and her children after her husband died, she took a job in a music camp in Maine. Nevertheless, she wrote to a friend late in 1938 that she expected to "go ahead as director" of the festival in 1939. Later, in a letter to Powell, she compared their "folk work" somewhat mystically to the building of Solomon's temple. "If our work is to continue at White Top," she said, "or if I myself am to continue there, a way will be opened." And in the spring of 1939, after a meeting with Blakemore, she reported that she was "still director, and just as much interested . . . as ever." The festival was in fact managed during its final two years (1938–39), however, by Blakemore, Powell, and Chase. Blakemore wrote to Powell in June 1938 (somewhat disingenuously, it would appear) that the idea of reviving the festival came up "rather hurriedly." "I have not said anything to Annabel about it," he wrote, "and I feel that the type of festival we want to have this year would not . . . justify Annabel giving her time to it from now on."[60]

The 1938 festival drew a crowd of about three thousand to hear many of the same performers who by then had become a regular White Top "stable"—the Cruises, the Blevinses, Wohlford and Barker, Albert Hash, and others. But the program was accommodated increasingly to the concept of traditional culture held by Chase. Much of the festival was taken up with his Punch and Judy shows and children's games, a folk play by Barter Theater, and a "special program" directed by Powell. Traditional musicians and dancers, whom the festival had been founded to celebrate, were crowded increasingly into the background.

The 1939 festival, the last, was put together mostly by a Mr. McDaniel, an employee of the White Top Company. Mrs. Buchanan told Powell early in the year that she expected to continue as director and asked Blakemore for a salary of $150 plus expenses, a financial statement of the festival, and one-half of any profit for "research or furthering festival activities." Blakemore replied that McDaniel offered $100. "[It] does not make any difference to him whether you are called Director or not," he continued, but "during the Festival he does not want you to take any part other than, possibly, to assist with the judging of the events." Mrs. Buchanan replied that she was "astonished" at the letter, could not take such a "flagrant discourtesy" seriously, and was too busy to do the festival again. "If you value my regard," she said, "please do not send me such a letter again."[61]

The 1939 festival was essentially a replay of the previous year, designed along lines favored by Powell and Chase. The Barter Theater company returned, and there were two "programs" (but no competition as in years past) by local musicians. Chase was apparently the center of attention. He presented a "Young Folks' Day" on Thursday and a puppet show on both Friday and Saturday, danced a "Morris Jig and Shepherd's Hey" (to Uncle Jim Chisholm's fiddling) on the "special program" on Saturday, and presented a Kirkby sword dance by some local people that he had shaped into the "Konnarock Sword Dance Team."

Trouble on the Mountain

A White Top festival was planned for 1940, but canceled. Situated though it was high on the sacred mountaintop, the festival did not escape the heavy rains and floods that blanketed the area, and which in an earlier time might have been viewed as a divine judgment upon a confused and conflicted cultural enterprise. However appropriate such symbolism—or such a judgment—might have been, there can be no doubt of the confusion and conflict. For the demise of the festival was at one level merely the public manifestation of the deeply crossed purposes, incompatible temperaments, and conflicting programs and aims of its three principals.

For all of John Powell and Annabel Morris Buchanan's enthusiasm for traditional music and dance, John Blakemore's major aim appears to have been to make money for the White Top Company by developing the mountain commercially as a recreation and tourism center. The festival was thus a mere instrument.

Blakemore was born in Muskogee, Oklahoma, in 1894, but his family on both sides had been in southwest Virginia since the eighteenth century. Brought back to Virginia as an infant, he graduated from local Emory and Henry College in 1917, served in World War I, took a law degree at the University of Virginia in 1927, and hung out his shingle in Abingdon. He was therefore a lifelong resident of the area, but from an upper-middle-class family which had little contact with (and no real interest in) the culture of their lower-class neighbors.[62] His entrepreneurial interest in the entire area was great, however.

Blakemore's White Top Company had grown out of a complicated land ownership case initiated in the 1870s. When the case was finally settled before Judge John A. Buchanan in the 1890s, some of the lawyers took title to part of the mountain in payment for their services. With several other private owners they formed the White Top Company in 1891. Having been willed his uncle Buchanan's interest in the company and having bought out some of the other partners, Blakemore had become the principal stockholder by the late 1920s.[63]

Commercial development of the property began quite early; one member of the company built a hotel on the mountain in the early 1890s. Beginning about 1906 another member of the company (L. C. Hassinger of Konnarock) erected a large band mill to process the timber that he was cutting at the lower elevations (below forty-eight hundred feet). As early as the autumn of 1928, Blakemore built a motor road to the top of the mountain—a move the *Bristol Herald-Courier* said was expected to help restore White Top "to its former position as one of the most popular resorts in the Southern Appalachians."[64] A gate was erected, and cars were charged one dollar to drive up the mountain.

Nearly fifty years after the advent of the festival, Blakemore candidly stated that "the basic reason" he liked Ike Sturgill's initial suggestion of a fiddlers' contest on the mountaintop was that it seemed likely to stimulate commercial development.[65] In late July 1931 he wrote to the southwest Virginia regional Chamber of Commerce that a festival on the mountain "would be a great idea in advertising this section of the country." A week later he wrote to the Chamber of Commerce in Bristol that he "would be glad to have you consider White Top in routing tourists to scenic points."[66]

From his relatively important position in local Democratic party politics (he was one of the strongest leaders in the Washington County party and an influential leader in the Ninth Congressional District), Blakemore also had some success in influencing where roads were built in the area.[67] Just after the first festival he wrote to J. P. McConnell that he was "working on . . . [getting] a State highway close to the mountain." By keeping careful records of the automobiles that went up the mountain, he was able to show a 360 percent increase in traffic resulting from the festival. "Our State Department of Highways has given us assurance," he wrote to Allen Eaton in August 1932, "that in case we do any worthwhile development on the mountain they will construct a suitable highway within reach of us." The state had in fact already begun to improve the access road, and by early 1933, Blakemore was able to report to Mrs. Buchanan that "Smyth County [road] reconstruction money in the St. Clair district seems to have been largely appropriated to the road crossing Iron Mountain and up to White Top." In midsummer he wrote to the district engineer of the Department of Highways that "the road up the mountain has been wonderfully improved, and all thanks are due to you for your assistance."[68]

Quite early, Mrs. Buchanan sensed the disparity between her own intentions and Blakemore's, which were solely entrepreneurial. "[The] advertising I've been sending all over the country for the festival will put your mountain on the map as nothing else will," she told him after the second festival, "but it is not a business proposition with me. . . . I am in it for the musical value and the worth of these folk traditions."[69]

By the time the festival had run for several more years, Mrs. Buchanan had become very critical of Blakemore's commercial plans, charging that he was commercializing the festival itself, using it for private gain, refusing to make a public financial accounting or to reimburse her for her expenses, and treating the performers shabbily in order to minimize expenses.[70]

When an Altavista, Virginia, woman wrote to Blakemore prior to the 1933 festival to ask if he would give meals and a place to sleep to a ballad singer whom she was bringing to the festival at her own expense and who "has been out of work for some time and has no money at all," Blakemore refused.[71] Other letters of the same period show, however, that Blakemore was providing food and lodging rather generously to various dignitaries he felt would lend prestige to the festival. He also consistently refused to pay musicians to perform (except in a few special cases), preferring a contest format, which obligated him merely to provide a small prize (rarely more than five to ten dollars) for the winner in each category.

Perhaps the most dramatic example of Blakemore's treating musicians shabbily involved Council Cruise. Cruise was a fine musician, a generous and thoughtful person who was invaluable to the festival. Each year he performed and brought both his neighbors and other members of his large family to perform. And each year, as he wrote to Mrs. Buchanan in 1933, "the minute I leave White Top Mtn. I start working and talking the one up that will be held next year." [72] He served as an informant for several collectors (including Buchanan and Powell), traveled with White Top performers when they performed elsewhere (as they often did), and was a valuable contact person in the surrounding communities. "I call [mountain folks] my people because they are," he wrote to Buchanan in pencil on a school child's tablet. "I walk I talk I sleep I work I weep I rejoice with them." [73]

But Cruise was poor, as were many of his neighbors, and the Depression was on. He drank some, and ran a still, for which he was periodically jailed. [74] Like most of his friends, he was usually out of work because there were few jobs to be had and what few there were paid little. Mrs. Buchanan knew his problems and eccentricities, but she also valued his intelligence, creativity, knowledge of tradition, and human concern. "Council Cruise stays on my mind," she told Powell shortly after the first festival; later she added that "we [need] him more than we [need] anyone else." "My eyes are suddenly beginning to be opened by Council Cruise," she confided on another occasion, recounting his sophisticated criticism of Elizabeth Burchenal's *American Country Dance Book*. "He *knows* all these things, through generations before him." [75]

Although Blakemore apparently did intercede once on Cruise's behalf when he was in trouble with the law, he refused more tangible aid, despite Cruise's great value to the festival and his substantial contributions of time and energy to it. A few days after the 1938 festival, Cruise wrote to ask Blakemore to cosign a note for $25.00 for ninety days, so he could get medical treatment for his father, who had cancer. Cruise was then making $2.00 per day and paying seventy-five cents of that for board (netting him $7.50 for a six-day week); he offered to repay the loan at $4.00 each week. Blakemore replied as follows:

> Your letter of the 23rd was duly received. When I was just a boy I was told by my uncle never to endorse a note for anybody else, and made a promise that I would not, and have kept that promise. I would be more than glad to help you in any way that I could, but with that in view I could not endorse the note.
>
> I was indeed sorry to hear that your father has cancer, and trust that he may be able to get some relief. [76]

Mrs. Buchanan, on the other hand, was deeply concerned about how

FIGURE 3-10
Council Cruise's family
(Southern Historical Collection, University of North Carolina
at Chapel Hill).

the musicians were treated, and continually urged Blakemore to treat them better. But Blakemore's Scrooge-like stinginess—together with Powell's conviction that the musicians should contribute their time and talent for the greater cultural glory of Virginia—constituted a nearly impregnable barrier. Throughout the nine years of the festival, money for performers was nearly nonexistent, but seemed relatively plentiful to feed and house "dignitaries."

The depth of Buchanan's concern is evident in two letters she wrote to Powell in 1932 asking for expenses for White Top musicians who were to perform at the Virginia State Choral Festival. The money was necessary, she said, "not because they demand it, but because they have nothing. They are so desperately pitiful now. . . . [They] give me everything they have of their best. . . . [These] men that have families to support and nothing to do it on, and that are giving *days* of their time to help me in this folk work . . . don't you think they are partly our responsibility, Mr. Powell?" Some of the musicians had taken in others who had no jobs or money, she said, and Council Cruise had turned down a job in California to stay and help with the "folk work." We must, she insisted two days later, "keep the goodwill of these men who are literally stripping themselves to help us. You cannot expect them to understand why they should give up days and days of their time and offer their own homes and food and living and the tiny bit of money they possess to help us, when we can spend as much for one costume and ticket to the Beaux Arts Ball as they will make in a week's time."

Since most of Powell's letters have disappeared, his response is unknown, but it may perhaps be inferred from another letter Mrs. Buchanan sent him two weeks later. She reiterated the desperate facts of the musician's lives and concluded, "Don't write back to me about their duty to Virginia—what do they care about that when they are almost begging for bread for their families?"[77]

Clearly, the White Top performers were squeezed between Powell's "duty to Virginia" and Blakemore's commercial development of the mountain. Blakemore seems to have overlooked few opportunities to minimize expenses connected with the latter. "If possible," he wrote to his White Top Company associates in the late 1930s, "the White Top Festival should be revived. . . . The festival would be an excellent source of advertising. . . . [A] school could be established as a training center for all types of the old folk arts. Such a school could possibly become the means of elimination of many questions concerning taxation. . . . The value to the people would be . . . the training in the old ways of honesty and good living, and above all, the happy feeling that the citizens of this country are still decent individuals."[78]

Mrs. Buchanan understood the multilayered irony of using a folk festival (or school) as a tax shelter while supposedly teaching "honesty" to folks whose culture was being obliterated by the corporation that owned the mountain where they fiddled and danced under the full moons of August for free. "I have begged you," she wrote to Blakemore, "to heed the criticism that our festival was being commercialized. We have no right to secure the aid of the state Chamber of Commerce in publicizing an undertaking . . . for private gain; we have no right to secure exemption from federal tax for a private undertaking benefiting, so far as the public can see, no one but the owner of the mountain-top." A week later she wrote to a friend that she had "withdrawn completely" from the festival until those policies could be changed.[79]

Throughout 1938 relations worsened between Mrs. Buchanan and her co-workers. Letters from her to both Powell and Blakemore attest to her gracious and earnest, but unsuccessful, attempts to continue working with them. Early in 1939, Blakemore wrote to Powell that he had talked with Buchanan and "raised all types of reasons why she should step down . . . without directly telling her she would have to." Powell's reply urged that no "injury" be done to her, recounted her great value to the festival, and urged that a face-saving compromise be worked out. A few weeks later, however, Buchanan wrote to Blakemore that she felt her future work to lie in New England.[80]

The final break between Buchanan and the White Top Folk Festival was precipitated by long-standing differences between her approach to traditional culture and Powell's, and by her tortuous personal relationship to him. Thus some of the history of White Top is social and cultural in the usual public sense of both terms. But at least as much of it must be approached through the private psychology and personal (and interpersonal) histories of Annabel Morris Buchanan and John Powell.

Personal History and "Folk Work"

Annabel (christened Annie Bell) Morris was born in the small east Texas town of Groesbeck in 1888.[81] Her father, William Caruthers Morris, had been born in northern Alabama to a Cumberland Presbyterian minister. Although he was founder and editor of the *Groesbeck, Texas, Journal*, as a young man he had been deeply influenced by the preaching and singing at a Moody-Sankey revival meeting. He became a Cumberland Presbyterian minister about 1897.

Some of Annabel's earliest memories were "all bound up with the music and singing of [her] parents": her father and her Grandmother Foster (the Fosters were native Texans) singing hymns at home; her father's singing with various traveling evangelists; her own browsing through the stacks of old shape-note hymnals stored in her father's newspaper office; and the family singing and playing music of all kinds—folk songs, operatic arias, hymns, popular songs, and Negro spirituals. Annabel herself was musically precocious; she began playing piano by ear at seven or eight. At fifteen she won a scholarship to Landon Conservatory in Dallas, where she studied violin, voice, piano, theory, and composition, and graduated with highest honors at eighteen.

After teaching piano in Texas and Oklahoma for a few months, she

FIGURE 3-11
John Powell and Annabel Morris Buchanan
(Southern Historical Collection, University of North Carolina
at Chapel Hill).

taught at Halsell College in Oklahoma for one year (1907–8) and then for three years (1909–12) at Stonewall Jackson College in Abingdon, Virginia. (In 1901 her parents had moved to central Tennessee, where her father had accepted a pastorate in Maury County.)

Her marriage in 1912 to John Buchanan and the birth of four children removed her from full-time teaching, but she found new outlets for her creative energies. She taught privately, directed church choirs and served as organist, gave rather frequent recitals, and began composing art songs. Her first published song ("You Came into My Life," which G. Schirmer brought out in 1919) was typical of the romantic art-song esthetic in which she was to work almost exclusively for more than a decade. Subsequently published songs bore such titles as "Pansies," "Peace," and "Come" (1920), "Tonight" (1921), "Wood Song" (1925), "My Candle" (1927), "Wild Geese" (1929), and "The Lamp," "An Old Song," "A Place of Dreams," and "A May Madrigal" (1931). In addition, she was writing and publishing poems, short stories, articles on gardening, and devotional articles for church publications.

There is relatively little evidence—despite her strong memories of music in her family—that Mrs. Buchanan became seriously interested in traditional or "folk" music before the late 1920s. A letter from a New York music publisher in 1919 rejecting one of her art songs and suggesting that "the great demand nowadays is for the melodious English ballad type of song" had no discernible effect upon her compositional efforts during the next few years.[82] She included a few "interpretations" of traditional songs and dances on programs of the Monday Afternoon Music Club, which she organized in Marion in 1923, but not until after her election as president of the Virginia Federation of Music Clubs in 1927—and her meeting shortly thereafter with John Powell—did she turn seriously to traditional music.[83] A major early project of her presidency was to organize the first Virginia State Choral Festival (1928), in which she collaborated with Powell to present performances by a few traditional musicians from southwest Virginia. It was the beginning of the road that led to White Top.[84]

John Powell was the closest thing to a classical musician of international stature that Virginia had ever produced. Born in 1882 in Richmond, he was raised in a home that doubled as the two-hundred-pupil Richmond Female Seminary (1873–1903), headed by his father.[85] A musical prodigy, he began to perform at age ten. He graduated from the University of Virginia at eighteen and commenced piano study with Leschetizky in Vienna when he was twenty. His Carnegie Hall debut occurred before his thirty-first birthday, and a period of intensive composing and international touring and performing followed. He performed with the New York Symphony in 1916 and had several European tours, including a major one in 1928.

For reasons that are not completely clear, Powell displayed an early interest in traditional music. Except perhaps through his Richmond childhood friend Henry Hurt, who played guitar and banjo and sang in the choir at the Episcopal church where Powell played organ, he seems to have had no contact with traditional music in his early life, as Annabel Morris did. Instead, he affected aristocratic manners and speech patterns. He was—says his only biographer, Pocahontas Wight Edmunds—"vain of pedigree."[86]

Nevertheless, once aroused, Powell's interest in traditional music continued throughout his life. His suite for piano *In the South* (begun about 1906) employed ragtime elements in one movement, Negro melodies in another and the fiddle tune "Arkansas Traveler" in its final movement, "Pioneer Dance." A stream of compositions based on folk themes followed: *Rhapsodie Negre* (1918), *Sonata Virginianesque* for violin and piano (1919), *In Old Virginia* (1921), *Natchez on the Hill* (1932), and other related compositions up to his *Symphony in A*, which he worked on for more than fifteen years, and which built its four movements on two fiddle tunes, Cecil Sharp's English tune "A Rosebud in May," the ballad "The Seven Sleepers," and two morris dance tunes ("Fine Times at Our House" and "Cluck Old Hen").[87]

Calling Powell "one of the few distinctly regional composers of any stature that the United States has produced," American music historian Gilbert Chase suggests that he was almost alone in trying to do with southern mountain music what Arthur Farwell and many others were doing with American Indian music: build an "American" music out of native materials to counter the current hegemony of German (and other European) classical music.[88]

In some finally inscrutable and ironic way, Powell's interest in traditional music seems to have been related to his apparently somewhat precarious sense of self-worth and the elitism, aloofness, and upper-class affectations with which he attempted to bolster it. Since virtually none of his letters survive, however, one can only tentatively infer the connection from some of his published writings.[89] In a piece he wrote for *Musical Courier* a few months after the first White Top festival, Powell sketched what appears to be something of a paradigm of his cultural situation as he understood it:

> For as long as I can remember, I have been the voice of one crying in the wilderness. It began when I was a child and heard older people saying, with sad shaking of their heads, "No, we are not a musical people. Music seems to have been left out of the Anglo-Saxon temperament."
>
> Instinctively I knew that something was wrong about this. . . . I turned to my mother, who had sung to me as she held me on her knee. . . . "It is not true," I asserted, "I know it is not true!" "Alas, my son," she answered, and she, too, shook her head, "I am afraid it is true. . . . [Wise] people who know say that the test of a people's musical gift lies in their folk music. . . . And of all peoples in the world, only the Anglo-Saxons have no folk music."

The child—later the young man—protests, but

> as I grew older I continued to meet the same statement on every side. During my school and university days, I was regarded as something of an anomaly in that music was evident to be my career. The general attitude was that it was a misfortune for an American and an Anglo-Saxon to spend his life working in music. . . .
>
> Abroad, again, I found that Europeans felt the same way. People who heard my music doubted . . . that I was a Virginian. . . . Anglo-Saxons, they all declared, were notoriously unmusical. And as proof they brought forth the staggering argument that the Anglo-Saxon people have no folk-music.[90]

Powell's public response to these presumed cultural slurs was at one level simply to seek out what he called "Anglo-Saxon folk music" and present it to the public at White Top and elsewhere. But existentially his response seems to have been more complex and ambivalent. On the one hand, he set out—as had so many Americans before him—to become as sophisticated as his European cultural and social betters. He adopted English spellings (*honour, practise, programme, centre, meagre*), schooled himself in Europe as a performer of European classical music, conducted himself with somewhat exaggerated elegance, and cultivated a public image as a rare musical genius, attired in a three-piece suit, seated at his Steinway.

On the other hand, Powell linked this posture—call it the anxious assimilationist yearning of the pianist son of a Richmond schoolmaster—with a certain cultural defiance expressed through his advocacy of American "folk music." In a way he remained throughout his life the eight year old of his sketch—stamping his foot at the cultural gainsayers, shouting

"It isn't true!" and running to the mother buried in his mind, who tells him that, alas, it *is* true.

Thus, even at his most culturally confident and assertive moments, Powell could not leave those domestic cultural treasures to stand on their own merits, whatever they could be argued to be. For him the standards of valuation were always (the ghostly voice of the cultural parent) essentially classical and European: "The discovery that folk-music existed in the Appalachians in inexhaustible quantities caught the attention of musicians at once. For this music is not, as some folk music is, a naive and primitive expression; it is highly developed and subtle, exquisitely beautiful even in its sturdiest manifestations. The melodies of which it consists both in beauty of line and variety of rhythm challenge comparison with the finest of composed tunes."[91] The "musicians" are of course classically trained; subtlety and "exquisite" beauty are higher qualities than sturdiness; the standard of judgment is clearly "the finest of composed tunes."

Powell's ambivalent posture is graphically (though presumably unintentionally) rendered in his account of himself as folk collector in the unlikeliest of surroundings—the annual Lee Ball at posh White Sulphur Springs:

> [At] the White Sulphur my vexation at being unable to dash to the mountains about me in search of folk-musicians was unexpectedly dissipated. Surrounded by the Greenbrier's splendid hospitality, at the very apex of the annual Lee Ball, a dancer actually left the floor to let me record "The Bailiff's Daughter of Islington" (Child 105) and "Get Up and Bar the Door" (Child 275) and another guest in the hotel contributed "The Elfin Knight" (Child 2). I got my three ballads without setting foot out of the hotel and without even seeing a mountaineer.

The image is extended in Powell's account of himself backstage at a Norfolk Symphony concert, on the evening of his appearance as guest soloist. "My eyes roved about for paper," he recalls of meeting a young man who knew a coveted tune, "and I explored in vain for a pencil in the pockets of my evening clothes." On still another occasion, he tells of "an invitation from a lady who is a collateral descendant of George Washington [which] brings an afternoon bubbling with fun as she shares with me those [songs] which were favorites by her fireside."[92]

Although Powell's explicit argument was that "folk music" can be found among lowlanders as well as among mountaineers, he implies the important corollary that the music is so good that it is valued by Lee Ball dancers and collateral descendants of George Washington. Indeed, the lad who offers him "Jockie to the Fair" and "Sir Patrick Spens" backstage at the symphony is no less than "a Tucker of Virginia." Powell and his Tucker informant then take a "motor" to a formal reception, and amidst appropriately elegant surroundings—"the phlox was white in the moonlight and its scent came up to me from the Colonial garden below"— Powell transcribes what he judges to be "the greatest ballad in any language, actually alive in our tradition."[93]

Such a posture allowed Powell to have it both ways—indeed, *every* way—at once. He could be a European-educated classical musician rubbing elbows in evening clothes at the Greenbrier with the Tuckers of Virginia, from whom one could excitedly collect "native" folk tunes whose roots lay ultimately in Europe and which formed a perfect basis for an "American" school of music built upon classical European high art forms and compositional techniques. Thus the image of the tuxedoed Richmond pianist-composer backstage at the symphony fumbling for a pencil to take down "Sir Patrick Spens" from a Tucker of Virginia is rich in its implications.

If this is how Powell seems to have seen himself in relation to "culture" in general, how did he see himself in relation to the folk themselves? "I am not a 'collector' in the accepted sense," he said.

> The music first came to me through a personal tradition. . . . [Each] tune that I hear for the first time . . . links its bearer to all that is dearest in life to me. We are drawn together into a cultural stream that has been sweeping our people along for thousands of years. The fact that I have studied music all my life in no wise invalidates the authenticity of my musical tradition. . . . Why must I be excluded because I was born far from mountain fastnesses, because I can read and write, because I have had a musical education?

Recalling the dramatist Percy MacKaye's protest that he should not be differentiated from the Kentucky mountaineers among whom he lived and wrote for a short while ("I, too, am a mountain man!"), Powell insisted, "I am a folk musician." Consequently, he said, "I feel qualified to speak up for whole classes of people who are being forgotten, perhaps suppressed."[94] To Powell, as best one can judge, culture was not conditioned in or transmitted by concrete social configurations, occupations, specific belief systems, or class linkages. Instead, it was somehow almost magically passed along in a "cultural stream" not unlike—or wholly separate from—

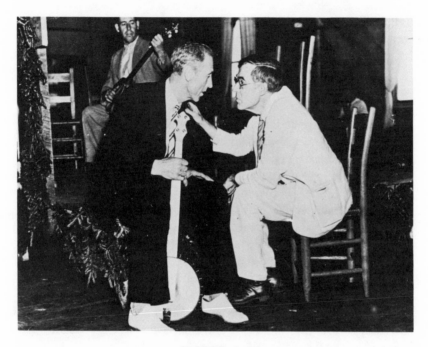

FIGURE 3-12
C. B. Wohlford (L) and John Powell (R)
(Southern Historical Collection, University of North Carolina
at Chapel Hill).

the bloodstream. The analogy, apt or not, was sufficiently powerful to draw him energetically into "folk work" among southern mountaineers.[95]

In any event, the history of the White Top festival cannot be understood apart from the conflicted personal and working relationship between John Powell and Annabel Morris Buchanan. To Buchanan, Powell was at once teacher, role model, co-worker, intellectual mentor, and partner in a personal relationship that was—for her at least—perilous and painful.

Buchanan was quite candid about her discipleship. She acknowledged repeatedly that Powell was her tutor and guide in "folk work." "[My] folk work belongs to you. . . . You started me on it," she wrote to him in 1932.[96]

In her numerous talks to women's clubs, schools, and professional groups about White Top, she rarely failed to characterize Powell as the primary authority to whom she turned for guidance and to quote his cultural theories liberally. "[Your] work is the greatest of all," she wrote to him just after the second festival, "but mine is to help you." Even the festival itself she saw as in a sense her offering to him, an instrument he might use for his larger and higher purposes. "It occurs to me," she wrote to him late in 1931, "that you might like the White Top Festival to play with, too. . . . You know that I should like nothing better than for you to be identified with it." "The principal thing I thought about it," she later wrote to Powell's wife, "[was] that it might give Mr. Powell an opportunity to carry out some of his ideas and incidentally help his career too." [97] In her judgment, Powell was "largely responsible for [the] present renaissance of folk interest in America." Thus almost plaintively she wrote to him, "I hope you . . . will count me in on this American folk music school. It surely is in my blood! I know so little, though." [98]

Discipleship under the best of circumstances is fraught with peril, but the discipleship of a creative, passionate, dynamic, but radically insecure woman whose marriage was troubled, to an aloof, self-important, cold, and deeply angry married man was fated for conflict. Although there is no evidence that Buchanan's personal relationship with Powell was anything other than scrupulously proper ("May I call you John," she asked in 1934. "You have been calling me Annabel for seven years"), it is nevertheless clear that she was deeply attached to and dependent upon him emotionally. [99]

Buchanan's relationship to Powell was conditioned partly by her own unsettled mind and mercurial temperament. "It is impossible for me to do *nothing*," she wrote to him before the first festival. "My brain keeps on working." A few days later she confided to his wife, "I CANNOT sleep . . . [Everything] I do seems to make me nervous." Her letters speak repeatedly of nervousness and insomnia, of her "mercurial disposition," of headaches, nightmares and "terrible depression." [100] Her temperament carried her through a recurrent cycle of nervousness, overwork, fatigue, and depression. "I wish I could get out from under this nervous strain," she confided to Powell in the winter of 1934. "I shall crack up soon if I don't." [101]

The problem was compounded by Buchanan's insecurities and incipient feelings of worthlessness, which she once characterized as a "terrible, heartsick feeling of unworthiness." [102] To both of the Powells she spoke of being "self-conscious and afraid of my own ability" and "wrapped up in fears and inhibitions." "Mr. Powell, I never could be great," she said in 1934. "Is there any use trying? If I could get over *littlenesses*, Mr. Powell, that is what hurts. . . . If we—or *I*—could free ourselves of little, petty things . . . [and] spiritual wastes—then we could get down to divinity and real greatness. Mr. Powell, do you think a woman could ever do that?" [103]

Hounded by such fears, she idolized Powell, who seemed to her the personification of greatness. It proved a deadly destructive combination. "You have typified all that is best and highest in Virginia music and American music to me," she told him. "You seemed to me an ideal to work for, and most of my best ideas . . . came from you." "I know that whatever you advise will be right," she said, "and whatever you disapprove of will be wrong necessarily." Her respect for Powell, she told his wife, "amount[s] to reverence." [104] Even as late as 1938, after years of conflict with Powell, she still was able to tell him, "You are great. . . . You are set apart to lead a great work." [105]

The structure of such a relationship made Buchanan acutely vulnerable to Powell's praise or blame. "If you think I don't amount to anything, then I just don't, that's all—I can't help it," she told him just before the first festival. A few months later she told his wife that if "[Mr. Powell] disapproves of me, it hurts me so all out of reason, it sets me perfectly wild, and I hardly know what to do or say." "I simply cannot stand your disapproving of my work and aims," she told Powell in the summer of 1932. "[If] I feel that I have failed, or disappointed you," she added later, "it makes me actually ill." [106]

Unfortunately, Powell's response to Buchanan appears to have left much to be desired. [107] The record suggests that he alternately praised and damned her work with him in musical analysis and composition, bolstered her confidence in herself and then dashed it without warning, was alternately (and quite unpredictably) approachable and coldly distant. Her many letters praising, thanking, and idolizing him are interspersed with other equally impassioned ones begging him not to hurt her again. "I don't believe you realize how terribly you hurt me," she told him in 1931, and a few days later she referred to his being "continually so sarcastic and contemptuous." Still later she implored, "Don't write me another nasty letter, or wait to say something even nastier to me when you see me, Mr. Powell, please." [108]

The historical irony is that Buchanan chose to deal with her insecurities partly through prodigious creativity and productivity, that the White Top festival was perhaps her most important attempt to do so, that her major collaborator in that enterprise turned out to be John Powell, and that the festival would probably have been better—treated its participants better, been less tied to the wishes and preconceptions of an academic art-music elite, adopted broader definitions of cultural authenticity, focused less attention on Powell's bizarre cultural ideas—had he not been involved. He remained aloof and little more than ceremonially present, while accepting—apparently without apology—the adulatory attention the festival focused upon him. "I wanted the festival for you in the first place," Buchanan wrote to him in 1934, "and you refused to have anything to do with starting it, or even to attend it, until just beforehand. . . . You apparently feel 'Annabel must be PUNISHED' and refuse to have anything to do with anything that means hard work . . . but graciously come in on the finale."[109]

As the years passed, and she had to cope with the increasing emotional and financial strain of a disintegrating marriage, Buchanan was less and less able to cope with Powell, as her letters throughout the 1930s attest. Her ultimate withdrawal from the festival appears to have been induced as much by that as by any other of the several contributing factors. "I seem," she had written to Powell somewhat prophetically on the eve of the first festival, "utterly helpless where my affections are involved. . . . As long as I can believe in myself . . . I have literally the 'strength of ten'. And if I don't feel believed in, I'm just not me any more than if a perfect stranger were surveying work I had planned to do."[110]

Thus beneath the public image of mountain dancers and musicians performing on top of Virignia's second highest mountain for throngs of people (Eleanor Roosevelt included) who rejoiced that the culture of the southern mountains was being celebrated and (presumably) preserved lay a tangled drama—not only because of its own internal dynamics but, more important, because it constituted an intentional, long-term, systematic intervention into that culture which it purported to celebrate and preserve.

To complete the story of White Top, one must therefore inquire into the standards it employed to select what was to be presented and celebrated, the images of Appalachian people and culture it projected, its impact upon them, its extractive use of the culture for "higher" art, and its function as a tactical instrument in broader political and cultural strategies.

Machinery against the Folk:
The White Top Festival as Intervention

Almost every time they were called upon to explain what they were doing at White Top, Buchanan and Powell responded with a little historical object lesson. It ran approximately as follows: Once upon a wonderful time in Merrie England, "the countryside rang with laughter and music." There was music at court, "every country village had its Morris side," and "summer nights . . . found the greens gay with [the] frolicsome measures" of country dances to fiddle, pipe, and tabor. Then came the dour Puritans, and "merriment was stripped from the land." Organs were taken from churches and burned; the people's songs and dances were forbidden, and England became "dumb and silent." With the Restoration, musicians were unfortunately "imported from the continent . . . [to bring] music to a [by then] unmusical people." But "the simple people refused to forget their [own] songs," and at length such collectors as Bishop Percy, Francis James Child, and, finally, Cecil Sharp took it upon themselves to "restore to us this musical tradition." Having exhausted the memories of his English informants, Sharp came to America, to the southern Appalachians, where there lived "a people—chiefly illiterate—with a beautiful musical tradition" brought by their foreparents from across the water.

And where had the best versions of the old ballads and fiddle tunes survived? In Virginia, of course, where although "some few, no doubt," of those who have remembered the folk tunes are illiterate, many are not. "Two of the loveliest tunes I have collected," Powell said, "came from a mountain district, but of the others I have found by far the most remarkable in those parts of the state which were centres of culture, where the high standard of taste either preserved the finer tunes or . . . improved and polished them."

But alas, modern life thrusts itself upon us through radios and motor cars, and if something isn't done to offset their influence, this great heritage will be lost forever. "I became more and more eager," said Powell, "to see established an agency for the preservation of the old music. . . . I determined to rouse Virginia's people to an enthusiasm for the music that I knew was lurking about them in the hills." [111]

Thus, White Top.

In an unpublished story left among her papers, Buchanan depicts a night conversation between three sophisticated friends before a blazing fire in a cabin on White Top. "We've got to get away from it," says one—a dramatist. "This is the age of machinery against the folk. We must find some way to re-create the old folk life, get back to simplicity of thought and beliefs, and put that simplicity into our own creative work—or else, be crushed under the weight of our own machinery." The yearned-for truth comes in the midst of a storm. "Brother Moses," a bearded old itinerant mountain preacher "famous for his simple faith, his knowledge of Scriptures, and the efficacy of his prayers," stumbles into the cabin. "We come before Thee," he prays a few moments later, "groping for the truth. Reveal . . . Thy way to us pore, ignorant children." [112] Within the logic of the historical paradigm and the symbolism of the mountaintop vision lies most of the rationale that Buchanan and Powell required to justify intervening in the cultural system that attracted their attention.

The festival was by no means the first instance of intervention in local culture. Josie Sheets Marshall, who performed with her father on White Top, recalled nearly fifty years later that as a student in the one-room school on the Douglas Land Company farm at Konnarock she and her classmates were required to take piano lessons as part of an attempt by the paternalistic owner of Hassinger Lumber Company to bring enlightenment to mountain people. Mrs. Marshall recalled performances by Chatauqua troupes in the early 1920s (with instruction in Dutch folk dances), piano recitals, and lantern-slide lectures by Mr. Hassinger. But there was no evidence that Mr. Hassinger valued local culture. Mountain people were invited to his Christmas parties, but there was no mountain music to be heard.[113]

Unlike Hassinger, the White Top organizers valued local culture. But they nevertheless shared his conviction that they knew both what was good and what was (therefore) good for mountain people. With apparently complete confidence in their own judgment, they set the standard for White Top—drew the boundaries that included or excluded. "Being folk, or of folk origin," Buchanan explained, "does not necessarily mean that a tune . . . is good. . . . In my own collecting . . . I am often offered crude versions perhaps of some modern ballad, based on a popular or revival tune."[114] "We must learn to discriminate," she told a high school class, "between the cheap 'hill billy' type and that which has true musical or literary worth."

To Buchanan and Powell, cultural history was essentially a process of natural decay, studded at unpredictable points by miraculous "pure" survivals. "So many of these old tunes have been used with modern words, very cheap," Buchanan wrote to a Galax woman in 1932, "and sometimes the tunes themselves have been altered beyond recognition—yet sometimes they come down to us in remarkable states of preservation. I have found a number myself, . . . maybe with modern verses of the poorest type, yet they are really old tunes, sometimes very lovely, and sometimes in the ancient folk modes."

Like many another collector, however, they were perplexed to find that some of their valued informants did not share their esthetic. "In seeking inspiration from the folk," Buchanan told a radio audience in 1941, "we are sometimes bewildered at hearing what seem to us crude, or even tawdry native songs and tunes. Folksong—of a sort—is pouring continually from our mountains and plains, from our cities and countrysides, even from our prisons and slums. Is this, we ask, the true, or the highest expression of American folklife? And can such cheap or vulgar tunes and texts be of any value?"[115]

The risk of celebrating folk culture in public was therefore that the folk, if left to themselves, might celebrate the wrong thing. Although Lamar Stringfield suggested that the judging at the first festival be done by an "assembly" of the musicians themselves, the idea was rejected, and strict "standards" were invoked. "We'd better designate types of songs to be sung," Buchanan warned. "If we don't, they are just as likely to sing When You and I Were Young, Maggie. . . ." Thus the performances were put "on a new basis," Powell explained later, "for the excellence and antiquity of the tune was to be given pre-eminence in awarding the prizes, and the judging was to be by persons whose experience and study qualified them for their task."[116]

The flyer announcing the first festival therefore stipulated, "Only old time music considered in contests: no modern songs, tunes, or dances." Getting the musicians to present the kind of "tradition" designated nevertheless proved difficult. Guitar player Lester Miller offered "Salty Dog" and "Don't Let Your Deal Go Down" (both out of black tradition, incidentally), but consented to play "Cumberland Gap" and "Jimmy Sutton" instead, which won him a blue ribbon. Although the instrumentalists performed rather readily, the singers held back. Finally, a later writer reported, "One 'un-shy' person, Council Cruise, came up and offered to sing an 'old' song; but it turned out that the song he wanted to sing was 'Rosie O'Grady', a far cry from the folk music sought." Finally, the wife of the president of a nearby college pleased the judges with "Barbara Allen."[117]

"[We] have endeavored . . . to keep the Festival purely for folk music," Buchanan told the WPA's Nicolai Sokoloff in 1935, "and have promptly eliminated . . . any of the musicians who have attempted to play modern music. Our real difficulty has been to hold the musicians to the original folk tunes. Some of our best players have insisted on bringing jazz into the tunes . . . ."[118]

But by and large, the folks got the message, and aimed to please. For the most part they showed up with archaic fiddle and banjo tunes and Child ballads, including the specially prepared ones noted by Charles Seeger in 1936. "[The] folk musicians are learning," Buchanan wrote in early 1932, "to discard many of their cheap later tunes . . . and teach their children their really lovely tunes before they are entirely forgotten."[119]

With dancing, Richard Chase pursued the same aims. His urgings to the native dancers ranged from reinstituting the morris and sword dances,

FIGURE 3-13
Group of dancers, early 1930s
(Virginia State Library and Blue Ridge Institute,
Ferrum College).

which had never been known in the culture, to attempting to alter rather dramatically those dances which were traditional in the area. "We want to try to get . . . [the square dance teams] out of overalls next year!," he wrote to Blakemore in 1939. "It is a problem to get some of them to get real *shape*, traditional or even 'waist swing,' into their sets." [120] And yet, Council Cruise, who organized a great many of the traditional dance groups that appeared at White Top, insisted that "there ain't no regular steps to these dances. . . . Don't try to keep 'em to standard, let 'em do any steps they please, just so they keep time and follow the figures; maybe the gent might . . . shuffle or clog, or [do] some other dance step . . . while a-waiting for his partner. Just keep 'em going with a good leader, and let your conscience be your guide." [121]

The White Top festival organizers were nevertheless confident that they knew best what "tradition" was and seem never to have questioned the wisdom of invoking their "standards."

Judging the impact of their actions upon the performers—or merely of the performers' participation in the festival—is difficult because most of those who performed most regularly (Sailor Dad Hunt, the Cruise family, Jack Reedy, C. G. Wohlford, and others) are dead. But some scraps of evidence remain.

As early as 1937, Virginia folklorist Arthur Kyle Davis expressed reservations about the impact of festival participation upon traditional musicians.

> A sound scholar might reasonably view with some alarm the springing up of folk festivals all over the country with their emphasis on performance, their high pressure publicity methods, their almost unfailing commercial basis. . . . One who has seen the effect of such festivals on several good folk singers may well doubt the value of such gatherings . . . although many a city-bred vacationist is by them provided with "quaint" entertainment and an abundance of so-called local color. The genuine folk singer is not likely to become a popular performer before either a sophisticated or an unsophisticated general audience, nor is the natural, unselfconscious quality of his singing . . . apt to survive this "ordeal by folk festival." . . .[122]

Davis's fears were more than justified, since there were important effects upon the musicians even outside the festival performance itself. A surprising portion of them derived from Powell and Buchanan's fascination with the archaic musical scales or modes that survived in southern mountain music.

According to their understanding, music had developed historically from simple monotone rhythms, through two-note "melodic" alternations, thence to three-, four-, or five-tone (pentatonic) scales, and finally to the seven-tone scales of modern music. At some vaguely premodern stage, folk musicians had instinctively employed many "gapped" or "modal" scales (Dorian, Mixolydian, and so forth) that had produced melodies of exquisite and subtle beauty.

But in the modern period, the popular music-induced hegemony of the major scale was driving out the lovely archaic modes, which therefore were to be cherished wherever they could still be found. Thus after Jack Reedy came by one afternoon to give Mrs. Buchanan some banjo tunes, she wrote to Powell that "all . . . were Dorian." Then, she said excitedly, "[He] played a breathtakingly fast piece he called the Fox Chase, all in dorian mode; (only of course he never plays them the same way twice). . . . I want him to play his Black Gal and Cluck Old Hen in the contest (he played it dorian again, then mixolydian! I showed him how to keep it dorian . . .)." [123]

Powell and Buchanan theorized that such urgings would lead mountain musicians to forsake their flirtations with modernity and—their cultural self-confidence restored—return to the superior traditional culture of their Anglo-Saxon forebears. In some few cases, it appears to have had approximately that effect. Fiddler Albert Hash, for example, was an insecure teenage boy in the early thirties. Raised in the isolated backcountry southeast of White Top, he recalls concealing his fiddle in a flour sack because fiddlers were "looked down on." But Hash played at White Top, and nearly fifty years later still recalled with pleasure how "a Colonel Kettlewell from England" took a picture of his homemade fiddle, how fine other players were, and how for the first time he "realized that it was something that was just more serious than I had heard that music was." For the first time, Hash recalled, "I felt justified in what I was doing." [124]

At the opposite extreme, however, was seventeen-year-old Myrtle Stout, who carried away the first prize for fiddling in 1932. Raised on a farm as one of eleven children, she had had polio at age five and had begun to learn to fiddle from an older sister who had in turn learned from her great grandfather. Since the family had neither radio nor phonograph, and so made its own music with neighbors and friends, Myrtle's repertoire was confined entirely to traditional tunes. At the request of one of "the Cruise boys," her parents reluctantly agreed to let her attend the festival in 1931 and to compete in 1932. She was closely chaperoned by an older sister.

Recalling the event after forty-seven years, Stout denied strongly that the festival had encouraged her to continue with her music. On the contrary, she said, she "sort of gave it up for awhile." Pressed to explain, she recalled that winning the contest had brought her offers from radio stations and concert managers as far away as Washington and New York. To a bright, aggressive, talented young woman who had never been out of southwest Virginia, the offers were attractive indeed. But her parents, understandably reluctant to allow a young daughter to launch forth in such a way, refused to allow her to accept any of them. "I love mountain music and I'll always love it," she still insisted in 1979. "I was brought up in it and I can't get away from it." But the anger and frustration she felt in encountering the seemingly unbridgeable chasm between the world defined for her by her parents and the world she had seen from the mountaintop were still poignantly evident. [125]

Other musicians responded to White Top in a variety of ways—some naively, some with a rather keen sophistication that belied the rustic perspectives that the festival's organizers assumed them to have. Konnarock fiddler Howard Wyatt wrote to Mrs. Buchanan in 1936, "I have learned two old songs that I plan to play. The Old Boatman and The Old Waterwheel." More sophisticated was fiddler Jess Johnson of Wolf Pen, West Virginia, who was entrepreneurial enough to perceive the possibilities of White Top for a quasi-professional performer and intelligent enough to understand the cultural program. "I have learned quite a few 'folk numbers' since I was up there," he wrote to Buchanan in 1936. Three years later he told Blakemore, "I have been working very hard on folk tunes since our last festival. I feel like I can render some numbers that will come up to the requirements." And prior to the projected 1940 festival he told Blakemore, "I am having a new collection of Folk Tunes which I hope you will like. . . . I am making a great effort to collect a number of Folk Tunes." In his letter it is clear that "folk" and "folk tunes" were not terms or categories he customarily employed.[126]

Ironically, then, a festival which purported to reflect the traditional culture of mountain people *as it was* in fact required a variety of accommodating responses from them, ranging from the learning of new repertoires and categories ("folk tunes"), to abandoning popular tunes they had recently come to like, to—for some of them, at least—foregoing their by then normal expectation that they would be paid for their services. Blakemore was aware of that expectation from the beginning, but was unwilling to meet it. Before the first year's festival opened, he wrote to the southwest Virginia Chamber of Commerce that "we are giving . . . $25.00 [in prizes] and trying to get up a little bit more to make the musicians think they have gotten something."[127]

For one of the most valued White Top performers, Horton Barker (1889–1973), the festival's effect was considerable. It continued for several years after the demise of the event itself. Barker was in his early forties when he was first visited by collector Winston Wilkinson about 1930. Born in Laurel Bloomery, Tennessee, he had moved as a child to the Good Hope community near Abingdon. Partially blind from early childhood (and later completely blind), Barker was educated at state schools for the blind in Tennessee and Virginia.[128]

Late in August 1931, Buchanan wrote to Powell that she had "spent Wednesday morning in a wild goose chase after Horton Barker. . . . [Finally] hauled him out of a church at Lebanon, got some Kodak pictures for my book . . . and induced him to come to Marion next morning by bus. . . . So yesterday he came and I worked the poor man for nearly five hours, spent a good part of it getting the words to four songs."[129] Although

FIGURE 3-14
Horton Barker, ballad singer, with winner's ribbon
(Southern Historical Collection, University of North Carolina
at Chapel Hill).

he had in fact learned his songs from a variety of sources ("He had a fine one about Queen Mab," Buchanan told Powell, "and I was ready to weep for joy, when he told me it was taught him from an old book at school when a child!"), Barker was accepted and presented by White Top organizers as an uncorrupted "folk singer" par excellence.

As a White Top performer, Barker continued to do what he had apparently always done, however—learn new songs if he happened to like them, regardless of their source or status in "tradition." From Sailor Dad Hunt he learned "Paddy Doyle," from George Pullen Jackson's Old Harp Singers he learned "Wayfaring Stranger," from John Powell (via Sharp's *English Folk Songs from the Southern Appalachians*) he learned "There Was an Old Lady," and from an unknown White Top singer he learned "At the Foot of Yonders Mountain."[130]

As a result of his appearances at White Top, Barker was recorded several times by the Archive of Folk Song at the Library of Congress, and in the early 1940s found himself under the "management" of Richard Chase, who presented him in a series of programs at colleges and universities. The programs featured Chase telling Jack tales (which he was collecting, editing, and publishing) and Barker (who, Chase said, "is in the opinion of John Powell . . . a true artist in his simple and straightforward handling of our genuine folk songs") singing ballads.[131]

Chase's use of Barker for his own essentially entrepreneurial purposes (however cloaked they were with cultural "concern") was a variant of what proved to be a much broader aim for some of the White Top promoters: to use traditional music for the creation of "higher" art compositions. Their work must therefore be seen as in some respects extractive.

As has already been noted, Powell had been using traditional musical materials as a basis for classical compositions for more than two decades before the advent of the festival. As Powell's student, Buchanan turned in a similar direction at the end of the 1920s. By the early 1930s she was convinced that her own salvation as a composer lay in understanding and employing folk materials. "I let composition go absolutely for folk study, for months," she wrote to Powell, "and then only a little, in folk style as far as possible, and I don't believe I could ever write a poor tune again. . . . A tawdry tune simply hurts me now."[132]

In 1934, in a speech to the Virginia Federation of Music Clubs, Buchanan described the "reason for this folk interest" as "trying to discover and preserve native folk material and make it available for use in American creative art. Trying to find the best tunes, ballads for our composers, writers, dramatists to build on as all great composers have built on their folk material." Great creators, she said, were "always close to folk life." Through his use of such materials, she said later, the composer "becomes so imbued with the spirit of his people that he . . . thinks in [their] . . . language, reflects their emotions and life. . . ." In a later radio speech she asserted that such an artist "has become so imbued with the spirit of his people that they speak through him. He becomes one with them in his creative utterance." [133]

In an illustrated lecture on her own settings of "Brother Green" and "Come All Ye Fair and Tender Ladies," Buchanan sketched a strikingly concentrated image of the extractive process and its possibilities as she envisioned them. Her tune, she said, came from Kentucky fiddler James W. Day, whom "traipsin' woman" Jean Thomas was marketing nationally as the homespun "Jilson Setters." The text was "from Mrs. Bishop of Marion, recorded in my living room . . . while Arthur Kyle Davis . . . recorded her tune on his phonograph and Berkeley Williams, young Richmond artist, made sketches of her and other mountain people which were afterwards to be elaborated into splendid canvases, to be exhibited in Philadelphia, New York, and Paris." [134]

Thus the inherent truth and beauty of folk musical materials would ennoble and purify the vision of the "creative artist" (traditional musicians themselves were never referred to as creative artists), who would then transmute them into great art. In such a process, Buchanan asserted, "we learn to discard vulgarity, over-writing, sentimentality, verbosity—none of these are found in folk music. . . . Nothing but *truth* can survive." So far it was—whether tenable or not—no more than a theory of composition or, at most, a philosophy of art. But it was in fact more than that. "We learn the basic impulses of the race," she continued, "whether good or evil, and how to treat them in art form." [135]

It was a hint of a most disturbing undercurrent in the White Top enterprise—an undercurrent to which Mrs. Buchanan had an ambivalent relationship. There is no evidence that she shared Powell's overt racism; whether she even knew of his earlier racist involvements is uncertain. But there is nevertheless no indication that she ever challenged Powell on the issue or attempted to bring black performers to White Top. [136]

Decontaminating the Cultural Stream:
John Powell and "Anglo-Saxon Culture"

For all his cultivated elegance, John Powell was a thoroughgoing racist who had for many years worked persistently to maintain the racist social and political structure of Virginia. For him, White Top was a tactical instrument to be used in a broader cultural and political strategy.

In her chapter on Powell in *Virginians Out Front* (1972), Edmunds notes that he was "vain of pedigree" and that "since 1910" he was "intent . . . on maintaining the purity of the Anglo-Saxon race." So enthralled was he with what he called "Anglo-Saxon culture," Edmunds says, that he and his wife "read to each other Beowulf and Norse books in order to understand the Anglo-Saxons better." [137]

Although the exact date is uncertain, it may be safely asserted that from the outset of his professional life just after the turn of the century, Powell was preoccupied with what he conceived to be the connections between race and culture; that around 1920 he turned from black to white folk materials in his compositions; that he played thereafter a major role in reinforcing racism in Virginia; that he linked his work with southern mountain music to his larger mission of developing a "national school of music" based on Anglo-Saxon culture; and that his involvement at White Top must finally be understood in the context that these facts provide.

Characterized by notions of purifying the American cultural and social order, Powell's racism exemplified a current of nativism which reached back to the foundations of the republic and which surfaced periodically in times of national stress and uncertainty: at the time of the notorious Alien Acts of the 1790s, in the "Know-Nothing" 1850s, in the socially and economically turbulent decade 1886–96, and in the years surrounding World War I. [138] Of the three primary strains of American nativism (anti-Catholicism, antiradicalism, and racial nativism), Powell embraced the third, and he did so near the end of the last great wave of such sentiment.

In contrast to the prewar period, with its nativist Know-Nothingism, the immediate post–Civil War years were good years for immigrants: territorial, industrial, and economic expansion nationally—together with social reconstruction in the South—put such a premium on immigrants that the Treasury Department calculated the value of each at eight hundred dollars, and individual states set up immigration bureaus and sent agents abroad to lure new workers. It was the heyday of the melting pot. But as frontier lands disappeared and the depression of the 1880s set in, immigrants began to be perceived as a social menace—and by American workers as a glut on the labor market. Thus after the Haymarket Riot of 1886, the Homestead Strike of 1892, and the severe depression of the mid-1890s, the country turned stridently nationalistic. The social turmoil was reflected in a rash of nativist organizations. One of the largest and strongest, the American Protective Association, was founded in Iowa in 1887. Many others, such as the Junior Order of United American Mechanics, the Immigration Restriction League, and the American Super Race Foundation, flourished in subsequent years.[139]

As economic confidence returned at the turn of the century, however, immigration increased dramatically again; roughly a million foreigners came ashore in the year 1907. As historian John Higham notes, the early years of the century were marked by a "prevailing progressive spirit," and most forms of nativism (antiradicalism, for example) were the province of more right-wing groups. But the advent of World War I brought nativist sentiments strongly into play again, especially in the notorious antiradical crusade of Attorney General Alexander Palmer.

This general sketch of the history of American nativism should not obscure the fact that the waxing and waning of each of its three contributing strains was not always completely synchronized with that of the other two. Racial nativism, which attracted Powell and apparently motivated much of his work with traditional music in the southern mountains, to an extent had its own history.

In general, nativism was late in coming to the South because southern states continued to need additional labor after the demand slackened in the North and West. Higham notes that southern congressmen were still opposing immigration restriction legislation in the early 1890s and that there were no nativist organizations south of Virginia. After the 1890s, however, the racial strain of nativism proved especially attractive in the South. The particular version of it that appealed to Powell was Anglo-Saxonism, which had its origins (and major exponents) not in the South at all, but among patrician New Englanders.

Higham locates the "first considerable impetus" for Anglo-Saxonism in the 1841 American (Philadelphia) edition of English writer Sharon Turner's *History of the Anglo-Saxons* (1799–1805). Originally written in connection with a "constitutional controversy," Turner's book was used by the emerging romantic Anglo-Saxon cult in this country to bolster their argument that in Anglo-Saxons "had been implanted . . . a gift for political freedom . . . a unique capacity for self-government and a special mission to spread its blessings" (p. 10).

By the 1870s and 1880s Anglo-Saxonism had become "a kind of patrician nationalism" attractive to many upper-class northern intellectuals. In 1876 Harvard awarded its first Ph.D. in political science to Boston Brahmin Henry Cabot Lodge, who wrote his dissertation on Anglo-Saxon law. Lodge built a part of his long career as a party-line Republican in the U.S. Senate (1893–1924) upon initiating and supporting legislation restricting immigration. With four other Harvard alumni (including lawyer Charles Warren—lately memorialized in Harvard's Charles Warren Center for Studies in American History), Lodge founded the Immigration Restriction League. By 1910, Lodge had emerged as one of three key "patrician nativists [who were] building a systematic ideology" for their romantic persuasion.[140]

The Anglo-Saxonist version of nativism espoused by Powell blended the patrician ethos of New England nativists (which as an aspiring FFV and classical composer-pianist he found quite congenial) with the specifically anti-Negro racism of the post–World War I period. This brand of nativism was by no means new or unfamiliar (Teddy Roosevelt had recently added his voice to the chorus of national magazine articles which were campaigning for "fecundity" and "unhyphenated Americanism" and against "race suicide"), but it had lately acquired a "scientific" basis that made it socially respectable.

Borrowing from (and conveniently reinterpreting) selected European ideas—primarily Mendelian genetics and the "eugenics" derived from it—Lodge and his like-minded associates attempted to put racial nativism on an empirical basis. The eugenics movement in particular, Higham concluded, "vindicated the hereditarian assumptions of the Anglo-Saxon tradition; . . . encouraged loose talk about race in reputable circles; . . . [and] put race-thinking on scientific . . . premises" (p. 152).

The most important nativist intellectually, Higham says, was Madison Grant, a Park Avenue bachelor socialite with "a razor sharp set of patrician values." Grant channeled his eugenicist-derived racial nativism into the founding of the New York Zoological Society and the writing of his magnum opus, *The Passing of the Great Race*, first published in 1916. On the basis of "a crude reinterpretation of Mendelian genetics," Grant argued for racial purity and in defense of class and race consciousness. Grant's book appeared at about the time Powell was completing his formal training as a musician, and it went through two more editions (1921 and 1923) just as he began to involve himself in racial politics in Virginia. And although the Ku Klux Klan (reborn in Atlanta in 1915) achieved its greatest popularity in the Midwest (Higham calls Ohio and Indiana the "leading Klan states" before the mid-twenties demise of the Klan), racial nativism was definitely on the rise in the South as Powell entered adulthood.

Two substrains within Anglo-Saxon racial nativism were salient in Powell's thought: an insistence upon race "purity" and the crude equation of race and culture. Early Anglo-Saxonists believed that a peculiar characteristic of the Anglo-Saxon "race" was its ability to assimilate other races and absorb their valuable qualities, but remain basically unchanged. As the pressure of immigration mounted in the 1890s, however, and a popularized Mendelianism came to dominate race thinking, that confidence was shaken, and maintaining the "purity" of the Anglo-Saxon bloodline assumed primary importance.

The equation of race and culture arose from similarly sloppy thinking. One of its more important exponents was Harvard-trained philosopher, Boston lawyer, and popular historian John Fiske (1842–1901), who was "enormously proud of the New Englander's ancestry in general," Higham says, and who believed more particularly that he himself was a lineal descendant of King Alfred. Blending orthodox religious beliefs, conventional patrician New England snobbism, and the social Darwinism of Herbert Spencer, Fiske celebrated the racial-cultural glories of America's English heritage. Fiske's books (such as *Old Virginia and Her Neighbors* of 1897) found a wide audience among those disposed to equate culture with ancestry.

Whether Powell read Fiske is not known, but he demonstrably drew upon—and skillfully used in the service of his own political-cultural mission—the jumbled grab bag of half-baked racial-cultural ideas which Fiske and others helped to popularize. He was one of the racial nativists who, as Higham says, "worshipped tradition in a deeply conservative spirit" (p. 139).

The first major event in Powell's racial-cultural work was his organizing the Anglo-Saxon Club of America in Richmond in the fall of 1922.[141] By June of the following year, the *Richmond News-Leader* reported that the club had more than four hundred members, and two years later Powell counted thirty-one "posts" in Virginia, some student posts in colleges, and a few in neighboring states. At the Richmond post's June 1923 meeting, Powell gave a talk entitled "Music and Nationalism," illustrated by "a programme of English and American folk songs."[142]

Membership in the club was open to white males, and its constitution (adopted 13 October 1923) committed it to "the maintenance of Anglo-Saxon institutions and ideals," the "wise limitation of immigration and the complete exclusion of unassimilable immigration," the "preservation of racial integrity," and "the supremacy of the white race in the United States, without racial prejudice or hatred." [143]

In an article published in the *Times-Dispatch* while the club was being formed, Powell aired his own views on racial purity and its relationship to the vitality of national culture. The "danger of racial amalgamation," he warned, is "a serious and fundamental peril," since "every race that has crossed blood with the Negro has failed to maintain its civilization and culture." Although the "dangers of injecting into a white population a mass of primitive savages" were well known even in slavery days, the current "increase in the number of hybrids born to white women . . . [is] too abhorrent to be discussed in the public press." To us is entrusted, Powell said, "the most sacred of all cultural heritages." And although he admitted there was no Anglo-Saxon race as such, he insisted that there is "no doubt in the mind of any as to the meaning of the words 'Anglo-Saxon Civilization.'" [144]

Nor was the Anglo-Saxon Club content with mere rhetoric. Within eighteen months of its founding, it had proposed, promoted, and gained the passage of Virginia's Racial Integrity Law of 1924.

Although Virginia had had antimiscegenation laws since 1691, aimed at preventing "abominable mixture and spurious issue," Powell considered them too lax. The true Anglo-Saxon, he asserted, has "an instinctive conviction that 'one drop of Negro blood makes the Negro.'" The color line must therefore be made absolute. The proposed law, he hoped, would "retard amalgamation sufficiently to insure the possibility . . . of achieving a final solution." [145]

Although the law as proposed by the Anglo-Saxon Club required every Virginia citizen to register according to race, the law as passed (20 March 1924) required registration only for those who desired to marry. It defined a white person as one who has "no trace whatsoever of any blood other than Caucasian." Those with one-sixteenth Indian blood or less were excluded, "to protect," as the state registrar explained, "the descendants of Pocahontas, of which some of our best families are quite proud." [146]

Powell was not reticent about claiming responsibility for the law, or about associating himself with its advocates. He described himself to one correspondent as its "originator" and offered to speak to the legislatures of several other states that were considering similar laws. [147] The advertising brochure used by his English agents for his 1928 European concert tour listed passage of the law among his accomplishments. An article in the *Wiener Illustrierte Zeitung* during the German segment of his tour quoted the English brochure and called Powell *"Ein hundert prozentiger Amerikaner aus den Sudstaaten"* ("a one-hundred-percent American from the South"). *"Seine Zusammenarbeit mit den Anglo-Saxon Clubs in Amerika,"* Powell's audiences were informed, *"schuf ein bemerkenwertes Gesetz in Virginia"* ("His work with the Anglo-Saxon Clubs of America brought a noteworthy law into being in Virginia").[148]

Ernest Sevier Cox, author of *The South's Part in Mongrelizing the Nation* (1926), called the law "probably the most perfect expression of the white racial ideal since the institution of caste in India some four thousand years ago," and Powell reciprocated by commending Cox's other book, *White America*, "to all Virginians." "If Virginia leads in making America a white nation," he said, "such service will be infinitely greater than any the state has performed throughout its glorious history."[149]

Although the reasons for Powell's leap from functional social and political racism to grandiose racial-cultural strategizing no doubt lay buried in the depths of his psyche, he explained it in the rational, "scientific" terms characteristic of the period. In his pamphlet on the Sorrels case, he derided the romanticism of the early racists and declared that

> the [racial] views of the succeeding generation have been formed under the influence of modern biology, by the new ethnology, by the new philosophy of cultural history, by the knowledge that institutions and civilizations are the effect and not the cause of racial psychology. . . . They realize why the inheritance of the more primitive, more generalized stock dominates that of the higher more specialized stock in the hybrid mixture. They know, too, that this dominance is more overwhelming in the intellectual . . . and the cultural fields than in the merely physical.[150]

Thus Powell's founding of the Anglo-Saxon Club and his support for the Racial Integrity Law neatly complemented his folk-based compositions and the cultural promotional work he did at White Top. The underlying aim was to develop a white national culture expressive of the values and esthetics of a white America.[151]

Four years before White Top he outlined his argument in a long article in *Etude*. Noting that many people had advocated developing a "distinctive American music," he grouped the advocates into six categories and quickly dismissed all but one: the Red Indian School of Farwell and others ("We Americans are not Red Indians . . . , we are Europeans in race and language"), the Negro School ("negro music . . . is almost as meagre and monotonous as the Indian music"), the Stephen Foster School ("too closely identified with a particular period"), the Popular Music School ("usually artificially manufactured by the lowest and most vulgar type of foreign musical parasite"), the Ultra Modern School ("nothing more nor less than cheap replicas of those of the recent European musical Bolshevists"), and finally, the Anglo-Saxon Folk Music School, which "promises a solution to our problem." [152]

The most valuable achievements in musical history, Powell asserted, "have been essentially national in spirit," citing Haydn, Mozart, Beethoven, Wagner, Brahms, Bizet, Rimsky-Korsakoff, and others as proof. "[If] we wish a living music in America," he argued, "we shall have to provide it with a folk basis." Our "only hope for a nation in America," he continued, "lies in grafting the stock of our culture on the Anglo-Saxon root. . . . [If] we desire a music characteristic of our racial psychology . . . it must be based upon Anglo-Saxon folk-song."

Having summarily dismissed all other possible musical idioms, Powell held up what he called Anglo-Saxon folk music as a paragon: "For perfection of line and richness of color, the beauty of Anglo-Saxon folk-music surpasses any other in the whole world. . . . Here, at last, we have a basic idiom thoroughly competent to express our national psychology. . . . [This] proves not only the innate musical gift of our race, but also the high plane of musical culture and taste that our forefathers . . . had reached, and which, consequently, is re-attainable by us, their descendents." Envisioning a "Golden Age of National Art," Powell—somewhat inconsistently, in view of his earlier work on behalf of the Racial Integrity Law—noted that "it has been wisely said, 'Let me write the songs of a nation and I care not who makes its laws.'" [153]

Although Powell had been in step with the racial nativist times when he founded the Anglo-Saxon Clubs, by the late twenties he was very much out of step. The Klan had more or less fallen apart in 1924–25, a boom economy had reappeared, and big business was opposing immigration restrictions and their associated social views. The advent of the White Top festival, therefore—in the heart of a supposed English-culture preserve in the southern mountains—offered Powell a new opportunity to pursue his racial-cultural goals.

Powell saw the festival—a showcase of white Anglo-Saxon music—as a major means by which a "high plane of [national] musical culture" might be rendered "reattainable." Recounting the first festival, he recalled Council Cruise's singing of "Pretty Polly," which he said was "a prophecy of the cultural future of Virginia." Stimulated by Virginia's example, others "throughout the length and breadth of the nation" were taking up the search for "Anglo-Saxon folk material." [154] As Mrs. Buchanan phrased it on one of the rare occasions when she employed Powell's terminology, the White Top festival was "not for the mountain people alone; not for one region alone, not for one class alone; . . . [it is] for a *race*." [155] "If we deprive ourselves or our children of the knowledge of their own racial instincts, racial culture, racial music," she had said earlier, "we deprive them of all the cultural and musical foundation that is their birthright." [156]

Whatever the broad historical-cultural implications of such a theory, one immediate result was that blacks and black music were summarily excluded from White Top. Prior to the 1933 festival, C. L. Miller of nearby Iron Mountain Lutheran School for Boys asked Blakemore if he could bring some CCC camp boys to do Negro spirituals. "We cannot feature the Negro spirituals," Blakemore replied, "because we are entirely limited to folk music of a date prior to . . . the induction [sic] of negro spirituals in the U.S.; the folk music coming from old English base." Thus the only spirituals on the mountain were those performed by a white group from Galax and by "white spirituals" scholar George Pullen Jackson's elegant Old Harp Singers from Vanderbilt University. [157]

Several years later, a doctor from Roanoke wrote jokingly to Blakemore that he wanted to enter the dancing contest, which he was sure he could win "unless you have some negro contestants." Blakemore, missing the joke, responded soberly: "Your letter has interested me more than most any letter I have received about the White Top Festival. No negro contestants are permitted, and there have never been any on the mountain. The only people we have on the mountain are the white people who live in this section of the country who have learned their art . . . from their ancestors, and those ancestors trace back to the original settlers of this country." [158] Indeed, the only blacks Blakemore ever allowed on the mountain during the festival were seventy-eight-year-old John Smith, Eleanor Roosevelt's father's servant, who came in 1933 to present a gift to her, and three black cooks who were allowed to prepare her meals (see Fig. 3-4, p. 195).

How numerous were blacks and black musicians in the White Top area in the 1930s? In an interview in 1979, Blakemore asserted that there had never been "more than twelve hundred" blacks in Washington County, but his facts were in error. The black population of the county in 1920 had been nearly 50 percent higher than that, and black residents in Washington, Smyth, and Grayson totaled more than thirty-four hundred. Although the total had dropped (both absolutely and as a percentage) by 1930, there were still nearly three thousand. Adding the black populations of another six or eight Virginia and North Carolina counties immediately around White Top (reasonable for an event promoted as an "interstate" festival) would have raised the total to approximately seventy-five hundred.[159]

It seems reasonable to suppose that there was a substantial number of black musicians and dancers among such a large population. A recent history of Grayson County contains a photograph taken in 1899 of about sixty blacks from the three black communities near Independence (directly adjacent to White Top); on the front row are a black fiddler, a banjo player, and a drummer.[160]

A recent carefully documented study of black banjo players in Virginia shows that there was in fact a rich banjo playing tradition among blacks at the time of the White Top festival in counties adjacent to the festival site. Among the black banjo players in Henry, Franklin, Floyd, and Bedford counties were Irvin Cook (b. 1924); several generations of the Kasey family; Robert Stuart (b. 1916) and the cousin from whom he learned, John Lawson Tyree (b. 1915); Stuart's uncles Torrance and Jack Wade; and John Calloway (b. 1906).[161] Clearly the black population was there, and the musical tradition was there; it was merely systematically excluded from the festival.[162]

Nor can one rationalize the festival's failure to include black performers as merely a characteristic of the times, challenged by no one. Sarah Gertrude Knott, who founded the National Folk Festival in 1934, presented a broad range of performers, including blacks, who shared the stage with whites. "[The] picture of our folk life today would not be complete," she said, "without the contributions of the Negro."[163] At her second annual festival in 1935, held in Chattanooga, Tennessee—surely as race-conscious an area as southwest Virginia—Knott's mountain fiddlers and ballad singers shared the program with a thousand-voice black chorus singing spirituals. In addition, a group of Pennsylvania anthracite miners brought by folklorist George Korson sang those industrial songs ("When the Breaker Starts Up Full Time," "Me Johnny Mitchell Man," "I'm a Celebrated Working Man") that Bruce Crawford had found so noticeably absent at White Top two years earlier.[164]

Critic Paul Rosenfeld, who attended the 1939 White Top festival, strongly criticized its racist basis.

> Cultural and social politics, of a sort [which] in the past [were] unhappy by-products of nationalistic movements are manifesting them-

FIGURE 3-15
John Smith presenting gift to Mrs. Roosevelt at White Top Festival, 1933
(Virginia State Chamber of Commerce and Southern Historical Collection,
University of North Carolina at Chapel Hill).

selves . . . among certain sophisticates engaged in encouraging and
spreading the American folksong: particularly among certain active
in behalf of the southern highland song. These politics are those of
regionalism and racialism: both are designed to "save" the highlanders and their song. . . . To sustain their . . . culture, the regionalist
wishes to draw a *cordon-sanitaire* about the region. . . . For the racial-
ist . . . [its] spiritual and economic salvation . . . is identical with its
bloodstream's retention of its "purity."

Although he did not mention Powell by name, Rosenfeld went on to refer
to "this fascist [who] introduces into the Virginia House of Burgesses bills
illegalizing marriage between whites and blacks, and is all for 'the true folk
manner.'" [165]

Conclusion

The White Top festival must finally be seen not as the presentation of a preexisting reality but as a manipulation of it—indeed at some levels as the *creation* of a "reality" tautologically certified as authentic by the self-assured promoters who presented it. The image of mountain people presented at White Top was one of a fragile and vulnerable cultural group that had naively and miraculously held on to its wholly premodern culture. But its hold on that culture—in the face of the destructive pressures of modern life—was tenuous, and would persist only through delicate but insistent reeducation by a group of cultural sophisticates sensitive to the esoteric beauty of selected traditional expressive forms. Sweet cultural children, mountain people were, preserved from the harsh modern world by their cultural parent-teacher-saviors. "Contented with little," said an article on Buchanan and the festival in the *Southern Literary Messenger*, "[the mountain people] have not contributed to the progress of the country, but as if in recompense they have preserved the 'best of the traditions' that the original settlers brought as contributions to a new country. . . . Wales has her Eisteddfodd, . . . and now America . . . has her White Top Festival." [166]

In hundreds of photographs published in newspapers, magazines, and festival programs, the image was commended to the public: fiddlers posed most artificially before a cabin door; a bonnetted banjo picker on a rock by the river; a Grant Wood-ish couple (Council Cruise's parents) against rough barn siding; two bearded patriarchs perched on a log with fiddle and zither; a mandolin player in boots, vest, and cowboy hat; a fiddler with pistol dangling from his belt. [167]

Nor can one (again) dismiss the essential dishonesty of the projected image as merely characteristic of the times. Many commentators, including those such as Bruce Crawford, Charles Seeger, and Paul Rosenfeld who actually attended the festival, viewed mountaineers and their cultural situation in far more complex (and tenable) terms.

A striking example was the novelist Sherwood Anderson, who after tiring of life in urban literary circles moved in the mid-1920s to Annabel Morris Buchanan's hometown of Marion, Virginia. [168] Twelve years before Rosenfeld was to attend the White Top festival, Anderson wrote to him of "my own efforts to get humanized here. To penetrate into the soil, plowed fields, people in little house[s] in hollows, to shake off, if possible, all smart-aleckness. . . . God knows, a lifetime would be little enough time to live in one valley like this." [169]

Through a mythical mountaineer reporter "Buck Fever," Anderson commented on mountain people, their values and ways. Although Anderson observed with Buchanan and her colleagues that "the basic stock of this section is Old American," he did not romanticize them. Men and women in Smyth County, he said, "sin and pay the price of sin"; they cope with industrialization, urbanization, the Depression, and the coming of the Tennessee Valley Authority. The world of the mountaineer as imaged by Anderson in the local newspapers he owned and edited was for the most part the familiar world of the late 1920s, full of radios, automobiles, bootleggers, economic instability, soup lines, and low-wage jobs in textile mills.[170]

If the White Top organizers' most ambitious plans had materialized, moreover, their "folk work" on the mountain would not have been confined to a single decade; it—and thus their views of traditional culture in the mountains—would have been permanently institutionalized. Even before the first festival in 1931, Buchanan and Blakemore were talking of a "permanent pavilion or . . . building of some kind" to allow the festival to become "big and permanent."[171] The next year Blakemore wrote to Allen Eaton about making White Top "the center for the display and sale of folk handicraft; not only at . . . the festival, but for all times." In 1933, H. K. Bowen, who was handling White Top publicity for the regional Chamber of Commerce, suggested establishing—possibly with Eleanor Roosevelt's help—a university on the mountain.[172] Buchanan envisioned establishing Powell's "folk classes" permanently "so that people will come to you from all over the country." Blakemore "wants to sell the mountain," she said, but "I [want it] to be set apart for folk activities." Two months later she referred cryptically to "the folk colony plans."[173] The following year Buchanan submitted the first of several grant applications to the Carnegie Corporation and the Guggenheim Foundation, requesting funds to create a permanent organization to present lectures, classes, performances, and other "folk activities" on White Top.[174]

The "folk work," as Mrs. Buchanan phrased it in a biblical image, was "bread cast upon the waters," valuable to mountain people (whose sense of the value of their own traditions it would shore up), to creative artists (who could create their best only when they assimilated their true folk cultural heritage), and to the larger community (which would grow in cultural pride and understanding).[175]

As late as 1951, more than a decade after she had ended her formal association with White Top and had retired to western Kentucky, Buchanan still hoped for "a permanent center for all my folklore undertakings." In an image that captured perfectly the polarities of her own temperament,

FIGURE 3-16
The parents of Council Cruise

she envisioned "a log cabin studio . . . on top of Huckleberry Mountain" in North Carolina "with windows looking out over a series of rock ledges, across a deep ravine, across to the sunset, mountains, hemlocks, birds and trees and enchanting view. High up, suspended in air, apparently, but with solid rock foundation." [176]

These were the polarities of her life and work as well. Paradoxically, the best and most durable work she did, she did alone. The work with Powell and Blakemore at White Top was frustrated and aborted by Blakemore's entrepreneurial obsessions and distorted and wrenched by Powell from its only possible historical and cultural foundation—not to float in the mountain air of Buchanan's romantic image, but to flounder in the miasma of his elegantly cloaked racism.

Ironically, the only permanent institution actually created to perpetuate the memories and work of any of the White Top festival organizers was the John Powell Foundation in Richmond. Meanwhile, the medium that best reflected the realities of mountain music in the 1920s and 1930s (although its reflection was also distorted in some respects) was not the White Top festival at all but the commercial recording industry so feared by the festival's organizers.

From our own historical perspective, one sees finally that White Top reflected dominant strands of our *whole* history and *all* of our conflict-ridden values in a way the newsmen and the photographers never came close to perceiving or projecting. Blakemore's entrepreneurial hustle was one with that of the first land speculators and canal builders; Powell's racism was merely the most recent outcropping of a layer of American consciousness that had given Virginia its first antimiscegenation law in 1691; and Buchanan's idealism and pluralism were consonant with the best in our formal values—those that are so often sacrificed to the demands of the wearyingly long line of Blakemores and Powells.

Buchanan challenged Blakemore repeatedly, and finally withdrew from the festival because she could not countenance his self-serving greed and his consequent ill treatment of mountain people. But she never summoned the courage to challenge Powell, and that she did not was her personal tragedy. She knew and felt and wished for so much more than she could ever bring together in such a distorted and conflicted mechanism as the White Top Folk Festival.

One of her finest social, cultural, and political statements in fact had nothing directly to do with the festival at all. It is an unpublished short story called "Rise, King Jesus," about the last shape-note singing held in a little backcountry Tennessee church about to be flooded by the waters of TVA's first dam.[177]

"Rise, King Jesus" stands in sharp contrast to TVA's own photographs, articles, and films, in which valley dwellers watch dumbly and gratefully— not unlike some primitive cargo cult—as TVA's technocratic shamans bring phosphate fertilizer, multipurpose dams, electric corn shellers, and washing machines from the faraway twentieth century. Such images encouraged the larger public to believe that there was little if anything of value in the people's own lifeways to salvage or build upon. The choice was between simple backwardness (economic and cultural) and pure progress.

As we now know, TVA was a mixed blessing even in the most limited economic terms.[178] But Buchanan knew from her work among mountain people that it was even more questionable culturally. She knew that cultural traditions had their roots in the very family and community structures that TVA found of so little value and so needful of change.

"Rise, King Jesus" is about Gideon Shands, a Tennessee mountaineer who refuses to lead the last singing at the church because he thinks it would imply that he approves of the flooding, which he believes will transgress the laws of God as they are revealed in the natural order. Thematically, the story is rich and complex. Oppositions multiply and intertwine: progress versus tradition; continuity versus discontinuity; the sacred natural order versus the contrived and profane social and technological order; durable values versus false values; the will of God versus man's will; reverence versus arrogance.

A more subtle theme is suggested, however, when the congregation sings its final hymn:

> When I can read my title clear
> To mansions in the skies,
> I'll bid farewell to every fear,
> And wipe my weeping eyes.

Conventionally one might hear the hymn as an expression of naive yearning for the world beyond. The events of the story, however, emphasize the first rather than the second line of the stanza. It is thus at one level an almost political (rather than eschatological) statement: in this world the have-nots are forever without clear titles, and therefore forever vulnerable, forever liable to being displaced, forever on the verge of forced wandering in search of a new home that will no doubt prove no more secure than the last. Heaven is that place where one may at last *hold clear title*—not only to one's dwelling place, but also to the values and meanings that inhere in it and to the mingled histories of the successive generations that have lived and died there.

In this, Gideon Shands and his neighbors at Sharon Church merge with the children of Israel and all who, yearning for home, have been displaced and forced to wander. Against that threat, human beings ancient and modern have built their communities and—in some ways more crucially—cherished images of a homeplace in their minds.

At the end of his *The Night Country* (1971), anthropologist and naturalist Loren Eiseley recalls a trip back to his boyhood Nebraska home in search of a tree he planted in his front yard with his father as a six year old. The tree has been growing in his mind ever since, remembered "because everyone died or moved away who was supposed to wait and grow old under its shade." His father's words are poignantly clear in his memory: "We'll plant a tree here, son, and we're not going to move any more. And when you're an old, old man you can sit under it and think how we planted it here, you and me, together." But at the end of his search, he finds that the tree has long since been cut down. "It was obvious," he says, that "I was attached by a thread . . . to a thing that had never been there, or certainly not for long. Something that had to be . . . sustained in the mind, because it was part of my orientation to the universe and I could not survive without it. . . . [It was] the attachment of the spirit to a grouping of events in time. . . ."

The social-political-cultural synthesis that Buchanan achieved in her story was not—could not have been—achieved at White Top. To do so would have taken an entirely new conception of the enterprise—something nearer to the analysis of Bruce Crawford and Paul Rosenfeld than to that of John Powell.

Cannibals and Christians
An Afterword

FOR A HALF-CENTURY after White Top, Albert Hash still built and played fiddles in the shadow of the mountain, musing at times about the festival days in August. But if one walks the slopes of the mountain today (now owned by the federal government), one will find the bricks and stones from the festival pavilion scattered amid the grass and weeds. In the more than forty years since the last festival was held there, many of the musicians and their families have left—gone on to other lives or on with the lives they led before, which had precious little to do with anything that ever happened on White Top the second weekend in August. Council Cruise and his family moved from the area years ago; dancer Harve Sheets died in his nineties in a Washington suburb; Myrtle Stout (Taylor) devotes her time to religious work and hasn't touched a fiddle in years; Frank Blevins, who was photographed endlessly with Mrs. Roosevelt, is an executive with a furniture company in Greenville, Tennessee; one of the Hensley boys is a California studio musician who now makes his living playing what John Powell would undoubtedly have called "tawdry" tunes for *The Waltons* and for Tennessee Ernie Ford, Eddie Arnold, and other latter-day practitioners of the commercial hillbilly and country music he and his brothers were discouraged from playing on White Top.

And yet to note the decay, the changes, the moving on is deceptive in a way, for much lingers. At Hindman, which has already passed its eightieth anniversary, one can still visit Uncle Sol's restored cabin and eat in the dining room where Pettit and Stone fed so many mountain children. The John C. Campbell Folk School is well into its second half-century, and one can still take a hard right at Mercer Scroggs's store, drive around the circular driveway in front of the weaving room, sit on the back porch of Keith

House, and look away across the fields to the Brasstown community where Mrs. Campbell's heart "turned most."

But more important than buildings are the shadows of people, programs, and ideas which still stretch across the intellectual and cultural landscape in the mountains. I knew that in a powerful way on an afternoon in 1981 in Stuart, Virginia—in that part of the mountains Cecil Sharp passed through without finding much music or culture he thought worthy of note—as I watched the son and grandson of fine black musicians who would never have been welcome upon lily White Top sit behind the counter of his father's roadside grocery store and read Richard Chase's *Jack Tales* for a course on Appalachian culture he was taking at Berea College.

Thus to note that many cultural intervention efforts "fail"—that the intervenors do not persevere individually, or that some of their institutions do not last—is too facile. Even when institutions pass from the scene, attitudes and assumptions remain, styles and designs persist, myths retain credibility.

Cultural intervention is, finally, a process which must be comprehended not only as an important element of the cultural history of one region in one period, but as a little understood feature of every cultural past, an inevitable component of every cultural present and future. Two episodes, far removed from the mountains in space and time but eerily close to some elements of its history, may lend weight to that assertion and perhaps help suggest some larger patterns.

The interaction of colonizing Englishmen and American Indians in coastal Virginia in the early seventeenth century proved to have a rather surprising predictive value for later encounters in the mountains, which were less violent but little less culturally complex. And the attempt more than a century later to "revive" Gaelic culture in Scotland took forms and brought forth consequences that give the viewer of cultural revival efforts in the southern mountains still another century later a disquieting sense of déjà vu.

In his recent study of the interaction between English colonizers and American Indians, Bernard Sheehan depicts a situation remarkably parallel in some respects to what transpired when missionaries, ballad collectors, festival organizers, and other cultural emissaries from "civilization" discovered southern mountaineers. What happened when Her Majesty's loyal subjects met the Indians in the coastal pine forests of Virginia throws the work of Katherine Pettit, May Stone, Olive Dame Campbell, Cecil Sharp, John Powell, Annabel Morris Buchanan, and their colleagues into sharp relief and reminds one yet again how perilous is the crossing between one cultural system and another.

The story of Englishmen and Indians in Virginia, argues Sheehan, is one of unrelieved "misperception" and cultural conflict, in which "perceptions of the actualities of Indian culture remained dim, scattered, tentative and invariably ethnocentric." Englishmen "never quite realized," Sheehan concludes, "that they had become enmeshed in a relationship with a traditional society made up of real people."[1]

Repeating patterns that had appeared earlier in both classical literature and the reflections of medieval travelers, Englishmen in the New World saw Indians as at once noble and ignoble savages. On the one hand, they were perceived as inhabitants of an earthly paradise (like the romantic "world of green and silver" that some ballad collectors saw in the mountains) in which the social structures, intellectual habits, manners, and economic arrangements familiar in European life were irrelevant (and therefore absent). On the other hand, they were bestial creatures, given to violence and treachery (like Kentucky feudists) who "neither use table, stoole or table cloth for comlinesse" (51). Because Indians "failed to replicate the civil order characteristic of European life," their very humanity remained "open to question" (65).

The Englishman's fundamental dependence upon the knowledge and skill of Indians for his very survival—for food, especially—in no way altered his ingrained perceptions. Englishmen were never able to admit the "inherent integrity" of the Indians' way of life (89). If Indians had a year of good crops and enjoyed eating and sharing of their bounty, they were viewed as "improvident." If crops were destroyed by fire or drought and food was scarce, they were inept and childlike (107). Even the Indians' beautiful human practice of gift-giving was seen as deriving from "the savagism of a simple and untutored people who had not yet acquired the wit to know the value of property" (38).

Despite evidence that the Indians' way of life was better suited than their own to actual conditions in Virginia in the early 1600s, Englishmen remained convinced that "Christ commanded [them] to spread his religion among the heathens" (a conviction that was shared by many a fotched-on missionary from the Bluegrass or New England to the southern mountains), and that savage people "ought to be grateful for the gifts of Christianity and civility" (116). As a learned Spaniard commented, Columbus's mission was "to unite the world and give to those strange lands the form of our own" (118). Thus colonial subjugation and religious conversion were linked (indeed, inseparable) aims.

Even the mechanisms chosen for the conversion endeavor cast a beam forward through the centuries—and westward to the mountains. English agent George Thorpe thought conversion would be facilitated by luring Indians into an English style of life through gifts of "apparell and house-holdstufe." "By opening their homes to the Indians, exchanging goods and knowledge, and exposing the natives to the proficiency of the white man's world," Sheehan observes, "the English thought that native society would be gradually recast." The summer encampments in Knott County were of course based upon precisely such a premise, and both Hindman Settlement School and the John C. Campbell Folk School derived from plans that resembled Englishman Robert Johnson's seventeenth-century one to "take their children, train them up in gentleness, teach them our English tongue and the principles of religion; [and] win the older sort by wisdom and discretion." You must, Johnson advised, "have patience and humanity to manage their crooked nature to your form of civility" (126).

In the seventeenth century, some few promising Indians were even sent to England to be educated and trained in civility, as mountain youngsters were sent from Hindman to Science Hill, Berea, and Wellesley three hundred years later. In 1617, plans were laid for Henrico College ("a colledge [sic] for infidels"), an institution designed to civilize and socialize scores of Indian youngsters. Henrico was remarkably similar in important respects to the Hindman and John C. Campbell schools, except that it did not include preserving the culture of its students among its formal aims. Historian Robert Land has noted the judgment of an earlier scholar that Henrico was similar to an industrial school, designed to teach Indians skills that would enable them to become farmers and planters. Henrico students were to concentrate on religious and academic studies to age twelve, and thereafter to be trained in "some lawful trade." Supporters in England sent money and religious books for the college (as did many a *New* Englander to the southern mountains). One anonymous friend sent "a communion cup, . . . a trencher plate for the bread, a carpet of crimson velvet, and a damask table cloth"—for "comlinesse," presumably. College deputy George Thorpe set out ten thousand grape vines in an attempt to use college lands (industrial school fashion) to develop a new staple crop, and also experimented with silk culture.[2]

But the Indians considered silkworms, Henrico College, and grapes a poor trade for what had been stolen from them, and in 1622 they rose and massacred the English colonists. Thorpe was killed and mutilated, and Henrico College was burned to the ground. An attempt was made to revive the college after the massacre, but the effort terminated with the revocation of the Virginia Company of London's charter in 1624.[3]

The parallels are not difficult to perceive. And while not exact by any means, they are more than close enough to be instructive. Much of what happened in the mountains at the Forks of Troublesome, at White Top, at Brasstown—and at many another location beyond the immediate scope of this book—was finally not that different from what happened in Virginia. The "savagism" of the Indians was functionally analogous to mountaineers' social and cultural "backwardness"; both derived from a culturally based misperception. Like the Indians, mountaineers were ambivalently characterized as noble ("100% Americans of the best stock") or ignoble (inbred degenerates, feudists, and moonshiners). Cultural intervention in the mountains was also fired by an ethnocentric conviction that bringing "advanced" (New England or Bluegrass) civilization to social and cultural premoderns was humane and enlightened despite its physical, social, and cultural costs to the indigenous population. Moreover, the acculturation process in both cases exerted subtle (and not so subtle) pressures on lifestyle (food, clothing, manners), and resulted in the building of special educational facilities (Henrico, Hindman, John C. Campbell) and the sending of children to schools in the mother country (England, New England, Bluegrass Kentucky). And in neither case did the light bringers apparently ever have the slightest doubts about the correctness and inherent superiority of their ethnocentric view of the world.

The costs to the Indians were ultimately much higher, of course, than were those to the mountaineers. At least the mountaineers were not exterminated. But the losses in the physical bases of life were more comparable than might first appear. Indians were gradually stripped of their land, fishing and hunting rights, and freedom to choose their own leaders and govern their own affairs. Mountaineers lost their land, too—though in most cases not directly to the selfsame bringers of social and cultural "light." They lost it to the timber cutters, railroad builders, tourism promoters, and coal operators—not a few of whom contributed money (and sympathy) to the settlement schools, folk schools, and cultural festivals.

Indeed, it seems reasonable to speculate that the very *fusion* of colonial subjugator and Christian missionary in the Englishman may have helped the Indians to retain a clearer sense of who the enemy was and what he was up to. Sheehan came away from his study impressed with the "inherent obduracy of culture"; I come to the end of this one amazed by the very plasticity and malleability of culture in the mountains. Indians preferred not to cooperate with the "collapse of their way of life" and were able to absorb "great quantities of European goods" without losing "the integrity of their society" (128ff.). And when the pressure became too great, they rose and massacred their self-appointed benefactors. But mountaineers did not, obviously. Why was there not more resistance—or at least hesitation?

One reason, apparently, is that the connection between social-cultural mission and economic exploitation in the mountains was more subtle and (therefore) confusing than it was in tidewater Virginia. The shift from saturnalian revel to Victorian Christmas trees, carols, and gifts bought with coal-money philanthropy (or fourth-generation New England slave, rum, or textile money) was not different in its human and cultural significance from teaching Indians to use tablecloths. But it was no doubt more difficult for mountaineers to perceive the connection between Christmas trees and John C. C. Mayo or the Bethlehem Steel Company than it was for Indians to see that the same breastplated Englishman was teaching them Christian prayers and stealing their land and corn.

The Indians were in another paradoxical sense more fortunate, since the cultural distances between them and the English were greater and the boundaries more sharply marked. In conflict situations, it is advantageous to be able to identify one's adversaries unambiguously. Unfortunately in some respects, the "quare women" were not quare *enough*.

If the cultural, social, economic, and spiritual collision between Indians and Englishmen in tidewater Virginia foreshadowed a part of what happened at mountain folk and settlement schools, the eighteenth-century Gaelic revival carries one forward to White Top—and to the extensive folk-revival aspects of the mountain schools as well.

According to Malcolm Chapman's account, the seventeenth century was a waning time for authentic Gaelic culture; the Gaelic language had been in declining use for five hundred years.[4] By the early eighteenth century, sophisticated southerners viewed Highlanders as both barbarous and (Englishmen and Indians again) noble savages. Following the 1745 uprising under Bonnie Prince Charlie, traditional Highland dress had been proscribed by the Disclothing Act of 1747, as part of a larger plan to "de-Gaelicise" the region. The plan gained assistance from the clergy, who were, Chapman says, "foremost in consigning to the . . . rubbish heap the old customs of their people" (15).

For a number of complicated reasons, however, the outside world began to take renewed interest in the Highlands in the mid-eighteenth century. The general rise of Romanticism found particular expression in the spu-

rious but attractive Gaelic poems of Ossian, which met with an enthusiastic audience in such cities as London and Edinburgh. In the late eighteenth century the latter, says Chapman, was "a world where Gaeldom and
its customs were used to satisfy a taste for exotic ephemera. It was a world
where Highland culture was little regarded except as it fluttered with its
decorative symbols, the clan and the claymore, the kilt and the bag pipe. It
was the Edinburgh where Ossian became the talk of every drawing room,
where the disappearance of the ancient Erse was anticipated, and where
rationalists and improvers constructed their economies" (68).[5]

Two of the patterns Chapman locates in the Gaelic revival are most instructive as one attempts to comprehend analogous efforts in the Appalachian region much later: the appetite of outsiders for the romantic,
picturesque aspects of an alien culture "distant enough to be exotic . . .
but close enough to be noticed" (19); and their skill in "reviving" a reconstructed version of that culture suited to their own psychic needs and social purposes. Thus, as Chapman astutely observes, trying to understand
Gaelic (or Appalachian, or native American) culture presents the central
problem of "find[ing] a voice independent of that which is supplied by a
dominant and manipulative external discourse" (108).

The discourse upon the culture of the Appalachian region which emanated from (in the worst case) John Powell on White Top was "manipulative and external" in the extreme. And although the messages from Brasstown and Hindman were softer, gentler, and on the whole more humane,
externality and manipulativeness have nevertheless been a central characteristic of the discourse associated with almost every encounter with the
culture of southern mountain people—from the 1830s to the 1980s.

From this perception, from the case studies presented earlier, and from
the parallels sketched quickly here, it is possible to make some final obser-
vations about cultural intervention as a process that is larger and more persistent than events of any one region and period could reveal.

Just as every act in a complex social order is inescapably political in
character, so is it also bound up—in origin, intent, and effect—with culture. Thus culture must inevitably be construed in political terms, *especially* in an encounter between two cultural systems that are socially or economically unequal. When studies similar to the ones I have presented here
are undertaken for other regions and among other cultural groups in the
United States—Cajuns in southwest Louisiana, Scandinavians in the Upper Midwest, Chicanos in the Southwest, blacks anywhere—patterns in
the politics of culture similar to those I have sketched here will undoubtedly emerge.

An intervenor, by virtue of his or her status, power, and established credibility, is frequently able to define what the culture *is*, to normalize and legitimize that definition in the larger society, and even to feed it back into the culture itself, where it may be internalized as "real" or "traditional" or "authentic," as in the case of Sharp's morris dances, Chase's Jack tales, Campbell's carved animals, Berea's weaving, or Hindman's Fireside Industries and Roycroft furniture.

The "culture" that is perceived by the intervenor (even before the act of intervention) is rarely congruent with the culture that is actually there. It is a *selection*, an *arrangement*, an *accommodation* to preconceptions— whether of mountaineers, or Indians, or Georgia blacks, or Scotch Highlanders. Thus the culture that is "preserved" or "revived" is a hybrid at best: mountain banjo players coached to "keep it Dorian" when they play their tunes; mountain dancers urged by a Harvard boy to dress better and get "hip swing" into their movements; metal finger picks and jazzy tunes forbidden; feud songs banished; Cherokee County boys and girls practicing the "Anders hop."

As an impulse, cultural intervention arises from a marvelously tangled skein of assumptions, preconceptions, motives, and rationales. Behind Hindman lay (to take only the bolder strands) the settlement houses of the North, the industrial schools of the South, some shopworn myths about the mountains, and the mingled spirits of Vassar, Berea, and Bluegrass Kentucky. Behind White Top lay nearly two hundred years of fiddlers' contests, some folk festivals organized by a promoter for the Canadian Pacific Railroad, Cumberland Presbyterianism, commercially recorded hillbilly music, FFV elitism and racism, and the lives of poor people buffeted by Depression times. Behind the Campbell Folk School lay the Russell Sage Foundation's southern mountains study, the handicrafts movement, the "ballad wars," the twin shades of Grundtvig and Kold, and the Rockefeller-funded General Education Board.

By directing attention away from dominant structural realities, such as those associated with colonial subjugation or resource exploitation or class-based inequalities, "culture" provides a convenient mask for other agendas of change and throws a warm glow upon the cold realities of social dislocation.

Relationships between culturally intervening institutions and the political, social, and economic contexts in which they operate vary greatly, but, in general, *functional* connections between the two are tenuous at best. Hindman grew up in an area dominated by unregulated, large-scale extractive industries, whose powerful executives were happy enough to hear mountain children sing old songs and see them dance new dances ("With their contributions they send the most sympathetic letters," Pettit said), but would have taken a dim view indeed of any effort to encourage those same children to question the consensus ideology of the coal industry. The folk school, on the other hand, was a hundred miles at least from the nearest coal mine, in the middle of a small-scale agricultural area changing rapidly in response to increasing tourism, TVA-related development, and diffuse modernization and urbanization. But Olive Dame Campbell chose to emulate the most conservative aspects of Danish folk school philosophy and practice, held to the model long after its obsolescence had become manifest, and therefore could not respond to the changes as they pressed upon her and her school. White Top sat at the center of an old agricultural area rich in both traditional music and the newer commercial sounds, ringed by small towns and increasingly dominated by small industries hit hard by the Depression. In such a context John Blakemore's entrepreneurial cynicism, John Powell's elitism and racism, and Annabel Morris Buchanan's romanticism and personal vulnerability proved to be great liabilities. Indeed in all three cases, conceptions of culture itself and of the relationship between culture and the social, political, and economic context were too limited to encompass even *present* realities, to say nothing of the dynamics of change.

"Rescuing" or "preserving" or "reviving" a sanitized version of culture frequently makes for rather shallow liberal commitment: it allows a prepared consensus on the "value" of preservation or revival; its affirmations lie comfortably within the bounds of conventional secular piety; it makes minimal demands upon financial (or other) resources; and it involves little risk of opposition from vested economic or political interests. It is, in a word, the cheapest and safest way to go.

In some respects, people's "ties" to tradition prove to be less strong and durable than is generally assumed, especially when maintaining those ties entails psychic, social, or economic costs. For every mountaineer who affirms and holds consciously to tradition, hundreds welcome (and even seek) the changes that intervenors introduce into even the most "traditional" parts of their lives. For every Albert Hash, there are hundreds of Rhoda Stacys who are eager to sing "yourn way, not ourn." Except in situations of highly concentrated or extreme cultural pressure (war, massive political repression, forced relocation), moreover, people appear not to conceive of their own culture and traditions as being nearly as fragile as they are frequently assumed to be by others. They contemplate, confront, and adapt to change with a quite remarkable enthusiasm, equanimity, and agility. More refined analysis is needed if one is to comprehend how and why people resist and accommodate, keep and let go.

Cultural objects, styles, and practices introduced by intervenors sometimes prove remarkably durable, regardless of how little prior basis they had in the culture. The tens of thousands of tourists who visit the publicly funded Folk Art Center at the entrance to the Blue Ridge Parkway or troop through the craft shops of Gatlinburg or Asheville, and the millions who listen to folk-revival musicians on National Public Radio, are "seeing" and "hearing" continuity that is partial at best; they are buying the fruits of hybrid cultural trees that were long ago severely pruned and grafted. What they have in their shopping bags as they climb back into station wagons and onto tour buses is, to use a term familiar to cultural anthropologists, "airport culture."

The energies that undergird cultural intervention efforts frequently arise from and are shaped by personal needs that have little or no logical relation to the enterprise as it is publicly described and justified. The most dramatic example in the foregoing case studies is of course John Powell's racism, but others are easy to find, as Jacquelyn Jones discovered in her study of the "soldiers of light and love" who came south after the Civil War to teach blacks in Georgia, and as Chapman and Sheehan have shown for the Scottish Highlands and seventeenth-century coastal Virginia.

In the mountains, to draw out for a moment an example passed over rather hurriedly in the initial case study, one reason that Katherine Pettit had trouble keeping teachers at her settlement schools was that so many Smith and Wellesley and Vassar girls (as well as Bluegrass belles) who came to teach hillbilly boys married them. The personal (and feminist) implications of *that* pattern seemed important enough to Lucy Furman to cause her to return to the theme again and again in her novels. The loftier theory of settlement work goes only so far in explaining motive; a major preoccupation of settlement teachers was their relationships with men and their attempts to find meaningful work in two different social orders (the mountains and either Bluegass Kentucky or male-dominated Victorian New England) which routinely denied it to them.

Although mountain society was depicted in the novels as the most repressively patriarchal (Uncle Lot tells Aunt Ailsie that he is her "God app'inted head"), Bluegrass women were attracted to the mountains—even if only temporarily—partly to escape the boredom, tediousness, and meaninglessness of lives as Bluegrass belles waiting anxiously to be Sleeping Beauty–ed by some Bluegrass gentleman. "What more truthful and appealing work, particularly for women, do these United States offer?" Ida

Tarbell asks in her introduction to Furman's *Sight for the Blind*. "If there is an idle or lonely woman anywhere revolting against the dullness of life, wanting work with the flavor and virility of pioneering in it, let her look to these mountains."

Some of the settlement women in the novels were fleeing disappointment elsewhere. The teacher who narrates *Mothering on Perilous* says her "dearest ambition" was to make a home and "have a houseful of children." Frustrated in that, she turns to mothering (a houseful of Hindman boys) on Perilous and finds a "wonderful resurrection from grief, despair and selfishness to life and love and service. . . . [My] once lonely and drifting barque is held in a fair harbor by twelve strong anchors" (*MP*, 309ff.).

Other women came temporarily—to grow up and find themselves as independent and self-reliant beings. "I . . . was born out of time," says Susannah Reeves. "I should have been a pioneer woman. . . . Or at the very least, I should have been born in these mountains, where life is still alive and interesting, men still do brave and daring things" (*Glass Window*, p. 220). Engaged to marry a Bluegrass surgeon, Susannah delays again and again returning to the "normal" life that awaits her. She was too "petted and pampered" there, she says, to have had an opportunity "to be a real woman." But during her year in the mountains, she writes to her fiance, "I have really grown to womanhood" (*GW*, p. 194).

One of the poignant differences between mountain and Bluegrass women—which forged a bond of sympathy between them—was that the latter had the substance, and therefore the leisure, not to have been forced early into oppressive marriages with sundry "God app'inted heads." Susannah nevertheless eventually marries her Bluegrass surgeon in the library of the settlement school, saying—when he reminds her that her work of gathering logs for the buildings is unfinished—"let somebody else do it!" Later when mountaineer Giles Kent marries New Englander Christina Potter, he asks her about "all the things you must give up for me." "I count them as nothing," she replies (*GW*, p. 276).

On the one hand, one need not accept the severe explanatory limits of a trite romantic literary convention. Obviously, women came to teach and work in the settlements (and left to live elsewhere) for a vast number of reasons—many of which undoubtedly had little or nothing to do with men. But on the other hand, one ignores this element—as well as many other less than obvious or "reasonable" ones—at one's peril.

That cultural intervenors may be on the whole decent, well-meaning, even altruistic people does not (indeed must not) excuse them from historical judgment. One may reasonably display great charity for the cross-purposes, confusions, and miscalculations of fallible individuals in diffi-cult circumstances. But insofar as those people actively intervene in the cultural (or other) lives of large numbers of people, their failures and mis-calculations, however "understandable," become a legitimate object of public concern. For the effects of what they do touch so many, and linger so long.

One can see that with some clarity in the current situation at both Hind-man Settlement School and the John C. Campbell Folk School. Both have only recently acquired their first native-born directors, and both are strug-gling to find a useful contemporary role that is to some degree congruent with the institution's past (and—necessarily—therefore agreeable to es-tablished contributors). But since each school's program was in major re-spects so *in*congruent with the local social, economic, and cultural situa-tion at every period, maintaining continuity is a decidedly mixed blessing. Thus a major barrier for each institution is precisely its own past and the inertias and pieties that attach to it.

Michael Mullins, current director of Hindman Settlement School, has searched diligently and with some success for a new role and functions for the institution. As the school entered its ninth decade, the dormitories no longer echoed with archaic ballads and sword-dance tunes. Instead there was a remedial learning program for dyslexic children, a National Wom-en's Health Network meeting, an annual workshop for young Appalachian writers, a "visual arts week" which drew both local and outside artists as instructors, workshops on childbirth, credit unions, and greenhouse con-struction, and an adult high-school equivalency program. These are all ad-mirable efforts in themselves, all perfectly consistent with the practice of settlement houses as it developed ninety years earlier. And all several An-ders hops beyond sword dances in their social utility.

And yet—one must reluctantly observe—they focus on the symptoms rather than the causes of social dislocations: on poor educational programs and housing and nutritional conditions rather than on the coal-dominated social, political, and economic system of the area.

The reasons for this emphasis are not hard to understand. First, eastern Kentucky history is replete with dramatic and sometimes gruesome evi-dence of the cost of calling a spade a spade. From Harlan County in the 1930s to the strip-mining wars of the 1960s and 1970s, the cost has been clear; one may as well read the system and weep, for it will tolerate (per-sonally or institutionally) only that which poses no real threat. Thus Mul-lins's choice is an agonizing one: sacrifice the school or steer it delicately between the channel markers placed by the industry, relieving as many personal hurts along the way as one can.

Second—and this harks back to the very beginning—the school's involvement with a safely defined "culture" gives it an arena of apparent legitimacy, connectedness, and usefulness which partly alleviates the sense of frustration and futility that might otherwise sweep over one and all. In Miss Watts's terms, the school has "successfully" avoided politics for eighty years; in Alfred North Whitehead's tougher terms, it has chosen a domain of misplaced concreteness as its major sphere of activity. It is as if the romantic version of local culture, introduced at the Forks of Troublesome by some Bluegrass ladies, now will not ever go away. Romantic "culture" and the myth of Uncle Sol are available for each new generation, and they blur the stark realities of life in eastern Kentucky.[6] Culture as "soft" legitimacy, as energy sink.

At Hindman the cultural ghosts linger on in the form of dulcimer concerts, "folk evenings," handicrafts classes, and "family folk weeks" interspersed with GED classes and greenhouse workshops. The culture featured at the 1982 "family folk week" had about as much basis in local tradition as the culture featured at the school had ever had: two Ritchie daughters presenting what D. K. Wilgus recognized more than twenty years ago as a special settlement school version of mountain music; Morris Amburgey making the same dulcimers his father learned to make from Uncle Ed Thomas, who shipped most of *his* dulcimers to New York; a local bluegrass band; a Lexington, Kentucky, hammered dulcimer maker, and a player from the Midwest whose role in the mountains currently bears an intriguing resemblance to that of Richard Chase or John Jacob Niles a half-century earlier; the McLain Family Band, led by Raymond McLain, who guided the school through its most intense morris- and sword-dance period; and the daughter of a former Berea College president, who is the latest link in Hindman's historic tie to the Berea versions of mountain dancing, weaving, and ballad singing.

At Brasstown, the situation is both more and less complicated than at Hindman. Less in that Clay and Cherokee counties had no coal, and therefore were spared some of the more dramatic upheavals of Knott County, Kentucky. Less also in that, lacking such a concentration of money and power, the area has spawned no monolithic local system which the school must confront. But more in the sense that throughout its history the folk school existed within a conceptual box that was even tighter than that at Hindman. Except for a brief (and surprisingly successful) foray into agriculture, the folk school focused most of its energies, programs, and facilities upon folk-revival enterprises of a romantic and essentially alien sort. Both its buildings and (more important) the people who take classes there and contribute money now reflect that focus; local people have very little to do with the folk school.

The dilemma for mountain-born director Esther Hyatt is acute: in order to maintain the staff and physical plant, donations and class fees must continue. But they will continue only if the programs preferred by benefactors and potential students are continued. And those programs remain rooted in the cultural vision of the Southern Highland Handicraft Guild, the settlement schools, Berea College, and the romantic cultural revivalism of the 1920s and 1930s. In effect, then, the school is a refuge from both local *and* national cultural reality. As such, it is more or less ignored by local people and frequented mostly by culturally dislocated middle-class visitors from other parts of the country. Local people are more likely to enroll at the tri-county vocational-technical school in Murphy—many of whose functions and emphases were vainly urged upon folk school trustees by Dagnall Folger and Howard Kester thirty years earlier.

In one way, then, the schools are reverse images: facing overwhelming needs, Michael Mullins has little freedom to act in Knott County; Esther Hyatt, having considerable freedom to act insofar as the local situation is concerned, is constrained by the preferences of her distant supporters and by the lack of a clear sense of precisely what local needs the school could at long last respond to.

A final word, both serious and playful. In early-seventeenth-century Virginia, Sheehan relates, it was a continual embarrassment to English colonizers—who considered themselves such admirable specimens of spiritual and cultural superiority—that so many of their number became convinced of the actual superiority of Indian life and "went over" to live with the "savages." It is perhaps perverse, but tantalizing, nevertheless, to speculate on what might have happened had more New England and Bluegrass ladies (and gentlemen) "gone over" to the enemy. The image of a shouting and slightly tipsy Lucy Furman riding hell-for-leather through the muddy streets of Hindman on an old-fashioned saturnalian (that is to say, "chair-flingin'") Christmas eve is no doubt too far fetched to contemplate, but had she sketched a scene in one of her novels of a recidivist Fighting Fult Fallon escaping in the nick of time—purple knee-britches and all—through the bushes with his mountain Nancibel in tow, it would at least have given William Aspenwall Bradley something disquietingly useful to ponder. Like the narrator of Tom T. Hall's country song "The Little Lady Preacher," he could have "sat and wondered who it was converted whom."

"The world," as the pagan Queequeg tells the New England idealist Ishmael in *Moby-Dick*, "is a joint-stock company. Us cannibals have to help those Christians."

Notes

The following abbreviations are used in the notes:

AMBP: Annabel Morris Buchanan Papers, Southern Historical Collection

BFP-LC: Breckinridge Family Papers, Library of Congress

CP-SHC: John C. and Olive Dame Campbell Papers, Southern Historical Collection

EFSSA: Cecil Sharp, *English Folk Songs of the Southern Appalachians*

GEB: General Education Board

HSS: Hindman Settlement School Archives

IAOS: Irish Agricultural Organisation Society

JABP: John A. Blakemore Papers, Southern Historical Collection

JAF: *Journal of American Folklore*

JPP: John Powell Papers, Alderman Library, University of Virginia

ODC: Olive Dame Campbell

SHC-UNC: Southern Historical Collection, University of North Carolina

SHHL: John C. Campbell, *The Southern Highlander and His Homeland*

Introduction

1. Sarah S. Gielow, *Uncle Sam* (New York: H. Revell, 1913), p. 18. The novel is discussed briefly in Cratis D. Williams, "The Southern Mountaineer in Fact and Fiction" (Ph.D. diss., New York University, 1961). I am grateful to the Alderman Library at the University of Virginia for supplying a copy.

2. Gielow, *Uncle Sam*, p. 60.

3. See for example Roy B. Clarkson, *Tumult on the Mountains: Lumbering in West Virginia, 1770–1920* (Parsons, W.Va.: McClain Printing Co., 1964); C. Vann Woodward, *The Origins of the New South, 1877–1913* (Baton Rouge: Louisiana State University Press, 1951); Ronald D. Eller, *Miners, Millhands and Moun-*

taineers: The Modernization of the Appalachian South, 1880–1930 (Knoxville: University of Tennessee Press, 1981); David Corbin, *Life, Work, and Rebellion in the Coal Fields: Southern West Virginia Miners, 1880–1922* (Urbana: University of Illinois Press, 1981); and John Gaventa, *Power and Powerlessness: Quiescence and Rebellion in an Appalachian Valley* (Urbana: University of Illinois Press, 1980).

4. For an overview, see Carl N. Degler, *The Other South: Southern Dissenters in the Nineteenth Century* (New York: Harper & Row, 1974).

5. See Bill C. Malone, *Southern Music American Music* (Lexington: University Press of Kentucky, 1979).

6. Most are described at least briefly in Allen H. Eaton, *Handicrafts of the Southern Highlands* (New York: Russell Sage Foundation, 1937).

7. The process is detailed in John Prebble, *The Highland Clearances* (London: Secker and Warburg, 1963). In the concluding chapter of my *Modernizing the Mountaineer: People, Power, and Planning in Appalachia* (Boone, N.C.: Appalachian Consortium Press, 1981), I sketched some parallels between the Highland clearances and recent "regional development" schemes in Appalachia, especially with regard to their cultural dimensions and implications.

8. The discussion that follows is based upon Jacqueline Jones, *Soldiers of Light and Love: Northern Teachers and Georgia Blacks, 1865–1873* (Chapel Hill: University of North Carolina Press, 1980).

9. Ibid., pp. 30–41, 210–18.

10. Ibid., p. 154. Cf. p. 9.

11. Ibid., p. 4.

12. Ibid., pp. 111–26, 25ff.

13. Ibid., pp. 5–20.

14. Ibid., pp. 99, 149.

15. The conscious and intentional shift of missionary effort from southern blacks to mountain whites has been ably chronicled in James Klotter, "The Black South and White Appalachia," *Journal of American History* 66 (March 1980): 832–49. An excellent discussion of the role of local-color fiction in bringing the region to public attention at the end of the century may be found in Henry D. Shapiro, "A Strange Land and a Peculiar People: The Discovery of Appalachia, 1870–1920" (Ph.D. diss., Rutgers University, 1967).

16. Mary Swain Routzhan, "Presenting Mountain Work to the Public," *Mountain Life and Work* 3 (July 1928): 17–30.

17. Ann Douglas, *The Feminization of American Culture* (New York: Knopf, 1979), pp. 57, 46.

18. Dena Epstein, *Sinful Tunes and Spirituals: Black Folk Music to the Civil War* (Urbana: University of Illinois Press, 1977), p. 30.

19. Ibid., pp. 89f.

20. Ibid., p. 275.

21. Ibid., pp. 297–300.

22. Douglas, *The Feminization of American Culture*, p. 35.

23. Ibid., p. 69.

Chapter 1

1. Raymond McLain, "Early Ballad Singing at Hindman," quoting Elizabeth Watts in an undated typescript in the Hindman Settlement School Archives, Hindman, Kentucky; and Hindman newsletter of January 1918. I am grateful to Michael Mullins, director of Hindman Settlement School, for making the Hindman archives available to me. The account of Hindman Settlement School which follows is based upon those archives (hereafter cited as HSS), upon published sources cited, and upon additional archival materials at the King Library at the University of Kentucky; the John C. Campbell Papers in the Southern Historical Collection at the University of North Carolina (hereafter cited as CP-SHC); the Breckinridge Family Papers in the Library of Congress (hereafter cited as BFP-LC); and in the personal papers of Elizabeth Watts. For valuable suggestions I am indebted to Anne Campbell, Archie Green, Loyal Jones, Michael Mullins, James Still, Fredrika Teute, and Elizabeth Watts.

2. Sharp's ballad collecting, in which he collaborated with Olive Dame Campbell, is treated in Chapter 2.

3. By the 1920s, Olive Dame Campbell was able to count more than 120 such schools. See Olive Dame Campbell, *Southern Highland Schools Maintained by Denominational and Independent Agencies* (rev. ed., New York: Russell Sage Foundation, 1929). For a brief discussion of the schools see John C. Campbell, *The Southern Highlander and His Homeland* (New York: Russell Sage Foundation, 1921), pp. 271–89.

4. The industrial school model will receive further attention below.

5. For an introduction, see Jane Addams's classic *Twenty Years at Hull House* (New York: Macmillan, 1910); Gaylord White, "The Settlement Idea after Twenty-Five Years," *Harvard Theological Review*, 4 (1911): 47–70; Arthur C. Holden, *The Settlement Idea* (1922; rpt. New York: Arno, 1970); Robert A. Woods, *Handbook of Settlements* (1911; rpt. New York: Arno, 1970); Robert A. Woods and Albert J. Kennedy, *The Settlement Horizon* (1922; rpt. New York: Arno, 1970); and especially Allen F. Davis, *Spearheads of Reform: The Social Settlements and the Progressive Movement, 1890–1914* (New York: Oxford University Press, 1967).

6. Davis, *Spearheads*, p. 3.

7. Quoted from the guild's first report in Holden, *Settlement Idea*, p. 15.

8. Davis, *Spearheads*, p. 12.

9. The following brief account is based upon Addams, *Twenty Years at Hull House*, from which all quotations are taken.

10. Two other important aspects of Hull House work—their efforts to preserve and use immigrant culture and their involvement in urban political reform—will be discussed later.

11. White, "The Settlement Idea," p. 49.

12. Addams, *Twenty Years at Hull House*, p. 312.

13. Davis, *Spearheads*, p. 33.

14. See David E. Whisnant, "Selling the Gospel News, or: The Strange Career of Jimmy Brown the Newsboy," *Journal of Social History* 5 (spring, 1972): 306n.; Joel H. Spring, *Education and the Rise of the Corporate State* (Boston: Beacon Press, 1972), pp. 69–71. On 4 August 1900 (p. 4), the *Lexington Morning Herald* reported

on New York's Russell Sage, who bought the little fifty-mile-long Poughkeepsie and Eastern Railroad, hoping to use it to connect the Hudson River with New England. When the scheme failed, he built an amusement park to try to generate traffic. When that failed also, he used the rail line to take poor children from Poughkeepsie on day-long excursions into the country.

15. John P. Gavit, "Rural Social Settlements," *Commons*, May 1899, pp. 5-6. The movement of the settlement idea to rural areas occurred concurrently with its movement to the South. The latter has been partially sketched in Milton Speizman, "The Movement of the Settlement House Idea into the South," *Southwestern Social Science Quarterly* 44 (December 1963): 237-46, which focuses on Kingsley House in New Orleans, established in 1899. Although Speizman calls Kingsley House the first "real" social settlement in the South, Noreen Dunn Tatum demonstrates in *A Crown of Service: A Story of Woman's Work in the Methodist Episcopal Church, South, from 1878-1900* (Nashville: Parthenon Press, 1960), pp. 242ff., that Methodist women established a series of "Wesley houses"—similar in many respects to settlements—much earlier in Birmingham (1877, five years before London's Toynbee Hall) and Atlanta (1882).

16. According to Woods's *Handbook of Settlements*, there were at least two settlements in rural areas in the South at the time Gavit wrote: the Calhoun Colored School and Settlement, established in Lowndes County, Alabama, in 1892 (p. 6), and the Log Cabin Settlement near Asheville, North Carolina, founded by Vassar graduate Susan Chester about 1893 (p. 249). See also Frances MacGregor Ingram, "The Settlement Movement in the South," *World Outlook*, May 1937, pp. 12-14, 38. On the Calhoun School, see *Negro Education: A Study of the Private and Higher Schools for Colored People in the United States* (2 vols., Washington, D.C.: U.S. Bureau of Education, 1917), 1:125, and 2:58-60.

Woods lists a half-dozen settlements as having been established in rural areas in the South by 1910 and a number of others in small to medium-sized cities, such as Atlanta (1903, 1909), Augusta (1908), and LaGrange (1908), Georgia; Bristol (1909), Knoxville (1908), and Nashville (1901-9), Tennessee; Hampton (1890), Portsmouth (1910), and Richmond (1900), Virginia; and Winston-Salem, North Carolina (1909).

17. For a survey of the popular fiction, see Cratis D. Williams, "The Southern Mountaineer in Fact and Fiction" (Ph.D. diss., New York University, 1961); and Henry D. Shapiro, "A Strange Land and a Peculiar People: The Discovery of Appalachia, 1870-1920" (Ph.D. diss., Rutgers, 1967). Shapiro's dissertation is in my view a more accessible and coherent treatment of the pertinent literary history than is his later *Appalachia On Our Mind: The Southern Mountains and Mountaineers in the American Consciousness, 1870-1920* (Chapel Hill: University of North Carolina Press, 1978).

18. For a contemporary account of the feuds, see S. S. MacClintock, "The Kentucky Mountains and Their Feuds," *American Journal of Sociology* 7 (July 1901): 1-28 and 171-87. MacClintock, drawing extensively upon George E. Vincent's earlier article "A Retarded Frontier," *American Journal of Sociology* 4 (July 1898): 1-22, and articles in the *Berea Quarterly*, called eastern Kentucky "a case of arrested development in civilization." Vincent's article was based upon a four-day horseback trip through three eastern Kentucky counties.

19. On some connections between the feuds and broader social and economic dynamics in the mountains, see Gordon B. McKinney, "Industrialization and Violence in Appalachia in the 1890s," in J. W. Williamson, ed., *An Appalachian Symposium: Essays in Honor of Cratis D. Williams* (Boone, N.C.: Appalachian State University Press, 1977), pp. 131–46.

20. May Stone, "Katherine Pettit's first trips to the Kentucky Mountains," undated typescript (HSS). Women's clubs multiplied rapidly in the South in the years 1884–87, as Anne Firor Scott shows in *The Southern Lady, 1830–1930: From Pedestal to Politics* (Chicago: University of Chicago Press, 1970), pp. 150ff. Scott notes (p. 161) that federations of such clubs "were formed in every southern state" between 1894 and 1907.

21. The scant information that is available on this episode is contained in a scrapbook compiled by Eva Bruner, "Camp Cedar Grove at Hazard, Ky., Summer of 1899" (HSS), and in an article by Madeline McDowell Breckinridge, "Rural Social Settlement in the Mountains of Kentucky" (BFP-LC, box 708). The summer camp may have been modeled upon the vacation schools and camps conducted by settlement school workers and others in northern cities after 1885. See Sadie American, "The Movement for Vacation Schools," *American Journal of Sociology* 4 (November 1898): 309–25; and Spring, *Education and the Rise of the Corporate State*, pp. 66–71. Descriptions of school and camp programs given by both American and Spring suggest that they were quite similar to those designed by Pettit and her co-workers. On 18 August 1901 (p. 4), the *Lexington Herald* reported on vacation schools run by Mrs. Schuyler Van Renssalaer in New York City.

22. Breckinridge, "Rural Social Settlement." Breckinridge's letters from this period in BFP-LC give no indication that she herself participated in the camp, although Melba Porter Hay reports in "Madeline McDowell Breckinridge: Kentucky Suffragist and Progressive Reformer" (Ph.D. diss., University of Kentucky, 1980), p. 34, that Breckinridge took a month-long trip through the mountains with Pettit in July (just before the six weeks of Camp Cedar Grove).

23. Information on the 1900 camp is taken mainly from Katherine Pettit's "Camp Industrial Diary" (HSS). A brief report on the camp by anthropologist Ellen C. Semple, "A New Departure in Social Settlements," appeared in *Annals of the American Academy of Political and Social Science* 15 (March 1900): 157–60. Semple (who had been May Stone's classmate at Wellesley), described the mountaineers as having degenerated as a result of isolation, inbreeding, moonshine, and "wretchedly cooked food." The "abiding excellencies of the Anglo-Saxon race" still lay within them, she said, but were "overlaid with ignorance, thriftlessness, and immorality."

24. From article by French Combs in *Lexington Morning Herald*, 26 August 1900, pp. 1, 10, 11. Laura Campbell was a teacher at London, Ky. Combs's article includes excellent photographs of the camp.

25. On Sunday, 23 June, the *Louisville Courier-Journal* devoted two-thirds of the front page of its third section to an elaborate account of plans for the settlement, illustrated with photographs taken the previous year. Most information on this settlement in the account that follows is from an unpublished journal Katherine Pettit kept during her work (HSS). The *Courier-Journal* account lists Elizabeth Taylor of Canada as the fourth member of the group, instead of McNab.

Mary E. McCartney was born 14 October 1851 at Cambridge, Ohio (forty miles from the West Virginia border). Her work in Utah followed a stint in the millinery trade (1883–87). See William M. Glasgow, *The Geneva Book* (Philadelphia: Presbyterian Historical Society, 1908). She came to the Sunderland School (1891ff.) around 1898. On the school, founded by the Northern Presbyterian church, see Francis E. Ufford, "Among Deserving Girls of the South," *Progress Magazine* (house organ of the Concord, North Carolina, Telephone Co.), winter 1971, pp. 19ff. For assistance in locating information on McCartney, I am indebted to Edwin C. Clarke, current president of Geneva College, and the Charles A. Cannon Memorial Library, Concord, N.C.

Mary McCartney's experience is part of a substantial body of evidence that problems in the southern mountains and "the enormities of Mormonism" may have been frequently linked in missionary appeals of the period. Certainly it was a period of intense Protestant mission work among Mormons. For that in which McCartney was involved, see A. J. Simmonds, *The Gentile Comes to Cache Valley* (Logan: Utah State University Press, 1976).

On the Presbyterian school at Richmond, see Simmonds, pp. 42–45, 75ff.; and Joel E. Ricks (ed.), *The History of a Valley* (Logan, Utah: Cache Valley Centennial Commission, 1956), pp. 310–13. For assistance in locating information on this school I am indebted to the Historical Department of the Church of Jesus Christ of Latter Day Saints and to Merrill Library at Utah State University.

In *The Galax Gatherers* (Richmond: Onward Press, 1910), a collection of sermons by the eastern Kentucky Presbyterian missionary E. O. Guerrant, there is evidence that Mormons, for their part, were sending missionaries to the Kentucky mountains (see "The Mormons in the Mountains," pp. 119–25; and "Satan and the Mormons," pp. 125–31). Guerrant refers to Mormonism as "this monster iniquity of the century," and says its missionaries, whom he has met in "the most distant and inaccessible parts of the mountains," are "winning perverts [sic] to their faith by the thousands."

26. *Lexington Morning Herald*, 24 June 1901, p. 6.

27. *Report of Committee on Mountain Settlement Work to Kentucky Federation of Women's Clubs* [1901] (one-page printed flier, HSS).

28. Katherine Pettit, Camp Industrial Diary, pp. 98, 104, 121. Mrs. Smith was otherwise unidentified, but was apparently a philanthropist; the gentleman was not identified.

29. *Lexington Morning Herald*, 24 June, p. 6. The *Herald* also noted that efforts were proceeding through the WCTU.

30. Katherine Pettit, Camp Industrial Diary, p. 43 (HSS). The image of barefoot "Uncle Sol," who became a central icon in both the school's later fund-raising efforts and treatments of the school in the popular press and fiction, will be considered subsequently.

31. *Report of Reception and Musicale. Miss Katherine Pettit and Miss May Stone: "The Kentucky Mountaineer"* (Boston: Eastern Kindergarten Assn., 1902), pp. 7–9 (HSS).

32. Mary A. Hill, "Social Settlement Work in the Kentucky Mountains," *Commons* 7 (May 1902): 13–14.

33. Lucy Furman, "The Work of Fotched-On Women," *Louisville Courier-Jour-*

nal, 6 September 1936; May Stone, "Katherine Pettit's First Trips to the Kentucky Mountains" (undated typescript, HSS).

There seems to have been some uncertainty about what to name the school. A letter from May Stone to Sophonisba Breckinridge, 16 March 1903, is on a printed letterhead of the "Log Cabin Social Settlement . . . in the mountains of Kentucky 45 miles from the railroad" (BFP-LC, box 740), but a letter of 1 September 1901 (Special Collections, Hutchins Library, Berea College) is on a "W.C.T.U. Settlement School" letterhead. The latter name was retained, however, until the school became independent as Hindman Settlement School.

In "The Women on Troublesome," *Scribner's Magazine* 62 (1918): 315–28, William Aspenwall Bradley reported that, in addition to seven hundred dollars contributed by local people, Pettit and Stone raised enough money on their trip to buy the old school building, four acres of land, and rent "an old rough plank cottage . . . as a residence for workers."

An anonymous typescript, "Hindman Settlement School," in the school's archive suggests that one acre of land and the schoolhouse were purchased by the WCTU. The schoolhouse was bought from (or perhaps donated by) Professor George Clarke (1862–1940), who came to Hindman from Greenup County in 1887 to practice law, but was persuaded by local citizens to open a school. See [Anon.], "'Fesser Clarke: Pioneer Educator in Feud County," *Appalachian Heritage* 2 (winter 1974): 87–93. Clarke was later state school inspector (1921–22) and superintendent of schools in Letcher County. My efforts to locate WCTU records of the settlement school at Hindman were unsuccessful.

The idea of a settlement *school* rather than a settlement *house* was new but not unqiue to the Hindman experiment. In a speech to the National Education Association in 1902, John Dewey suggested expanding neighborhood schools into settlement-type institutions. Columbia University established the Speyer School Settlement in the same year, and by 1910 there was a national movement to transform existing schools in a similar fashion. See Davis, *Spearheads*, pp. 76–79.

34. In her journal for 30 November 1908 (SHC), Olive Dame Campbell reported after a visit to the school that there had been "two fires (one incendiary)."

35. Grace M. Hatch, "The Hindman Settlement School," *Kentucky Magazine* 1 (September 1917): 385–93.

36. The school's January 1910 newsletter reported a waiting list of seven hundred. Illiteracy figure from *Thirteenth Census of the United States, 1910*, 3:731ff.

37. Newsletter, January 1906.

38. Interview with Elizabeth Watts, 22 January 1980; Katherine Pettit to John C. Campbell, 7 January 1910 (CP-SHC).

39. Pettit to John C. Campbell, 27 September 1911 (CP-SHC). James S. Greene's "Progressives in the Kentucky Mountains: The Formative Years of the Pine Mountain Settlement School, 1913–1930" (Ph.D. diss., Ohio State University, 1982) appeared too late for me to make use of it here.

40. Campbell to Glenn, 15 and 19 June 1914 (CP-SHC). The feelings were so hostile, Campbell reported, that Stone insisted that if Butler left Hindman, she should leave mountain work altogether, rather than accept Pettit's invitation to come to Pine Mountain.

41. Stone to John C. Campbell, 26 November 1918 (CP-SHC).

42. See Elisabeth S. Peck, "Triumph over Trachoma," *Louisville Courier-Journal*, 11 November 1956 (unpaged clipping in HSS). Stucky's work at Hindman, which led to cooperative efforts by the Kentucky State Board of Health and the U.S. Public Health Service, and to the establishment of three trachoma hospitals, was widely publicized at the time. A letter from John C. Campbell to John Glenn of 8 May 1913 (CP-SHC), however, suggests that the publicity had serious negative effects upon the school's own staff at Hindman—so serious that Pettit declined to invite Stucky to do similar work at Pine Mountain. See also J. A. Stucky, "Trachoma: Scourge of the Mountains," *Mountain Life and Work* 2 (October 1926): 3–6. Some letters concerning the school's involvement in the trachoma program may be found in the Linda Neville Papers, University of Kentucky Library (see especially Katherine Pettit to Linda Neville, 13 November 1908, 13 October 1909, and 16 and 23 November 1909), and Hutchins Library of Berea College (Katherine Pettit to Dr. J. A. Stucky, 26 April and 2 July 1911, 3 July, 3 October, and 2 December 1912). Linda Neville (1873–1961) was a Lexington native, the daughter of a university professor, and a graduate of Bryn Mawr (1895). She became involved in the trachoma work after a visit to the school in 1908. For assistance in finding these materials I am indebted to Anne G. Campbell and Gerald Roberts.

43. Some of these tensions and contradictions contributed to Katherine Pettit's decision to found Pine Mountain Settlement School in 1913. Her efforts to persuade John C. and Olive Dame Campbell to join her in creating a "model school for the mountains" (letter of 14 October 1911; CP-SHC) apparently derived partly from her awareness that Campbell was exploring the idea of adapting the Danish folk school model to the southern mountains.

As much as a decade before Hindman Settlement School experienced another minor crisis occasioned by the contemplated departure of founder May Stone in 1918, Campbell had urged that its "public school" program be dropped and the institution turned into a cooperative "educative center" along Danish lines (Campbell to John Glenn of the Russell Sage Foundation, 4 December 1918; May Stone to Campbell, 26 November 1918; Campbell to Glenn, 11 February 1919; and Glenn to Campbell, 26 February 1919, all in CP-SHC).

At Pine Mountain, Pettit appears to have attempted to resolve some of the Hindman contradictions by accepting only full-time boarding students for a program that was much more culturally oriented than that at Hindman (Pettit to Campbell, 19 June 1913, CP-SHC). Two early impressions of Pine Mountain Settlement School are to be found in "The Far Side of Pine Mountain," *Survey*, 3 March 1917, pp. 627–30; and Lucy Furman, "The Work of Fotched-On Women," *Louisville Courier-Journal*, 6 September 1936.

44. Pettit to Campbell, 19 June 1913 (SHC-UNC).

45. Davis, *Spearheads*, pp. 2–11. In later years, Hindman Settlement School recruited many teachers from, and sent a number of its graduates to, the Seven Sisters colleges, especially Wellesley.

46. Elizabeth Watts to Mrs. Henry W. Boynton, 4 December 1911 (Elizabeth Watts papers); Elizabeth Watts typescript biographical sketch, 1927 (HSS); *Louisville Courier-Journal*, 3 September 1936 (Pettit obituary); interview with Elizabeth Watts, 22 January 1980; and Elisabeth S. Peck, "Katherine Pettit," in *Notable American Women* (Cambridge: Harvard University Press, Belknap Press, 1971),

pp. 56–58. Pettit's mother was Clara Mason (Barbee) Pettit.

47. Pettit took a normal four-course curriculum in 1885 and 1887 but only one course in 1886 (untitled yearly average grade roster, Sayre School archive, pp. 67–100). Pettit's sisters Minnie (Mrs. Waller Bullock), Martha (Mrs. Joseph Van Meter), and Lillian (Mrs. Higgins Lewis) also attended Sayre. Alumnae rosters in J. Winston Coleman, Jr., *History of Sayre School* (Lexington: Winburn Press, 1954), do not list Katherine Pettit among Sayre graduates.

48. Peck, *Notable American Women*, p. 37.

49. "May Stone—the Ladyest," undated reprint from *Mountain Life and Work* (HSS); Elizabeth Watts to Mrs. Henry W. Boynton, 11 January 1913 (Elizabeth Watts papers); *Hindman News*, 1 May 1952, pp. 1, 6; *Who's Who in Kentucky: A Biographical Assembly of Notable Kentuckians* (Louisville: Standard Printing Company, 1936), p. 384; Lucy Furman, "The Work of Fotched-On Women," *Louisville Courier-Journal*, 6 September 1936; *Wellesley Alumnae Magazine* 38 (July 1954): 7; and (on Henry Stone) *National Cyclopedia of American Biography*, 19:96f. Henry Stone served as city attorney of Louisville (1896–1904), and as general counsel for the L & N Railroad (1905–21). For some details on May Stone, I am indebted to Stephanie Welch of the Margaret Clapp Library at Wellesley College.

50. Inspired by a speech by Chicago settlement leader Graham Taylor, two local theology students (Archibald Hill and W. E. Wilkins) opened Neighborhood House in September 1896. It offered kindergarten classes, a library, classes in pottery, dance, and dramatics, a playground and gymnasium, and manual training and instruction in domestic skills for men and women. See *Neighborhood House: A Social Settlement* (Louisville: Neighborhood House, 1910).

51. During a one-week period in 1899 (11–18 June), the *Lexington Morning Herald* carried six accounts (all except one on the front page) of the White-Howard, Taylor-Lee, and Baker-Howard feuds in eastern Kentucky.

52. A brief account of Pettit's life by her co-worker Lucy Furman notes that as a young woman she had heard of conditions in eastern Kentucky from Guerrant (Furman, "The Work of Fotched-On Women"). The following sketch of Guerrant and his work is based upon Edward Owings Guerrant, *The Soul Winner* (Lexington, Ky.: J. B. Morton & Co., 1876), *The Gospel of the Lilies* (Boston: Sherman, French & Co., 1912), and *The Galax Gatherers* (Richmond: Onward Press, 1910); and Eunice Tolbert Johnson (comp.), *History of Perry County, Kentucky* (Hazard, Ky.: Daughters of the American Revolution, 1953), pp. 23–28, 71; J. Gray McAllister and Grace Owings Guerrant, *Edward O. Guerrant: Apostle to the Southern Highlanders* (Richmond: Richmond Press, 1950); and Williamson Lee Cooper, *Stuart Robinson School and Its Work* (Nashville: Parthenon Press, 1936).

Whether May Stone knew Guerrant is uncertain, but it is likely that she did. Her family's residence in Mt. Sterling (1878–85) overlapped one year with Guerrant's tenure there (1875–79) as a Presbyterian minister. Mt. Sterling was a small town, and Guerrant was a prominent minister. His work in eastern Kentucky had not yet begun, however. Because Guerrant's later mountain work was well known through his own writing and organizational work, and was covered extensively in the church and secular press, it is of course not necessary that Pettit or Stone must have known him personally to have felt his influence.

53. The report (1877) is reprinted in Guerrant, *The Soul Winner*, pp. 121ff.

McAllister reports in *Edward O. Guerrant*, pp. 76ff., that Robinson spent part of the Civil War period in self-imposed exile in Canada because of his "forthright Confederate convictions." Robinson, who had been a professor at Danville Theological Seminary (1856–58) while Guerrant was a student at Centre College (Danville), spent his last years (d. 1881) as pastor of Louisville's Second Presbyterian Church, where he served while Guerrant was pastor (1879–81) of First Presbyterian. Guerrant's papers in SHC contain several letters from Robinson (March-April 1875). For a more extended treatment of Robinson, see Louis Weeks, "Stuart Robinson: Kentucky Presbyterian Leader," *Filson Club Historical Quarterly* 54 (1980): 360–77.

54. My brief account of Guerrant's work is intended merely to suggest some possible historical and conceptual connections between it and the later settlement effort at Hindman. Although I discovered no primary evidence that Guerrant and Pettit were acquainted before she started her work at Hindman (e.g., no correspondence between them), that they knew each other personally is suggested by a report of one of Guerrant's trips into the mountains late in 1902. Retired general O. O. Howard (former chief commissioner of the Freedmen's Bureau) accompanied Guerrant on a preaching tour of the area in September and wrote of a day they spent in Jackson. At dinner with President Dinwiddie (of the local Collegiate Institute) they talked with "Mrs. Beauchamp and her teacher Miss Pettit, [who] urged me to go further up the North Fork to Hindman, where they are working in the name of the WCTU, and are becoming well known in the industrial lines of training" (Oliver Otis Howard, "My Tour among the Mountain Whites," *Christian Herald*, 15 October 1902, p. 843). Guerrant's diary for this period (vol. 105, 2 July–7 November 1902, pp. 89–110, SHC) records Howard's visit and the preaching tour, including the meal with Dinwiddie, but does not refer to Pettit.

55. Both Guerrant's *The Soul Winner* and McAllister's biography contain extensive extracts from diaries that Guerrant kept throughout his work in the mountains.

56. Guerrant, *The Soul Winner*, pp. 204, 213, 220–25.

57. On Fox, see Cratis Williams, "The Southern Mountaineer in Fact and Fiction," pp. 888–967, 1013–74, and 1144–1200.

58. See James C. Klotter, "The Breckinridges of Kentucky: Two Centuries of Leadership" (Ph.D. diss., University of Kentucky, 1975). For assistance in locating materials on the Breckinridges, I am indebted to Professor Klotter. Most of what follows is drawn from BFP-LC.

59. Vida Scudder to Sophonisba Breckinridge, 9 August 1892, and fellowship brochure (both in BFP-LC, box 740). It is not clear whether she actually applied for or received the fellowship.

60. May Stone to Sophonisba Breckinridge, 16 March 1903 (BFP-LC, box 740). On Sophonisba, see Peck, *Notable American Women*, pp. 233–36. It is perhaps worth noting that the Breckinridges knew Guerrant. In a letter to Curry of 23 July 1891 (BFP-LC), W. C. P. Breckinridge mentions having spoken with Guerrant at a railway station in Louisville.

61. See Sophonisba P. Breckinridge, *Madeline McDowell Breckinridge* (Chicago: University of Chicago Press, 1921); Peck, *Notable American Women*, pp. 232–33;

and Melba Porter Hay, "Madeline McDowell Breckinridge: Kentucky Suffragist and Progressive Reformer" (Ph.D. diss., University of Kentucky, 1980).

62. Hay, her most recent biographer, says that at her death Madeline was "the most famous and influential woman in Kentucky" (p. v).

63. Hay, "Madeline McDowell Breckinridge," p. 34. Letters in BFP-LC (Desha to Curry, 21 July 1899; W. C. P. to Curry, 24 July; W. C. P. to Sophonisba, 26 and 30 July, and 14 August; and W. C. P. to Curry, 28 July 1899) indicate that Madeline's trip extended from at least mid-July to early August. They do not make clear whether she was actually involved in Camp Cedar Grove. Her papers contain both an extensive manuscript account of the trip, and her article "Rural Social Settlement in the Mountains of Kentucky," which is about Camp Cedar Grove and related plans for a permanent settlement (BFP-LC, box 708). She also spoke of the experiment in "The Regeneration of Rural New England," *Lexington Herald*, 25 March 1900 (unpaged clipping in BFP-LC). Pettit's friendship with Madeline continued for years. Olive Dame Campbell's journal, vol. 3 (9–11 January 1909, CP-SHC) records her visit with Pettit and Breckinridge at the Breckinridge home in Lexington.

64. See Hay, pp. 33–34; Sophonisba Breckinridge, *Madeline McDowell Breckinridge*, pp. 29–32; Henderson Daingerfield, "Among the Mountaineers of the Diocese of Lexington," *Spirit of Missions* 67 (December 1902): 885–87; Lillie B. Mahan, "In the Mountain Missions of Kentucky," ibid., 69 (January 1904): 56–59; and Lillie B. Mahan, "What the Church Kindergarten Does for the Children of the Kentucky Mountains," ibid., 69 (February 1904): 110–12. Madeline was also quite aware of the industrial school movement in the South, as is indicated by her twenty-fifth-anniversary article on the Industrial School of Lexington (founded in 1876), *Lexington Morning Herald*, 16 December 1900, p. 14. Her papers also show that she corresponded with Jane Addams, Florence Kelly, and Chicago's Neighborhood House (see for example Addams to Breckinridge, 21 August 1903, BFP-LC, box 680).

65. W. C. P. to Curry, 1 September 1891; and W. C. P. to Sophonisba, 6 July 1899, and 11 December 1901 (BFP-LC). See also clipping from *Richmond* (Ky.) *Climax*, 7 November 1917, p. 1 (BFP-LC).

66. W. C. P. to Sophonisba, 5 November 1897 (BFP-LC, box 778).

67. W. C. P. to Sophonisba, 13 June and 2 September 1900, respectively (BFP-LC, box 508). About 1901, Curry established a night school for boys unable to attend school in the daytime. Eventually, she was able to study nursing in New York and Chicago, where she graduated from the Presbyterian Hospital Training School in 1908. Putting her training to use in situations of social need, she became one of the first trained nurses to care for the insane (at Northern State Hospital for the Insane, Elgin, Illinois); worked in a tuberculosis hospital in Chicago; conducted pioneer public health surveys in rural Michigan; aided flood victims in Dayton, Ohio; and eventually died from illness and exhaustion brought on by work in the ambulance service in France during World War I. See Curry to W. C. P., 18 September 1891 (BFP-LC, box 845); W. C. P. to Sophonisba, 24 January 1901 (BFP-LC, vol. 510); Desha Breckinridge, "Mary Curry Desha Breckinridge," *Lexington Herald*, 25 June 1918 (BFP-LC, box 845); memorial tribute to

Sophonisba, *Lexington Herald*, 6 August 1918 (clipping in BFP-LC, box 845); and Curry Breckinridge, "My Experience at Elgin," typescript (ca. 1908) in Lyman Chalkley Papers, University of Kentucky Library. One of the speakers at the memorial service for Curry in Chicago in June 1918 was Jane Addams (unidentified newspaper clipping, BFP-LC, box 845, and typed copy of memorial tribute from the *Bulletin of the Presbyterian Hospital of the City of Chicago*, July 1918, pp. 16–21, in Linda Neville Papers, University of Kentucky). The stresses in Curry's life prior to her World War I service are apparent in a series of family letters of 11 June 1914 through 5 May 1915, in the Lyman Chalkley Papers.

68. Pettit, Camp Industrial Diary, p. 122 (HSS).

69. Furman, "The Work of Fotched-On Women," *Louisville Courier-Journal*, 3 September 1936.

70. Pettit, Camp Industrial Diary, pp. 3–5, and untitled ms. (HSS).

71. On the other hand, New Englander Elizabeth Watts, who came to teach at Hindman in 1909 as a nineteen-year-old girl, found a 1912 baptizing in the creek at the Forks of Troublesome "an awfully impressive service." A few months later, however, she was disturbed by the shooting, drunkenness, fighting, and dynamiting that accompanied local voting in the 1912 presidential election. Elizabeth Watts to Mrs. Henry W. Boynton, 11 March and 12 November 1912 (Elizabeth Watts papers).

72. *Who Was Who in American History—Arts and Letters* (Chicago: Marquis, 1975), p. 51, and interview with Elizabeth Watts, 22 January 1980.

73. Sarah McIntosh Lloyd, *A Singular School: Abbot Academy, 1828–1973* (Hanover, N.H.: University Press of New England, 1979), pp. 175–87.

74. Elizabeth Watts, "Hindman Settlement School," *Abbot Academy Bulletin*, series 14 (May 1947), and letter to Mrs. Henry W. Boynton, 9 September 1911 (Elizabeth Watts papers); *Louisville Courier-Journal*, 27 April 1956. The "Little Colonel" books, written by Annie Fellows Johnson (b. 1863), were published in Boston by L. C. Page (1901ff.). In "Miss Watts—A Remarkable Woman," included in the brochure *Elizabeth Watts: Seventy Years of Service* (Hindman, Ky.: Hindman Settlement School, 1980), p. 5, Ruby Allen recalls that Watts was still reading the Little Colonel stories to Hindman students in the 1930s.

75. Elizabeth Watts to Mrs. Henry W. Boynton, 30 January 1912, and 26 April 1913, respectively (Elizabeth Watts papers). Arriving at Hindman at about the same time Watts did was Smith College graduate (1901) Ethel DeLong of Montclair, N.J. Daughter of businessman George DeLong, Ethel decided—following a Christmas visit in 1907—to go to Hindman to teach. She remained there until she left to help Katherine Pettit found Pine Mountain Settlement School in 1913. She married Pine Mountain worker Luigi Zande in 1918, and died in 1928. See Thomas A. De Long, *The DeLongs of New York and Brooklyn: A Huguenot Family Portrait* (Southport, Conn.: Sasco Associates, 1972), pp. 121 and 138–41. For another contemporary account of a Wellesley graduate's coming to Hindman, see Dorothy Stiles ('14), "The Settlement on Troublesome," *Wellesley College News* 24 (January 1916): 20–28.

76. Davis, *Spearheads*, pp. 6–10. In *War and Welfare: Social Engineering in America, 1860–1925* (Westport, Conn.: Greenwood Press, 1980), John F. McClymer comments at length on the "generalized, cultural sense of superiority"

among settlement workers. "Cultural blessedness," he says, "a secularized version of middle-class Protestantism, was the theme [they] returned to again and again" (pp. 19–22).

77. Addams, *Twenty Years at Hull House*, pp. 231–34.

78. Veblen and Lewis quoted in Davis, *Spearheads*, p. 17; A. H. Fromerson, "The Years of Immigrant Adjustment," *National Conference of Jewish Charities Proceedings* (1904), pp. 12off. Quoted in Cary Goodman, "(Re)Creating Americans at the Educational Alliance," *Journal of Ethnic Studies* 6 (no. 4): 22. Davis himself notes (p. 45) that while some settlement programs taught "useless skills, such as the art of serving tea from a silver service or accepting a calling card on a tray," most taught more serviceable skills. Some of the prissiness to which Lewis's character refers is evident in Gaylord White, "The Social Settlement after Twenty-Five Years," *Harvard Theological Review* 4 (1911): 47–70.

79. Nicholas John Cords, "Music in Social Settlement and Community Music Schools, 1893–1939: A Democratic-Esthetic Approach to Musical Culture" (Ph.D. diss., University of Minnesota, 1970), pp. 42, 70–71, 200.

80. Interview with Elizabeth Watts, 22 January 1980.

81. Camp Industrial Diary, p. 77.

82. Camp Industrial Diary, pp. 77, 66, 62, and letter to Mrs. Henry W. Boynton, 28 January 1912 (Elizabeth Watts papers).

83. Pettit diaries, passim. Edward W. Billups's *The Sweet Songster: A Collection of the Most Popular and Approved Songs, Hymns and Ballads* (originally published in Ohio in 1854) appears from the diaries to have been in widespread use in the area. Despite its title, it contained only hymns. Of its approximately 275 hymns (words only), nearly 50 were also to be found in B. F. White's *Original Sacred Harp* of 1844. *The Sweet Songster*'s reflection of the sacred repertoire in eastern Kentucky is also suggested by the fact that nearly a quarter of its hymns were also included in Elder E. D. Thomas's later *Choice Selection of Hymns and Spiritual Songs* (1877), which became a standard hymnal among Old Regular Baptists. In "'Following Music' in a Strange Land," *Musical Quarterly*, July 1918, p. 382, Josephine McGill reported that during her collecting trip to Knott County in 1914 she found *The Sweet Songster* and the Thomas hymnal "owned by nearly every mountain family."

84. Camp Industrial Diary, pp. 18–19; Elizabeth Watts to Mrs. Henry W. Boynton, 29 December 1912, 26 April 1913, and 20 September 1914 (Elizabeth Watts papers) and Pettit journal of 1901, p. 6. Montgomery Ward issued its first mail-order catalog in 1872, and Rural Free Delivery made mail-order merchandise widely available to rural people after 1896, immediately before the onset of the settlement experiments.

85. Camp Industrial Diary, passim. Although Rev. Guerrant had carried a similar organ on his evangelistic tours in the 1880s and early 1890s (Guerrant, *The Soul Winner*, pp. 177–221), the instrument was still considered a novelty in the area.

86. Pettit, Diary of 1901, passim. A decade later, the school's newsletter reported that the girls "have already forgotten that fingers (or knives) were made before forks; they are past masters of the gentle art of Fletcherizing; they know what to do with their napkins" (Newsletter, 1912).

87. James Mooney, "Folk-Lore of the Carolina Mountains," *Journal of American Folklore* 2 (April, 1889): 98. For a general treatment, see Chester R. Young, "The

Observance of Old Christmas in Southern Appalachia," in Jerry Williamson, ed., *An Appalachian Symposium: Essays Written in Honor of Cratis D. Williams* (Boone, N.C.: Appalachian State University Press, 1977), pp. 147–58.

88. Tom Carter and Blanton Owen, *Old Originals, Vol. I: Old Time Instrumental Music Recently Recorded in North Carolina and Virginia* (Rounder 0057).

89. Pine Mountain Settlement School newsletter, 24 January 1917 (HSS). How long it took the settlement school version of Christmas to displace local customs completely is unclear. On 24–25 December 1908, Olive Dame Campbell, on a visit to Hindman, recorded in her diary (vol. 3, CP-SHC) that she "went to sleep to pistol shots," but awakened Christmas (i.e., 25 December) morning to the sound of Lucy Furman and her boys singing "old, old Christmas carols." Paradoxically, the "shootin', . . . chair-flingin'" Christmas celebration was of greater antiquity by far than the genteel Christmas "customs" the women introduced. As Susan G. Davis shows in her recent study of similar transformations in late-nineteenth-century Philadelphia, "shooting" at Christmas time was an ancient pan-European custom marking the death of the old year. See Susan G. Davis, "'Making Night Hideous': Christmas Revelry and Public Order in Nineteenth-Century Philadelphia," *American Quarterly* 34 (summer 1982): 185–99.

90. Pettit, Diary of 1901, p. 82; Newsletter of January 1910 and 30 December 1912; Elizabeth Watts to Mrs. Henry W. Boynton, 29 December 1912 (Elizabeth Watts papers); and Louise Moody Merrill diary of 1924 (HSS). For a related discussion see Williams, "The Southern Mountaineer in Fact and Fiction," pp. 1131, 1187. The shift from Old to New Christmas is the focus of chapters 18 and 19 of Lucy Furman's *Mothering on Perilous* (New York: Macmillan, 1913), and of chapter VII of her *The Glass Window* (Boston: Little, Brown, 1925). See also Ann Cobb, *Kinfolks: Kentucky Mountain Rhymes* (privately printed, 1922), pp. 52–58. In *Singing Family of the Cumberlands* (New York: Oxford University Press, 1955), Perry County native Jean Ritchie recalled her family's first celebration of New Christmas. Although several of the Ritchie children attended Hindman and Pine Mountain settlement schools, Jean says (pp. 162–64) that her mother probably got the idea from a magazine.

91. Hindman was not alone in this role. Fragmentary evidence suggests that introducing contemporary mainstream holiday celebrations was common among mountain settlements. *Women's Work in Tennessee* (Memphis: Tennessee Federation of Women's Clubs, 1916) reported that women who started a settlement in Walker's Valley in 1902 introduced a Fourth of July celebration, and that a Greenbrier Valley (Sevier County) settlement gave local people their first Christmas tree in 1910. Earlier (ca. 1895), Susan G. Chester's Log Cabin Settlement in Asheville played a similar role. On the first Christmas celebration at Pine Mountain Settlement School, see Virginia Anne Chambers, "Music in Four Kentucky Mountain Settlement Schools" (Ph.D. diss., University of Michigan, 1970), pp. 67ff. and 124ff.

92. Letter to Mrs. Henry W. Boynton, 19 October 1912 (Elizabeth Watts papers).

93. In "A New Departure in Social Settlements," *Annals of the American Academy of Political and Social Science* 15 (March 1900), Ellen C. Semple said that the

cooking instructor at the 1899 summer settlement had "taken a course in the school of hygienic cooking at Battle Creek" (p. 159).

94. For an extended discussion of Child, his collection, and the ensuing scholarly "ballad wars," see D. K. Wilgus, *Anglo-American Folksong Scholarship since 1898* (New Brunswick: Rutgers University Press, 1959).

95. *An Opportunity to Help in an Important Work* (U.S. Bureau of Education, Department of the Interior, Special Inquiry, November 1913).

96. Pettit Diary of 1901, pp. 101, 74. Cf. Camp Industrial Diary, p. 19.

97. G. L. Kittredge (ed.), "Ballads and Rhymes from Kentucky," *Journal of American Folklore* 20 (1907): 251–76. Although Kittredge said Pettit had collected the ballads, it seems likely that they came primarily from Hindman student Josiah Combs. See Wilgus, *Anglo-American Folksong Scholarship*, p. 178. Combs's relationship to Hindman is discussed more fully below.

98. H. E. Krehbiel, in "Kentucky Versions of Some English Ballads," *New York Tribune*, 30 April 1916, reported that four of the ballads McGill collected were being performed by the Edith Rubel Trio (violin, cello, piano) in New York. Elizabeth Watts wrote to Mrs. Henry W. Boynton on 5 September 1914 that McGill was then at Hindman. Some items from her collection (which she numbered at "over a hundred" ballads and play-party songs) were published as *Folk-songs of the Kentucky Mountains* (New York: Boosey, 1917).

99. The quotations that follow are from Josephine McGill, " 'Following Music' in a Mountain Land," *Musical Quarterly*, July 1917, pp. 364–84. See also her "Old Ballad Burthens," *Musical Quarterly*, April 1918, pp. 293–306, which examines ballad refrains as evidence of the "communal origin" some scholars claimed for them.

100. In " 'Following Music,' " pp. 376ff., McGill refers to the Furman stories (to be considered subsequently) and to a ballad "interpretation" by "Mr. Bispham." Bispham may have been David Bispham, a British singer referred to in Maud Karpeles, *Cecil Sharp: His Life and Work* (Chicago: University of Chicago Press, 1967), p. 13.

101. Katherine Pettit to John C. Campbell, 5 May 1916 (CP-SHC). The Hindman Settlement School guest book shows that Wyman and Brockway arrived there on 15 May. On Brockway, see *Who Was Who in America*, 3:105.

102. (New York: H. W. Gray, 1916), with piano accompaniments by Brockway. The concert took place on 29 October 1916, at the Cort Theater, 48th Street and Broadway.

103. The following summary is based upon Howard Brockway, "The Quest of the Lonesome Tunes," *Art World* 2 (June 1917): 227–30, from which all quotations are taken.

104. William Aspenwall Bradley, "In Shakespeare's America," *Harper's Magazine*, August 1915, pp. 436–44; and January 1914 newsletter.

105. Elizabeth Watts to Mrs. Henry W. Boynton, 3 November 1920 (Elizabeth Watts papers); and Newsletter of January 1933.

106. Newsletter, January 1938. Ten years later, Ann Cobb wrote in "Hindman Settlement School's First Forty-Five Years," *Mountain Life and Work* 24 (summer 1948): 15–18, that the school's current Ballad Club was "only an oasis, alas!, in the

desert of 'hillbilly' songs falsely called ballads and sung for the most part by people outside our mountains."

107. For a longer discussion of this point, see Oscar Lovell Triggs, *Chapters in the History of the Arts and Crafts Movement* (Chicago: Bohemian Guild of the Industrial Arts League, 1902), pp. 62–129.

108. William Morris, "The Revival of Handicrafts," in *The Collected Works of William Morris*, with an introduction by his daughter May Morris (London: Longmans, 1914), 22:331–41.

109. Ibid., p. 374.

110. Morris, "The Arts and Crafts of Today," *Collected Works*, 22:359.

111. See Triggs, *Chapters in the History of the Arts and Crafts Movement*, pp. 69ff.

112. Ibid., pp. 85, 147ff.

113. Ibid., p. 58.

114. See ibid., pp. 159ff., 189ff.; and Max West, "The Revival of Handicrafts in America," *Bulletin of the Bureau of Labor* 9 (November 1904): 1573–1622.

115. Davis, *Spearheads*, passim.

116. The following discussion is based primarily upon Allen H. Eaton, *Handicrafts of the Southern Highlands* (New York: Russell Sage Foundation, 1937).

117. Eaton, *Handicrafts of the Southern Highlands*, pp. 61ff.

118. Ibid., pp. 66–108. For a summary of some of these efforts, see Pamela M. Henson, "An Analysis of Cultural Change Factors Affecting the Development of Handicrafts Cooperatives in Appalachia" (M.A. thesis, George Washington University, 1976), pp. 22–72.

119. Pettit, Diary of 1901, pp. 44, 65, 104–6.

120. *Kentucky White Ribbon* (Morehead, Ky.), October 1904, p. 1 (HSS). I have been unable to locate additional issues of this publication.

121. A Hindman brochure of ca. 1912 in the Linda Neville Papers at the University of Kentucky notes that $10,500 worth of handicrafts had been sold by the school in ten years.

122. Baskets produced at Hindman in the early 1930s may be seen in "Mountain Baskets," *American Magazine of Art* 26 (December 1933): 506–49.

123. Hindman Newsletter, January 1913, and pamphlet, 1913–14 (HSS). An exception was dulcimer maker Jethro Amburgey, who will be treated briefly later.

124. Ethel DeLong letter of late 1906, quoted in January 1907 Newsletter. A letter from Belle Breck, 1 December 1908 (HSS), mentions Roycroft furniture in Hindman buildings.

125. Elisabeth S. Peck, *Berea's First Century, 1855–1955* (Lexington: University Press of Kentucky, 1955), pp. 116–18; Eaton, *Handicrafts of the Southern Highlands*, pp. 60–63; letters from Pettit to Frost, 30 April and 21 May 1903 (Hutchins Library, Berea College); and Hattie Wright Graham, "The Fireside Industries of Kentucky," *Craftsman*, January 1902, pp. 45–48. Graham instituted the first significant crafts program at Berea.

126. Jennie Lister Hill, "Fireside Industries in the Kentucky Mountains," *Southern Workman* 32 (April 1903): 208–12. I have discovered no published statements by the directors of Hindman's own Fireside Industries.

127. Elizabeth Watts to Mrs. Henry W. Boynton, 15 March 1913 (Elizabeth Watts papers).

128. Johnson, *History of Perry County*, p. 57.

129. See Richard B. Drake, "The Mission School Era in Southern Appalachia, 1880–1940," *Appalachian Notes* 6 (1978): 1–8. Episcopalians established a mission school at Valle Crucis in western North Carolina as early as the 1840s.

130. Davis, *Spearheads*, p. ix.

131. Quotation from ibid., p. 17.

132. Ibid., pp. 105, 80, 170–93.

133. Ibid., pp. 123ff.

134. Woods, *Handbook of Settlements*, p. 285. In "Whither the Settlement Movement Tends," *Charities and the Commons* 15 (3 March 1906): 840–44, Graham Taylor listed "civic realization of social ideals" and "industrial democracy" as two of the six areas of major concern among settlements.

135. Davis, *Spearheads*, pp. 148ff.

136. Addams, *Twenty Years at Hull House*, pp. 198ff.

137. Davis, *Spearheads*, pp. 105ff.

138. Jane Addams, "Trades Unions and the Public Duty," *American Journal of Sociology* 4 (November 1898): 448–62, and *Twenty Years at Hull House*, p. 227, respectively.

139. This brief historical sketch of the industrial school idea is based upon Berenice M. Fisher, *Industrial Education: American Ideals and Institutions* (Madison: University of Wisconsin Press, 1967).

140. A. D. Mayo, *Industrial Education in the South* (Washington, D.C.: Government Printing Office, 1888), p. 9.

141. *Lexington Morning Herald* for June 1899; 26 August 1901, p. 1; and June–September 1908.

142. George T. Winston, "Industrial Education for White and Black in the South," *Southern Workman* 30 (February 1901): 58–66; and Woodward, *Origins of the New South*, p. 356, respectively.

143. *Southern Workman* 30 (February 1901): 65.

144. On industrial schools for blacks, see *Lexington Morning Herald*, 15 July 1900, p. 1; 22 June 1901, p. 15; 8 and 24 July 1901, p. 2. On the shift of concern to mountain whites, see Mrs. A. A. Myers, "Mountain White Work in Kentucky," *American Missionary* 38 (January 1884): 12–16. For an excellent retrospective analysis of the shift, see James C. Klotter, "The Black South and White Appalachia," *Journal of American History* 66 (March 1980): 832–49.

145. Pettit, Diary of 1901, p. 65; and *Lexington Morning Herald*, 13 September 1901, p. 5.

146. S. S. MacClintock, "The Kentucky Mountains and Their Feuds," *American Journal of Sociology* 7 (July 1901): 3, 9–10, and *Lexington Morning Herald*, 18–20, 28 June; 7, 10, 13, 14, 19 July; 4 August; 3 September.

147. Campbell to Glenn, 8 March 1913 (CP-SHC).

148. P. M. Sherwin, "Development of the Hazard Coal Field," *Coal Industry*, 1 (June 1918): 222–23; Ronald D. Eller, "Miners, Millhands and Mountaineers: the Modernization of the Appalachian South, 1880–1930" (Ph.D. diss., University of North Carolina, 1979), p. 223. Production figures are from *Mineral Resources of the United States, 1889–1890*, pp. 219–21; ibid., 1922, pt. 2, p. 598; ibid., 1923, pt. 2, p. 675; ibid., 1928, pt. 2, p. 547.

149. See Woodward, *Origins of the New South*, pp. 291ff.

150. Ibid., p. 295.

151. Thomas J. Brown, "The Roots of Bluegrass Insurgency: An Analysis of the Populist Movement in Kentucky," *Register of the Kentucky Historical Society* 78 (summer 1980): 219–42.

152. Woodward, *Origins of the New South*, p. 377ff. See also James C. Klotter, *William Goebel: The Politics of Wrath* (Lexington: University Press of Kentucky, 1977).

153. ODC Journal, vol. 3, 18 January 1909 (CP-SHC).

154. Eller, "Miners, Millhands and Mountaineers," pp. 103ff., 155. See also Harry M. Caudill, "The Strange Career of John C. C. Mayo," *Filson Club History Quarterly* 56 (July 1982): 258–89.

155. Elizabeth Watts to Mrs. Henry W. Boynton, 28 January 1912 (Elizabeth Watts papers). Even the Rev. E. O. Guerrant had kept more abreast of early conflict in the eastern Kentucky coalfields. Several months after Hindman Settlement School opened, he noted in his diary: "Conference of Coal operators & miners with President Roosevelt . . . *failed*. A pity & a shame & a sin. Operators refused any concessions to miners and refused arbitration" (Edward O. Guerrant diary, 4 October 1902, vol. 105, p. 145, SHC-UNC).

156. Had the school offered any challenge to the system, it would undoubtedly have encountered resistance, as did Jane Addams and her co-workers. In 1931 Pine Mountain Settlement School director Glyn Morris came under surveillance by the infamous local sheriff J. H. Blair because of his Union Seminary-induced humanitarian sympathies for striking coal miners and their families. Summoned to Blair's office, Morris moved to clear himself of all suspicion. "All my behavior, as I recounted it, had been that of an innocent person," he recalled. "In the end, Blair agreed, and gave me a clean bill of health." He joined the county chamber of commerce and kept himself distant from all coal-industry politics and issues. "When I left there after fifteen years of service," Morris said, "there were [a] few inhabitants who continued to have doubts as to my loyalty to the United States, so deep and menacing is the fear of Communism among some people." Glyn Morris, *Less Travelled Roads* (New York: Vantage Press, 1977), pp. 62ff. Red-baiting was of course a favorite coal-industry tactic in eastern Kentucky in the 1930s.

157. In fairness it should be said that Hindman was not the only settlement to retreat into "culture" during this period (1920s–1930s). Allen Davis notes that in the late 1920s Albert Kennedy led a movement among urban settlements to concentrate on cultural programs as populations shifted and new social and political problems arose. Concurrently, however, other settlements were redoubling their social-political efforts (*Spearheads*, pp. 235ff.).

158. The director was Marie Marvel, a Missouri native with a master's degree from Columbia University. See newsletters of May and September 1936, and January 1937. Marvel later worked as recreation leader for the Council of the Southern Mountains.

159. Newsletter, January 1937. The school had hired a music teacher as early as 1904 (*Hindman News*, 1 May 1952, sect. 3, p. 14).

160. Ibid.

161. Pauline Ritchie, "Hindman and Recreation," *Country Dancer*, April 1943, pp. 26, 29–31.

162. Newsletter, February 1949. On the council, see David E. Whisnant, *Modernizing the Mountaineer: People, Power and Planning in Appalachia* (Boone, N.C.: Appalachian Consortium Press, 1981), pp. 3–39.

163. Newsletters of October 1954 and January 1956. McLain, son of a former president of Lexington's Transylvania University, was a graduate of Denison University (Ohio) and had done graduate work at Harvard and the University of North Carolina.

164. Sharp and Macilwaine, *The Morris Book, Part I* (1906; rpt. Yorkshire: E. P. Publishing, 1974), p. 47. On Sharp's dance revival efforts in England, see Maud Karpeles, *Cecil Sharp: His Life and Work* (Chicago: University of Chicago Press, 1967), pp. 25, 68–76, 99–104. The earliest revival performance of a sword dance in the United States of which I am aware occurred in 1906. Orrie C. Hatcher reported in *Modern Language Notes* 21 (June 1906) that the medieval *Revesby Sword Play* had recently been presented at Bryn Mawr College.

165. Sharp and Karpeles, *English Folk Songs from the Southern Appalachians* (London: Oxford University Press, 1932), p. xxx. In *The Puritans and Music in England and New England* (New York: Russell and Russell, 1962), Percy A. Scholes reported the survival of one possible morris fragment in New England, but there is no substantial evidence of significant morris survivals in the United States, from the seventeenth century onward. See, however, note 169 below.

166. Sharp and Macilwaine argued in *The Morris Book, Part I*, p. 17, that "almost every representative figure of the Country-dance can be traced to its origin in the Morris or Sword-dance."

167. Campbell to Glenn, 23 March 1916, quoted in Olive Dame Campbell, *The Life and Work of John Charles Campbell, September 15, 1868–May 2, 1919* (privately printed, 1958), p. 472.

168. Some of the photographs were published in *Scenic South*, May 1955, pp. 4–5. On the dancing at Pine Mountain, see Morris, *Less Travelled Roads*, pp. 131ff.; and a letter (1931) from Pine Mountain's Evelyn Wells quoted in Karpeles, *Cecil Sharp*, p. 161. In an interview on 22 January 1980, Elizabeth Watts recalled that earlier attempts to do traditional mountain square dancing at Hindman had brought criticism because local churches considered it "wicked." To skirt the criticism, "singing games" were started instead, and those led to "folk dances" of the type favored in public recreation programs. In fairness it must be noted that notions of strict traditionality and cultural authenticity were not widespread in such programs at the time. An early (1913) photograph shows young (presumably Jewish) women at Louisville's Neighborhood House, for example, dressed in Japanese kimonos doing a "folk dance" at a settlement house "play festival." Neighborhood House appears to have been operated by and for Louisville's Jewish community.

169. John A. Forrest, "Matachin and Morris: A Study in Comparative Choreography" (M.A. thesis, University of North Carolina, 1977), pp. 65 and 34. I am grateful to Daniel W. Patterson for calling this study to my attention. For the conventional explanation of morris origins, see Curt Sachs, *World History of the Dance* (New York: Norton, 1937), p. 333; Walter Raffe, *The Dictionary of the Dance*

(New York: A. S. Barnes, 1964), p. 333; and Anatole Chujoy, *Dance Encyclopedia* (New York: Simon and Schuster, 1967). Oddly enough, Forrest notes that Indians in the southwestern United States preserve a form of matachin, introduced by Spanish explorers (see Forrest, pp. 52ff.).

170. William Aspenwall Bradley, "The Women on Troublesome," *Scribner's Magazine* 63 (1918): 317f.

171. For versions of the Uncle Sol story dating from 1900 to 1981, see newsletters and brochures in HSS; Furman, *The Quare Women*, pp. 19–21, 57, 207; May Stone, "Uncle Solomon Everidge," *Mountain Life and Work* 4 (April 1928): 17–18; Pauline Ritchie Kermiet, "May Stone: The Ladyest" (HSS); J'May Bertrand (Rivara), "The Appalachian Settlement Schools: The Rural Response to an Urban Concept" (M.A. thesis, Bryn Mawr College, 1975); Bernice A. Stevens, "The Quare Women" (typescript, HSS, 1979); *Troublesome Creek Times* (Knott County), 5 June 1980, p. 1; John Ed Pearce, "Knott County," *Louisville Courier-Journal Magazine*, 10 August 1980, p. 4; and Mercy Coogan, "At the Forks of Troublesome Creek: The Hindman Settlement School," *Appalachia* 14 (March 1981): 33–40. The earliest account is in Katherine Pettit's Camp Industrial Diary (1900), p. 43 (HSS).

172. Bradley, "The Women on Troublesome," pp. 316–19. There is no evidence elsewhere that such armed men ever accompanied the women.

173. *Hindman News*, 1 May, 1952, sect. 3, p. 5.

174. For a general discussion of Furman's work, see Cratis D. Williams, "The Southern Mountaineer in Fact and Fiction" (Ph.D. diss., New York University, 1961), pp. 1144–1201. Furman's *The Lonesome Road* (Boston: Little, Brown, 1927) is not based upon Hindman Settlement School. Williams also discusses (pp. 1123–43) earlier fiction about mountain schools, including Barton's *Life in the Kentucky Hills* (1890) and *Pine Knot* (1900), Opie Read's *The Jucklins* (1895), Louise R. Baker's *Cis Martin* (1898), and Sarah E. Ober's *Ginsey Kreider* (1900).

175. Two chapters from *The Glass Window* were anthologized several times: "Christmas on Bee Tree" in M. L. Becker's *Golden Tales of Our America* (New York: Dodd, Mead, 1929) and *Home Book on Christmas* (New York: Dodd, Mead, 1941), and "Uncle Tutt's Typhoids" in N. B. Fagin, *America Through the Short Story* (Boston: Little, Brown, 1936), C. A. Hibbard, *Stories of the South* (New York: Norton, 1931), and F. H. Spencer, *American Family Album* (New York: Harper & Bros., 1946). Furman's story "Mothering on Perilous" appeared in *Century Magazine* in December 1910; and "The Most Knowingest Child" in *Century* for March 1913. Five chapters of *The Quare Women* were published in *Atlantic Monthly* in late 1922.

Boston-born Emily Reed, who came from Smith College to teach at Hindman in 1922, had learned of the school from Furman's novels and stories (telephone interview with Emily Reed, Clarksville, Indiana, 20 April 1980). Reed had also read the "Little Colonel" stories that had earlier fascinated Elizabeth Watts.

176. Lucy Furman, *Sight to the Blind* (New York: Macmillan, 1914).

177. A subordinate concern in Furman's novels—the feminist dimensions of the settlement school impulse—will be commented upon later.

178. *New York Herald-Tribune*, 1 November 1925, p. 8; *Outlook* 141 (25 November 1925): 485; and *Literary Review*, 31 October 1925, p. 2, respectively.

179. John Fox, Jr., *The Heart of the Hills* (1913), pp. 3, 130, 151; and Bradley, "The Women on Troublesome," pp. 320, 322–23.

180. Two of Hindman's oldest graduates (Oliver Stamper, '14, and Clark Pratt, '19) agreed more than sixty years after they left the settlement that the cultural activities had for them been at best secondary to a desire to get strong academic preparation for college. Both went to one-room grade schools before entering Hindman; both went from Hindman to college and thence to law school. Stamper recalled that very few who managed to get a "first class education" went back to the mountains. He himself planned to return to practice law after he finished Harvard Law School, but stopped in Cleveland, got a job, and never returned to Kentucky. Clark Pratt returned to Hindman, however, where he still lives. Interview with Clark Pratt, 18 January 1980, and with Oliver Stamper, 20 April 1980. In his memoir of Pine Mountain Settlement School in the 1930s and early 1940s, Glyn Morris (*Less Travelled Roads*, p. 87) reported that he knew of "no pupil who finished at Pine Mountain who returned to his mountain community."

181. The following sketch of Combs's life and his relationship to the settlement is based upon an article in the *Hindman News*, 1 May 1952, sect. 2, pp. 1, 15; Josiah H. Combs, *Folk-Songs of the Southern United States*, ed. D. K. Wilgus (1925; rpt. Austin: University of Texas Press, 1967), pp. ix-xv; an obituary in the *Fort Worth Star-Telegram*, 3 June 1960; D. K. Wilgus, "Josiah H. Combs, 1886–1960," *Journal of American Folklore* 75 (1962): 354ff.; Josiah Combs, "Breaking Out of the Sticks," undated typescript in HSS; Combs's letter to Katherine Pettit, 20 August 1932, and a typescript copy of his letter to Lucy Furman, 1 May 1933 (both in HSS).

182. George L. Kittredge, "Ballads and Rhymes from Kentucky," *Journal of American Folklore* 20 (1907): 251ff. On the attribution of some items to Combs (who was not mentioned or credited in the *JAF* article) see the Wilgus introduction to Combs, *Folk-Songs of the Southern United States*, p. ix.

183. Combs, "Breaking Out of the Sticks."

184. Combs was professor of French and German at the University of Oklahoma (1923–27) and head of the foreign languages departments at Texas Christian University (1927–47) and Mary Washington College of the University of Virginia (1947–56). His other published works (in addition to many articles in scholarly journals) included *All That's Kentucky* (1915) and *Folk Songs from the Kentucky Highlands* (1935).

185. Combs letters to Pettit and Furman, 20 August 1932 and 1 May 1933, respectively (HSS).

186. Josiah Combs, *The Kentucky Highlanders from a Native Mountaineer's Viewpoint* (Lexington: J. L. Richardson, 1913), p. 41. Subsequent quotations are from this source.

187. In *Folk-Songs of the Southern United States*, p. 80, Combs observed that Negro folksongs "can hardly stand inspection alongside the songs of whites."

188. Combs, *Folk-Songs of the Southern United States*, p. 99.

189. Combs, *Folk-Songs of the Southern United States*, pp. 99–101.

190. Older daughters Mallie and Una attended Hindman; Edna, Jewel, Pauline, May, and Patty went to Pine Mountain. See Jean Ritchie, *Singing Family of the Cumberlands* (New York: Oxford University Press, 1955), pp. 34, 250–56.

191. Archive of Folk Culture files at the Library of Congress show that Jean was recorded for the archive in 1946 and 1951.

192. *Folk Songs of the Southern Appalachians as Sung by Jean Ritchie*, p. 12; and *Louisville Courier-Journal RotoMagazine* (undated clipping in HSS), respectively.

193. I use the word *myth* here not in the sense of a fabrication or untruth, but to distinguish between factual history and the historical construct projected to the public through selected images and narratives.

194. On her learning from Jason, see Jean Ritchie, "Living Is Collecting: Growing Up in a Southern Appalachian 'Folk' Family," in J. W. Williamson, ed., *An Appalachian Symposium: Essays in Honor of Cratis D. Williams* (Boone, N.C.: Appalachian State University Press, 1977), pp. 188–98.

195. Ritchie, *Singing Family*, pp. 79–83; Niles, "The Singing Ritchies"; and Alan Lomax, foreword to *Folk Songs . . . as Sung by Jean Ritchie*, p. 5.

196. Ritchie, *Singing Family*, p. 252.

197. Pauline returned to Hindman as recreation director in 1940 (Pauline Ritchie, "Hindman and Recreation," *Country Dancer*, April 1943). In a telephone interview on 20 April 1980, Una recalled her days at Hindman with great affection. May Ritchie (Deschamps) remained in the mountains, first as a teacher at Pine Mountain and later at the John C. Campbell Folk School and Warren Wilson College. See also Edna Ritchie, "Folkways and Customs," in Eunice Johnson, ed., *History of Perry County* (Hazard, Ky.: Daughters of the American Revolution, 1953), pp. 35–40, and Hindman newsletter of June, 1943.

198. Ritchie, *Singing Family*, p. 273. The account of Una and Pauline performing for Sharp is in Ritchie, "Living Is Collecting," p. 189.

199. This brief sketch of Ritchie's public career is based upon Jean Ritchie, *Jean Ritchie's Dulcimer People* (New York: Oak Publications, 1975), pp. 8–15.

200. Olive Dame Campbell Journal, vol. 3, ca. 4 December 1908 (CP-SHC). On 14 December, Campbell heard a young man on Tracy Fork [?] of Lott's Creek play "Ground Hog" on a dulcimer, and two weeks later visited an 85-year-old man near the school who had until recently sung and played dulcimer.

201. L. Allen Smith, "Toward a Reconstruction of the Development of the Appalachian Dulcimer," *Journal of American Folklore* 93 (October 1980): 392ff.; and Eaton, *Handicrafts of the Southern Highlands*, p. 202.

202. Eaton, *Handicrafts of the Southern Highlands*, p. 202.

203. Ibid., p. 201.

204. Ibid., p. 202. Eaton called Thomas "the most outstanding dulcimer maker of the Highlands" prior to his death in 1933, and Amburgey "probably the best maker in the mountains today." Amburgey's dulcimers were memorialized in Hindman librarian James Still's 1935 poem "Dulcimer," which said, "The dulcimer's three strings are the heart's cords" (*Mountain Life and Work* 11 [October 1935]: 10). The importance of Eaton's book itself in legitimizing the dulcimer should not be overlooked. In his treatment of "mountain music and instruments" (pp. 197ff.), he mentions other instruments briefly, but concentrates upon the dulcimer, which he says is the one "most frequently used to accompany the singer." He also cites the settlement schools as important centers for the dulcimer version of mountain music and quotes extensively from the dulcimer poems of Hindman teacher and poet Ann Cobb in her *Kinfolks* (Boston: Houghton-Mifflin, 1922).

205. Amburgey letters in HSS; his work is sketched briefly in Ritchie, *Jean Ritchie's Dulcimer People*, p. 23. Ritchie's featuring of the instrument was by no means the sole reason for its relatively sudden growth in popularity. From the 1930s onward, it was also promoted by several other players who performed widely, such as John Jacob Niles, Paul Clayton, and Howie Mitchell.

206. Such ironies are not uncommon in the record. In his excellent notes to Edna Ritchie's Folk-Legacy recordings (FSA-3), D. K. Wilgus emphasizes that there was a "settlement school tradition of songs and singers" and a definable settlement school musical taste. He demonstrates that a number of what have come to be known as "Ritchie family" songs ("May Day Carol," "Gentle Fair Jenny," "Old Man in the Woods," "Aunt Sal's Song," "Jackero") in fact entered the family repertoire only after having been learned by one of the Ritchie daughters at Hindman or Pine Mountain.

In "Information, Please," *Mountain Life and Work* 36 (summer 1960): 32–33, former Pine Mountain Settlement School teacher Evelyn K. Wells commented on the influence of settlement teachers upon the musical repertoires of settlement school children and others (such as Texas Gladden and Aunt Molly Jackson) who became widely known as performers of "traditional" eastern Kentucky music. In particular, Wells mentioned the song "Father Grumble," listed as a "Kentucky folksong" in *Songs of All Time*, but which "actually came from New Jersey with Mrs. Ethel de Long Zande who learned it there in her childhood and taught it to the Pine Mountain children." Wells article cited in Virginia Anne Chambers, "Music in Four Kentucky Mountain Settlement Schools" (Ph.D. diss., University of Michigan, 1970), p. 67.

207. Mercy Coogan, "At the Forks of Troublesome Creek," *Appalachia* 14 (March 1981): 33ff.

208. Ritchie, *Singing Family of the Cumberlands*, p. 278.

Chapter 2

1. The letters from which the epigraphs for this chapter were drawn are both in CP-SHC. A letter from Pettit to Campbell, 21 April 1911, identifies "Miss Jackson" as Katherine Jackson of London, Kentucky.

2. The study was published two years after John C. Campbell's death, but under his name, as *The Southern Highlander and His Homeland* (New York: Russell Sage Foundation, 1921)—hereafter referred to as *SHHL*. On the writing of *SHHL* see Edith Canterbury, "Background Years," *Mountain Life and Work* 30 (autumn 1954): 11–12. The southern mountain survey was funded by the Sage Foundation at the same time as its better-known Pittsburgh survey. On the Russell Sage Foundation, see John F. McClymer, *War and Welfare: Social Engineering in America, 1890–1925* (Westport, Conn.: Greenwood Press, 1980), pp. 30–49, and Robert F. Arnove, ed., *Philanthropy and Cultural Imperialism: The Foundations at Home and Abroad* (Boston: Hall, 1980).

3. Olive Dame Campbell Journal, vol. 3, 2 October 1908 (CP-SHC).

4. Olive Dame Campbell, *The Life and Work of John Charles Campbell, September 15, 1868–May 2, 1919* [offset from typescript; 1968], pp. 104f. The Campbells

were married 21 March 1907 in Medford. Olive Dame received the "Woman of Arts" degree with honors from Tufts, the institution's "female equivalent of the A.B." until 1910 (letter to author from Robert Johnson-Lally, 28 January 1981).

5. ODC letters to her family, 12 April–12 November 1907 (CP-SHC); and ODC, *Life and Work*, pp. 104–8. The Campbells apparently returned to America in late November 1907.

6. One major article on the formation of the foundation appeared in the *New York Times* before they left for Europe (13 March 1907, p. 1), and one afterwards (14 May 1907, p. 6).

7. See letters from ODC to Warren H. Wilson, 12 February 1937, and from Margaret Gleason to Marion Simonds, 12 February 1947 (CP-SHC). Several brief biographical accounts of Campbell are available, including Henry Shapiro's introduction to the 1969 reprint of *SHHL* (pp. xxii–xxxi), and David E. Whisnant, "John C. Campbell," in William S. Powell, ed., *Dictionary of North Carolina Biography* (Chapel Hill: University of North Carolina Press, 1979), 1:316–17. The fullest account is Mrs. Campbell's *Life and Work*, cited earlier.

8. Shapiro's introduction to *SHHL*, p. xxiii, gives Campbell's wife's death date as 1905, but an unidentified clipping in CP-SHC gives it as March 1904. Grace Buckingham Campbell was from Flint, Michigan, and was a Smith College graduate.

9. On the Sage fortune, and the means used to assemble it, see Gustavus Myers, *History of the Great American Fortunes* (1908; rpt. New York: Random House, 1937), pp. 447–77. The following brief account of the foundation's early orientation is based primarily upon John M. Glenn et al., *The Russell Sage Foundation, 1907–1946*, 2 vols. (New York: Russell Sage Foundation, 1947).

10. See Luther H. Gulick, *The Healthful Art of Dancing* (New York: Doubleday, Page, 1910).

11. Copy of resolution in CP-SHC.

12. Glenn et al., *Russell Sage Foundation*, p. 76.

13. ODC Journal, vol. 3, 1–4 October 1908 (CP-SHC).

14. Ibid., 6 October 1908.

15. Ibid., 8 October and 1 December 1908.

16. Ibid., 8 October and 4 December 1908.

17. Itineraries at end of ODC Journals, vols. 3 and 4 (CP-SHC).

18. ODC Journal, vol. 4, 12 March 1909 (CP-SHC).

19. ODC Journal, vol. 3, ca. 4 December 1908 (CP-SHC).

20. The first edition of the Sharp-Campbell *English Folksongs of the Southern Appalachians* (1917; hereafter cited as *EFSSA*) lists her version of "Barbara Allen" as having been collected from Ada B. Smith in Knott County, Kentucky, on 16 December 1907. Only two other titles have 1907 dates. By 1905–6, scholars Phillips Barry and H. M. Belden were beginning to bring New England and Missouri ballads to public attention. Barry did his first collecting in New England in 1902–3.

21. James Mooney, "Folk-Lore of the Carolina Mountaineers," *JAF* 2 (April 1889): 95–190; Lila Edmonds, "Songs from the Mountains of North Carolina," *JAF* 6 (January 1893): 131ff.; and Haywood Parker, "Folk-Lore of the North Carolina Mountaineers," *JAF* 20 (October 1907): 241–50. In *American Folk Song Scholarship since 1898* (New Brunswick, N.J.: Rutgers University Press, 1959),

D. K. Wilgus argues that there was no significant American ballad scholarship before 1898, and that E. C. Perrow's series "Songs and Rhymes from the South" (*JAF*, 1912–15) was the first significant collection of Southern folksong. The earliest graduate thesis on ballads listed in Alan Dundes's *Folklore Theses and Dissertations* is G. C. D. Odell's of 1892; during the next seventeen years, there were only five more.

22. ODC Journal, vol. 3, 14–24 December 1908 (CP-SHC).

23. ODC Journal, vol. 4, 20 January 1909 (CP-SHC).

24. Mary W. Glenn to ODC, 23 July 1909 (CP-SHC).

25. Glenn to JCC, 11 March 1910 (CP-SHC). Dates and locations from *EFSSA*.

26. Glenn to JCC, 17 June 1910; JCC to Glenn, 23 June 1910; L. R. Lewis to Glenn, 14 March 1911 (CP-SHC).

27. Kittredge subsequently encouraged Mrs. Campbell, made technical suggestions, and offered to write an introduction if her collection were published. G. L. Kittredge to ODC and to Glenn, 16 March 1911, and Glenn to JCC, 7 April 1911 (CP-SHC).

28. On the "wars" provoked by such issues as communal versus individual authorship and the relative worth of certain types of ballads, see Wilgus, *Anglo-American Folk Song Scholarship since 1898*, passim.

29. Pettit to ODC, 23 March 1911 (CP-SHC). "Joshua" is presumably Josiah Combs, former Hindman student and rising ballad scholar; "professor Sharon" is Hubert G. Shearin, Combs's teacher at Transylvania, who was just then publishing an article entitled "British Ballads in the Cumberland Mountains" in *Sewanee Review* (1911). I encountered no evidence that Mrs. Campbell participated in the "wars."

30. The following account of the Sharp-Campbell collaboration is based upon Maude Karpeles, *Cecil Sharp: His Life and Work* (London: Routledge and Kegan Paul, 1967), *Cecil Sharp's Collection of Folk Songs*, 2 vols. (London: Oxford University Press, 1974), and correspondence and other documents in CP-SHC as cited.

31. See Marian P. Michael, "Child, Sharp, Lomax and Barry: A Study in Folksong Collecting" (M.A. thesis, University of Texas, 1960), pp. 6–8.

32. Langdon to ODC, 4 June 1915 (CP-SHC).

33. Accounts of the meeting may be found in Karpeles, *Cecil Sharp*, pp. 130–31, and in Olive D. Campbell, *Life and Work of John Charles Campbell*, pp. 419ff.

34. JCC to Lee F. Hanmer, 13 June 1915, and Sharp to ODC, 24 June 1915 (CP-SHC).

35. ODC to Sharp, 3 July 1915 (CP-SHC). For the time, Mrs. Campbell's collection was almost unique in the United States in according major importance to ballad tunes, instead of solely to the texts so prized by most American ballad scholars, still tied to the primarily literary origins of their enterprise. In her "Songs and Ballads of the Southern Mountains," *Survey* 33 (1915), Mrs. Campbell noted the general lack of attention to ballad tunes.

36. Glenn to JCC, 8 July 1915; Sharp to ODC, 15 July and 15 August 1915; and ODC to Sharp, 4 September 1915 (CP-SHC).

37. In *Appalachia on Our Mind: The Southern Mountains and Mountaineers in the*

American Consciousness, 1870–1920 (Chapel Hill: University of North Carolina Press, 1978), Henry Shapiro treats the Sharp-Campbell collaboration as though it were based upon the same jealousy, greed, and self-aggrandizement that characterized the work of so many other collectors of the period. "[Mrs. Campbell] owned the mine, and he would do the digging," he says (p. 254), adding that her proprietary "holdings" in Georgia and North Carolina were especially attractive to Sharp because "substantial claims had already been laid in Virginia and Kentucky as collecting fields." In fact, there is no evidence in all of the Sharp-Campbell correspondence (none of which Shapiro cites) that either of them ever conceived of the enterprise in such a way. The forty-niner terminology is Shapiro's own. In *The Life and Work of John C. Campbell*, p. 441, Mrs. Campbell quotes a letter (27 September 1915) in which Sharp says he would not presume "to ravage your preserves." In context, however, it appears that the comment arose mainly from his assumption before he became well acquainted with Mrs. Campbell that she probably would be as territorially jealous as most of her contempoary collectors. It was a reasonable assumption, but it did not prove tenable in her case.

Shapiro also hints (p. 254) that Sharp may have hoped to use John C. Campbell's ties with the Sage Foundation to finance "his campaign to popularize English folk dancing in America." In fact, John Glenn did provide some travel money for Sharp at the beginning, but stated quite early that the foundation would not provide major funding (cf. note 117 below). Further, Sharp's major overtures were to the Carnegie Corporation rather than to Sage, as his letters in CP-SHC make clear.

38. From a second letter from ODC to Sharp dated 4 September 1915 (CP-SHC).

39. Mrs. Campbell also noted that she had approached other collectors with the idea of a cooperative endeavor, but had encountered "personal and financial considerations and sectional jealousies."

40. Sharp to ODC, 20 December 1915, and to JCC, 25 February 1916 (CP-SHC). Shapiro suggests (p. 254) that Sharp hoped to make a lot of money from his work in the United States, but I found no evidence whatever of such a motive in the scores of Sharp's letters in CP-SHC. Shapiro's evidence consists of one sentence from a letter quoted by Karpeles; I found Karpeles's transcriptions of Sharp's letters to be somewhat unreliable. In his letter of 27 September 1915, Sharp told Mrs. Campbell he had four children to support and a wife who was ill and might be an invalid "for some time to come."

41. Sharp to JCC, 10 March 1916, and to ODC, 26 March 1916 (CP-SHC). Shapiro (p. 254) says that Sharp was not impressed with "the intrinsic merit" of Mrs. Campbell's material. All of the Sharp-Campbell correspondence in CP-SHC, however, shows that quite the opposite was the case (see especially his letter to John Glenn of 26 March 1916).

42. Sharp to Glenn, 26 March 1916 (CP-SHC).

43. Karpeles, *Cecil Sharp*, p. 146; and Sharp to ODC, 27 September 1915 (CP-SHC).

44. JCC to Glenn, 5 April 1916 (CP-SHC).

45. Sharp to ODC, 27 September 1915 (CP-SHC); and Karpeles, *Cecil Sharp*, p. 133.

46. A subtler problem—the extent to which Sharp's aural conditioning and es-

thetic preferences may have altered the tunes he "heard" and recorded in his note-books—is difficult to assess. In the Sharp-Campbell correspondence there are scat-tered references to his wish to "take phonographic records" and to his having consulted with recording companies (Sharp to ODC, 15 August 1915; and JCC to Sharp, 5 May 1916). But his efforts, whatever their extent, were unavailing. He found one of the Victrola Corporation's representatives "a most egregious person," with "a sloppy untidy mind and simply no artistic conscience, and therefore from our point of view a very dangerous person." It is unlikely in any case that recording equipment available then could have been carried on the journey that lay ahead. Bertrand Bronson, the foremost student of ballad tunes, said when the 1932 edi-tion of the Sharp collection was reissued in 1954 that Sharp was "almost the ideal recorder" of tunes. "One never feels," Bronson said, "that Sharp has heard only what he was listening for, nor that he has imposed upon, distorted, or falsified the truth of his rendition" (*JAF* 67 [January 1954]: 94–95).

47. Sharp to ODC, 24 May and 6 June 1916; and to JCC, 25 July 1916 (CP-SHC). Mrs. Campbell describes the flood and the difficulties attending Sharp's ar-rival in *The Life and Works of John C. Campbell*, pp. 485ff.

48. Sharp to ODC, 1 August 1916; JCC to Frances Goodrich, 7 August 1916; and Sharp to ODC, 13 August 1916 (CP-SHC). Although Mrs. Campbell was Sharp's primary collaborator, the recent birth of a daughter made it impossible for her to accompany him. Mr. Campbell went along initially to guide him and make arrangements and introductions.

49. JCC to Glenn, 26 August 1916; and Sharp to JCC, 12 September 1916 (CP-SHC). Sharp's itinerary may be found in the 1932 edition of his collection, vol. 1, p. 13.

50. Sharp to JCC, 20 September 1916, and to ODC, 28 September 1916 (CP-SHC).

51. Karpeles to John Campbell's secretary, Miss Dickey, 23 August 1916; and ODC, *Life and Work of John C. Campbell*, p. 495. Sharp left Virginia for Chicago around 1 October and returned to England in December (Sharp to JCC, 9 October 1916; to ODC, 31 October 1916; to Ruth Coolidge [Mrs. Campbell's sister], 29 November 1916; and ODC to Sharp, 20 December 1916 [all in CP-SHC]).

52. ODC to Sharp, 20 December 1916 (CP-SHC). In her letter of 20 February 1917, Mrs. Campbell suggested some softening and qualifying changes in Sharp's draft introduction (e.g., "rude log cabins" to "log cabins more or less water-tight"). All were incorporated into the final text.

53. All quotations from Sharp's introduction to Olive D. Campbell and Cecil J. Sharp, *English Folk Songs From the Southern Appalachians* (New York: Putnam, 1917), pp. iii–ix.

54. The volume included almost 40 Child ballads, two dozen more non-Child English ballads, nearly sixty "songs" (including a number of native American bal-lads), and a dozen nursery songs.

55. JCC to Sharp, 29 November 1916 (CP-SHC).

56. *Nation*, 3 February 1917, pp. 618–19.

57. *New York Times*, 2 December 1917, sect. 3, p.3; H. M. Belden, "Folk-Song in America—Some Recent Publications," *Modern Language Notes* 34 (1919): 139–45.

58. Sharp to ODC, 8 January and 25 August 1917 (CP-SHC). The authority Sharp referred to was apparently Miss A. G. Gilchrist, a member of the English Folk-Song Society (see Karpeles, *Cecil Sharp*, p. 49).

59. From tabulation of dates and locations in the 1932 edition, p. xiii.

60. These are discussed at some length in the study of the White Top Folk Festival in Chapter 3.

61. Plans for his return are discussed in Sharp to Ruth Coolidge, 29 November 1916; ODC to Sharp, 20 December 1916; and Sharp to ODC, 8 March 1917 (CP-SHC).

62. Sharp to JCC, 13 April 1917 (CP-SHC). The *Times Literary Supplement* review of the Sharp-Campbell volume the following January said "a volume of fiddle tunes is promised later."

63. Sharp to ODC, 20 April 1917, and to JCC, 30 April 1917 (CP-SHC).

64. Sharp to JCC, 5 May 1917 (CP-SHC).

65. Karpeles, *Cecil Sharp*, p. 157; *EFSSA* (1932), I:xiv.

66. JCC to Glenn, 21 May 1917; JCC to Glenn, 13 June 1917; and Sharp to Ruth Coolidge, 17 June 1917, and to JCC, 23 July 1917 (CP-SHC).

67. *EFSSA*, (1932), I: xii.

68. Although the *amount* of time Sharp spent at the two schools has been exaggerated in earlier accounts (it was actually less than two out of forty-six weeks), the *significance* of his collecting there has not been adequately understood.

69. Sharp to ODC, 15, 20, 27 August 1917 (CP-SHC).

70. Sharp to Glenn, 2 September 1917 (typed copy in CP-SHC). A somewhat different text of the letter is in Karpeles, *Cecil Sharp*, p. 159.

71. Sharp to ODC, 15 August 1917, and to JCC, 20 September 1917 (CP-SHC).

72. Karpeles, *Cecil Sharp*, p. 158.

73. Pettit to JCC, 16 February 1916; and Sharp to JCC, 9 September 1917 (CP-SHC).

74. Sharp to Mrs. Storrow, 13 September 1916, quoted in Karpeles, *Cecil Sharp*, p. 153. Sharp's severest criticism of a mission school was aimed at Oneida Institute, where he judged that children were scandalously ill-fed. "If it were my own country," he told John Campbell, "I should report the case to the Society for the Prevention of Cruelty to Children." "People such as we met at Oneida," he added a week later, "should be exiled to the slums of the large cities and not allowed to drag down the mountaineer to their low and crude level" (Sharp to JCC, 23 August and 2 September 1917, [CP-SHC]).

75. Sharp to JCC, 2 September 1917 (CP-SHC).

76. ODC to Sharp, 4 September 1915; Sharp to ODC, 2 September 1917, and to JCC, 20 September 1917 (CP-SHC). Sharp's reference to the dance as "the Running Set" suggests that his lack of familiarity with local terminology led to semantic confusion that has since been preserved in other accounts of dance in the mountains. His use of capitals implies that he considered "the Running Set" to be the *name* of a dance which had a certain well-defined *form*, such as "the waltz" or "the fox trot." More likely, however, "running sets" would have been used locally to refer to an *activity* (like "playing ball") that might in fact be quite free in form. Thus what Sharp probably saw was a "big circle" mountain square dance, in

which the overall form and the sequence of figures is determined by the caller, more or less at his own discretion. On the history of the square dance, and especially the role of the caller, see S. Foster Damon, "The History of Square-Dancing," *Proceedings of the American Antiquarian Society* 62 (1952): 63–98.

77. Sharp to JCC, 20 September 1917 (CP-SHC). The illness of the Campbell's second daughter and her death in late October made it impossible for either of them to stay closely in touch with Sharp during this period of his work.

78. Sharp to JCC, 30 April 1918 (CP-SHC).

79. Sharp to JCC, 16 July 1918, and to Glenn, 3 September 1918 (CP-SHC). Quotations from the latter. John C. Campbell was ill during much of the last half of 1918; he and Mrs. Campbell spent most of the time on Nantucket. Mr. Campbell died in May 1919.

80. Sharp to Mrs. Storrow, 17 December 1918, quoted in Karpeles, *Cecil Sharp*, p. 138.

81. Sharp to Glenn, 3 September 1918 (CP-SHC). It was not true that Sharp had not (as he asserted) been anywhere in the mountains where blacks were much in evidence. He had stayed with the Campbells in Asheville on several occasions, where the black population was quite substantial.

82. The following brief references are based exclusively upon Tom Carter and Blanton Owen's excellent notes to *Old Originals, Volume I* (Rounder 0057), an album derived from their fieldwork on the Virginia–North Carolina border in 1974–75.

83. *TLS*, 17 January 1918.

84. Shapiro, *Appalachia on Our Mind*, p. 255; and Archie Green, "A Folklorist's Creed and a Folksinger's Gift," *Appalachian Journal* 7 (autumn-winter 1979–80): 37–50. Green points out that Sharp "had been touched by both Fabian Socialism and British cultural nationalism" (p. 39).

85. Sharp to Glenn, 27 October 1920 (typed copy in CP-SHC).

86. ODC Journal, 7 October 1908 (CP-SHC).

87. The GEB was an outgrowth of the Conference for Southern Education (1898ff.) and its executive committee, the Southern Education Board. John D. Rockefeller gave $53 million to the GEB between 1902 and 1909. See C. Vann Woodward, *The Origins of the New South, 1877–1913* (Baton Rouge: Louisiana State University Press, 1951), pp. 402–6 for a brief account of the GEB.

88. Claxton to Fred Brownlee, 5 April 1953 (CP-SHC). Claxton (1862–1957) was born in middle Tennessee's Bedford County. He became superintendent of schools in Kinston, Wilson, and Asheville, N.C., and later a university professor of education. When the Campbells met him, he was teaching at the University of Tennessee. See *Who's Who in America* (1914), 8:456.

89. John Glenn to Claxton, 27 August 1910; Claxton to JCC, 2 and 20 January 1911; JCC to Claxton, 17 January 1911; JCC to Glenn, 17 December 1913; Claxton to JCC, 13 February 1914 and 19 December 1916 (CP-SHC).

90. Rolland G. Paulston's *Folk Schools in Social Change: A Partisan Guide to the International Literature* (Pittsburgh: University Center for International Studies, 1974) is an excellent annotated bibliography on the origins, development, and proliferation of folk schools throughout the world.

91. L. L. Friend, *Folk Schools of Denmark*, bulletin 5 (Washington, D.C.: U.S. Bureau of Education, 1914); and H. W. Foght, *The Danish Folk High Schools*, bulletin 22 (Washington, D.C.: U.S. Bureau of Education, 1914).

92. *New York Times*, 10 May 1914.

93. American Consular Service to JCC, 30 April 1909; A. Bolijerg [?] to JCC, 28 April 1909; Reverend Teelweg [?] to JCC, 12 June 1909; and Christian Bay to JCC, 30 June 1909 (CP-SHC).

94. Glenn to JCC, 12 July 1909 (CP-SHC). Campbell declined an offer from Claxton to go as an agent of the bureau (JCC to Glenn, 5 November 1912, CP-SHC).

95. Glenn to JCC, 23 July and 27 August 1913; JCC to Glenn, 18 June 1914; Glenn to JCC, 17 and 25 July and 5 August 1914 (CP-SHC).

96. Glenn to JCC, 15 January 1915 (CP-SHC).

97. Woodward Finley to JCC, 26 June 1916 (CP-SHC); and JCC to Glenn, 17 April 1917 (CP-SHC, film M-3800).

98. See an account of one of his folk school addresses in *Home Mission Monthly*, July 1914, and his pamphlet *The Future of the Church and Independent Schools in the Southern Highlands* (New York: Russell Sage Foundation, 1917).

99. John C. [and Olive Dame] Campbell, *The Southern Highlander and His Homeland* (New York: Russell Sage Foundation, 1921). Quotations following are from the 1969 reprint by the University Press of Kentucky, pp. 260–98.

100. In 1921 she listed and categorized more than 150 mission schools, seminaries, industrial schools, academies, institutes, normal schools, settlement schools, training schools, and others. See Olive Dame Campbell, *Southern Mountain Schools Maintained by Denominational and Independent Agencies* (1921; rev. ed. New York: Russell Sage Foundation, 1929). Her journals record visits to the Berry School in Georgia (vol. 3, 30 October 1908); "Buckhorn College" (vol. 3, 11 December 1908); Hazel Green Academy (vol. 3, 28 November 1908), and Oneida Institute (vol. 3, 17 January 1909) in eastern Kentucky; Maryville College (vol. 4, 26 January 1909) and Tusculum College (vol. 4, 2 February 1909) in east Tennessee; and Valle Crucis (vol. 4, 3 March 1909), Asheville Home Industrial (vol. 4, 8 March 1909), and Asheville Farm School (vol. 4, 12 March 1909) in western North Carolina, as well as numerous others.

101. Siegfried Munch to ODC, 13 January 1922; American-Scandinavian Foundation to ODC, 10 April 1922; ODC Journal, vol. 6, 13 August 1922; and ODC to F. J. Clark, 6 October 1922 (CP-SHC).

102. ODC to American friends, 13 April 1923 (CP-SHC). The wedding ceremony is also described in Olive Dame Campbell, *The Danish Folk School: Its Influence in the Life of Denmark and the North* (New York: Macmillan, 1928), pp. 209f.

103. The following discussion is based upon both the journals and *The Danish Folk School*. Page numbers in parentheses refer to the book.

104. Daily schedule for Askov Folk High School, *Danish Folk School*, p. 101.

105. The history of the cooperative movement in Scandinavia is well documented and need not be recited here. See, for example, Marquis Childs, *Sweden: The Middle Way* (New Haven: Yale University Press, 1936). Mrs. Campbell visited the great Irish nationalist and co-operator George Russell ("AE") while she was abroad and reported later that he "deeply influenced" her thinking on "the coun-

try life problem" (John C. Campbell Folk School newsletter no. 11, April 1931, CP-SHC). See also ODC, "Testing AE's Philosophy," *Mountain Life and Work* 7 (April 1931): 2ff. Russell (1867–1935) edited the *Irish Homestead* (1904–23) and the *Irish Nationalist* (1923–30).

106. Almost a decade after Mrs. Campbell visited the folk schools, Don West and Myles Horton followed her, again studying the schools as possible models for adult education in the southern mountains. They focused more on the urban schools for workers, however—a focus reflected in the Highlander Folk School they founded in east Tennessee in 1932. See Myles Horton, "The Community Folk School," in Samuel Everett (ed.), *The Community School* (New York: Appleton-Century, 1938), pp. 265–97; and Frank Adams, *Unearthing Seeds of Fire: The Idea of Highlander* (Winston-Salem, N.C.: John F. Blair, 1975), esp. pp. 19–24.

107. ODC Journal, vol. 6, 14 September and 6 October 1922, and ODC to Hanmer, 26 February 1925 (CP-SHC).

108. Dean G. Larson, "A Comparison of the Spread of the Folk High School Idea in Denmark, Finland, Norway, Sweden, and the United States" (Ed.D., Indiana University, 1970), p. 147.

109. Elkhorn, Iowa (1878); Grant, Michigan (1882); West Denmark, Wisconsin (1884); Nysted, Nebraska (1887); Tyler, Minnesota (1888); Des Moines, Iowa (1896); and Kenmore, North Dakota (1902). See Paulston, *Folk Schools in Social Change*, p. 97, for a synopsis of Hannah M. Nyholm, "Grundtvig and His Impact on America" (M.A. thesis, University of Wisconsin, 1951).

110. John H. Bille, "A History of the Danes in America," *Transactions of the Wisconsin Academy* 11 (1896–97): 1–49.

111. Bille's findings were substantiated more than a half-century later by Frank M. Paulson, who undertook investigations of cultural survivals among Danes in California, Nebraska, and Iowa. He found that not only folk schools but also Danish language newspapers and fraternal organizations fared poorly among Danish immigrants. The Elkhorn, Iowa, school became an old folks' home in 1918, and Atterdag College (Solvang, California) was turned into a children's camp. Paulson argues that folk schools in the United States were "ailing" in the 1920s and dead by the 1930s. See Frank M. Paulson, "Danish-American Folk Traditions: A Study of Fading Survivals" (Ph.D. diss., Indiana University, 1967), pp. 19f., 38–41. Paulson's interview with A. C. Nielsen (pp. 269ff.), who attended the Nysted folk school in 1908–9, confirmed that many students attended the schools primarily to learn English. In 1928 there was an attempt to convert the long-closed folk high school at Ashland, Michigan, into the Ashland School for Adult Education. See John E. Kirkpatrick, "In Danish Shoes," *Survey* 60 (1 June 1928), 277–79, 310.

112. Foght, *The Danish Folk High Schools*, p. 91.

113. Olive Dame Campbell, "Danish People's Colleges and Their Relation to Southern Mountain Problems," *Public Health Nurse*, August 1924, pp. 391–96 See also her "Impressions of the People's College of Denmark," *Scandinavian*, March 1924, pp. 17–21. She used "people's college" rather than "folk high schools" to make clear that the schools were for adults rather than high-school-age students.

114. ODC, "The People's College of Denmark and What It May Mean to the

Highlands," in *Two Addresses Delivered at the Conference of Southern Mountain Workers, Knoxville, Tennessee, April 8–10, 1924* (Knoxville: Conference of Southern Mountain Workers, [1924]).

115. Miss McCord to ODC, 26 November 1923; John Glenn to ODC, 1 December 1923; ODC to F. S. Bennett, 20 May 1924; ODC to John Glenn, 26 June 1924; May Stone to ODC, 4 December 1924; ODC to Glenn, 11 March 1925 (CP-SHC).

116. ODC to Glenn, 21 June 1924 (CP-SHC).

117. ODC to Glenn, 13 October 1924, and to unidentified correspondent, 6 April 1925 (CP-SHC). Mrs. Campbell hoped for major funding for the school from the Sage Foundation, but it did not materialize. As McClymer has shown (*War and Welfare*, pp. 51–64), the foundation's resources were severely strained in this period by its involvement in starting the "model" upper-class community of Forest Hills Gardens in New York. The project cut foundation income virtually in half between 1909 and 1913.

118. ODC to Glenn, 23 January 1925 (CP-SHC). The Berea experiment, described in *Mountain Life and Work* 1 (July 1925): 16–17, took place 2–28 January 1925.

119. Pat McNelley, *The First 40 Years: John C. Campbell Folk School* (Atlanta: McNelley, Rudd Printing Service, 1966) pp. 6–7.

120. Frederick C. Brownlee, *The John C. Campbell Folk School, 1925–52*, p. 9; *Asheville* (N.C.) *Citizen*, 18 November 1925; *Cherokee Scout*, 2 October and 20 November 1925; A. Cartwright of Carnegie Corporation to ODC, 2 December 1925 (CP-SHC). Georg Bidstrup came to manage the farm in May 1926. The fullest of Mrs. Campbell's many published statements on the school's concept, design, and programs is "I Sing behind the Plow," *Journal of Adult Education* 2 (June 1930): 248–59. My account is based upon (in addition to published materials cited) interviews with former students and teachers Oscar Cantrell, Mr. and Mrs. Leon Deschamps, Herman Estes, Dagnall Folger, Hayden and Bonnie Hensley, Maggie Masters, Mrs. F. O. Scroggs, Mercer Scroggs, and Claude Stalcup and current director Esther Hyatt.

121. Articles of Incorporation of the John C. Campbell Folk School, 23 November 1925 (CP-SHC). Original trustees were Mrs. Campbell; Edna Voss of the Presbyterian church's Board of National Missions; Fred Brownlee, secretary of the American Missionary Association; and J. H. Dillard, a local lawyer (ODC to Carnegie Corporation, 5 December 1925, CP-SHC).

122. ODC to Glenn, 3 May 1924 (CP-SHC). In *Mountain Life and Work* 2 (July 1926): 26–28, Mrs. Campbell reiterated that "the ultimate form which the . . . school is to take must grow out of community need." In an interview on 16 July 1981, former student Hayden Hensley reported that community people were generally enthusiastic about the school's coming to the community.

123. *Cherokee Scout*, 15 July 1927, p. 1; unidentified clipping (26 December 1931) in John C. Campbell Folk School scrapbook no. 1; *Cherokee Scout*, 27 May, 10 June, 11 November 1932 (all p. 1); and interviews with Mrs. Fred O. Scroggs and Mercer Scroggs, 17 July 1981.

124. Newsletter 2 (August 1926); *Cherokee Scout*, 5 February 1926, pp. 1, 6; 22 July 1927, p. 1; and 9 September 1927, p. 1; "Notes from the John C. Campbell Folk School," *Mountain Life and Work* 6 (January 1928): 25–29; Leon Deschamps,

"Building in Stone," *Mountain Life and Work* 7 (January 1932): 18–19. Deschamps remained at the school until 1943 (interview with Leon Deschamps, Swannanoa, N.C., 20 March 1981).

125. ODC to Agnes Macphail, 16 September 1927; ODC to Mr. and Mrs. Lange, 14 February 1928 (CP-SHC). In an interview on 21 March 1981, Leon Deschamps attributed the small number of students (in the early years and later as well) to the school's policy of not giving regular academic credit for its courses.

126. ODC to Ralph S. Rounds, 13 April and 19 June 1929; annual report of 1929 (CP-SHC).

127. *Mountain Life and Work* 2 (July 1926): 26–28; annual report, 1931; ODC to Herbert C. Morris, 25 June 1930 (CP-SHC). See also ODC, "I Sing behind the Plow." In "The Winter Session of the John C. Campbell Folk School," *Mountain Life and Work* 8 (April 1932): 4–6, Mrs. Campbell voiced her "renewed conviction of the wisdom of the general plan" for the school.

128. ODC to Ralph S. Rounds, 2 March 1931 (CP-SHC).

129. Annual reports, 1931–33.

130. ODC, "I Sing behind the Plow," p. 252.

131. The following discussion is based upon statistics in *Historical Statistics of the United States, Colonial Times to 1970*, 1:457–68; *Fourteenth Census of the United States, 1920*, vol. 6, part 2: Agriculture, pp. 221–64; and *Sixteenth Census of the United States, 1940*, Agriculture, vol. 2, part 2, 140–204.

132. *Mountain Life and Work* 2 (July 1926): 26–28.

133. ODC to American friends, 13 April 1923; Plunkett to ODC, 11 September 1923; IAOS to ODC, 1 October 1923 (CP-SHC).

134. *Cherokee Scout*, 23 April 1926, p. 1; Marguerite Butler, "The Brasstown Savings and Loan Association," *Mountain Life and Work* 2 (July 1926): 41; Newsletter 6 (1 November 1928); "Brasstown Savings and Loan Association," *Mountain Life and Work* 4 (January 1928): 35; ODC, "A Cooperating Community," *Mountain Life and Work* 5 (April 1929): 20; ODC, "Are We Developing Dependence or Independence?," *Mountain Life and Work* 5 (July 1929): 10–16; John C. Campbell Folk School annual report for 1931; and Brasstown Savings and Loan Association monthly report, October 1932. Records of the association are scanty in CP-SHC, but it appears that it still existed at least as late as 1934. In *Farmer Movements in the South, 1865–1933* (Berkeley: University of California Press, 1960), p. 219, Theodore Saloutos notes that "the first successful co-operative credit union in North America" was organized in Quebec in 1900. Saloutos says that North Carolina's credit union enabling legislation (1915) was "among the best of its kind in the nation" (p. 220).

135. Saloutos, *Farmer Movements*, pp. 263f.

136. Saloutos, *Farmer Movements*, pp. 60 ff.; Woodward, *Origins of the New South*, pp. 175ff.; and Stuart Noblin, *The Grange in North Carolina, 1929–1954* (Greensboro: North Carolina State Grange, 1954).

137. *Cherokee Scout*, 21 January 1927, p. 1; ODC to Mr. and Mrs. Lange, 14 February 1928; Newsletter 6 (November 1928) (CP-SHC); ODC, "A Cooperating Community," *Mountain Life and Work* 5 (April 1929): 19–21.

138. Fred O. Scroggs to J. R. Pitman, 12 April 1931; monthly and annual reports, 1931–34 (CP-SHC).

139. *Cherokee Scout*, 7 December 1928 and 30 August 1929 (both p. 1); ODC to Mr. Lange, 9 March 1929 (CP-SHC); *Cherokee Scout*, 9, 12, 16 August 1932, p. 1.

140. Report to board of directors, 15 March 1934; and John C. Campbell Folk School and Mountain Valley Creamery annual reports, 1931–48. In 1935 the Creamery and the Farmers' Association merged to become the Mountain Valley Co-operative, so that early and later sales totals are not fully comparable (*Mountain Life and Work* 12 [April 1936]: 24).

141. ODC to Poe, 12 July 1937 (CP-SHC).

142. "Confidential Report to Directors," February 1938; ODC to J. R. Pitman, 24 October 1940 (CP-SHC).

143. Loans went to W. J. Martin, Glenn and Wayne Holland, G. R. Ford, Verlin Reese, Hayden Hensley, Frank Hogan, Wallace Massey, Cecil Tipton, and perhaps others.

144. Farm report for 1951; school annual report for 1952. Paradoxically, part of the problem may have been competition from James G. K. McClure's Asheville-based Farmer's Federation co-operative (founded in 1920), which moved into the Cherokee-Clay area around 1937. Two letters from ODC to John Glenn (22 October and 18 December 1937, CP-SHC) suggest that the federation had decided, over her protests, to open an agency in the area. "I am inclined to think that it is the beginning of the end in regard to our own development," Mrs. Campbell said. Ironically, fifteen years earlier, she had written an admiring article on the federation, "Agricultural Co-operation in the Southern Highlands," *Home Lands* 4 (June, 1922): 4, 16–17. See also James G. K. McClure, "Ten Years of the Farmer's Federation," *Mountain Life and Work* 7 (April 1931): 23–25.

145. *Cherokee Scout*, 22 November 1930, p. 1.

146. ODC to Ralph Rounds, 9 February 1929; Rounds to ODC, 15 May 1929; memo to Rounds, 19 November 1929 and 1 April 1930; ODC to Rounds, 27 October 1930 and 12 March and 10 April 1931; 1931–33 annual reports; Rounds to ODC, 2 June 1933 (CP-SHC).

147. Marguerite Butler to Ralph Rounds, 22 December 1933; unidentified newspaper clippings in CP-SHC (January 1936), and John C. Campbell Folk School scrapbook no. 2.

148. 1940 annual report; 1 March 1949 financial report; Georg Bidstrup to ODC, 10 April 1952 and 18 November 1953 (CP-SHC).

149. Confidential report to directors, 21 January 1942; ODC to Morris Mitchell, 21 January 1942; report of school staff meeting, 10 April 1942 (CP-SHC).

150. John Glenn to ODC, 11 February 1909; and ODC Journal, vol. 4, 12 March 1909, 115f. (CP-SHC).

151. ODC Journal, vol. 3, 26 November 1908 (CP-SHC).

152. Pettit to John C. Campbell, 23 July 1912 (CP-SHC).

153. Additional photographs of John C. Campbell Folk School craftspeople and their products appear facing pages 209, 220, 223, 238, 239, 288, and 330. In *Mountain Life and Work* 10 (October 1934), Mrs. Campbell wrote of Ullman's "rare and sympathetic insight" and called her photographs "a remarkable record of mountain life and character." In recent years, John Jacob Niles and Jonathan Williams have resurrected and republished a large collection in *The Appalachian Photographs of Doris Ullman* (Highlands, N.C.: Jargon Society, 1971).

154. See Eaton, *Handicrafts*, p. 258, for a brief account of the staging of the photographs.

155. ODC Journal, vol. 4, 25 January 1909 (CP-SHC).

156. Ibid., vol. 3, 3 November 1908 (CP-SHC).

157. Ibid., vol. 3, 28 November and 6, 7, 31 December 1908 (CP-SHC). A letter from Pettit to ODC, 12 July 1909, indicates that an eastern Kentucky dulcimer maker was making an instrument for Mrs. Campbell.

158. ODC Journal, vol. 4, 19 February 1909 (CP-SHC). Goodrich was "a woman of means," John Campbell told John Glenn, connected with the family of a former president of Yale University (JCC to Glenn, 17 March 1914, CP-SHC). She worked under the auspices of the Presbyterian church. She retired in 1931 and died in 1944. See Frances Goodrich, *Mountain Homespun* (New Haven: Yale University Press, 1931).

159. See Blackwell P. Robinson, ed., *The North Carolina Guide* (Chapel Hill: University of North Carolina Press, 1955), pp. 135, 140f. Cost figure is from Carl A. Schenck, *The Birth of Forestry in America: Biltmore Forest School, 1898–1913* (1955; rpt. Santa Cruz: Forest History Society and Appalachian Consortium Press, 1974), p. 82.

160. Eaton, *Handicrafts*, p. 70.

161. ODC Journal, vol. 4, 11 March 1909 (CP-SHC).

162. Ruth Dame Coolidge, "Vibrations from a Danish Bell," *American-Scandinavian Review* 33 (June 1945): 106; Marguerite Butler, "Pulling Together Through Play," *Mountain Life and Work* 8 (April 1932): 25–26; and "Course on Singing Games," *Mountain Life and Work* 8 (July 1932): 28. Compare Butler's later reminiscences in *Mountain Life and Work* 30 (autumn 1954): 23ff. In an interview on 21 March 1981, school director (1946–49) D. F. Folger recalled that Butler considered local square dances less graceful and attractive than the Danish and English dances. Several former students interviewed in mid-1981 said that local dances could be done only in Butler's absence.

163. See *Singing Games Old and New, Collected and Translated by the John C. Campbell Folk School* (Swannanoa, N.C.: Asheville Farm School, 1933). The two non-Scandinavian tunes were German.

164. Butler to Rounds, 28 June 1931; ODC to Rounds, 21 November 1932, respectively (CP-SHC). Also ODC to Rounds, 3 September 1929, to Herbert C. Morris, 25 June 1930, to Rounds, 27 October 1930; and 7 May 1932 annual report (all in CP-SHC).

165. May 1934 annual report (CP-SHC).

166. 1946 annual report (CP-SHC). An undated [1940s?] price list in CP-SHC shows that the carved animals sold for from 75 cents to $1.35 each.

167. *Cherokee Scout*, 26 June 1925, p. 6.

168. *Newark* (N.J.) *Star-Eagle*, 22 November 1937, p. 13; and Edward L. Dupuy, *Artisans of the Appalachians* (Asheville, N.C.: Miller Printing Company, 1967), pp. 108–19. I encountered no evidence to establish the origins of weaving patterns or techniques used at the John C. Campbell Folk School.

169. Ruth D. Coolidge, "Vibrations from a Danish Bell," p. 116.

170. Newsletter 30 (November 1948).

171. Dupuy, *Artisans of the Appalachians*, p. 102. Even so admiring an observer

of Berea as Eaton makes clear that the handicraft industry there was based only partly, at best, on southern mountain traditional designs and techniques.

Estes (b. 1897) was from Lee County, Kentucky, the son of a farmer and river-man. After two years at Berea (1911–13), he spent five years in the army, and then held a succession of jobs with railroads, construction companies, and the like, until he settled into woodworking and cabinetmaking. He had taught woodworking at the Presbyterian school at Guerrant, Kentucky, and was teaching at Beattyville un-der the New Deal National Youth Administration program when the opportunity came to go to the folk school in 1939. Interview with Herman Estes, 15 July 1981.

172. This sketch of Hensley is based upon an interview with him on 15 July 1981.

173. ODC to Ralph Rounds, 21 November 1932 (CP-SHC); and *New York Sun*, 21 November 1935.

174. *Mountain Life and Work* 30 (autumn 1954); ODC to John Glenn, 7 March 1928 (CP-SHC). She also urged Glenn to put up the Sage Foundation money that eventually led to the Allen Eaton crafts study and the publication of his *Handicrafts of the Southern Highlands* in 1937.

175. ODC to John Glenn, 1 January 1929 (CP-SHC); and "A Southern Moun-tain Handicraft Association: Report of Penland Conference," *Mountain Life and Work* 5 (July 1929): 31–32. See Eaton's account of the early years of the guild in *Handicrafts*, pp. 237–54, from which most details of the following brief discussion are taken. The guild was officially formed a year later, in December 1929.

176. Pamela Henson, "An Analysis of Cultural Change Factors Affecting the Development of Handicrafts Co-operatives in Appalachia" (M.A. thesis, George Washington University, 1976), p. 84.

177. See David E. Whisnant, *Modernizing the Mountaineer: People, Power, and Planning in Appalachia* (Boone, N.C.: Appalachian Consortium Press, 1981), pp. 3–39 on the CSMW.

178. Lucy Morgan of Penland School (one of the guild's founders) had studied weaving with Chicagoan Edward F. Worst, whom she later brought to Penland many times as a weaving teacher. See Bonnie W. Ford, "Learning From a Great Teacher," *Mountain Life and Work* 7 (October 1931): 22–23. In his "review" of mountain weaving at the 1927 Conference of Southern Mountain Workers meet-ing—"Exhibits at the Conference of Mountain Workers," *Mountain Life and Work* 3 (July 1927): 27–28—Worst made numerous "suggestions [for] better techniques and selection of materials."

179. On the exhibit, see "Mountain Baskets," *American Magazine of Art* 26 (December 1933): 546–48; and vol. 27 (September 1934): 36–38. The guild was also a major contributor to the later Rural Arts [handicrafts] Exhibition staged in connection with the seventy-fifth anniversary of the U.S. Department of Agricul-ture, 14 November–5 December 1937, which received extensive coverage in major newspapers. See Clementine Douglas, "The Rural Arts Exhibition," *Mountain Life and Work* 13 (January 1938): 8–10.

180. Henson, "An Analysis," pp. 85–98. Late in 1933, Mrs. Campbell and TVA chairman Arthur Morgan spoke at a program on handicrafts in Knoxville (ODC to Ralph Rounds, 6 November 1933, CP-SHC). The resulting Labor De-partment study by Bertha M. Nienburg, *Potential Earning Power of Southern*

Mountaineer Handicraft (Washington, D.C.: Women's Bureau, U.S. Department of Labor, 1935), argued that the possible market was substantial (on the order of $20 million per year), but average earnings were small (an average of $52 per craftworker per year) and abuses were frequently akin to those in sweatshop, piecework industries (see esp. pp. 4–5).

181. Clementine Douglas, "The Southern Highlanders: A New Craft Service," *Mountain Life and Work* 12 (April 1936): 21–23. The guild craft shop at Big Meadows Lodge on the Skyline Drive opened 5 May 1941. See *Mountain Life and Work* 17 (fall 1941): 24.

182. Eaton, *Handicrafts*, p. 241. The 1940 Guild annual report argued for establishing formal "apprentice," "craftsman," and "master craftsman" designations among members, betokening the strong shift to formal training and concern for "artful" design.

183. Eaton, *Handicrafts*, p. 251.

184. Guild memorandum, 3 October 1943 (CP-SHC).

185. Eaton to ODC, 18 November 1943; Heard to ODC, 9 December 1943 and 30 [sic] February 1944; ODC to O. J. Mattil, 18 January 1944 (CP-SHC). Heard held degrees in ceramic arts and fine arts from Alfred University and Columbia University. The guild appears to have received about fourteen thousand dollars from GEB. A grant of $45,000 for a five-year study was approved but never given, because of problems with the guild's tax-exempt status (Louise Pitman to ODC, 4 January 1944; GEB to Winogene Redding, 5 April 1945; ODC to John Glenn, 20 November 1945; GEB to ODC, 5 December 1945; unsigned letter to ODC, 11 January 1950; all in CP-SHC).

186. Henson, "An Analysis," p. 145. Henson also notes (p. 128) that a 1960 survey of guild members revealed that only half of the active guild craftspeople were natives of the mountains, and nearly a quarter were college educated.

187. Jonathan Williams, "The Southern Appalachians," *Craft Horizons* 27 (June 1966): 47–66. In *Encouraging American Craftsmen* (Washington, D.C.: Government Printing Office, 1972), a report written for the Federal Interagency Crafts Committee, guild member Charles Counts argued that "since [economic] success in handcraft development will depend to a large degree on the quality of the craft product, the *whole effort* should be directed and coordinated by professionals in the art and craft fields" (italics added).

188. Dupuy, *Artisans of the Appalachians*, pp. 92–93.

189. A full-scale study of the guild is unfortunately beyond the scope of this study. Supporting details for the brief analysis here are easily available in the published record (e.g., *Mountain Life and Work*), however.

190. ODC to board members, 1 June 1946 (CP-SHC); D. F. Folger, "The History and Aims of Cumberland Homesteads," *Mountain Life and Work* 11 (July 1935): 5–7. Folger became director on 1 September 1946. The following account of his brief tenure is based upon documents cited and upon an interview with D. F. Folger in Black Mountain, N.C., on 21 March 1981.

191. Brownlee to ODC, 28 January 1949 (CP-SHC).

192. Louise Pitman to Brownlee, 13 February 1949; and board to Folger, 24 March 1949 (CP-SHC).

193. The following brief summary is based upon Folger's report, "A Critical

Appraisal of the John C. Campbell Folk School with Suggested Plans for the Future" (14 April 1949, CP-SHC).

194. More than twenty years earlier, John Kirkpatrick had noted similar patterns among former students (and their children) of Michigan's Ashland Folk School (Kirkpatrick, "In Danish Shoes," p. 277).

195. In an interview on 20 March 1981, Leon and May Ritchie Deschamps, former folk school staff members of the period, confirmed that there was hostility between the community and the school.

196. Minutes of board meeting, 30 April 1949; ODC to William G. Klein, 17 May 1949 (CP-SHC); interview with Herman Estes, 15 July 1981. Although Mrs. Campbell added that "necessary adaptations" could be considered, those of the order Folger suggested clearly could not be countenanced.

197. See his *Revolt of the Sharecroppers* (New York: Covici, 1936), and George B. Tindall, *The Emergence of the New South, 1913–1945* (Baton Rouge: Louisiana State University Press, 1967), pp. 418, 551, 634f. For an excellent study of Kester and other southerners who were working at the time for progressive change in the South, see Anthony Dunbar, *Against the Grain: Southern Radicals and Prophets, 1929–1959* (Charlottesville: University of Virginia Press, 1981). Robert F. Martin's excellent article on Kester, "A Prophet's Pilgrimage: The Religious Radicalism of Howard Anderson Kester, 1921–1941," *Journal of Southern History* 48 (November 1982): 511–30, appeared too late for me to make use of it here.

198. Herman Estes to ODC, 11 October 1949; staff letter to ODC, 13 October 1949 (CP-SHC); interview with Estes, 15 July 1981.

199. *Cherokee Scout*, 20 July 1950, p. 1; undated clipping [late 1951]; memorandum from Fred Brownlee, 21 January 1952 (CP-SHC). Kester said his resignation resulted from "the discussion within the Board of Directors regarding [my] plans for developing a school-community program." In Pat McNelley's official history of the folk school, *The First 40 Years of the John C. Campbell Folk School* (Atlanta: McNelley-Rudd Printing Service, 1966), the five-year tenure of Fogler and Kester as directors is passed over in a single sentence (p. 71).

200. Minutes of May 1952 annual meeting; Bidstrup to ODC, 6 October 1949, 13 January 1950, and 10 December 1952 (CP-SHC).

201. Newsletter of September 1952 (CP-SHC). During the postwar period, the folk school whittlers received considerable press coverage. See Dale Carnegie's nationally syndicated column for 27 October 1945; *Pittsburgh Press*, 9 December 1945; *Motor Court Age*, April 1946; *American Magazine*, August 1946; and *Atlanta Journal Magazine*, 17 August 1947.

202. Newsletter, October 1953; "Suggested Plans for the Future" (typescript, 14 April 1954). Mrs. Campbell was apparently distressed by Bidstrup's sketch of the future; on 20 April 1954 he wrote to apologize for having caused her "so much worry" (CP-SHC).

203. Georg Bidstrup, "The Folk School Faces the Future," *Mountain Life and Work* 31 (winter 1955): 35–42 (italics in original). Bidstrup was not alone in his estimate, for folk schools continued to be established—in Manitoba after 1940, and among Indians in rural Ontario in the 1960s (Paulston, *Folk Schools in Social Change*, pp. 19, 42). In the 1960s humanistic psychologists such as Abraham Maslow and Carl Rogers were arguing for folk schools, as was Paul Goodman in his

Compulsory Mis-Education (1964; cf. Paulston, pp. 5 ff.). The latest folk school to be established in the Appalachian region was eastern Kentucky's short-lived Marrowbone Folk School, founded by community activist Edith Easterling in Pike County in the late 1960s upon the encouragement of Myles Horton. On Marrowbone, see *People's Appalachia* 1 (spring 1971). In the late 1970s, the Folk School Association of America was formed. Its second (1980) meeting was held at the John C. Campbell Folk School. See *Appalachian Center Newsletter* [Berea College] 9 (summer 1980): 1.

204. Bidstrup, "The Folk School Faces the Future," p. 39. Detailed studies of dance in the region are very scarce, but one study which confirms the point is Margaret Counts, "Dance Traditions in the Blue Ridge" (Appalachian Studies Conference, March 1981).

205. Among other (sometimes overlapping) segments of the population, stereotypes traceable to commercial recorded "hillbilly" music of the 1920s and 1930s predominate.

206. ODC to Olive V. Marsh, 5 September 1924 (CP-SHC). Marsh was associated with the Carr Creek Community Center. See her article on the center in *Mountain Life and Work* 2 (January 1927): 17–20. By 1930, Mrs. Campbell had become more keenly aware of the ethical risks of intervention. "How far," she asked herself, "should one's own ideas of what is needed shape plans for others in a different environment?" ("I Sing behind the Plow," p. 254).

207. ODC to unidentified family member, December 1925 (CP-SHC). She also asked for "those old college [song books] we used to have years ago."

208. Daisy Dame to her family, 25 February 1926 (CP-SHC). Photographs of most of the furnishings may be found in Daisy Dame's photo album (1925ff.); they provide an excellent index to local traditional styles.

209. ODC to Rounds, 19 June 1929; and Newsletter 19 (May 1936) (CP-SHC).

210. ODC to Claxton, 27 February 1931; Newsletter 19 (May 1936); Bidstrup to ODC, 30 November 1949 (CP-SHC). As early as 27 February 1931, Mrs. Campbell wrote to A. C. Nielsen that Bidstrup had already had "such a great influence" upon gymnastics and singing games at the school.

211. ODC to Dingman, 14 March 1939 (CP-SHC).

212. Annual report for 1933 (CP-SHC). On 18 July 1938, Harvey Moorehead of Antioch College wrote to Mrs. Campbell that he was trying to start a local group to do the dances he had learned in a folk school short course. See Willie Fay Allen, "Ten Days of Work and Play at Brasstown," *Mountain Life and Work* 6 (October 1930): 28–30, an account of Danish exercises and games under Georg Bidstrup's direction; and Marguerite Butler, "Folk Festival Plans," *Mountain Life and Work* 10 (January 1935): 5–6, and *Mountain Life and Work* 11 (January, 1936): 12–14, two accounts of the Berea College festivals which drew heavily upon *Singing Games Old and New*.

213. Annual report for 1945 (CP-SHC).

214. Annual reports for 1945 and 1946 (CP-SHC).

215. Through its Appalachian Center, under the direction of Loyal Jones, Berea has in recent years also promoted and presented a more authentic version of mountain music.

216. ODC to friends in the United States, 13 April 1923 (CP-SHC).

217. ODC, *Adult Education in Scandinavia and America: Two Addresses Delivered at the Conference of Southern Mountain Workers, Knoxville, Tennessee, April 8–10, 1924* (Knoxville: Conference of Southern Mountain Workers, 1924), pp. 13–14. From the perspective of left, labor-oriented groups, of course, the schools' religious cast probably would have been considered the least of their problems. Cherokee County was not immune to the Red-baiting fears witnessed broadly during the post-World War I period. On 1 October 1932 the *Cherokee Scout* made front-page news out of the Communist party's attempt to get on the ballot in North Carolina, going so far as to assert that even the ACLU was "affiliated with the Communist party."

218. ODC to unidentified correspondent, 6 April 1925 (CP-SHC).

219. Indeed, her observation in 1929, that "floating, unsettled" unemployed mountaineers become "a problem to the economist, the social workers, the police, and the state in general" is reminiscent of the "dangerous classes" rhetoric of conservative social workers at the turn of the century. See ODC, "Adjustment to Rural Industrial Change with Special Reference to Mountain Areas," *National Education Association Proceedings* 67 (1929): 486.

220. See Tyndall, *Emergence of the New South*, esp. pp. 318–53, 391–432, and 607–49.

221. The following discussion is based upon Martin Duberman, *Black Mountain College: An Exploration in Community* (New York: Dutton, 1972).

222. Ibid., p. 73.

223. Ibid., p. 43.

224. Raymond and Charlotte Koch, *Educational Commune: The Story of Commonwealth College* (New York: Schocken Books, 1972), p. 9. The brief account that follows is based upon the Kochs's book.

225. On Emma Dusenberry, see Koch and Koch, *Educational Commune*, pp. 18, 55, 93. Some of Dusenberry's singing can be heard on the Library of Congress album *Versions and Variants of Barbara Allen* (AFS L-54). See also Vance Randolph, "Utopia in Arkansas," *Esquire* 9 (January 1938): 60–63. Among the folklore collectors of the 1920s and 1930s, Randolph was a spirited iconoclast who accepted the lore more as he found it than as it could be made to fit accepted norms and assumptions about the folk. His early collection of bawdy Ozark stories saw the light of day only in the 1970s as *Pissing in the Snow and Other Ozark Folk Tales* (Urbana: University of Illinois Press, 1978).

226. Koch and Koch, *Educational Commune*, p. 144.

227. On Hays, see R. Serge Denisoff, *Great Day Coming: Folk Music and the American Left* (Urbana: University of Illinois Press, 1971), pp. 28, 78–81. The folk school play appears in *Mountain Life and Work* 9 (October 1935): 4–9.

228. The following brief account is based upon W. Edward Orser, *Searching for a Viable Alternative: The Macedonia Cooperative Community, 1937–1958* (New York: Burt Franklin, 1981).

Chapter 3

1. See Margaret R. Wolfe, "J. Fred Johnson, His Town and His People: A Case Study of Class Values, the Work Ethic, and Technology in Southern Appalachia, 1916–1944," *Appalachian Journal* 7 (autumn-winter 1979–80): 70–83.

2. The commercial discovery of southern mountain musicians has begun to be explored in a growing body of descriptive and analytical literature. Useful points of entry are the special "hillbilly" issues of *JAF* 78 (July-September 1965) and *Western Folklore* (July 1971); Bill C. Malone, *Country Music USA: A Fifty-Year History* (Austin: Univ. of Texas Press, 1968); and David E. Whisnant, "Thicker Than Fiddlers in Hell: Issues and Resources in Appalachian Music," *Appalachian Journal* 5 (autumn 1977): 103–15.

3. See Archie Green, "Hillbilly Music: Source and Symbol," *Journal of American Folklore* 78 (1965): 204ff.

4. However faulty the logic may have been in some respects, it was true that commercial recordings were moving traditional music away from its roots. In "The Skillet Lickers: A Study of a Hillbilly String Band and Its Repertoire," *JAF* 78 (July-September 1965): 229–44, Norman Cohen notes that 70 percent of the first 100 southern mountain records released in Columbia's 15000-D series (1926–31) were traditional, but of the last 100, only 10 percent were. Fragmentary evidence suggests that such a pattern was more or less typical of many commercial recording companies. Thus what the public was offered as "authentic" mountain music in the late 1920s was in fact becoming less and less so. On the other hand, Cohen also notes that Columbia discouraged its "hillbilly" musicians from recording the jazz and popular tunes many of them were interested in; to that extent the company functioned as a conservative influence. For a detailed account of one such case, see Charles Wolfe, "Clayton McMichen: Reluctant Hillbilly," *Bluegrass Unlimited*, May 1979, pp. 56–61. I am grateful to Mia Boynton for calling this article to my attention.

5. See Malone, *Country Music, U.S.A.: A Fifty-Year History*, pp. 68ff. For an excellent account of some of the earliest mountain musicians to "go commercial" (Henry Whitter, Fiddlin' John Carson, Ernest Stoneman, Gid Tanner), see Norman Cohen, "Early Pioneers," in Bill C. Malone and Judith McCulloh, eds., *Stars of Country Music: Uncle Dave Macon to Johnny Rodriguez* (Urbana: University of Illinois Press, 1975), pp. 3–39. D. K. Wilgus's article on Bradley Kincaid, in the same volume, pp. 40–63, chronicles the career of a mountain-born musician on the WLS radio barn dance.

6. Alan P. Merriam, in *The Anthropology of Music* (Evanston: Northwestern University Press, 1964), pp. 242–44, discusses the opposition to jazz mounted by clergymen, doctors, and others in the 1920s and 30s who viewed it as a symbol of barbarism, savagery, animalism, and even Bolshevism.

7. On Lunsford's festival, see David E. Whisnant, "Finding the Way between the Old and the New: The Mountain Dance and Folk Festival and Bascom Lamar Lunsford's Work as a Citizen," *Appalachian Journal* 7 (autumn-winter 1979–80): 135–54; on Knott's, see Archie Green, "Commercial Music Graphics 32: The National Folk Festival Association," *John Edwards Memorial Foundation Quarterly* 11 (spring 1975): 23–32. See also Angus K. Gillespie, "Pennsylvania Folk Festivals

of the 1930s," *Pennsylvania Folklife* 26 (fall 1976), 2–11; and David E. Whisnant, *Folk Festival Issues: Report from a Seminar* (Los Angeles: John Edwards Memorial Foundation, 1979).

8. "And the Mountains Sing With Joy," *Southern Magazine* 2 (April 1935): 10; *Bristol* (Va.) *Herald-Courier*, 6 August 1933; Charles B. Coale, *The Life and Adventures of Wilburn Waters . . . Embracing the Early History of Southwestern Virginia* (Richmond: G. W. Gary, 1878), pp. 17–24.

9. See Joseph T. Wilson's liner notes to *A Fiddler's Convention at Mountain City, Tennessee, in 1925* (County 505); *Fields Ward and His Buck Mountain Band* (Historical BC-2433); and *Ernest V. Stoneman and His Dixie Mountaineers* (Historical HLP-8004).

10. See the recollections of Pearl D. Hensley in Bettye-Lou Fields, comp., *Grayson County: A History in Words and Pictures* (Independence, Va.: Grayson County Historical Society, 1976), p. 237.

11. The account of the White Top Festival which follows is based upon the private papers of John A. Blakemore and Annabel Morris Buchanan in the Southern Historical Collection at the University of North Carolina (cited as JABP and AMBP, respectively) and the private papers of John Powell in the Alderman Library at the University of Virginia (cited as JPP); an interview with John A. Blakemore on 5 May 1979; interviews with former White Top performers Francis Atkins, Albert Hash, Harold Hensley, Harve G. Sheets, Josie Sheets Marshall, and Myrtle Stout Taylor; and published materials as cited. Valuable leads and suggestions were provided by Francis N. Atkins, James R. Billings, Bill Blanton and Steven Fisher of *The Plow*, Mrs. George P. [Buchanan] Crounse, Archie Green, Mrs. W. M. Hensley, Kip Lornell, J. Roderick Moore, Paul Morris, Daniel Patterson, Charles Perdue, Mrs. Jack Reedy, David A. Sturgill, and Joseph T. Wilson.

12. Printed programs of 21 May and 24 September 1923, in AMBP.

13. Ulrich Troubetzkoy, "Music on the Mountain," *Virginia Cavalcade* 2 (summer 1961): 6; and Buchanan to Powell, 14 June 1931 (JPP). Troubetzkoy said there had been "fiddlers' contests" on the mountain before, but I was unable to find corroborating evidence.

14. Blakemore to H. K. Bowen, 22 July 1931 (JABP). Buchanan, Powell, and Blakemore are cited hereafter as AMB, JP, and JAB.

15. JAB to Mrs. Edgar Umbarger, 29 July 1931 (JABP); JAB to Lamar Stringfield, 5 August 1931 (JABP).

16. See John A. Burrison, "Fiddlers in the Alley: Atlanta as an Early Country Music Center," *Atlanta Historical Bulletin* 21 (summer 1977): 63; Bill C. Malone, *Southern Music American Music* (Lexington: University Press of Kentucky, 1979), p. 8; AMB to JAB, 17 July 1931 (JABP); John Murray Gibbon, "The Music of the People," Empire Club of Canada *Addresses* (1929), pp. 278–88; and *Canadian Mosaic: The Making of a Northern Nation* (Toronto: McClellan & Stewart, 1938), pp. 225–353 and 424ff. An article in the *Albertan*, 30 June 1945, says Gibbon began his festivals at Quebec City in the early twenties. On 15 December 1928, the *Edmonton Journal* reported that he had recently inaugurated the Folklore and Handicrafts Festival at Winnepeg.

17. Letters to JAB, 31 July–12 August 1931 (JABP). These and many other letters from early White Top performers are preserved in JABP.

18. Correspondence in JABP suggests that some of the string bands may have been both formed and named especially for the White Top event.

19. AMB to JP and Mrs. John Powell, 2 and 6 August 1931, respectively (JPP).

20. JAB to C. F. Holland, 23 August 1931 (JABP).

21. Figures are approximate; multiple lists of contestants in JABP do not agree completely.

22. Letter to author from Francis N. Atkins, 15 June 1979, and interview 24 September 1979. See L. Allen Smith, "Toward a Reconstruction of the Development of the Appalachian Dulcimer," *JAF* 93 (October-December 1980): 385–96.

23. J. B. Wells to JAB, 1 August 1932 (JABP), and AMB to JAB, 22 June 1932 (JABP), respectively.

24. AMB to JAB, 1 September 1932 (JABP); and AMB to JP, 15 September 1932 (JPP), respectively.

25. Eleanor Roosevelt to AMB, 1 March 1933 (AMBP). Eleanor Roosevelt was concerned for the poor and downtrodden from early in life, when as a six year old she helped serve Thanksgiving dinner at a newsboys' lodging house. Her later efforts to help the handicapped, and especially to relocate Scott's Run (W.Va.) miners into the planned community of Arthurdale, have often been recounted. See Tamara K. Hareven, *Eleanor Roosevelt: An American Conscience* (Chicago: Quadrangle, 1966); Eleanor Roosevelt, *This I Remember* (New York: Harper and Row, 1949), pp. 126ff.; Stella K. Hershan, *A Woman of Quality* (New York: Crown, 1970); and Joseph P. Lash, *Eleanor and Franklin* (New York: Norton, 1971), pp. 393–417.

26. *Galax* (Va.) *Gazette*, 5 September 1972, p. 1-B. Clipping (on the building's demolition) courtesy of Mrs. Jack Reedy, Damascus, Va.

27. George Pullen Jackson, "White Top Festival Keeps Folk Music Alive," *Musical America* 53 (September 1933): 7ff., and "The White Top Festival," *Music Clubs Magazine*, September-October, 1933, pp. 25–27. See also *New York Times*, 13 August 1933, sect. 2, p. 4, and Eleanor G. Pierce, "White Top Musical Festival," *Norfolk and Western* [Railway] *Magazine* 11 (September 1933): 313–17.

MacKaye (1875–1956) had long been interested in what he called "civic theatre" and "community drama" (see his volumes by those titles, 1912 and 1917, respectively, and *The New Citizenship: A Civic Ritual Devised for Places of Public Meeting in America*). In the early 1920s he began a sojourn in the Kentucky mountains (mostly at Pine Mountain Settlement School), out of which came *This Fine-Pretty World: A Comedy of the Kentucky Mountains* (1923), *Tall Tales of the Kentucky Mountains* (1926), *Kentucky Mountain Fantasies: Three Short Plays for an Appalachian Theatre* (1928), and *The Gobbler of God: A Poem of the Southern Appalachians* (1928). In his introduction to *This Fine-Pretty World*, MacKaye called for an Appalachian theater "founded upon Diversity versus Standardization; a theatre of the soil, synthetic of our native lores . . . ; a theatre of living 'spoken' speech . . . ; of reconciliation between society and solitude, between the tamed and the untamable, the eternally social and the eternal-lonely; a theatre of the mountains . . . as far from sophistication as it is near to serenity and wild nature. . . ."

28. John Powell, "Treasure Recovered (Folk Music)," *Home and Garden Review*, July-August 1934, p. 6.

29. Douglas Land Company articles of incorporation (JABP). My account of

Elliott Roosevelt in southwest Virginia is based upon Goodridge Wilson, "When a Roosevelt Found Health in the Virginia Hills," *Richmond* (Va.) *Times-Dispatch Sunday Magazine*, 24 February 1935, sect. 5, pp. 1ff.; *New York Times*, 6 August 1933, sect. 2, p. 4, and 13 August 1933, sect. 2, p. 4; JAB to H. K. Bowen, 17 July 1931 (JABP); *Roanoke* (Va.) *Times*, 13 August 1933, p. 1; and Elliott Roosevelt letters in the Roosevelt Library, Hyde Park, N.Y. Robinson built a summer home on the northeast side of White Top, and his wife Corinne later published a sentimental poem entitled "The Trail to White Top." See Corinne Roosevelt Robinson, *The Call of Brotherhood and Other Poems* (New York: Charles Scribner's Sons, 1912), p. 23.

30. See Fields, *Grayson County*, p. 236.

31. Roosevelt to his daughter, 20 August 1893, and to "little Nell," July 19, 1894 (Roosevelt Library, Hyde Park).

32. Jackson, "White Top Festival," pp. 7ff.

33. AMB to JP, 16 and 17 May 1933 (JPP).

34. Bruce Crawford, "Folk Music at White Top," *New Republic* 76 (30 August 1933), 74–75. Crawford contributed "Harlan County and the Press" to *Harlan Miners Speak* (New York: Harcourt, Brace, 1932), the published record of the hearings.

35. Documentary records of the 1934 festival are quite sparse compared to other years.

36. George Pullen Jackson, "Ballad Art Revived at White Top Festival," *Musical America*, 54 (September 1934): 8ff. See also Annabel Morris Buchanan, "The Fourth Annual White Top Festival," *Music Clubs Magazine* 14 (September-October 1934): 19–20.

37. *New York Times*, 19 August 1934, p. 24. At the festival conference, R. W. Gordon spoke on "The Crisis in American Folk Song" and stressed the "fragility of the art" under modern conditions. The larger question of the festival's impact upon participants will be discussed below.

38. Powell, "Treasure Recovered (Folk Music)," p. 6. Powell's notion of the "mind of the race" will be discussed more fully below.

39. JAB to Johnston, 10 August 1935, and AMB to JAB, 11 August 1935 (JABP). For general contemporary accounts of the 1935 festival, see "White Top Folk Festival," *Musical America* 55 (September 1935): 12; and Annabel Morris Buchanan, "White Top Folk Festival," *Music Clubs Magazine*, September-October 1935, pp. 17–19. See also George Schuan, "Musical Treasure in the Appalachians," *Baltimore Sun Magazine*, 4 August 1935, p. 8.

40. JAB to AMB, 27 July 1935 (JABP). See *New York Times*, 21 April 1935, sect. 9, p. 13; 28 July 1935, sect. 10, p. 4; and 12 August 1935, p. 13.

41. In his article "In the Lowlands Low," *Southern Folklore Quarterly* 1 (March 1937): 3, John Powell wrote, "My wonder never ceases that Morris tunes . . . should have persisted in their transplantation, although the ritual dances . . . had been left behind and utterly forgotten." Quotation from Winston Wilkinson, "Virginia Dance Tunes," *Southern Folklore Quarterly* 6 (March 1942): 2. Wilkinson collected extensively from Albemarle County fiddler Uncle Jim Chisholm, who had been one of Sharp's informants, but who played no fiddle tunes for him because

"he never asked me." Tunes in Chisholm's repertoire that Wilkinson identified as morris tunes included "Haste to the Wedding," "The Fisher Laddie," "Getting Upstairs," "The Foggy Dew," and "Fine Times at Our House." Sharp himself was careful to note that transferring the morris tunes from pipe to fiddle or concertina had altered many of them so as to render them unplayable on the original instruments. "We have found," he said, "that of the old tunes which we have noted down from fiddlers . . . only a few are capable of being played on the more ancient instruments" (Sharp and Macilwaine, *The Morris Book, Part I*, p. 34). Some of Wilkinson's morris parallels are so distant even from the transformed tunes published by Sharp that considerable charity would appear to be necessary to admit that they are the "same" tunes.

42. Angelica Gibbs, "Profiles: May Gadd," *New Yorker*, 1 February 1953, 36ff.

43. AMB to JAB, 13 August 1935 and 19 May 1936 (JABP).

44. Paul Rosenfeld, "Folksong and Culture-Politics," *Modern Music* 17 (November-December 1939): 18–19. Attempts to associate morris dances with Appalachian tradition have proved remarkably durable, given the paucity of the evidence. West Virginia's state cultural magazine *Goldenseal* recently reported (6 [January-March 1980]: 6) that the Monroe (W.Va.) 4-H Dance Team would perform "Morris, English, Irish, Scottish and Appalachian traditional dances" at a local high school homecoming. For an account of the most recent morris dance revival in major U.S. cities, see David M. Schwartz, "Morris Dancers Are Coming," *Smithsonian Magazine*, May 1981, pp. 118–24.

45. See Annabel Morris Buchanan, "Traditional Dances Lure Virginians Back," *Richmond Times-Dispatch*, 13 December 1936, pp. 2, 10, for an account of Chase's teaching morris dances in Richmond.

46. Details from interview with Richard Chase, Hendersonville, North Carolina, 17 June 1981. On Rabold, see Maude Karpeles, *Cecil Sharp: His Life and Work* (London: Routledge and Kegan Paul, 1967), pp. 129f.

47. AMB to JP and JAB, 30 August 1936 (JABP). Chase was quite skillful at self-promotion, and newspapers proved—as the years passed—to lack the discrimination necessary to pierce the veil. "As the Grimm brothers ferreted out the old tales of Germany," one newspaper reported, "as Joel Chandler Harris put together Negro tales . . . so Chase has been searching" for old songs and dances in southwest Virginia (unidentified clipping in Chase file, Archive of Folk Culture, Library of Congress). Twenty years later the *Charlotte* (N.C.) *Observer* gushed that Chase was "the American Hans Christian Andersen" (22 July 1957, sect. B, p. 12). Chase's published collections of folk material include *Traditional Ballads, Songs and Singing Games* (1935), *Old Songs and Singing Games* (1938), *Jack Tales* (1943), *Grandfather Tales* (1948), *Wicked John and the Devil* (1951), and others.

48. Unidentified clipping in JABP, 18 July 1939.

49. Richard Chase, "Folk Traditions and Our Cultural Destiny," *Commonwealth*, January 1939, pp. 30–32.

50. On Chase's early suggestion, see Jackson, "Ballad Art Revived," pp. 8ff. Vollmer wrote folk plays such as *Sun-Up* (1923), *The Dunce Boy* (1925), and *Moonshine and Honeysuckle* (1933). In "Making a Native Folk Drama," *Southern Folklore Quarterly* 1 (September 1937): 29, the Playmakers' Frederick H. Koch defined folk

drama as "the work of a single artist dealing consciously with . . . the folkways of our less sophisticated and more primitive people, living simple lives apart from the responsibilities of a highly organized social order."

Frederick Koch started the Carolina Playmakers theater group in 1919, having earlier founded and directed the Dakota Playmakers in North Dakota. Although Lula Vollmer, Thomas Wolfe, and other early Playmakers dramatists used folk elements in a way that was consistent with Koch's definition, others read the life of the folk in more political terms. The Playmakers' 1919–20 season included Harold Williamson's *Peggy: A Tragedy of the Tenant Farmer* and Minnie S. Sparrows's *Who Pays? A Tragedy of Industrial Conflict*. In 1931, J. O. and Loretto Carroll Bailey wrote and produced *Strike Song*, based on the 1929 Gastonia textile strike. *Strike Song* was denounced in the January 1932 issue of the industry-oriented *Southern Textile Bulletin*. See *The Carolina Playmakers*, vol. 1 (1918–20) and vol. 16 (1934–35), scrapbooks in the North Carolina Collection, University of North Carolina. See also F. H. Koch, *Carolina Folk Plays* (New York: Holt, 1941), Samuel Selden, *Frederick Henry Koch, Pioneer Playmaker* (Chapel Hill: University of North Carolina Library, 1954), and Walter Spearman, *The Carolina Playmakers: The First Fifty Years* (Chapel Hill: University of North Carolina Press, 1970).

51. AMB to JAB, 17 April 1936; and JAB to AMB, 30 April, 18 May, and 25 July 1936 (all in JABP).

52. JAB to AMB, 16 September 1936 (JABP). Since 1936 was an election year, Blakemore wanted to invite political speakers to swell the crowds, but Buchanan convinced him not to do so (JAB to AMB, 22 June 1936; and AMB to JAB, 19 July 1936 [JABP]).

53. See "Folklore Is Theme of White Top Conference," *Musical America* 56 (September 1936): 14, 17; and *Baltimore Sun*, 2 August 1936, p. 2.

54. AMB to JAB, 1 August 1933 (JABP), and *Roanoke Times*, 30 July 1933.

55. *Musical America* 56 (September 1936): 14, 17.

56. Handicrafts were never a major feature of the White Top Festival, but were often displayed and sold on a limited scale, and were discussed seriously at the conferences. A major handicrafts revival was under way in the southern mountains, partly as a result of the handicraft programs of the scores of settlement and denominational schools, and the advent of the Southern Highlands Handicraft Guild (1929), discussed in chapter 2 above. When he spoke at the 1936 White Top conference, Eaton was completing his Russell Sage–sponsored study, *Handicrafts of the Southern Highlands* (New York: Russell Sage, 1937).

57. Seeger to Adrian Dornbush, 21 August 1936, in U.S. Farm Security Administration, *Miscellaneous Printed Matter*, 2 vols. (unpaged), Music Division, Library of Congress. I am grateful to Archie Green for calling this document to my attention. Although Seeger's account tends toward parody, the documentary record of the festival confirms its essential accuracy. An article in *Musical America* 56 (September 1936): 14, 17, reported that Seeger spoke on "Musical Acculturation Problems Met With in the Southern Appalachians" at the conference, but I was unable to locate a text of his remarks.

58. John A. Blakemore, *Buchanan: A Genealogical History* (Bristol: Quality Printers, 1977), p. 232; AMB to JP, undated [ca. 1933] [JPP]. John P. Buchanan died 15 September 1937.

59. AMP to JP, 8 and 21 June 1937, respectively (JPP).

60. AMB to J. B. Orrick, 26 September 1938 (AMBP); AMB to JP, 11 December 1938 [JPP]; AMB to Joe Russell, 13 April 1939 (AMBP); and JAB to JP, 25 June 1938 (JABP). Blakemore refused Buchanan's request for a financial statement on the 1938 festival (JAB to AMB, 1 September 1938 [JABP]).

61. AMB to JP, 18 February 1939; AMB to JAB, 28 February 1939; JAB to AMB, 7 March 1939; and AMB to JAB, 9 May 1939, respectively (all in JABP).

62. Interview with John Blakemore, Emory, Virginia, 27 May 1979. On his mother's side, Blakemore was related to the Buchanan family into which Annabel Morris married.

63. Interview with John Blakemore, 27 May 1979.

64. *Bristol Herald-Courier*, 8 and 16 September 1928.

65. Interview with John Blakemore, 27 May 1979.

66. JAB to H. K. Bowen and H. W. Hodges, 22 and 29 July 1931, respectively (JABP).

67. Blakemore ran unsuccessfully for commonwealth attorney in 1931, but was successful in 1935 (interview with David Daniel Brown, 4 June 1979).

68. JAB to J. P. McConnell, 2 September 1931 (JABP); "Record of Automobiles Admitted to the Grounds of White Top Company . . . September 1929 to 4 July 1931," and "Record . . . September 1929 to 31 December 1935" (JABP). Auto traffic increased from an average of 47 per month before the festival began to more than 169 per month thereafter. JAB to Allen Eaton, 16 August 1932; JAB to Munsey Slack, 1 August 1932; JAB to AMB, 15 February 1933; JAB to W. W. McClevy, 24 July 1933 (all in JABP).

69. AMB to JAB, 1 September 1932 (JABP).

70. AMB to JAB, 12 October 1933 (AMBP). Although Blakemore kept actual expenses as low as possible, financial statements remaining in JABP suggest that his accounting practices tended to maximize expense items so that the festival would not show a profit.

71. Juliet Fauntleroy to JAB, 29 July 1933, and JAB reply, 5 August 1933 (JABP).

72. Cruise to AMB, 7 October 1933 (AMBP). The Cruise family group that performed at White Top included Council's brothers John, Thurman, Carl, and several others.

73. Cruise to AMB, 7 October 1933 (AMBP).

74. A perceptive and humane account of the impact of the depression, big-time illicit distillers from the cities, and biased law enforcement on southwest Virginia moonshiners is to be found in Sherwood Anderson's "City Gangs Enslave Moonshine Mountaineers," *Liberty*, 2 November 1935, pp. 12–13.

75. AMB to JP, 20 November 1931, 16 July 1932, and 17 April 1932, respectively (JPP).

76. Council Cruise to JAB, 23 August 1938, and JAB reply of 26 August 1938 (JABP).

77. AMB to JP, 17 and 19 April and 6 May 1932 (JPP). Mrs. Buchanan pleaded unsuccessfully with Blakemore in 1935 for "special prizes" that would make it possible for some performers to attend (AMB to JAB, 11 August 1935 [JABP]). A preliminary budget for 1939 (JABP) lists $250 for publicity, $100 for Richard

Chase, and $100 for all the performers combined. On 8 February 1940, Chase wrote to Blakemore to ask for $450 to do work on the 1940 festival similar to what Mrs. Buchanan had for years done without remuneration.

78. "Part of a Report to the White Top Company Prepared about 1933 et seq.," undated report by Blakemore in JABP.

79. AMB to JAB, 1 June 1937, and to Mrs. Eldridge Copenhaver, 8 June 1937 (both in JPP).

80. JAB to JPP, 20 February 1939; JPP to JAB, 28 February 1939; and AMB to JAB, 18 May 1939 (all in JABP).

81. The following sketch is based upon Annabel Morris Buchanan, "Recollections of Groesbeck," *Groesbeck, Texas, Journal*, 28 March 1963, p. 3; 4 April 1963, sect. 2, p. 2; and 11 April 1963, sect. 2, p. 3; *Paducah Sun-Democrat*, 3 January 1978; and extensive correspondence in AMBP, especially a letter to George Pullen Jackson, 21 June 1937.

82. John Church Co. to AMB, 18 June 1919 (AMBP).

83. The 24 September 1923 program of the Monday Afternoon Music Club included a talk on "Ballads from the Southern Appalachians" by Mrs. Bascom Copenhaver and some dulcimer songs by Mrs. J. H. Rouse.

84. I have discovered no evidence that Buchanan met Powell earlier than 1927–28.

85. The following sketch of Powell's life is based upon Gilbert Chase, *America's Music* (rev. ed. New York: McGraw Hill, 1966), 401ff.; Pocahontas Wight Edmunds, *Virginians Out Front* (Richmond: Whittet and Shepperson, 1972), pp. 337–71; clippings from the *Roanoke Times*, 16 September 1930; *Richmond Times-Dispatch*, 21 September 1931, 28 May 1932, 12 May 1935, 26 January 1936, 12 June 1938, and 26 August 1963 (obituary); *Washington Post*, 21 January 1934; *Washington Herald*, 21 January 1934; *Who's Who in America* (1930–31), p. 1796; and Powell's papers in the Alderman Library at the University of Virginia. Powell was born 6 September 1882 and died 15 August 1963. For sketches of the Richmond Female Seminary see Virginius Dabney, *Richmond: The Story of a City* (Garden City: Doubleday, 1976), pp. 230f., and Margaret Meagher, *History of Education in Richmond* (Richmond: Works Progress Administration, 1939), p. 85.

86. Edmunds, *Virginians Out Front*, p. 356. Edmunds's book, while amateurish and filiopietistic, is one of the few available sources on Powell's early life. Besides Powell, the other "Virginians out front" it treats include Woodrow Wilson, Booker T. Washington, Ellen Glasgow, Douglas Southall Freeman, and others of similar stature.

87. Recordings of Powell's *Rhapsodie Negre* and *Sonata Teutonica* (1913) were still on the market in 1979. Gilbert Chase concluded in 1966 that Powell's "ambitious" *Symphony in A* "leaves one with the suspicion that its aesthetic premise and its technical apparatus are outmoded."

88. Following Powell by about ten years, North Carolinian Lamar Stringfield (b. 1897) also used traditional (Indian, black, southern mountain) music extensively as compositional material. His symphonic suite *From the Southern Mountains* won a Pulitzer Prize for music in 1928. He became acquainted with Powell in the late twenties, and was involved in the White Top Festival during its early years. How important his influence was cannot be ascertained, since his papers from that

period of his life have apparently disappeared. Buchanan's letters to Powell and Blakemore suggest that she was in touch with Stringfield regularly about the festival in 1931.

89. A major body of evidence—Powell's activities as one of Virginia's leading racists of the 1920s—will be discussed subsequently.

90. John Powell, "Virginia Finds Her Folk Music," *Musical Courier*, 23 April 1932, p. 5.

91. Powell, "Treasure Recovered (Folk Music)," p. 6.

92. John Powell, "In the Lowlands Low," pp. 3–5.

93. Ibid., pp. 5–6.

94. Ibid., p. 2.

95. The specifically racial dimensions of this figure are explored subsequently.

96. AMB to JP, 21 October 1932 (JPP); and grant application to Guggenheim Foundation, 1 November 1934 (AMBP).

97. AMB to JP, 15 September 1932, to JP, ca. late 1931, and to Louise Burleigh Powell, 20 October 1931, respectively (all in JPP).

98. Annabel Morris Buchanan, "English-American Folksong and Its Value in Composition," unpublished ms. in AMBP; and AMB to JP, 22 June 1931 (JPP).

99. AMB to JP, 16 July 1934 (JPP).

100. AMB to JP, 5 July 1931, to Mrs. Powell, 11 July 1931 and 1 August 1931, and to JP, 4 March 1933 (all in JPP).

101. AMB to JP, 24 January 1934 (JPP).

102. AMB to JP, 8 February 1933 (JPP).

103. AMB to Mrs. Powell, 3 August 1931, to JP, 24 January 1934, and to JP, 1 May 1934 (JPP, emphasis in original).

104. AMB to JP, 17 July 1931 and 2 August 1932; and to Mrs. Powell, 11 February 1933 (JPP).

105. AMB to JP, 11 December 1938 (JPP).

106. AMB to JP, 17 July 1931, to Mrs. Powell, 20 October 1931, to JP, 24 July 1932, and to JP, 7 March 1933 (all in JPP).

107. Since virtually all of Powell's letters seem to have disappeared, his response to her must be inferred from Buchanan's letters, his references to himself in his published writings (which fortunately are rather numerous), and documentary evidence on other aspects of his life which reveal salient features of his personality. Even allowing for some instability and paranoia on Buchanan's part, I believe the inferences I have drawn here are reasonable.

108. AMB to JP, 17 and 21 July 1931, and undated (ca. April 1934) (JPP). These are typical of many such statements in Buchanan's letters to Powell. In an interview on 17 June 1981, Richard Chase recalled that Buchanan "worshiped" Powell, and he "scorned" her in return.

109. AMB to JP, undated (ca. April 1934) (JPP). The voluminous records of the festival which remain offer more than adequate confirmation of the charge that Powell allowed Buchanan to do most of the work while he himself claimed most of the praise.

110. AMB to JP, 11 August 1931 (JPP).

111. This précis is based primarily upon Powell's "Virginia Finds Her Folk Music," pp. 5ff.; and Annabel Morris Buchanan, "English-American Folksong and

Its Value in Composition," unpublished ms. in AMBP. Quotations are from the former.

112. Annabel Morris Buchanan, "Moses Asks for a Sign," unpublished ms. story in AMBP.

113. Interview with Josie Sheets Marshall, 25 May 1979, Manassas, Virginia.

114. Unpublished ms., "English-American Folksong and Its Value in Composition" (AMBP). The example of a "bad" tune Mrs. Buchanan chose was "Omie Wise," which collector Frank C. Brown later called "North Carolina's principal single contribution to American folk song." See Harry M. Belden and Arthur Palmer Hudson, eds., *The Frank C. Brown Collection of North Carolina Folklore* (Durham, N.C.: Duke University Press, 1952), 2:690-98.

115. AMB to Mrs. Guy Carr, 12 April 1932 (JPP); ms. notes for talk to Richmond school class, 22 October 1936 (AMBP); and text of talk on WWNC (Asheville, N.C.), 31 July 1941 (AMBP).

116. AMB to JP, JAB, and Stringfield, 11 and 13 July 1931 (JABP); and Powell, "Treasure Recovered (Folk Music)," p. 6.

117. List of 1931 winners (JABP); and Troubetzkoy, "Music on the Mountain," p. 6. Judges normally included Powell, Buchanan, Stringfield, and several of the academic folklorists, professional musicians, and critics who attended. In an interview on 25 May 1979, ninety-five-year-old fiddler Harve Sheets recalled that the White Top judges would never let him play his "fancy tunes."

118. AMB to Sokoloff, 2 August 1935 (JABP).

119. AMB to Mrs. Guy Carr, 8 April 1932 (JPP).

120. Chase to JAB, 14 August 1939 (JABP).

121. Quoted in Annabel Morris Buchanan, "Adventures in Virginia Folkways," *Richmond Times-Dispatch*, 21 June 1936, p. 3.

122. A. K. Davis, "Some Recent Trends in the Field of Folksong," *Southern Folklore Quarterly*, 1 (June 1937): 22. It is important to note, however, that not all the White Top performers were "unselfconscious" before their appearances at the festival. Some (including at least banjo player Jack Reedy, fiddler Frank Blevins, and several other fiddlers) had recorded and performed commercially before 1931 (interview with Mrs. Jack Reedy, 18 May 1979). In a letter to Powell and Blakemore of 27 August 1931, Buchanan herself expressed fears that by arousing "too much public interest," "our musicians will be so rotten spoiled . . . they'll be worthless." "I hate to exploit them so much," she concluded, but "maybe . . . [they] will inspire [classical composers] to employ our folk themes" (JABP).

123. AMB to JP, ca. July 1931 (JPP). Some of the tunes Buchanan transcribed from Reedy may be found in AMBP, series B, folder 270.

124. Interview with Albert Hash (b. 1917), White Top, Virginia, 28 May 1979. See also Cay Cotton, "Albert Hash: Fiddle Maker, Fiddle Master," *Bluegrass Unlimited*, April 1979, pp. 88-92.

125. Interview with Myrtle Stout (Taylor), Mountain City, Tennessee, 17 July 1979. Some insights into Mrs. Taylor's life are contained in her two privately printed books, *Carry a Little Honey* (Radford, Va.: Commonwealth Press, 1974), and *Mock of the Forest* (Iowa Falls, Iowa: General Publishing and Binding Co., 1978). In the latter Taylor quotes a newspaper clipping about her winning at White Top and says her musical career "was not pursued because of strict parental disci-

pline" (p. 3).

126. Johnson to AMB, 21 July 1936, and to JAB, 11 July 1939 and 18 June 1940 (all in JABP).

127. JAB to H. K. Bowen, 23 July 1931 (JABP).

128. For some recollections of Barker, see W. Amos Abrams, "Horton Barker: Folk Singer Supreme," *North Carolina Folklore Journal* 22 (November 1974): 141–53.

129. Data on Barker from *Bristol Virginia-Tennessean*, 13 August 1973; notes to Sandy Paton, *Horton Barker: Traditional Singer* (Folkways FA 2362); and *Washington Post*, 24 March 1963, sect. G, p. 6. Quotation from AMB to JP, 28 August 1931 (JPP).

130. See liner notes to *Horton Barker* (Folkways FA 2362).

131. Barker was recorded by Herbert Halpert in April 1939 and by Sam Eskin in January 1950. See Alan Lomax to Chase, 28 April 1942, and Chase to Lomax, 5 May and 7 September 1942 (all in Archive of Folk Culture, Library of Congress). Other Library of Congress recordings of White Top musicians are listed in Charles L. Perdue, Jr., comp., *The Archive of Folk Song Virginia Folklore Index* (1979, typescript on file in Library of Congress).

132. AMB to JP, undated (ca. 1933) (JPP). Buchanan arranged and published solo and choral settings for many folk tunes in the 1930s.

133. Notes for speech to VFMC, 25 October 1934; text of speech to Richmond DAR, 25 February 1941; and speech on WWNC (Asheville, N.C.), 31 July 1941 (all in AMBP).

134. Speech in Washington, D.C., undated [January, 1934?] (AMBP). On Berkeley Williams see *St. Christopher's* [School] *News* (1978), pp.1–4. St. Christopher's is a private school in Richmond.

135. Speech over WWNC, 31 July 1941 (AMBP, emphasis in original).

136. In 1920, Buchanan's husband published a racist story in *Scribner's Magazine* about "Uncle John Goode," a stereotypical black who cheerfully performs the usual menial chores "with a grey head filled with sense and a heart full of love and loyalty for his white folks" [68 (December 1920): 711–19], but nothing of the sort apparently ever came from Mrs. Buchanan's pen. Her own politics were liberal. Just prior to the 1932 election, she wrote to Powell (7 November 1932 [JPP]), "I'm voting for Roosevelt, but I really admire Norman Thomas about as much as any of them, or more." As late as 9 January 1932 she wrote to him in connection with an article by Lamar Stringfield, "I'd hate to have you involved in a racial controversy" (JPP).

137. Edmunds, *Virginians Out Front*, p. 366.

138. The brief discussion of nativism which follows is based upon John Higham, *Strangers in the Land: Patterns of American Nativism, 1860–1925* (New York: Atheneum, 1977). All quotations are from this source; page numbers are in parentheses.

139. Ibid., passim.

140. The other two were Harvard geologist (and head of its Lawrence Scientific School) Nathaniel S. Shaler and Massachusetts Institute of Technology president Francis A. Walker.

141. Virginia State Registrar to Stone Deavours of the Mississippi State Bar

Association, 15 April 1925, and JP to Deavours, 20 April 1925 (JPP). In the endeavor, Powell collaborated with Dr. Lawrence Price of Richmond.

142. *Richmond News-Leader*, 5 June 1923, p. 18; and JP to Stone Deavours, 20 April 1925 (JPP).

143. *Constitution of Anglo-Saxon Club of America* (Richmond, 1923) (JPP).

144. John Powell, "Is White America to Become a Negroid Nation?" *Richmond Times-Dispatch Sunday Magazine*, 22 July 1923, p. 2.

145. Ibid., p. 2.

146. Richmond *News-Leader*, 5 June 1923, p. 18; registrar to JP, 5 June 1925 (JPP). The law as enacted may be found in *Acts and Joint Resolutions of the General Assembly of the State of Virginia, 1924*, chapter 371. It appears as title 45, chapter 204, §5099a of the Code of 1924. The law remained on the books until 1967, when it was declared unconstitutional by the U.S. Supreme Court in *Loving* v. *Virginia*. See Robert J. Sickels, *Race, Marriage and the Law* (Albuquerque: University of New Mexico Press, 1972), pp. 64ff. Sickels notes that thirty-eight states had anti-miscegenation laws at one time or another (Maryland's dated from 1661); thirty-one still had them by the end of World War II.

147. JP to George H. Roberts, Ohio House of Representatives, 28 February 1925, and to James Davis of Atlanta, 30 May 1925 (JPP). Georgia enacted such a law in 1927.

148. "John Powell the American Pianist" (London: Ibbs and Tillett, 1928), and *Wiener Illustrierte Zeitung*, 21 October 1928, pp. 13–14 (both in JPP).

149. Cox quoted in Sickels, *Race, Marriage and the Law*, p. 65; Powell quote from Cox's advertising brochure in JPP. For years, the Virginia state registrar sent Powell copies of all letters he wrote in the course of enforcing the law. Powell's activities on behalf of racism in Virginia were too extensive to explore fully here. He apparently led an effort to harass Hampton Institute in 1925 (see *Richmond News-Leader*, 14 July 1925, p. 1, and *Newport News Daily Press*, 28 November 1925) and helped lead a protest against a judicial decision in the so-called Sorrels Case brought under the Racial Integrity Law. See John Powell, *The Breach in the Dike: An Analysis of the Sorrels Case, Showing the Danger to Racial Integrity from Intermarriage of Whites with So-Called Indians* (Richmond: Anglo-Saxon Club of America, n.d.).

150. Powell, *The Breach in the Dike*, p. 2.

151. Powell was of course not alone in advocating a folk-based national musical culture. His contemporaries Ralph Vaughan Williams (1872–1958) in England and Zoltan Kodaly (1882–1958) in Hungary were similarly disposed, though they did not share Powell's racism. Vaughan Williams's first folk-based compositions were *The Fen Country* (1904) and *Norfolk Rhapsodies* (1905–7). His ideas on the topic were set forth in his book *National Music* (1934). Kodaly insisted upon a folk-based national music, but argued that the creative infusion of other cultural strains was an essential part of the process. "Without the effect of foreign culture a national culture will waste away," he said in "Thirteen Young Hungarian Composers" (1925), in Ferenc Bones, ed., *The Selected Writings of Zoltan Kodaly* (London: Boosey and Hawkes, 1974), pp. 70–74. I am grateful to Beverly Boggs for this reference.

152. These and subsequent quotations are from John Powell, "How America Can Develop a National Music," *Etude*, May 1927, pp. 340f.

153. Along with some of his contemporaries, Powell followed a desire for folk-based "national culture" into racism and anti-Semitism. His close associate Daniel Gregory Mason had advocated a national music as early as 1918 ("Folk-Song and American Music," *Musical Quarterly* 4 [July 1918], 323–32), and elaborated his ideas in *The Dilemma of American Music* (1929) and *Tune In, America: A Study of Our Coming Musical Independence* (1931). In his 1918 article, however, Mason had dismissed rising interest in "British folk songs" such as those found in the Kentucky mountains as "an enthusiasm that overshoots the mark." The virulent anti-Semitism that surfaced in Mason's musical nationalism is discussed by Gilbert Chase in *America's Music* (1966), p. 402, and is clearly evident in Mason's *Tune In, America*, pp. 160f. Chase discusses at length (pp. 385ff.) the larger national movement of which Powell and Mason were a part. The two maintained their relationship throughout the White Top Festival years. See Mason to JP, 21 August 1926 (JPP), an undated [ca. 1933] letter from AMB to JP, which mentions her receiving "a nice letter from Daniel Gregory Mason" (JPP), and JAB to Mason, 19 August 1938 (JABP).

154. John Powell, "Virginia Finds Her Folk Music," *Musical Courier*, 23 April 1932, pp. 5–6.

155. Annabel Morris Buchanan, "The Function of a Folk Festival," *Southern Folklore Quarterly* 1 (March 1937): 34. In her WWNC radio speech of 31 July 1941, she reiterated that "The traditional music and balladry we seek as inspiration for American art belongs to our race."

156. Undated [ca. 1932] typescript, "A National Music for America" (JPP).

157. C. L. Miller to JAB, 18 July 1933; JAB to Miller, 20 July 1933 (JABP). In *White Spirituals in the Southern Uplands* (1933; rpt. New York: Dover Publications, 1965), p. 273, and his later *White and Negro Spirituals* (1943) Jackson subscribes to the position that black spirituals derive predominantly from white music. The argument over the relationship between black and white spirituals is too complex to enter here. It is sufficient to note that White Top policy was a de facto endorsement of Jackson's position.

158. Hugh H. Trout to JAB, 20 July 1938, and JAB to Trout, 21 July 1938 (JABP).

159. Statistics from *Negroes in the United States, 1920–1932* (Washington, D.C.: Government Printing Office, 1935), pp. 18ff.

160. Fields, ed., *Grayson County*, p. 322. I am grateful to J. Roderick Moore for calling this item to my attention.

161. Robert B. Winans, "The Black Banjo-Playing Tradition in Virginia and West Virginia," *Folklore and Folklife in Virginia* 1 (1979): 7–30. Winans's list includes only those players who were still living (and could be located to interview) in 1979.

162. A few local black musicians were recorded commercially also just prior to the advent of the White Top festival. Martin, Martin, and Armstrong (the "Tennessee Chocolate Drops") recorded for Vocalion in 1930; Steve Tarter (ca. 1895–ca. 1935) and Harry Gay (b. 1904) of Johnson City recorded two sides for Victor in

1928. See Kip Lornell, "Tarter and Gay," *Living Blues #27*, May-June 1976, p. 18. I am grateful to Lornell for numerous suggestions about the role of blacks in commercial recorded music in the Tennessee-Virginia border area.

163. Sarah Gertrude Knott, "The National Folk Festival—Its Problems and Reasons," *Southern Folklore Quarterly* 3 (1939): 117. "Since our language and laws are English, and there is much to be found here of British origin," she noted, "we might have featured only those traditions." She chose otherwise, however, rejecting the White Top theory of culture.

164. See Archie Green, "The National Folk Festival Association," *John Edwards Memorial Foundation Quarterly* 11 (Spring 1975): 23-32.

165. Paul Rosenfeld, "Folksong and Culture Politics," *Modern Music* 17 (November-December 1939): 23. Rosenfeld (1890-1946) had been music critic of the *Dial* (1920-27) and editor of *American Caravan* (1928-36). See *New York Times*, 22 July 1946, p. 21. Rosenfeld's reactions to Powell and the festival are consistent with my reading of the documentary record.

166. "Real Southerner and the White Top Folk Festival," *Southern Literary Messenger* 1 (June 1939): 404f.

167. The final photo, used to illustrate Powell's "Treasure Recovered (Folk Music)," p. 5, was captioned "Where They Wear Shooting Irons to Music Practice."

168. See Annabel Morris Buchanan, "Sherwood Anderson: Country Editor," *World Today* 3 (February 1929): 249-53.

169. Howard M. Jones and Walter B. Rideout, eds., *Letters of Sherwood Anderson* (Boston: Little, Brown, 1952), p. 172 (letter of 19 May 1927).

170. See Ray Lewis White, ed., *Return to Winesburg: Selections from Four Years of Writing* [1927-31] *for a Country Newspaper* (Chapel Hill: University of North Carolina Press, 1967); and Welford D. Taylor, ed., *The Buck Fever Papers* (Charlottesville: University Press of Virginia, 1971). In a series of articles, Anderson examined working conditions endured by mountaineers (and others) employed in textile mills: "Cotton Mill," *Scribner's* 88 (July 1930): 1-11; "Danville, Virginia," *New Republic* 65 (1 January 1931): 266-68; and "Mill Girls," *Scribner's* 91 (January 1932): 8-12ff.

171. AMP to JP, 14 June and 21 July 1931 (JPP).

172. JAB to Allen Eaton, 16 August 1932, and H. K. Bowen to JAB, 27 July 1933 (JABP).

173. AMB to JP, 29 July and 1 October 1933 (JPP).

174. See AMB to Guggenheim, 30 October 1934; Carnegie to Blakemore, 15 October 1935; AMB to Guggenheim, 5 September and 15 October 1936; and AMB to JAB, 18 July 1938 (all in AMBP). Buchanan reapplied as late as 1940.

175. Annabel Morris Buchanan, "Enriching the Community through Folk Activities," ms. speech to National Federation of Music Clubs, St. Louis, Missouri, 24 October 1933 (JPP).

176. AMB to Duncan Emrich, 31 May 1951 (Archive of Folk Culture, Library of Congress).

177. AMB, "Rise, King Jesus" (AMBP). I have analyzed this story at greater length in John Shelton Reed and Merle Black, eds., *Perspectives on the American South: An Annual Review of Politics, Society, and Culture* (New York: Gordon and Breach, 1983).

178. See for example Philip Selznick, *TVA and the Grass Roots* (Berkeley: University of California Press, 1949); and Whisnant, *Modernizing the Mountaineer*, pp. 43–69.

Afterword

1. Bernard W. Sheehan, *Savagism and Civility: Indians and Englishmen in Colonial Virginia* (London: Cambridge University Press, 1980), p. ix. Subsequent page numbers in parentheses.

2. Robert H. Land, in "Henrico and Its College," *William and Mary Quarterly*, 2nd ser., 18 (1938), 453–98; John S. Flory, "The University of Henrico," *Publications of the Southern History Association* 8 (January 1903): 40–52; and *Proceedings of the Virginia Company of London*, 1:42–46 (as quoted by Flory).

It is worth noting that the industrial school idea remained compelling for the federal government throughout its period of intense work with Indian education at the end of the nineteenth century. Robert Trennert has noted in "Peaceably if They Will, Forcibly if They Must: The Phoenix Industrial School, 1890–1901," *Journal of Arizona History* 20 (1979): 297–322 that twenty-five such schools were started in the two decades after 1880. Trennert's account shows that the cultural justifications used for such schools among Indians are remarkably similar to those used a decade or so later among mountaineers.

3. Land, "Henrico and Its College," pp. 492f.

4. Malcolm Chapman, *The Gaelic Vision in Scottish Culture* (London: Croome-Helm, 1979), p. 10. The account that follows is drawn entirely from Chapman. Subsequent page numbers in parentheses.

5. The relationship between exploitative economic "improvement" schemes, cultural destruction, and romantic cultural revival is explored at length in John Prebble, *The Highland Clearances* (London: Secker and Warburg, 1963). Some analogues between the Highland clearances and "Appalachian development" strategies are outlined in my *Modernizing the Mountaineer: People, Power, and Planning in Appalachia* (Boone, N.C.: Appalachian Consortium Press, 1981), pp. 266ff.

6. For the most recent retreading of the Uncle Sol myth, see Mercy Coogan, "At the Forks of Troublesome Creek: Hindman Settlement School," *Appalachia* 14 (March 1981): 33–40. *Appalachia* is the magazine of the state-federal Appalachian Regional Commission.

Index